Reading Women's Lives

The Faculty of the Department of
Women's Studies at The Ohio State University

Compiled by

Ms. Ingrid I. Sabio
Introduction to Women's Studies
WMST 101
Community College of Baltimore County -
History & Women's Studies

Pearson Learning Solutions

New York Boston San Francisco
London Toronto Sydney Tokyo Singapore Madrid
Mexico City Munich Paris Cape Town Hong Kong Montreal

Senior Vice President, Editorial and Marketing: Patrick F. Boles
Senior Sponsoring Editor: Natalie Danner
Development Editor: Mary Kate Paris
Editorial Assistant: Jill Johnson
Marketing Manager: Brian T. Berkeley
Operations Manager: Eric M. Kenney
Production Manager: Jennifer Berry
Rights Manager: Jillian Santos
Art Director and Cover Designer: Renée Sartell

Special thanks to the contributors: The Faculty of the Department of Women's Studies at the Ohio State University.

Cover Art: Art Collage, Copyright © Joanne Stichweh, *Four Faces* courtesy of Kaadaa / Veer Incorporated.

Printed in the United States of America.

Please visit our website at *www.pearsoncustom.com.*

Attention bookstores: For permission to return any unsold stock, contact us at *pe-uscustomreturns@pearson.com.*

Pearson Learning Solutions, 501 Boylston Street, Suite 900, Boston, MA 02116
A Pearson Education Company
www.pearsoned.com

10 11 12 13 14 15 16 17 18 19 20 V092 14 13 12

ISBN 10: 0-536-79011-6
ISBN 13: 978-0-536-79011-8

Contents

Declaration of Sentiments and Resolutions (1848)

The Seneca Falls Women's Rights Convention of 1848

This document, drawn in 1848, was a product of the first meeting on women's rights in the United States. Written in a style similar to the Declaration of Independence, *the document presents the many injustices women faced in the nineteenth century. From a contemporary viewpoint, the document provides important historical information on the origins of social movements seeking improvement in the quality of women's lives.*

When, in the course of human events, it becomes necessary for one portion of the family of man to assume among the people of the earth a position different from that which they have hitherto occupied, but one to which the laws of nature and of nature's God entitle them, a decent respect to the opinions of mankind requires that they should declare the causes that impel them to such a course.

"Declaration of Sentiments and Resolutions," from The Seneca Falls Women's Rights Convention of 1848.

We hold these truths to be self-evident: that all men and women are created equal; that they are endowed by their Creator with certain inalienable rights; that among these are life, liberty, and the pursuit of happiness; that to secure these rights governments are instituted, deriving their just powers from the consent of the governed. Whenever any form of government becomes destructive of these ends, it is the right of those who suffer from it to refuse allegiance to it, and to insist upon the institution of a new government, laying its foundation on such principles, and organizing its powers in such form, as to them shall seem most likely to effect their safety and happiness. Prudence, indeed, will dictate that governments long established should not be changed for light and transient causes; and accordingly all experience hath shown that mankind are more disposed to suffer, while evils are sufferable, than to right themselves by abolishing the forms to which they were accustomed. But when a long train of abuses and usurpations, pursuing invariably the same object evinces a design to reduce them under absolute despotism, it is their duty to throw off such government, and to provide new guards for their future security. Such has been the patient sufferance of the women under this government, and such is now the necessity which constrains them to demand the equal station to which they are entitled.

The history of mankind is a history of repeated injuries and usurpations on the part of man toward woman, having in direct object the establishment of an absolute tyranny over her. To prove this, let facts be submitted to a candid world.

He has never permitted her to exercise her inalienable right to the elective franchise.

He has compelled her to submit to laws, in the formation of which she had no voice.

He has withheld from her rights which are given to the most ignorant and degraded men—both natives and foreigners.

Having deprived her of this first right of a citizen, the elective franchise, thereby leaving her without representation in the halls of legislation, he has oppressed her on all sides.

He has made her, if married, in the eye of the law, civilly dead.

He has taken from her all right in property, even to the wages she earns.

He has made her, morally, an irresponsible being, as she can commit many crimes with impunity, provided they be done in the presence of her husband. In the covenant of marriage, she is compelled to promise obedience to her husband, he becoming, to all intents and purposes, her master—the law giving him power to deprive her of her liberty, and to administer chastisement.

He has so framed the laws of divorce, as to what shall be the proper causes, and in case of separation, to whom the guardianship of the children shall be given, as to be wholly regardless of the happiness of women—the law, in all cases, going upon a false supposition of the supremacy of man, and giving all power into his hands.

After depriving her of all rights as a married woman, if single, and the owner of property, he has taxed her to support a government which recognizes her only when her property can be made profitable to it.

He has monopolized nearly all the profitable employments, and from those she is permitted to follow, she receives but a scanty remuneration. He closes against her all the avenues to wealth and distinction which he considers most honorable to himself. As a teacher of theology, medicine, or law, she is not known.

He has denied her the facilities for obtaining a thorough education, all colleges being closed against her.

He allows her in Church, as well as State, but a subordinate position, claiming Apostolic authority for her exclusion from the ministry, and, with some exceptions, from any public participation in the affairs of the Church.

He has created a false public sentiment by giving to the world a different code of morals for men and women, by which moral delinquencies which exclude women from society, are not only tolerated, but deemed of little account in man.

He has usurped the prerogative of Jehovah himself, claiming it as his right to assign for her a sphere of action, when that belongs to her conscience and to her God.

He has endeavored, in every way that he could, to destroy her confidence in her own powers, to lessen her self-respect, and to make her willing to lead a dependent and abject life.

Now, in view of this entire disfranchisement of one-half the people of this country, their social and religious degradation—in view of the unjust laws above mentioned, and because women do feel themselves aggrieved, oppressed, and fraudulently deprived of their most sacred rights, we insist that they have immediate admission to all the rights and privileges which belong to them as citizens of the United States.

In entering upon the great work before us, we anticipate no small amount of misconception, misrepresentation, and ridicule; but we shall use every instrumentality within our power to effect our object. We shall employ agents, circulate tracts, petition the State and National legislatures, and endeavor to enlist the pulpit and the press in our behalf. We hope this Convention will be followed by a series of Conventions embracing every part of the country.

Resolutions

WHEREAS, The great precept of nature is conceded to be, that "man shall pursue his own true and substantial happiness." Blackstone in his Commentaries remarks, that this law of Nature being coeval with mankind, and dictated by God himself, is of course superior in obligation to any other. It is binding over all the globe, in all countries and at all times; no human laws are of any validity if contrary to this, and such of them as are valid, derive all their force, and all their validity, and all their authority, mediately and immediately, from this original; therefore,

Resolved, That such laws as conflict, in any way, with the true and substantial happiness of woman, are contrary to the great precept of nature and of no validity, for this is "superior in obligation to any other."

Resolved, That all laws which prevent woman from occupying such a station in society as her conscience shall dictate, or which place her in a position inferior to that of man, are contrary to the great precept of nature, and therefore of no force or authority.

Resolved, That woman is man's equal—was intended to be so by the Creator, and the highest good of the race demands that she should be recognized as such.

Resolved, That the women of this country ought to be enlightened in regard to the laws under which they live, that they may no longer publish their degradation by declaring themselves satisfied with their present position, nor their ignorance, by asserting that they have all the rights they want.

Resolved, That inasmuch as man, while claiming for himself intellectual superiority, does accord to woman moral superiority, it is pre-eminently his duty to encourage her to speak and teach, as she has an opportunity, in all religious assemblies.

Resolved, That the same amount of virtue, delicacy, and refinement of behavior that is required of woman in the social state, should also be required of man, and the same transgressions should be visited with equal severity on both man and woman.

Resolved, That the objection of indelicacy and impropriety, which is so often brought against woman when she addresses a public audience, comes with a very ill-grace from those who encourage, by their attendance, her appearance on the stage, in the concert, or in feats of the circus.

Resolved, That woman has too long rested satisfied in the circumscribed limits which corrupt customs and a perverted application of the Scriptures have marked out for her, and that it is time she should move in the enlarged sphere which her great Creator has assigned her.

Resolved, That it is the duty of the women of this country to secure to themselves their sacred right to the elective franchise.

Resolved, That the equality of human rights results necessarily from the fact of the identity of the race in capabilities and responsibilities.

Resolved, therefore, That, being invested by the Creator with the same capabilities, and the same consciousness of responsibility for their exercise, it is demonstrably the right and duty of woman, equally with man, to promote every righteous cause by every righteous means; and especially in regard to the great subjects of morals and religion, it is self-evidently her right to participate with her brother in teaching them, both in private and in public, by writing and by speaking, by any instrumentalities proper to be used, and in any assemblies proper to be held; and this being a self-evident truth growing out of the divinely implanted principles of human nature, any custom or authority adverse to it, whether modern or wearing the hoary sanction of antiquity, is to be regarded as a self-evident falsehood, and at war with mankind.

[At the last session Lucretia Mott offered and spoke to the following resolution:]

Resolved, That the speedy success of our cause depends upon the zealous and untiring efforts of both men and women, for the overthrow of the monopoly of the pulpit, and for the securing to woman an equal participation with men in the various trades, professions, and commerce.

QUESTIONS

1. Explain the significance of the author's decision to use the same format as the Declaration of Independence in this document. What might this choice of format have accomplished for women in a nineteenth century context? What were the goals of the authors? What might have been the response to the document?
2. What echoes from the Seneca Falls document do you hear in contemporary feminist concerns? What contemporary concerns were not relevant for inclusion in the document at that time? What social changes might account for both the echoes and the emergence of other concerns today?
3. Who does "women" refer to in this document? What language from the text leads you to these conclusions?
4. Why is this an important document in the history of the women's movement?

On Voluntary Motherhood (1855)

Sarah Grimké

Grimké (1792–1873) was an abolitionist and women's rights activist, who pioneered in the development of feminist theory in the U.S. Denied a college education because of her sex, she studied the condition and status of women throughout history and wrote a number of essays justifying women's demands for equality and autonomy. In her essay, "Marriage," she argued that women's oppression in marriage resulted from their economic dependence and their inability to control pregnancies. Grimké's demand for women's control of their own bodies, for their right to say no to their husbands' sexual desires, was radical in its day. In an era when contraception was unreliable and abortion dangerous, she advocated that women control reproduction by sexual abstinence. Sarah Grimké, who never married, lived with her sister Angelina Grimké Weld and her husband and helped care for their three children.

"On Voluntary Motherhood," by Sarah Grimké, reprinted from *Marriage, Weld Grimké Papers*, 1855. The William L. Clements Library, University of Michigan

An eminent physician of Boston once remarked that if in the economy of nature, the sexes alternated in giving birth to children no family would ever have more than three, the husband bearing one & the wife two. But the *right* to decide this matter has been almost wholly denied to woman. How often is she forced into an untimely motherhood which compels her to wean her babe, thus depriving it of that nutriment provided by nature as the most bland & fitting, during the period of dentition. Thousands of deaths from this cause, in infancy, are attributed by superstition & ignorance to the dispensations of Divine Providence. How many thousand, too, of miscarriages are forced upon woman by the fact that man lives down that law of his being which would protect her from such terrible consequences just as animal instinct protects the female among brutes. To save woman from legalized licentiousness is then one of the reasons why we plead for *equality of rights*.

No one can fail to see that this condition of things results from several causes:

1. Ignorance of those physical laws which every man & woman *ought* to know before marriage, the knowledge of which has been withheld from the young, under a false & fatal idea of delicacy. Many a man ruins his own health & that of his wife & his children too, thro' ignorance. A diffusion of knowledge respecting these laws would greatly defuse existing evils.

2. A false conception in man & woman of *his* nature & necessities. The great truth that the most concentrated fluid of the body has an office to perform in the product of *great tho'ts & original ideas*, as well as in the reproduction of the species is known to few & too little appreciated by all. The prodigal waste of this by legalized licentiousness has dwarfed the intellect of man. . . .

3. The fact that many legal marriages are not love marriages. In a pure, true relation between the sexes, no difficulties can ever arise, but a willing recognition of each other's right & mutual wants, naturally & spontaneously resulting in voluntary motherhood, a joyful appreciation of the blessedness of parentage, the birth of healthy, comely children & a beautiful home.

But it may be asked, what is to be done in cases of uncongenial marriages. Are not such men & women to follow their attractions outside of the legal relation. I unhesitatingly answer No! Where two persons have established a false marriage relation, *they are bound to abide by the consequences* of the mistake they have made.

Perhaps they did love each other, but a nearer intimacy has frozen this love or changed it into disgust. Or, theirs may have been a marriage of *convenience*, or one for the sake of obtaining a house, a fortune, a position in life: or it may have been a mere act of obedience to parents, or of gratitude, or a means of canceling a monied obligation. Multiform are the *unworthy* motives which seduce men & women into this sacred relation. In all these cases, let them abide the consequences of their own perversion of marriage, in exchanging personal chastity for the pride of life, vanity in dress, position or a house to live in, without that *love* which alone can make that house a *home*.

In some cases, it may be duty for the parties to separate, but let both keep themselves pure, so long as both are living. Let them accept the discipline thus afforded, & spiritual strength & growth will be their reward.

The Doctrine that human beings are to follow their attractions, which lies at the base of that miscalled "free love" system, is fraught with infinite danger. We are too low down to listen for one moment to its syren voice. . . .

Let me then exculpate "the woman's rights movement," from the charge of "tending directly and rapidly to the Free Love system, & nullifying the very idea of Marriage as anything more than a partnership at will." On the contrary our great desire is to purify & exalt the marriage relation & destroy *all* licentiousness. . . .

. . . Man seems to feel that Marriage gives him the control of Woman's person just as the Law gives him the control of her property. Thus are her most sacred rights destroyed by that very act, which, under the laws of Nature should enlarge, establish & protect them. In marriage is the origin of Life—in it woman finds herself endowed with a creative energy she never possessed before. In it new aspirations take possession of her, an indescribable longing after motherhood as the felt climax of her being. She joyfully gives herself away, that she may receive the germ of a new being, & true to nature, would fain retire within herself & absorb & expend all her energies in the development of this precious germ. But alas! How few are permitted, unmolested to pursue that end, which for the time being, has become the great object of life. How often is she compelled by various considerations to yield to the *unnatural* embraces of her husband, & thus to endanger the very existence of her embryo babe. How often is it sacrificed to the ungoverned passion of its own father, & the health of the mother seriously impaired. Every unnatural process is deleterious, hence abortions are destructive to the constitution & many women are broken down in the prime of life by them alone, & their haggard countenances too plainly reveal their secret sorrows. A lady once said to me I have but one child, but I have had 12 miscarriages—another had 4 children & 15 abortions. And why I would ask this untimely casting of her fruit? Do the beasts of the field miscarry? Why not? *They* are governed by instinct. Are the *brutes* safe during the period of gestation whilst *Woman* is not! . . .

. . . Again—look at the burdens imposed upon her by the care of many children following in quick succession. How can any mother do her duty to her family, if in 8 years she have 6 children. Look at the unnatural tug upon her constitution, her night watches, her sore vexations & trials & causes nameless & numberless, that wear away her life. If men had to alternate with their wives, the duties of the nursery, fewer & further between would be its inmates.

Questions

1. What are the arguments that Grimké makes for voluntary motherhood, or women's right to control pregnancy? What does she cite as consequences resulting from women's inability to control her body?
2. What assumptions does Grimké make about male sexuality and female sexuality?
3. How does Grimké respond to the charge that feminists advocate "free love?"
4. Why do you think Grimké advocates that voluntary motherhood be practiced through sexual abstinence? How does that position separate her from most contemporary feminists?

Civil Rights Act, Title VII from *Women's America: Refocusing the Past* (1964)

Linda K. Kerber and
Jane Sherron De Hart, eds.

According to Linda K. Kerber, history professor at the University of Iowa, and Jane Sherron De Hart, history professor at the University of California Santa Barbara, Title VII of the 1964 Civil Rights Act had tremendous significance for women. Below is their discussion of the history of how women were added to the law as well as sections of the law.

The Civil Rights Act of 1964 was a comprehensive law of enormous significance. It was a complex statute, twenty-eight printed pages long and divided into eleven major sections, or *Titles.* Title I dealt with voting rights; Title III with the desegregation of public facilities; Title V established a Commission on Civil Rights. Title VII defined a long list of practices that would be forbidden to employers and labor unions, obliged the federal government to undertake an "affirmative" program of equal employment opportunity for all employees and job applicants, and created an Equal Employment Opportunity Commission (EEOC) to monitor compliance with the law.

Title VII was notable in that it outlawed discrimination on the basis of gender as well as of race. Sex was added to the categories "race, color, religion and national origin" by Congressman Howard Smith of Virginia, who hoped to defeat the legislation; he joked that an amendment adding the category "sex" would guarantee the "right" of every woman to a husband. Representative Martha Griffiths of Michigan and other congresswomen supported the bill, ironically receiving support from conservative colleagues who spoke on behalf of the amendment in the hope that the prospect of sexual equality might cause the entire bill to fail.

The Equal Employment Opportunity Commission, which began to operate in the summer of 1965, anticipated that virtually all its complaints would come from blacks. They were surprised to discover that 25 percent of the complaints received during the first year were from women. In the course of responding to these complaints, both the commission and the courts were driven to a more subtle analysis of female job categories and work patterns. Section 703(e)l required that employers wishing to define a job category by sex had to show that sex was a "bona fide occupational qualification"; it was not enough to say that men or women had traditionally filled any given job.

The act was amended in 1972 and again in 1978; on both occasions the EEOC was given substantial additional powers and responsibilities. The three major areas of EEOC activity are: (1) furnishing assistance to comparable state agencies, (2) furnishing advice to employers and labor unions about compliance, and (3) enforcing compliance by conciliation and by legal action. In 1978 Congress passed the Pregnancy Discrimination Act, which amplified the definition of *sex* to include pregnancy, childbirth, or related medical conditions. EEOC has been willing to view sexual harassment as a form of sex discrimination but has not endorsed the concept of comparable worth.

> Sec. 703. (a) It shall be an unlawful employment practice for an employer—

(1) to fail or refuse to hire or to discharge any individual, or otherwise to discriminate against any individual with respect to his compensation, terms, conditions, or privileges of employment, because of such individual's race, color, religion, sex, or national origin; or

(2) to limit, segregrate, or classify his employees in any way which would deprive or tend to deprive any individual of employment opportunities or otherwise adversely affect his status as an employee, because of such individual's race, color, religion, sex, or national origin.

(b) It shall be an unlawful employment practice for an employment agency to fail or refuse to refer for employment, or otherwise to discriminate against, any individual because of his race, color, religion, sex, or national origin, or to classify or refer for employment any individual on the basis of his race, color, religion, sex, or national origin.

(c) It shall be an unlawful employment practice for a labor organization

(1) to exclude or to expel from its membership, or otherwise to discriminate against, any individual because of his race, color, religion, sex, or national origin;

(2) to limit, segregate, or classify its membership, or to classify or fail or refuse to refer for employment any individual, in any way which would deprive or tend to deprive any individual of employment opportunities, or would limit such employment opportunities or otherwise adversely affect his status as an employee or as an applicant for employment, because of such individual's race, color, religion, sex, or national origin; or

(3) to cause or attempt to cause an employer to discriminate against an individual in violation of this section. . . .

(e) Notwithstanding any other provision of this title, (1) it shall not be an unlawful employment practice for an employer to hire and employ employees, for an employment agency to classify, or refer for employment any individual, for a labor organization to classify its membership or to classify or refer for employment any individual, or for an employer, labor organization, or joint labor-management committee controlling apprenticeship or other training or retraining programs to admit or employ any individual in any such program, on the basis of his religion, sex, or national origin in those certain instances where religion, sex, or national

origin is a bona fide occupational qualification reasonably necessary to normal operation of that particular business or enterprise.
. . .

Sec. 705. (a) There is hereby created a Commission to be known as the Equal Employment Opportunity Commission, which shall be composed of five members, not more than three of whom shall be members of the same political party, who shall be appointed by the President by and with the advice and consent of the Senate.
. . .

(g) The Commission shall have power—

(1) to cooperate with and, with their consent, utilize regional, State, local, and other agencies, both public and private, and individuals; . . .

(3) to furnish to persons subject to this title such technical assistance as they may request to further their compliance with this title or an order issued thereunder;

(4) upon the request of (i) any employer, whose employees or some of them, or (ii) any labor organization, whose members or some of them, refuse or threaten to refuse to cooperate in effectuating the provisions of this title, to assist in such effectuation by conciliation or such other remedial action as is provided by this title;

(5) to make such technical studies as are appropriate to effectuate the purposes and policies of this title and to make the results of such studies available to the public;

(6) to refer matters to the Attorney General with recommendations for intervention in a civil action brought by an aggrieved party under section 706, or for the institution of a civil action by the Attorney General under section 707, and to advise, consult, and assist the Attorney General on such matters. . . .

U.S. Statutes at Large, 78:253-66. For a full discussion of Title VII, see Donald Allen Robinson, "Two Movements in Pursuit of Equal Employment Opportunity," *Signs: Journal of Women in Culture and Society* 4 (1979):413–33.

Questions

1. How and why was sex added as a protected status to the 1964 Civil Rights Act? Why was this important to women? Did women take advantage of these new legal protections against discrimination?
2. According to Sec. 703, what specific employment practices are unlawful? How does the law apply to labor organizations and employment agencies?
3. What is the Equal Employment Opportunities Commission and why was it created? According to Sec. 705 what power does the Commission have?

"A Day without Feminism" & "Third Wave Manifesta: A Thirteen-Point Agenda" (2000)

Jennifer Baumgardner and Amy Richards

What if the American women's movement never happened? What if conditions for women today resembled those of 1970? "A Day Without Feminism," prologue to the popular feminist text, Manifesta, *provides possible answers to these questions, describing a time when employment ads were segregated by sex, teachers could be demoted or fired for pregnancy, and women had little control over their own reproductive lives. Women today owe much to the changes activists initiated in the 1960s and 70s, a period of the women's movement commonly referred to as the "second wave." Yet as the authors' "Third Wave Manifesta" details— much work remains to be done.*

We were both born in 1970, the baptismal moment of a decade that would change dramatically the lives of American women. The two of us grew up thousands of miles apart, in entirely different kinds of families, yet we both came of age with the awareness that certain rights had been won by the women's movement. We've never doubted how important feminism is to people's lives—men's and women's. Both of our mothers went to consciousness-raising-type groups. Amy's mother raised Amy on her own, and Jennifer's mother, questioning the politics of housework, staged laundry strikes.

With the dawn of not just a new century but a new millennium, people are looking back and taking stock of feminism. Do we need new strategies? Is feminism dead? Has society changed so much that the idea of a feminist movement is obsolete? For us, the only way to answer these questions is to imagine what our lives would have been if the women's movement had never happened and the conditions for women had remained as they were in the year of our births.

Imagine that for a day it's still 1970, and women have only the rights they had then. Sly and the Family Stone and Dionne Warwick are on the radio, the kitchen appliances are Harvest Gold, and the name of your Whirlpool gas stove is Mrs. America. What is it like to be female?

Babies born on this day are automatically given their father's name. If no father is listed, "illegitimate" is likely to be typed on the birth certificate. There are virtually no child-care centers, so all preschool children are in the hands of their mothers, a baby-sitter, or an expensive nursery school. In elementary school, girls can't play in Little League and almost all of the teachers are female. (The latter is still true.) In a few states, it may be against the law for a male to teach grades lower than the sixth, on the basis that it's unnatural, or that men can't be trusted with young children.

In junior high, girls probably take home ec; boys take shop or small-engine repair. Boys who want to learn how to cook or sew on a button are out of luck, as are girls who want to learn how to fix a car. *Seventeen* magazine doesn't run feminist-influenced current columns like "Sex + Body" and "Traumarama." Instead the magazine encourages girls not to have sex; pleasure isn't part of its vocabulary. Judy Blume's books are just beginning to be published, and *Free to be . . . You and Me* does not exist. No one reads much about masturbation as a natural activity; nor do they learn that sex is for anything other than procreation. Girls do read mystery stories about Nancy Drew, for whom there is no sex, only her blue roadster and having "luncheon." (The real mystery is how Nancy gets along without a purse and manages to meet only white people.) Boys read about the Hardy Boys, for whom there are no girls.

In high school, the principal is a man. Girls have physical-education class and play half-court basketball, but not soccer, track, or cross country; nor do they have any varsity sports teams. The only prestigious physical activity for girls is cheerleading, or being a drum majorette. Most girls don't take calculus or physics; they plan the dances and decorate the gym. Even when girls get better grades than their male counterparts, they are half as likely to qualify for a National Merit Scholarship because many of the test questions favor boys. Standardized tests refer to males and male experiences much more than to females and their experiences.[1] If a girl "gets herself pregnant," she loses her membership in the National Honor Society (which is still true today) and is expelled.[2]

Girls and young women might have sex while they're unmarried, but they may be ruining their chances of landing a guy full-time, and they're probably getting a bad reputation. If a pregnancy happens, an enterprising gal can get a legal abortion only if she lives in New York or is rich enough to fly there, or to Cuba, London, or Scandinavia. There's also the Chicago-based Jane Collective, an underground abortion-referral service which can hook you up with an illegal or legal termination. (Any of these options are going to cost you. Illegal abortions average $300 to $500, sometimes as much as $2,000.) To prevent pregnancy, a sexually active woman might go to a doctor to be fitted for a diaphragm, or take the high-dose birth-control pill, but her doctor isn't likely to inform her of the possibility of deadly blood clots. Those who do take the Pill also may have to endure this contraceptive's crappy side effects: migraine headaches, severe weight gain, irregular bleeding, and hair loss (or gain), plus the possibility of an increased risk of breast cancer in the long run. It is unlikely that women or their male partners know much about the clitoris and its role in orgasm unless someone happens to fumble upon it. Instead, the myth that vaginal orgasms from penile penetration are the only "mature" (according to Freud) climaxes prevails.

Lesbians are rarely "out," except in certain bars owned by organized crime (the only businessmen who recognize this untapped market), and if lesbians don't know about the bars, they're less likely to know whether there are any other women like them. Radclyffe Hall's depressing early-twentieth-century novel *The Well of Loneliness* pretty much indicates their fate.

The Miss America Pageant is the biggest source of scholarship money for women.[3] Women can't be students at Dartmouth, Columbia, Harvard, West Point, Boston College, or the Citadel, among other all-male institutions. Women's colleges are referred to as "girls' schools." There are no Take Back the Night marches to protest women's lack of safety after dark, but that's okay because college girls aren't allowed out much after dark anyway. Curfew is likely to be midnight on Saturday and 9 or 10 p.m. the rest of the week. Guys get to stay out as late as they want. Women tend to major in teaching, home economics, English, or maybe a language—a good skill for translating someone else's words.[4] The women's studies major does not exist, although you can take a women's studies course at six universities, including Cornell and San Diego State College.[5] The absence of women's history, black history, Chicano studies, Asian-American history, queer studies, and Native American history from college curricula implies that they are not worth studying. A student is lucky if he or she learns that women were "given" the vote in 1920, just as Columbus "discovered" America in 1492. They might also learn that Sojourner Truth, Mary Church Terrell, and Fannie Lou Hamer were black abolitionists or civil-rights leaders, but not that they were feminists. There are practically no tenured female professors at any school, and campuses are not racially diverse. Women of color are either not there or they're lonely as hell. There is no nationally recognized Women's History Month or Black History Month. Only 14 percent of doctorates are awarded to women. Only 3.5 percent of MBAs are female.

Only 2 percent of everybody in the military is female, and these women are mostly nurses. There are no female generals in the U.S. Air Force, no female naval pilots, and no Marine brigadier generals. On the religious front, there are no female cantors or rabbis, Episcopal canons, or Catholic priests. (This is still true of Catholic priests.)

Only 44 percent of women are employed outside the home. And those women make, on average, fifty-two cents to the dollar earned by males. Want ads are segregated into "Help Wanted

Male" and "Help Wanted Female." The female side is preponderantly for secretaries, domestic workers, and other low-wage service jobs, so if you're a female lawyer you must look under "Help Wanted Male." There are female doctors, but twenty states have only five female gynecologists or fewer. Women workers can be fired or demoted for being pregnant, especially if they are teachers, since the kids they teach aren't supposed to think that women have sex. If a boss demands sex, refers to his female employee exclusively as "Baby," or says he won't pay her unless she gives him a blow job, she either has to quit or succumb—no pun intended. Women can't be airline pilots. Flight attendants are "stewardesses"—waitresses in the sky—and necessarily female. Sex appeal is a job requirement, wearing makeup is a rule, and women are fired if they exceed the age or weight deemed sexy. Stewardesses can get married without getting canned, but this is a new development. (In 1968 the Equal Employment Opportunity Commission—EEOC—made it illegal to forcibly retire stewardesses for getting hitched.) Less than 2 percent of dentists are women; 100 percent of dental assistants are women. The "glass ceiling" that keeps women from moving naturally up the ranks, as well as the sticky floor that keeps them unnaturally down in low-wage work, has not been named, much less challenged.

When a woman gets married, she vows to love, honor, and obey her husband, though he gets off doing just the first two to uphold his end of the bargain. A married woman can't obtain credit without her husband's signature. She doesn't have her own credit rating, legal domicile, or even her own name unless she goes to court to get it back. If she gets a loan with her husband—and she has a job—she may have to sign a "baby letter" swearing that she won't have one and have to leave her job.

Women have been voting for up to fifty years, but their turnout rate is lower than that for men, and they tend to vote right along with their husbands, not with their own interests in mind.[6] The divorce rate is about the same as it is in 2000, contrary to popular fiction's blaming the women's movement for divorce. However, divorce required that one person be at fault, therefore if you just want out of your marriage, you have to lie or blame your spouse. Property division and settlements, too, are based on fault. (And at a time when domestic violence isn't a term, much less a crime, women are legally encouraged to remain in abusive marriages.) If fathers ask for custody of their children, they get it in 60 to 80 percent of the cases. (This is still true.) If a husband or a lover hits his partner, she has no shelter to go to unless she happens to live near the one in northern California or the other in upper Michigan. If a woman is downsized from her role as a housewife (a.k.a. left by her husband), there is no word for being a displaced homemaker. As a divorcée, she may be regarded as a family disgrace or as easy sexual prey. After all, she had sex with one guy, so why not *all* guys?

If a woman is not a Mrs., she's a Miss. A woman without makeup and a hairdo is as suspect as a man with them. Without a male escort she may be refused service in a restaurant or a bar, and a woman alone is hard-pressed to find a landlord who will rent her an apartment. After all, she'll probably be leaving to get married soon, and, if she isn't, the landlord doesn't want to deal with a potential brothel.

Except among the very poor or in very rural areas, babies are born in hospitals. There are no certified midwives, and women are knocked out during birth. Most likely, they are also strapped down and lying down, made to have the baby against gravity for the doctor's convenience. If he has a schedule to keep, the likelihood of a cesarean is also very high. *Our Bodies, Ourselves* doesn't exist, nor does the women's health movement. Women aren't taught how to look at their cervixes, and their bodies are nothing to worry their pretty little heads about; however, they are supposed to worry about keeping their little heads pretty. If a woman goes under the knife to see if she has breast cancer, the surgeon won't wake her up to consult about her options before performing a Halsted mastectomy (a disfiguring radical procedure, in which the breast, the muscle wall, and the nodes under the arm, right down to the bone, are removed). She'll just wake up and find that the choice has been made for her.

Husbands are likely to die eight years earlier than their same-aged wives due to the stress of having to support a family and repress an emotional life, and a lot earlier than that if women have followed the custom of marrying older, authoritative, paternal men. The stress of raising kids, managing a household, and being undervalued by society doesn't seem to kill off women at the same rate. Upon a man's death, his beloved gets a portion of his Social Security. Even if she has worked outside the home for her entire adult life, she is probably better off with that portion than with hers in its entirety, because she has earned less and is likely to have taken time out for such unproductive acts as having kids.[7]

Has feminism changed our lives? Was it necessary? After thirty years of feminism, the world we inhabit barely resembles the world we were born into. And there's still a lot left to do.

Third Wave Manifesta: A Thirteen-Point Agenda

1. To out unacknowledged feminists, specifically those who are younger, so that Generation X can become a visible movement and, further, a voting block of eighteen- to forty-year-olds.
2. To safeguard a woman's right to bear or not to bear a child, regardless of circumstances, including women who are younger than eighteen or impoverished. To preserve this right throughout her life and support the choice to be childless.
3. To make explicit that the fight for reproductive rights must include birth control; the right for poor women and lesbians to have children; partner adoption for gay couples; subsidized fertility treatments for all women who choose them; and freedom from sterilization abuse. Furthermore, to support the idea that sex can be—and usually is—for pleasure, not procreation.
4. To bring down the double standard in sex and sexual health, and foster male responsibility and assertiveness in the following areas: achieving freedom from STDs; more fairly dividing the burden of family planning as well as responsibilities such as child care; and eliminating violence against women.
5. To tap into and raise awareness of our revolutionary history, and the fact that almost all movements began as youth movements. To have access to our intellectual feminist legacy and women's history; for the classics of radical feminism, womanism, *mujeristas*, women's liberation, and all our roots to remain in print; and to have women's history taught to men as well as women as a part of all curricula.
6. To support and increase the visibility and power of lesbians and bisexual women in the feminist movement, in high

schools, colleges, and the workplace. To recognize that queer women have always been at the forefront of the feminist movement, and that there is nothing to be gained—and much to be lost—by downplaying their history, whether inadvertently or actively.

7. To practice "autokeonony" ("self in community"): to see activism not as a choice between self and community but as a link between them that creates balance.
8. To have equal access to health care, regardless of income, which includes coverage equivalent to men's and keeping in mind that women use the system more often than men do because of our reproductive capacity.
9. For women who so desire to participate in all reaches of the military, including combat, and to enjoy all the benefits (loans, health care, pensions) offered to its members for as long as we continue to have an active military. The largest expenditure of our national budget goes toward maintaining this welfare system, and feminists have a duty to make sure women have access to every echelon.
10. To liberate adolescents from slut-bashing, listless educators, sexual harassment, and bullying at school, as well as violence in all walks of life, and the silence that hangs over adolescents' heads, often keeping them isolated, lonely, and indifferent to the world.
11. To make the workplace responsive to an individual's wants, needs, and talents. This includes valuing (monetarily) stay-at-home parents, aiding employees who want to spend more time with family and continue to work, equalizing pay for jobs of comparable worth, enacting a minimum wage that would bring a full-time worker with two children over the poverty line, and providing employee benefits for freelance and part-time workers.
12. To acknowledge that, although feminists may have disparate values, we share the same goal of equality, and of supporting one another in our efforts to gain the power to make our own choices.
13. To pass the Equal Rights Amendment so that we can have a constitutional foundation of righteousness and equality upon which future women's rights conventions will stand.

NOTES

1. Phyllis Rosser pioneered the research that named the gender gap in SAT and PSAT scores. She wrote to us as we were finishing the book that in the past couple of years "the gender gap on the PSAT has narrowed from 45 to 20 points (in SAT terms). This means that women will achieve about $1,500,000 more in scholarship money in 2000 than in previous years." See Rosser's book, *The SAT Gender Gap: Identifying the Causes,* published by the center for Women's Policy Studies (1989) for more information.

2. In 1999, the Women's Rights Project of the American Civil Liberties Union (ACLU) won a landmark Title IX case. Two high-school girls from Covington, Kentucky, brought suit against the National Honor Society for ignoring their qualifying GPAs in light of their pregnancy and parental status. The school district argued that the girls weren't denied admission because of their parental status (and implicitly acknowledged that such a practice would be unlawful) but because "they engaged in premarital sex." The school relied solely on pregnancy as proof of sexual activity, though, a determining factor that can apply only to women. (No males had ever been excluded from the school's chapter of the National Honor Society on grounds of having had sex—Title IX prevailed!)

3. Beauty contests are still the largest source of college scholarships for women. For example, the Miss America winner receives upward of $50,000, and the Miss America Organization has given more than $100 million in grants since 1945, when it began awarding scholarships. It remains the largest "scholarship organization" in the world.

4. Anonymous was a woman, as were the translators of most "great" works. For instance, the first English translation of *The Communist Manifesto* was done by a woman, Helen McFarlane. We intend to have any translations of *Manifesta* done by a man.

5. Before 1969, there were no women's studies departments, and very few individual courses. As of 2000, the National Women's Studies Association counted 728 women's studies courses in their database in the United States alone.

6. The McGovern-Nixon election of 1972 marked the emergence of a "gender gap," the first election in which there was a clear difference between men's and women's voting patterns. During the 1980 Carter-Reagan election, the gap had become wide enough for politicians to worry about getting the women's vote. (Only 46 percent of

women voted for Reagan, according to the Gallup poll, but 54 percent of men did.)

7. Statistics and facts from "A Day without Feminism" come from a few sources: *The American Woman 1994–95: Where We Stand, Women and Health,* edited by Cynthia Costello and Anne J. Stone for the Women's Research and Education Institute (New York: W. W. Norton, 1994); *The Book of Women's Firsts,* by Phyllis J. Read and Bernard L. Witlieb (New York: Random House, 1992); *Mother's on Trial: The Battle for Children and Custody,* by Phyllis Chesler; *The Reader's Companion to U.S. Women's History;* and the U.S. Bureau of Labor Statistics. (For full citations of all other books mentioned, see the Bibliography.)

QUESTIONS

1. Why might the authors have chosen the term "Manifesta" for their book? How does the tone of the "thirteen-point agenda" compare with documents from other periods in the women's movement?
2. How did conditions in the pre-feminist world prevent the achievement of equality between men and women and limit women's opportunities and growth? What educational inequalities do the authors describe? What economic distinctions are detailed? Which of these conditions still exist for women today?
3. What conditions described in "A Day Without Feminism" surprised you? Why?
4. What kind of list might women write 30 years from now about today's social conditions? What conditions, according to the authors, still need to be changed?

Equal Rights Amendment (1972)

Linda K. Kerber
and Jane Sherron De Hart, eds.

The words of the Equal Rights Amendment (ERA) were concise, elegant and straightforward. Yet their interpretation sparked great controversy. Would men and women have to share the same bathrooms? Would women be subject to the draft and be forced to serve in military combat situations? Would it be worth it to low-wage and working-class women, who often worked in potentially unsafe workplaces, to give up "protective" labor legislation such as limits on lifting and working long hours? Some business interests opposed the ERA because equality would be expensive to implement. Cultural conservatives opposed it because they feared a radical re-ordering of traditional gender roles. Despite a well financed opposition feminists continued to lobby for its passage until all avenues were exhausted. Historians Linda K. Kerber and Jane Sherron De Hart provide a brief background to the Equal Rights Amendment printed below.

An equal rights amendment, with wording slightly different from that passed by Congress in 1972, was sponsored in 1923 by the National Woman's Party. It seemed to party members the logical corollary to suffrage. But that amendment was vigorously opposed by the League of Women Voters and other progressive reformers, lest it undermine the protective legislation for which they had fought so hard.

An equal rights amendment was introduced regularly in Congress virtually every year thereafter, but it received little attention until after World War II. In 1950 and 1953 it was passed by the Senate but ignored by the House.

By 1970 much protective legislation had been applied to both men and women. It was possible to support an equal rights amendment without risking the undoing of labor law reforms. The hope that the Supreme Court would apply the Fourteenth Amendment's "equal protection of the laws" clause to cases involving discrimination on the basis of sex as firmly as it applied the clause to cases involving racial discrimination had not been fulfilled. When the current Equal Rights Amendment was introduced in 1970, it was endorsed by a wide range of organizations, some of which had once opposed it; these organizations included groups as disparate as the United Automobile Workers and the Woman's Christian Temperance Union. Its main sponsor in the House was Martha Griffiths of Michigan; in the Senate, Birch Bayh of Indiana.

The ERA was passed by Congress on March 22, 1972, and sent to the states for ratification. There was much initial enthusiasm; within two days six states had ratified. But the pace of ratification slowed after 1975, and only thirty-five of the needed thirty-eight states had ratified it by 1978. (Four state legislatures voted to rescind ratification, although the legality of that move was open to question.) In October 1978 Congress extended the deadline for ratification to June 30, 1982; the extension expired with no additional ratifications. The amendment was reintroduced in Congress in 1983 but has not been passed.

Section 1. Equality of rights under the law shall not be denied or abridged by the United States or by any State on account of sex.

Section 2. The Congress shall have the power to enforce, by appropriate legislation, the provisions of this article.

Section 3. The amendment shall take effect two years after the date of ratification.

QUESTIONS

1. Why was the Equal Rights Amendment proposed in the first place? What is it modeled after?
2. Why did many progressive reformers oppose the Equal Rights Amendment? What happened in the 1970s that made them change their minds?
3. What is the legislative history of the ERA? How did it end?

A Black Feminist Statement (1977)

The Combahee River Collective

The Combahee River Collective was a black feminist group that was formed in 1974 during the second wave of the feminist movement. The distinctive name was taken from a South Carolina river where Harriet Tubman led an effort to free 750 slaves during the Civil War. In 1977, the group released a statement of purpose, printed below, that articulates its philosophy and the importance of the women's liberation movement for women of color. The manifesto—a classic in movement history—describes the development of black feminism and the importance of addressing the issue of homophobia within the black feminist community.

We are a collective of black feminists who have been meeting together since 1974.[1] During that time we have been involved in the process of defining and clarifying our politics, while at the same time doing political work within our own group and in

"A Black Feminist Statement," by The Combahee River Collective, reprinted from *Capitalist Patriarchy and the Case for Socialist Feminism*, edited by Zillah R. Eisenstein, 1979, Monthly Review Press.

coalition with other progressive organizations and movements. The most general statement of our politics at the present time would be that we are actively committed to struggling against racial, sexual, heterosexual, and class oppression and see as our particular task the development of integrated analysis and practice based upon the fact that the major systems of oppression are interlocking. The synthesis of these oppressions creates the conditions of our lives. As black women we see black feminism as the logical political movement to combat the manifold and simultaneous oppressions that all women of color face.

We will discuss four major topics in the paper that follows: (1) The genesis of contemporary black feminism; (2) what we believe, i.e., the specific province of our politics; (3) the problems in organizing black feminists, including a brief herstory of our collective; and (4) black feminist issues and practice.

1. THE GENESIS OF CONTEMPORARY BLACK FEMINISM

Before looking at the recent development of black feminism, we would like to affirm that we find our origins in the historical reality of Afro-American women's continuous life-and-death struggle for survival and liberation. Black women's extremely negative relationship to the American political system (a system of white male rule) has always been determined by our membership in two oppressed racial and sexual castes. As Angela Davis points out in "Reflections on the Black Woman's Role in the Community of Slaves," black women have always embodied, if only in their physical manifestation, an adversary stance to white male rule and have actively resisted its inroads upon them and their communities in both dramatic and subtle ways. There have always been black women activists—some known, like Sojourner Truth, Harriet Tubman, Frances E. W. Harper, Ida B. Wells Barnett, and Mary Church Terrell, and thousands upon thousands unknown—who had a shared awareness of how their sexual identity combined with their racial identity to make their whole life situation and the focus of their political struggles unique. Contemporary black feminism is the outgrowth of countless generations of personal sacrifice, militancy, and work by our mothers and sisters.

A black feminist presence has evolved most obviously in connection with the second wave of the American women's movement beginning in the late 1960s. Black, other Third World, and working women have been involved in the feminist movement from its start, but both outside reactionary forces and racism and elitism within the movement itself have served to obscure our participation. In 1973 black feminists, primarily located in New York, felt the necessity of forming a separate black feminist group. This became the National Black Feminist Organization (NBFO).

Black feminist politics also have an obvious connection to movements for black liberation, particularly those of the 1960s and 1970s. Many of us were active in those movements (civil rights, black nationalism, the Black Panthers), and all of our lives were greatly affected and changed by their ideology, their goals, and the tactics used to achieve their goals. It was our experience and disillusionment within these liberation movements, as well as experience on the periphery of the white male left, that led to the need to develop a politics that was antiracist, unlike those of white women, and antisexist, unlike those of black and white men.

There is also undeniably a personal genesis for black feminism, that is, the political realization that comes from the seemingly personal experiences of individual black women's lives. Black feminists and many more black women who do not define themselves as feminists have all experienced sexual oppression as a constant factor in our day-to-day existence.

Black feminists often talk about their feelings of craziness before becoming conscious of the concepts of sexual politics, patriarchal rule, and, most importantly, feminism, the political analysis and practice that we women use to struggle against our oppression. The fact that racial politics and indeed racism are pervasive factors in our lives did not allow us, and still does not allow most black women, to look more deeply into our own experiences and define those things that make our lives what they are and our oppression specific to us. In the process of consciousness-raising, actually life-sharing, we began to recognize the commonality of our experiences and, from that sharing and growing consciousness, to build a politics that will change our lives and inevitably end our oppression.

Our development also must be tied to the contemporary economic and political position of black people. The post-World War II generation of black youth was the first to be able to minimally partake of certain educational and employment options, previously closed completely to black people. Although our economic position is still at the very bottom of the American capitalist economy, a handful of us have been able to gain certain tools as a result of tokenism in education and employment which potentially enable us to more effectively fight our oppression.

A combined antiracist and antisexist position drew us together initially, and as we developed politically we addressed ourselves to heterosexism and economic oppression under capitalism.

2. What We Believe

Above all else, our politics initially sprang from the shared belief that black women are inherently valuable, that our liberation is a necessity not as an adjunct to somebody else's but because of our need as human persons for autonomy. This may seem so obvious as to sound simplistic, but it is apparent that no other ostensibly progressive movement has ever considered our specific oppression a priority or worked seriously for the ending of that oppression. Merely naming the pejorative stereotypes attributed to black women (e.g., mammy, matriarch, Sapphire, whore, bulldagger), let alone cataloguing the cruel, often murderous, treatment we receive, indicates how little value has been placed upon our lives during four centuries of bondage in the Western hemisphere. We realize that the only people who care enough about us to work consistently for our liberation is us. Our politics evolve from a healthy love for ourselves, our sisters, and our community which allows us to continue our struggle and work.

This focusing upon our own oppression is embodied in the concept of identity politics. We believe that the most profound and potentially the most radical politics come directly out of our own identity, as opposed to working to end somebody else's oppression. In the case of black women this is a particularly repugnant, dangerous, threatening, and therefore revolutionary concept because it is obvious from looking at all the political movements that have preceded us that anyone is more worthy of liberation than ourselves. We reject pedestals, queenhood, and walking ten paces behind. To be recognized as human, levelly human, is enough.

We believe that sexual politics under patriarchy is as pervasive in black women's lives as are the politics of class and race. We also often find it difficult to separate race from class from sex oppression because in our lives they are most often experienced simultaneously. We know that there is such a thing as racial-sexual oppression which is neither solely racial nor solely sexual, e.g., the history of rape of black women by white men as a weapon of political repression.

Although we are feminists and lesbians, we feel solidarity with progressive black men and do not advocate the fractionalization that white women who are separatists demand. Our situation as black people necessitates that we have solidarity around the fact of race, which white women of course do not need to have with white men, unless it is their negative solidarity as racial oppressors. We struggle together with black men against racism, while we also struggle with black men about sexism.

We realize that the liberation of all oppressed peoples necessitates the destruction of the political-economic systems of capitalism and imperialism as well as patriarchy. We are socialists because we believe the work must be organized for the collective benefit of those who do the work and create the products and not for the profit of the bosses. Material resources must be equally distributed among those who create these resources. We are not convinced, however, that a socialist revolution that is not also a feminist and antiracist revolution will guarantee our liberation. We have arrived at the necessity for developing an understanding of class relationships that takes into account the specific class position of black women who are generally marginal in the labor force, while at this particular time some of us are temporarily viewed as doubly desirable tokens at white-collar and professional levels. We need to articulate the real class situation of persons who are not merely raceless, sexless workers, but for whom racial and sexual oppression are significant determinants in their working/economic lives. Although we are in essential agreement with Marx's theory as it applied to the very specific economic relationships he analyzed, we know that this analysis must be extended further in order for us to understand our specific economic situation as black women.

A political contribution which we feel we have already made is the expansion of the feminist principle that the personal is political. In our consciousness-raising sessions, for example, we have in many ways gone beyond white women's revelations because we are dealing with the implications of race and class as well as sex. Even our black women's style of talking/testifying in black language about what we have experienced has a resonance that is both cultural and political. We have spent a great deal of energy delving into the cultural and experiential nature of our oppression out of necessity because none of these matters have ever been looked at before. No one before has ever examined the multilayered texture of black women's lives.

As we have already stated, we reject the stance of lesbian separatism because it is not a viable political analysis or strategy for us. It leaves out far too much and far too many people, particularly black men, women, and children. We have a great deal of criticism and loathing for what men have been socialized to be in this society: what they support, how they act, and how they oppress. But we do not have the misguided notion that it is their maleness, per se—i.e., their biological maleness—that makes them what they are. As black women we find any type of biological determinism a particularly dangerous and reactionary basis upon which to build a politic. We must also question whether lesbian separatism is an adequate and progressive political analysis and strategy, even for those who practice it, since it so completely denies any but the sexual sources of women's oppression, negating the facts of class and race.

3. PROBLEMS IN ORGANIZING BLACK FEMINISTS

During our years together as a black feminist collective we have experienced success and defeat, joy and pain, victory and failure. We have found that it is very difficult to organize around black feminist issues, difficult even to announce in certain contexts that we *are* black feminists. We have tried to think about the reasons for our difficulties, particularly since the white women's movement continues to be strong and to grow in many directions. In this section we will discuss some of the general reasons for the organizing problems we face and also talk specifically about the stages in organizing our own collective.

The major source of difficulty in our political work is that we are not just trying to fight oppression on one front or even two, but instead to address a whole range of oppressions. We do not have racial, sexual, heterosexual, or class privilege to rely upon, nor do we have even the minimal access to resources and power that groups who possess any one of these types of privilege have.

The psychological toll of being a black woman and the difficulties this presents in reaching political consciousness and doing political work can never be underestimated. There is a very low value placed upon black women's psyches in this society, which is both racist and sexist. As an early group member once said, "We are all damaged people merely by virtue of being black women." We are dispossessed psychologically and on every other level, and yet we feel the necessity to struggle to change our condition and the condition of all black women. In "A Black Feminist's Search for Sisterhood," Michele Wallace arrives at this conclusion:

> We exist as women who are black who are feminists, each stranded for the moment, working independently because there is not yet an environment in this society remotely congenial to our struggle—because, being on the bottom, we would have to do what no one else has done: we would have to fight the world.[2]

Wallace is not pessimistic but realistic in her assessment of black feminists' position, particularly in her allusion to the nearly classic isolation most of us face. We might use our position at the bottom, however, to make a clear leap into revolutionary action. If black women were free, it would mean that everyone else would have to be free since our freedom would necessitate the destruction of all the systems of oppression.

Feminism is, nevertheless, very threatening to the majority of black people because it calls into question some of the most basic assumptions about our existence, i.e., that gender should be a determinant of power relationships. Here is the way male and female roles were defined in a black nationalist pamphlet from the early 1970s.

> We understand that it is and has been traditional that the man is the head of the house. He is the leader of the house/nation because his knowledge of the world is broader, his awareness is greater, his understanding is fuller and his application of this

> information is wiser. . . . After all, it is only reasonable that the man be the head of the house because he is able to defend and protect the development of his home. . . . Women cannot do the same things as men—they are made by nature to function differently. Equality of men and women is something that cannot happen even in the abstract world. Men are not equal to other men, i.e., ability, experience, or even understanding. The value of men and women can be seen as in the value of gold and silver—they are not equal but both have great value. We must realize that men and women are a complement to each other because there is no house/family without a man and his wife. Both are essential to the development of any life.[3]

The material conditions of most black women would hardly lead them to upset both economic and sexual arrangements that seem to represent some stability in their lives. Many black women have a good understanding of both sexism and racism, but because of the everyday constrictions of their lives cannot risk struggling against them both.

The reaction of black men to feminism has been notoriously negative. They are, of course, even more threatened than black women by the possibility that black feminists might organize around our own needs. They realize that they might not only lose valuable and hard-working allies in their struggles but that they might also be forced to change their habitually sexist ways of interacting with and oppressing black women. Accusations that black feminism divides the black struggle are powerful deterrents to the growth of an autonomous black women's movement.

Still, hundreds of women have been active at different times during the three-year existence of our group. And every black women who came, came out of a strongly felt need for some level of possibility that did not previously exist in her life.

When we first started meeting early in 1974 after the NBFO first eastern regional conference, we did not have a strategy for organizing, or even a focus. We just wanted to see what we had. After a period of months of not meeting, we began to meet again late in the year and started doing an intense variety of consciousness-raising. The overwhelming feeling that we had is that after years and years we had finally found each other. Although we were not doing political work as a group, individuals continued their involvement in lesbian politics, sterilization abuse and abortion rights work, Third World Women's International Women's

Day activities, and support activity for the trials of Dr. Kenneth Edelin, Joan Little, and Inez Garcia. During our first summer, when membership had dropped off considerably, those of us remaining devoted serious discussion to the possibility of opening a refuge for battered women in a black community. (There was no refuge in Boston at that time.) We also decided around that time to become an independent collective since we had serious disagreements with NBFOs bourgeois-feminist stance and their lack of a clear political focus.

We also were contacted at that time by socialist feminists, with whom we had worked on abortion rights activities, who wanted to encourage us to attend the National Socialist Feminist Conference in Yellow Springs. One of our members did attend and despite the narrowness of the ideology that was promoted at that particular conference, we became more aware of the need for us to understand our own economic situation and to make our own economic analysis.

In the fall, when some members returned, we experienced several months of comparative inactivity and internal disagreements which were first conceptualized as a lesbian-straight split but which were also the result of class and political differences. During the summer those of us who were still meeting had determined the need to do political work and to move beyond consciousness-raising and serving exclusively as an emotional support group. At the beginning of 1976, when some of the women who had not wanted to do political work and who also had voiced disagreements stopped attending of their own accord, we again looked for a focus. We decided at that time, with the addition of new members, to become a study group. We had always shared our reading with each other, and some of us had written papers on black feminism for group discussion a few months before this decision was made. We began functioning as a study group and also began discussing the possibility of starting a black feminist publication. We had a retreat in the late spring which provided a time for both political discussion and working out interpersonal issues. Currently we are planning to gather together a collection of black feminist writing. We feel that it is absolutely essential to demonstrate the reality of our politics to other black women and believe that we can do this through writing and distributing our work. The fact that individual black feminists are living in isolation all over the country, that our own numbers are small, and that we have some skills in writing, printing, and publishing makes us want to carry out these kinds of projects as a means of organizing black feminists as we continue to do political work in coalition with other groups.

4. Black Feminist Issues and Practice

During our time together we have identified and worked on many issues of particular relevance to black women. The inclusiveness of our politics makes us concerned with any situation that impinges upon the lives of women, Third World, and working people. We are of course particularly committed to working on those struggles in which race, sex, and class are simultaneous factors in oppression. We might, for example, become involved in workplace organizing at a factory that employs Third World women or picket a hospital that is cutting back on already inadequate health care to a Third World community, or set up a rape crisis center in a black neighborhood. Organizing around welfare or daycare concerns might also be a focus. The work to be done and the countless issues that this work represents merely reflect the pervasiveness of our oppression.

Issues and projects that collective members have actually worked on are sterilization abuse, abortion rights, battered women, rape, and health care. We have also done many workshops and educationals on black feminism on college campuses, at women's conferences, and most recently for high school women.

One issue that is of major concern to us and that we have begun to publicly address is racism in the white women's movement. As black feminists we are made constantly and painfully aware of how little effort white women have made to understand and combat their racism, which requires among other things that they have a more than superficial comprehension of race, color, and black history and culture. Eliminating racism in the white women's movement is by definition work for white women to do, but we will continue to speak to and demand accountability on this issue.

In the practice of our politics we do not believe that the end always justifies the means. Many reactionary and destructive acts have been done in the name of achieving "correct" political goals. As feminists we do not want to mess over people in the name of politics. We believe in collective process and a nonhierarchical distribution of power within our own group and in our vision of a revolutionary society. We are committed to a continual examination of our politics as they develop through criticism and self-criticism as an essential aspect of our practice. As black feminists and lesbians we know that we have a very definite revolutionary task to perform and we are ready for the lifetime of work and struggle before us.

NOTES

1. This statement is dated April 1977.
2. Michele Wallace, "A Black Feminist's Search for Sisterhood," *The Village Voice,* 28 July 1975, pp. 6–7.
3. Mumininas of Committee for Unified Newark, *Mwanamke Mwananchi* (*The Nationalist Woman*), Newark, N.J., © 1971, pp. 4–5.

QUESTIONS

1. How did Black feminism develop? Why is it needed? Why isn't just "feminism" enough? What do the authors mean by the statement that the "personal is political"?
2. What specific concerns do black feminists have that the women's liberation movement has not adequately addressed? What do the authors mean by black women's "multiplicity of oppressions"?
3. Why do the authors of this piece believe that lesbian separatism is not an acceptable answer to the challenges black lesbians face?

4. Why do the authors believe that black women need to feel solidarity with progressive black men around the subject of race?

5. What challenges to organizing do black women face? Why is political work nevertheless so vital to the position of black women?

Becoming the Third Wave (1992)

Rebecca Walker

Rebecca Walker is the editor of To Be Real *(1995) and co-founder of the Third Wave Direct Action Corporation, a national non-profit organization that promotes young women's leadership and activism in the United States. In this 1992 selection, Walker explores what it means to be part of Third Wave feminism. In her first person narrative, she insists on the need to move beyond political theory and toward "tangible action."*

I am not one of the people who sat transfixed before the television, watching the Senate hearings. I had classes to go to, papers to write, and frankly, the whole thing was too painful. A black man grilled by a panel of white men about his sexual deviance. A black woman claiming harassment and being discredited by other women. . . . I could not bring myself to watch that sensationalized assault [of] the human spirit.

To me, the hearings were not about determining whether or not Clarence Thomas did in fact harass Anita Hill. They were about checking and redefining the extent of women's credibility and power.

"Becoming the Third Wave," by Rebecca Walker, reprinted from *Ms. Magazine*, January/February 1992.

Can a woman's experience undermine a man's career? Can a woman's voice, a woman's sense of self-worth and injustice, challenge a structure predicated upon the subjugation of our gender? Anita Hill's testimony threatened to do that and more. If Thomas had not been confirmed, every man in the United States would be at risk. For how many senators never told a sexist joke? How many men have not used their protected male privilege to thwart in some way the influence or ideas of a woman colleague, friend, or relative?

For those whose sense of power is so obviously connected to the health and vigor of the penis, it would have been a metaphoric castration. Of course, this is too great a threat.

While some may laud the whole spectacle for the consciousness it raised around sexual harassment, its very real outcome is more informative. He was promoted. She was repudiated. Men were assured of the inviolability of their penis/power. Women were admonished to keep their experiences to themselves.

The backlash against U.S. women is real. As the misconception of equality between the sexes becomes more ubiquitous, so does the attempt to restrict the boundaries of women's personal and political power. Thomas's confirmation, the ultimate rally of support for the male paradigm of harassment, sends a clear message to women: "Shut up! Even if you speak, we will not listen."

I will not be silenced.

I acknowledge the fact that we live under siege. I intend to fight back. I have uncovered and unleashed more repressed anger than I thought possible. For the umpteenth time in my 22 years, I have been radicalized, politicized, shaken awake. I have come to voice again, and this time my voice is not conciliatory.

The night after Thomas' confirmation I ask the man I am intimate with what he thinks of the whole mess. His concern is primarily with Thomas' propensity to demolish civil rights and opportunities for people of color. I launch into a tirade. "When will progressive black men prioritize my rights and well-being? When will they stop talking so damn much about 'the race' as if it revolved exclusively around them?" He tells me I wear my emotions on my sleeve. I scream "I need to know, are you with me or are you going to help them try to destroy me?"

A week later I am on a train to New York. A beautiful mother and daughter, both wearing green outfits, sit across the aisle from me. The little girl has tightly plaited braids. Her brown skin is glowing and smooth, her eyes bright as she chatters happily while looking out the window. Two men get on the train and sit directly behind me, shaking my seat as they thud into place. I bury myself in *The Sound and the Fury*. Loudly they begin to talk about women. "Man, I fucked that bitch all night and then I never called her again." "Man, there's lots of girlies over there, you know that ho, live over there by Tyrone? Well, I snatched that shit up."

The mother moves closer to her now quiet daughter. Looking at her small back I can see that she is listening to the men. I am thinking of how I can transform the situation, of all the people in the car whose silence makes us complicit.

Another large man gets on the train. After exchanging loud greetings with the two men, he sits next to me. He tells them he is going to Philadelphia to visit his wife and child. I am suckered into thinking that he is different. Then, "Man, there's a ton of females in Philly, just waitin' for you to give 'em some." I turn my head and allow the fire in my eyes to burn into him. He takes up two seats and has hands with huge swollen knuckles. I imagine the gold rings on his fingers slamming into my face. He senses something, "What's your name, sweetheart?" The other men lean forward over the seat.

A torrent explodes: "I ain't your sweetheart, I ain't your bitch, I ain't your baby. How dare you have the nerve to sit up here and talk about women that way, and then try to speak to me." The woman/mother chimes in to the beat with claps of sisterhood. The men are momentarily stunned. Then the comeback: "Aw, bitch, don't play that woman shit over here 'cause that's bullshit." He slaps the back of one hand against the palm of the other. I refuse to back down. Words fly.

My instinct kicks in, telling me to get out. "Since I see you all are not going to move, I will." I move to the first car. I am so angry that thoughts of murder, of physically retaliating against them, of separatism, engulf me. I am almost out of body, just shy, of being pure force. I am sick of the way women are negated, violated, devalued, ignored. I am livid, unrelenting in my anger at those who invade my space, who wish to take away my rights, who refuse to hear my voice.

As the days pass, I push myself to figure out what it means to be a part of the Third Wave of feminism. I begin to realize that I owe it to myself, to my little sister on the train, to all of the daughters yet to be born, to push beyond my rage and articulate an agenda. After battling with ideas of separatism and militancy, I connect with my own feelings of powerlessness. I realize that I must undergo a transformation if I am truly committed to women's empowerment. My involvement must reach beyond my own voice in discussion, beyond voting, beyond reading feminist theory. My anger and awareness must translate into tangible action.

I am ready to decide, as my mother decided before me, to devote much of my energy to the history, health, and healing of women. Each of my choices will have to hold to my feminist standard of justice.

To be a feminist is to integrate an ideology of equality and female empowerment into the very fiber of my life. It is to search for personal clarity in the midst of systemic destruction, to join in sisterhood with women when often we are divided, to understand power structures with the intention of challenging them.

While this may sound simple, it is exactly the kind of stand that many of my peers are unwilling to take. So I write this as a plea to all women, especially the women of my generation: Let Thomas' confirmation serve to remind you, as it did me, that the fight is far from over. Let this dismissal of a woman's experience move you to anger. Turn that outrage into political power. Do not vote for them unless they work for us. Do not have sex with them, do not break bread with them, do not nurture them if they do not prioritize our freedom to control our bodies and our lives.

I am not a postfeminism feminist. I am the Third Wave.

Questions

1. What characteristics of third wave feminism are evident in Walker's article? How does Walker see these characteristics as different from previous concerns of the women's movement?

2. Why does Walker begin and end the article with references to the Hill/Thomas decision? What effects of sexism are evident in that decision?

3. How does Walker's story of her train ride through New York support the idea that words are powerful actions? How do the other riders on the train illustrate the effects of sexism?

Fear of Feminism: Why Young Women Get the Willies (1994)

Lisa Maria Hogeland

Despite the accomplishments of the women's movement, and widespread attention to women's issues in the media and in education, a great deal of confusion remains about feminism—what the term means, who it represents, why it is necessary. Accompanying this confusion has been discomfort with the feminist label. In this 1994 Ms. Magazine *essay, Lisa Hogeland, Assistant Professor of English and Women's Studies at the University of Cincinnati, responds to these fears and clarifies some of the tenets and implications of feminism.*

I began thinking about young women's fear of feminism, as I always do in the fall, while I prepared to begin another year of teaching courses in English and women's studies. I was further prodded when former students of mine, now graduate students elsewhere and teaching for the first time, phoned in to complain about their young women students' resistance to feminism. It

"Fear of Feminism: Why Young Women Get the Willies," by Lisa Maria Hogeland, reprinted from *Ms.* magazine, November/December 1994.

occurred to me that my response—"Of course young women are afraid of feminism"—was not especially helpful. This essay is an attempt to trace out what that "of course" really means; much of it is based on my experience with college students, but many of the observations apply to other young women as well.

Some people may argue that young women have far less to lose by becoming feminists than do older women: they have a smaller stake in the system and fewer ties to it. At the same time, though, young women today have been profoundly affected by the demonization of feminism during the 12 years of Reagan and Bush—the time when they formed their understanding of political possibility and public life. Older women may see the backlash as temporary and changeable; younger women may see it as how things are. The economic situation for college students worsened over those 12 years as well, with less student aid available, so that young women may experience their situation as extremely precarious—too precarious to risk feminism.

My young women students often interpret critiques of marriage—a staple of feminist analysis for centuries—as evidence of their authors' dysfunctional families. This demonstrates another reality they have grown up with: the increased tendency to pathologize any kind of oppositional politics. Twelve years of the rhetoric of "special interests versus family values" have created a climate in which passionate political commitments seem crazy. In this climate, the logical reasons why all women fear feminism take on particular meaning and importance for young women.

To understand what women fear when they fear feminism—and what they don't—it is helpful to draw a distinction between gender consciousness and feminist consciousness. One measure of feminism's success over the past three decades is that women's gender consciousness—our self-awareness as women—is extremely high. Gender consciousness takes two forms: awareness of women's vulnerability and celebration of women's difference. Fear of crime is at an all-time high in the United States; one of the driving forces behind this fear may well be women's sense of special vulnerability to the epidemic of men's violence. Feminists have fostered this awareness of violence against women, and it is to our credit that we have made our analysis so powerful; at the same time, however, we must attend to ways this awareness can be deployed for nonfeminist and even antifeminist purposes, and most especially to ways it can be used to serve a racist agenda.

Feminists have also fostered an awareness of women's difference from men and made it possible for women (including non-feminists) to have an appreciation of things pertaining to women—perhaps most visible the kinds of "women's culture" commodified in the mass media (soap operas and romance, self-help books, talk shows, and the like). Our public culture in the U.S. presents myriad opportunities for women to take pleasure in being women—most often, however, that pleasure is used as an advertising or marketing strategy.

Gender consciousness is a necessary precondition for feminist consciousness but they are not the same. The difference lies in the link between gender and politics. Feminism politicizes gender consciousness, inserts it into a systematic analysis of histories and structures of domination and privilege. Feminism asks questions—difficult and complicated questions, often with contradictory and confusing answers—about how gender consciousness can be used both for and against women, how vulnerability and difference help and hinder women's self-determination and freedom. Fear of feminism, then, is not a fear of gender, but rather a fear of politics. Fear of politics can be understood as a fear of living in consequences, a fear of reprisals.

The fear of political reprisals is very realistic. There are powerful interests opposed to feminism—let's be clear about that. It is not in the interests of white supremacy that white women insist on abortion rights, that women of color insist on an end to involuntary sterilization, that all women insist on reproductive self-determination. It is not in the interests of capitalism that women demand economic rights or comparable worth. It is not in the interests of many individual men or many institutions that women demand a nonexploitative sexual autonomy—the right to say and mean both no and yes on our own terms. What would our mass culture look like if it didn't sell women's bodies—even aside from pornography? It is not in the interests of heterosexist patriarchy that women challenge our understandings of events headlined Man Killed Family Because He Loved Them, that women challenge the notion of men's violence against women and children as deriving from "love" rather than power. It is not in the interests of any of the systems of domination in which we are enmeshed that we see how these systems work—that we understand men's violence, male domination, race and class supremacy, as systems of permission for both individual and institutional exercises of power, rather than merely as individual pathologies. It is not in the interests of white supremacist capitalist patriarchy that women ally across differences.

Allying across differences is difficult work, and is often thwarted by homophobia—by fears both of lesbians and of being named a lesbian by association. Feminism requires that we confront that homophobia constantly. I want to suggest another and perhaps more subtle and insidious way that fear of feminism is shaped by the institution of heterosexuality. Think about the lives of young women—think about your own. What are the arenas for selfhood for young women in this culture? How do they discover and construct their identities? What teaches them who they are, who they want to be, who they might be? Our culture allows women so little scope for development, for exploration, for testing the boundaries of what they can do and who they can be, that romantic and sexual relationships become the primary, too often the only, arena for selfhood.

Young women who have not yet begun careers or community involvements too often have no public life, and the smallness of private life, of romance as an arena for selfhood, is particularly acute for them. Intimate relationships become the testing ground for identity, a reality that has enormously damaging consequences for teenage girls in particular (the pressures both toward and on sex and romance, together with the culturally induced destruction of girls' self-esteem at puberty, have everything to do with teenage pregnancy). The feminist insistence that the personal is political may seem to threaten rather than empower a girl's fragile, emergent self as she develops into a sexual and relational being.

Young women may believe that a feminist identity puts them out of the pool for many men, limits the options of who they might become with a partner, how they might decide to live. They may not be wrong either: how many young men feminists or feminist sympathizers do you know? A politics that may require making demands on a partner, or that may motivate particular choices in partners, can appear to foreclose rather than to open up options for identity, especially for women who haven't yet discovered that all relationships require negotiation and struggle. When you live on Noah's ark, anything that might make it more difficult to find a partner can seem to threaten your very survival. To make our case, feminists have to combat not just homophobia, but also the rule of the couple, the politics of Noah's ark in the age of "family values." This does not mean that heterosexual feminist women must give up their intimate relationships, but it does mean that feminists must continually analyze those pressures, be clear about how they operate in our lives, and try to find ways around and through them for ourselves, each other, and other women.

For women who are survivors of men's violence—perhaps most notably for incest and rape survivors—the shift feminism enables, from individual pathology to systematic analysis, is empowering rather than threatening. For women who have not experienced men's violence in these ways, the shift to a systematic analysis requires them to ally themselves with survivors—itself a recognition that *it could happen to me.* Young women who have not been victims of men's violence hate being asked to identify with it; they see the threat to their emergent sense of autonomy and freedom not in the fact of men's violence, but in feminist analyses that make them identify with it. This can also be true for older women, but it may be lessened by the simple statistics of women's life experience: the longer you live, the more likely you are to have experienced men's violence or to know women who are survivors of it, and thus to have a sense of a range and scope of that violence.

My women students, feminist and nonfeminist alike, are perfectly aware of the risks of going unescorted to the library at night. At the same time, they are appalled by my suggesting that such gender-based restrictions on their access to university facilities deny them an equal education. It's not that men's violence isn't real to them—but that they are unwilling to trace out its consequences and to understand its complexities. College women, however precarious their economic situation, and even despite the extent of sexual harassment and date rape on campuses all over the country, still insist on believing that women's equality has been achieved. And, in fact, to the extent that colleges and universities are doing their jobs—giving women students something like an equal education—young women may experience relatively little overt or firsthand discrimination. Sexism may come to seem more the exception than the rule in some academic settings—and thus more attributable to individual sickness than to systems of domination.

Women of all ages fear the existential situation of feminism, what we learned from Simone de Beauvoir, what we learned from radical feminists in the 1970s, what we learned from feminist women of color in the 1980s: feminism has consequences. Once you have your "click!" moment, the world shifts, and it shifts in some terrifying ways. Not just heterosexism drives this fear of political commitment—it's not just fear of limiting one's partner-pool. It's also about limiting oneself—about the fear of commitment to something larger than the self that asks us to examine the consequences of our actions. Women fear anger, and change, and challenge—who doesn't? Women fear taking a public stand, entering public discourse, demanding—and perhaps getting—attention. And for what? To be called a "feminazi"? To be denounced as traitors to women's "essential nature"?

The challenge to the public-private division that feminism represents is profoundly threatening to young women who just want to be left alone, to all women who believe they can hide from feminist issues by not being feminists. The central feminist tenet that the personal is political is profoundly threatening to young women who don't want to be called to account. It is far easier to rest in silence, as if silence were neutrality, and as if neutrality were safety. Neither wholly cynical nor wholly apathetic, women who fear feminism fear living in consequences. Think harder, act more carefully; feminism requires that you enter a world supersaturated with meaning, with implications. And for privileged women in particular, the notion that one's own privilege comes at someone else's expense—that my privilege *is* your oppression—is profoundly threatening.

Fear of feminism is also fear of complexity, fear of thinking, fear of ideas—we live, after all, in a profoundly anti-intellectual culture. Feminism is one of the few movements in the U.S. that produce nonacademic intellectuals—readers, writers, thinkers, and theorists outside the academy, who combine and refine their knowledge with their practice. What other movement is housed so substantially in bookstores? All radical movements for change struggle against the anti-intellectualism of U.S. culture, the same anti-intellectualism, fatalism, and disengagement that make even voting too much work for most U.S. citizens. Feminism is work—intellectual work as surely as it is activist work—and it can be very easy for women who have been feminists for a long time to forget how hard-won their insights are, how much reading and talking and thinking and work produced them. In this political climate, such insights may be even more hard-won.

Feminism requires an expansion of the self—an expansion of empathy interest, intelligence, and responsibility across differences, histories, cultures, ethnicities, sexual identities, othernesses. The differences between women, as Audre Lorde pointed out over and over again, are our most precious resources in thinking and acting toward change. Fear of difference is itself a fear of consequences; it is less other women's difference that we fear than our own implication in the hierarchy of differences, our own accountability to other women's oppression. It is easier to rest in gender consciousness, in one's own difference, than to undertake the personal and political analysis required to trace out one's own position in multiple and overlapping systems of domination.

Women have real reasons to fear feminism, and we do young women no service if we suggest to them that feminism itself is safe. It is not. To stand opposed to our culture, to be critical of institutions, behaviors, discourses—when it is so clearly not in your immediate interest to do so—asks a lot of a young person, of any person. At its best, the feminist challenging of individualism, of narrow notions of freedom, is transformative, exhilarating, empowering. When we do our best work in selling feminism to the unconverted, we make clear not only its necessity, but also its pleasures: the joys of intellectual and political work, the moral power of living in consequences, the surprises of coalition, the rewards of doing what is difficult. Feminism offers an arena for selfhood beyond personal relationships but not disconnected from them. It offers—and requires—courage, intelligence, boldness, sensitivity, relationality, complexity, a sense of purpose, and, lest we forget, a sense of humor as well. Of course young women are afraid of feminism—shouldn't they be?

QUESTIONS

1. What are the various reasons young women fear feminism? How does Hogeland respond to these fears? Which fears are significant? Why?
2. What is gender consciousness? Feminist consciousness? What is the distinction Hogeland makes between these ideas? How are they related? How does Hogeland's defi-

nition of feminism differ from other definitions you are familiar with?

3. Why is feminism necessary, according to Hogeland? What does it offer? What challenges does it pose?

Oppression (1983)

Marilyn Frye

Marilyn Frye is a philosopher and the author of numerous articles, essays and books including Willful Virgin: Essays in Feminism *(1992) and* The Politics of Reality: Essays in Feminist Theory *(1983). In this 1983 essay, Frye attempts to clarify the meaning of the term "oppression"—a forceful, value-laden term that is nonetheless significant for understanding women's experiences. Most illuminating in Frye's essay is her use of several metaphors and images to illustrate the complex nature of oppression. Through these key metaphors, Fry emphasizes how multiple factors intersect to place individuals in oppressive situations.*

It is a fundamental claim of feminism that women are oppressed. The word 'oppression' is a strong word. It repels and attracts. It is dangerous and dangerously fashionable and endangered. It is much misused, and sometimes not innocently.

"Oppression," by Marilyn Frye, reprinted from *The Politics of Reality: Essays in Feminist Theory*, 1983, by permission of Crossing Press.

The statement that women are oppressed is frequently met with the claim that men are oppressed too. We hear that oppressing is oppressive to those who oppress as well as to those they oppress. Some men cite as evidence of their oppression their much-advertised inability to cry. It is tough, we are told, to be masculine. When the stresses and frustrations of being a man are cited as evidence that oppressors are oppressed by their oppressing, the word 'oppression' is being stretched to meaninglessness; it is treated as though its scope includes any and all human experience of limitation or suffering, no matter the cause, degree or consequence. Once such usage has been put over on us, then if ever we deny that any person or group is oppressed, we seem to imply that we think they never suffer and have no feelings. We are accused of insensitivity; even of bigotry. For women, such accusation is particularly intimidating, since sensitivity is one of the few virtues that has been assigned to us. If we are found insensitive, we may fear we have no redeeming traits at all and perhaps are not real women. Thus are we silenced before we begin: the name of our situation drained of meaning and our guilt mechanisms tripped.

But this is nonsense. Human beings can be miserable without being oppressed, and it is perfectly consistent to deny that a person or group is oppressed, without denying that they have feelings or that they suffer.

We need to think clearly about oppression, and there is much that mitigates against this. I do not want to undertake to prove that women are oppressed (or that men are not), but I want to make clear what is being said when we say it. We need this word, this concept, and we need it to be sharp and sure.

I

The root of the word 'oppression' is the element 'press.' *The press of the crowd; pressed into military service; to press a pair of pants; printing press; press the button.* Presses are used to mold things or flatten them or reduce them in bulk, sometimes to reduce them by squeezing out the gasses or liquids in them. Something pressed is something caught between or among forces and barriers which are so related to each other that jointly they restrain, restrict or prevent the thing's motion or mobility. Mold. Immobilize. Reduce.

The mundane experience of the oppressed provides another clue. One of the most characteristic and ubiquitous features of the world as experienced by oppressed people is the double bind—situations in which options are reduced to a very few and all of them expose one to penalty, censure or deprivation. For example, it is often a requirement upon oppressed people that we smile and be cheerful. If we comply, we signal our docility and our acquiescence in our situation. We need not, then, be taken note of. We acquiesce in being made invisible, in our occupying no space. We participate in our own erasure. On the other hand, anything but the sunniest countenance exposes us to being perceived as mean, bitter, angry or dangerous. This means, at the least, that we may be found "difficult" or unpleasant to work with, which is enough to cost one one's livelihood; at worst, being seen as mean, bitter, angry or dangerous has been known to result in rape, arrest, beating and murder. One can only choose to risk one's preferred form and rate of annihilation.

Another example: It is common in the United States that women, especially younger women, are in a bind, where neither sexual activity nor sexual inactivity is all right. If she is heterosexually active, a woman is open to censure and punishment for being loose, unprincipled or a whore. The "punishment" comes in the form of criticism, snide and embarrassing remarks, being treated as an easy lay by men, scorn from her more restrained female friends. She may have to lie and hide her behavior from her parents. She must juggle the risks of unwanted pregnancy and dangerous contraceptives. On the other hand, if she refrains from heterosexual activity, she is fairly constantly harassed by men who try to persuade her into it and pressure her to "relax" and "let her hair down"; she is threatened with labels like "frigid," "uptight," "man-hater," "bitch" and "cocktease." The same parents who would be disapproving of her sexual activity may be worried by her inactivity because it suggests she is not or will not be popular, or is not sexually normal. She may be charged with lesbianism. If a woman is raped, then if she has been heterosexually active she is subject to the presumption that she liked it (since her activity is presumed to show that she likes sex), and if she has not been heterosexually active, she is subject to the presumption that she liked it (since she is supposedly "repressed and frustrated"). Both heterosexual activity and heterosexual nonactivity are likely to be taken as proof that you wanted to be raped, and hence, of course, weren't *really* raped at all. You can't win. You are caught in a bind, caught between systematically related pressures.

Women are caught like this, too, by networks of forces and barriers that expose one to penalty, loss or contempt whether one works outside the home or not, is on welfare or not, bears children or not, raises children or not, marries or not, stays married or not, is heterosexual, lesbian, both or neither. Economic necessity; confinement to racial and/or sexual job ghettos; sexual harassment; sex discrimination; pressures of competing expectations and judgments about *women, wives,* and *mothers* (in the society at large, in racial and ethnic subcultures and in one's own mind); dependence (full or partial) on husbands, parents or the state; commitment to political ideas; loyalties to racial or ethnic or other "minority" groups; the demands of self-respect and responsibilities to others. Each of these factors exists in complex tension with every other, penalizing or prohibiting all of the apparently available options. And nipping at one's heels, always, is the endless pack of little things. If one dresses one way, one is subject to the assumption that one is advertising one's sexual availability; if one dresses another way, one appears to "not care about oneself " or to be "unfeminine." If one uses "strong language," one invites categorization as a whore or slut; if one does not, one invites categorization as a "lady"—one too delicately constituted to cope with robust speech or the realities to which it presumably refers.

The experience of oppressed people is that the living of one's life is confined and shaped by forces and barriers which are not accidental or occasional and hence avoidable, but are systematically related to each other in such a way as to catch one between and among them and restrict or penalize motion in any direction. It is the experience of being caged in: all avenues, in every direction, are blocked or booby trapped.

Cages. Consider a birdcage. If you look very closely at just one wire in the cage, you cannot see the other wires. If your conception of what is before you is determined by this myopic focus, you could look at that one wire, up and down the length of it, and be unable to see why a bird would not just fly around the wire any time it wanted to go somewhere. Furthermore, even if, one day at a time, you myopically inspected each wire, you still could not see why a bird would have trouble going past the wires to get anywhere. There is no physical property of any one wire, *nothing* that the closest scrutiny could discover, that will reveal how a bird could be inhibited or harmed by it except in the most accidental way. It is only when you step back, stop looking at the wires one by one, microscopically, and take a macroscopic view of the whole cage, that you can see why the bird does not go anywhere; and then you will see it in a moment. It will require no great subtlety of mental powers. It is perfectly *obvious* that the bird is surrounded by a network of systematically related barriers, no one of which would be the least hindrance to its flight, but which, by their relations to each other, are as confining as the solid walls of a dungeon.

It is now possible to grasp one of the reasons why oppression can be hard to see and recognize: one can study the elements of an oppressive structure with great care and some good will without seeing the structure as a whole, and hence without seeing or being able to understand that one is looking at a cage and that there are people there who are caged, whose motion and mobility are restricted, whose lives are shaped and reduced.

The arresting of vision at a microscopic level yields such common confusion as that about the male door-opening ritual. This ritual, which is remarkably widespread across classes and races, puzzles many people, some of whom do and some of whom do not find it offensive. Look at the scene of the two people approaching a door. The male steps slightly ahead and opens the door. The male holds the door open while the female glides through. Then the male goes through. The door closes after them. "Now how," one innocently asks, "can those crazy womens-libbers say that is oppressive? The guy *removed* a barrier to the lady's smooth and unruffled progress." But each repetition of this ritual has a place in a pattern, in fact in several patterns. One has to shift the level of one's perception in order to see the whole picture.

The door-opening pretends to be a helpful service, but the helpfulness is false. This can be seen by noting that it will be done whether or not it makes any practical sense. Infirm men and men burdened with packages will open doors for able-bodied women who are free of physical burdens. Men will impose themselves awkwardly and jostle everyone in order to get to the door first. The act is not determined by convenience or grace. Furthermore, these very numerous acts of unneeded or even noisome "help" occur in counterpoint to a pattern of men not being helpful in many practical ways in which women might welcome help. What *women* experience is a world in which gallant princes charming commonly make a fuss about being helpful and providing small services when help and services are of little or no use, but in which there are rarely ingenious and adroit princes at hand when substantial assistance is really wanted either in mundane affairs or in situations of threat, assault or terror. There is no help with the (his) laundry; no help typing a report at 4:00 a.m.; no help in mediating disputes among relatives or children. There is nothing but advice that women should stay indoors after dark, be chaperoned by a man, or when it comes down to it, "lie back and enjoy it."

The gallant gestures have no practical meaning. Their meaning is symbolic. The door-opening and similar services provided are services which really are needed by people who are for one reason or another incapacitated—unwell, burdened with parcels, etc. So the message is that women are incapable. The detachment of the acts from the concrete realities of what women need and do not need is a vehicle for the message that women's actual needs and interests are unimportant or irrelevant. Finally, these gestures imitate the behavior of servants toward masters and thus mock women, who are in most respects the servants and caretakers of men. The message of the false helpfulness of male gallantry is female dependence, the invisibility or insignificance of women, and contempt for women.

One cannot see the meanings of these rituals if one's focus is riveted upon the individual event in all its particularity, including the particularity of the individual man's present conscious intentions and motives and the individual woman's conscious perception of the event in the moment. It seems sometimes that people take a deliberately myopic view and fill their eyes with things seen microscopically in order not to see macroscopically. At any rate, whether it is deliberate or not, people can and do fail to see the oppression of women because they fail to see macroscopically and hence fail to see the various elements of the situation as systematically related in larger schemes.

As the cageness of the birdcage is a macroscopic phenomenon, the oppressiveness of the situations in which women live our various and different lives is a macroscopic phenomenon. Neither can be *seen* from a microscopic perspective. But when you look macroscopically you can see it—a network of forces and barriers which are systematically related and which conspire to the immobilization, reduction and molding of women and the lives we live.

II

The image of the cage helps convey one aspect of the systematic nature of oppression. Another is the selection of occupants of the cages, and analysis of this aspect also helps account for the invisibility of the oppression of women.

It is as a woman (or as a Chicana/o or as a Black or Asian or lesbian) that one is entrapped.

> "Why can't I go to the park; you let Jimmy go!"
>
> "Because it's not safe for girls."

> "I want to be a secretary, not a seamstress; I don't want to learn to make dresses."
>
> "There's no work for negroes in that line; learn a skill where you can earn your living."[1]

When you question why you are being blocked, why this barrier is in your path, the answer has not to do with individual talent or merit, handicap or failure; it has to do with your membership in some category understood as a "natural" or "physical" category. The "inhabitant" of the "cage" is not an individual but a group, all those of a certain category. If an individual is oppressed, it is in virtue of being a member of a group or category of people that is systematically reduced, molded, immobilized. Thus, to recognize a person as oppressed, one has to see that individual as belonging to a group of a certain sort.

There are many things which can encourage or inhibit perception of someone's membership in the sort of group or category in question here. In particular, it seems reasonable to suppose that if one of the devices of restriction and definition of the group is that of physical confinement or segregation, the confinement and separation would encourage recognition of the group as a group. This in turn would encourage the macroscopic focus which enables one to recognize oppression and encourages the individuals' identification and solidarity with other individuals of the group or category. But physical confinement and segregation of the group as a group is not common to all oppressive structures, and when an oppressed group is geographically and demographically dispersed the perception of it as a group is inhibited. There may be little or nothing in the situations of the individuals encouraging the macroscopic focus which would reveal the unity of the structure bearing down on all members of that group.[2]

A great many people, female and male and of every race and class, simply do not believe that *woman* is a category of oppressed people, and I think that this is in part because they have been fooled by the dispersal and assimilation of women throughout and into the systems of class and race which organize men. Our simply being dispersed makes it difficult for women to have knowledge of each other and hence difficult to recognize the shape of our common cage. The dispersal and assimilation of women throughout economic classes and races also divides us against each other practically and economically and thus attaches *interest* to the inability to see: for some, jealousy of their benefits, and for some, resentment of the others' advantages.

To get past this, it helps to notice that in fact women of all races and classes *are* together in a ghetto of sorts. There is a women's place, a sector, which is inhabited by women of all classes and races, and it is not defined by geographical boundaries but by function. The function is the service of men and men's interests as men define them, which includes the bearing and rearing of children. The details of the service and the working conditions vary by race and class, for men of different races and classes have different interests, perceive their interests differently, and express their needs and demands in different rhetorics, dialects and languages. But there are also some constants.

Whether in lower, middle or upper-class home or work situations, women's service work always includes personal service (the work of maids, butlers, cooks, personal secretaries),[3] sexual service (including provision for his genital sexual needs and bearing his children, but also including "being nice," "being attractive for him," etc.), and ego service (encouragement, support, praise, attention). Women's service work also is characterized everywhere by the fatal combination of responsibility and powerlessness: we are held responsible and we hold ourselves responsible for good outcomes for men and children in almost every respect though we have in almost no case power adequate to that project. The details of the subjective experience of this servitude are local. They vary with economic class and race and ethnic tradition as well as the personalities of the men in question. So also are the details of the forces which coerce our tolerance of this servitude particular to the different situations in which different women live and work.

All this is not to say that women do not have, assert and manage sometimes to satisfy our own interests, nor to deny that in some cases and in some respects women's independent interests do overlap with men's. But at every race/class level and even across race/class lines men do not serve women as women serve men. "Women's sphere" may be understood as the "service sector," taking the latter expression much more widely and deeply than is usual in discussions of the economy.

III

It seems to be the human condition that in one degree or another we all suffer frustration and limitation, all encounter unwelcome barriers, and all are damaged and hurt in various ways. Since we are a social species, almost all of our behavior and activities are structured by more than individual inclination and the conditions of the planet and its atmosphere. No human is free of social structures, nor (perhaps) would happiness consist in such freedom. Structure consists of boundaries, limits and barriers; in a structured whole, some motions and changes are possible, and others are not. If one is looking for an excuse to dilute the word 'oppression,' one can use the fact of social structure as an excuse and say that everyone is oppressed. But if one would rather get clear about what oppression is and is not, one needs to sort out the sufferings, harms and limitations and figure out which are elements of oppression and which are not.

From what I have already said here, it is clear that if one wants to determine whether a particular suffering, harm or limitation is part of someone's being oppressed, one has to look at it *in context* in order to tell whether it is an element in an oppressive structure: one has to see if it is part of an enclosing structure of forces and barriers which tends to the immobilization and reduction of a group or category of people. One has to look at how the barrier or force fits with others and to whose benefit or detriment it works.

As soon as one looks at examples, it becomes obvious that not everything which frustrates or limits a person is oppressive, and not every harm or damage is due to or contributes to oppression.

If a rich white playboy who lives off income from his investments in South African diamond mines should break a leg in a skiing accident at Aspen and wait in pain in a blizzard for hours before he is rescued, we may assume that in that period he suffers. But the suffering comes to an end; his leg is repaired by the best surgeon money can buy and he is soon recuperating in a lavish suite, sipping Chivas Regal. Nothing in this picture suggests a structure of barriers and forces. He is a member of several oppressor groups and does not suddenly become oppressed because he is injured and in pain. Even if the accident was caused by someone's malicious negligence, and hence someone can be blamed for it and morally faulted, that person still has not been an agent of oppression.

Consider also the restriction of having to drive one's vehicle on a certain side of the road. There is no doubt that this restriction is almost unbearably frustrating at times, when one's lane is not moving and the other lane is clear. There are surely times, even, when abiding by this regulation would have harmful consequences. But the restriction is obviously wholesome for most of us most of the time. The restraint is imposed for our benefit, and does benefit us; its operation tends to encourage our *continued* motion, not to immobilize us. The limits imposed by traffic regulations are limits most of us would cheerfully impose on ourselves given that we knew others would follow them too. They are part of a structure which shapes our behavior, not to our reduction and immobilization, but rather to the protection of our continued ability to move and act as we will.

Another example: The boundaries of a racial ghetto in an American city serve to some extent to keep white people from going in, as well as to keep ghetto dwellers from going out. A particular white citizen may be frustrated or feel deprived because s/he cannot stroll around there and enjoy the "exotic" aura of a "foreign" culture, or shop for bargains in the ghetto swap shops. In fact, the existence of the ghetto, of racial segregation, does deprive the white person of knowledge and harm her/his character by nurturing unwarranted feelings of superiority. But this does not make the white person in this situation a member of an oppressed race or a person oppressed because of her/ his race.

One must look at the barrier. It limits the activities and the access of those on both sides of it (though to different degrees). But it is a product of the intention, planning and action of whites for the benefit of whites, to secure and maintain privileges that are available to whites generally, as members of the dominant and privileged group. Though the existence of the barrier has some bad consequences for whites, the barrier does not exist in systematic relationship with other barriers and forces forming a structure oppressive to whites; quite the contrary. It is part of a structure which oppresses the ghetto dwellers and thereby (and by white intention) protects and furthers white interests as dominant white culture understands them. This barrier is not oppressive to whites, even though it is a barrier to whites.

Barriers have different meanings to those on opposite sides of them, even though they are barriers to both. The physical walls of a prison no more dissolve to let an outsider in than to let an insider out, but for the insider they are confining and limiting while to the outsider they may mean protection from what s/he takes to be threats posed by insiders—freedom from harm or anxiety. A set of social and economic barriers and forces separating two groups may be felt, even painfully, by members of both groups and yet may mean confinement to one and liberty and enlargement of opportunity to the other.

The service sector of the wives/mommas/assistants/girls is almost exclusively a woman-only sector; its boundaries not only enclose women but to a very great extent keep men out. Some men sometimes encounter this barrier and experience it as a restriction on their movements, their activities, their control or their choices of "lifestyle." Thinking they might like the simple nurturant life (which they may imagine to be quite free of stress, alienation and hard work), and feeling deprived since it seems closed to them, they thereupon announce the discovery that they are oppressed, too, by "sex roles." But that barrier is erected and maintained by men, for the benefit of men. It consists of cultural and economic forces and pressures in a culture and economy controlled by men in which, at every economic level and in all racial and ethnic subcultures, economy, tradition—and even ideologies of liberation—work to keep at least local culture and economy in male control.[4]

The boundary that sets apart women's sphere is maintained and promoted by men generally for the benefit of men generally, and men generally do benefit from its existence, even the man who bumps into it and complains of the inconvenience. That barrier is protecting his classification and status as a male, as superior, as having a right to sexual access to a female or females. It protects a kind of citizenship which is superior to that of females of his class and race, his access to a wider range of better paying and higher status work, and his right to prefer unemployment to the degradation of doing lower status or "women's" work.

If a person's life or activity is affected by some force or barrier that person encounters, one may not conclude that the person is oppressed simply because the person encounters that barrier or force; nor simply because the encounter is unpleasant, frustrating or painful to that person at that time; nor simply because the existence of the barrier or force, or the processes which maintain or apply it, serve to deprive that person of something of value. One must look at the barrier or force and answer certain questions about it. Who constructs and maintains it? Whose interests are served by its existence? Is it part of a structure which tends to confine, reduce and immobilize some group? Is the individual a member of the confined group? Various forces, barriers and limitations a person may encounter or live with may be part of an oppressive structure or not, and if they are, that person may be on either the oppressed or the oppressor side of it. One cannot tell which by how loudly or how little the person complains.

IV

Many of the restrictions and limitations we live with are more or less internalized and self-monitored, and are part of our adaptations to the requirements and expectations imposed by the needs and tastes and tyrannies of others. I have in mind such things as women's cramped postures and attenuated strides and men's restraint of emotional self-expression (except for anger). Who gets what out of the practice of those disciplines, and who imposes what penalties for improper relaxations of them? What are the rewards of this self-discipline?

Can men cry? Yes, in the company of women. If a man cannot cry, it is in the company of men that he cannot cry. It is men, not women, who require this restraint; and men not only require it, they reward it. The man who maintains a steely or tough or laid-back demeanor (all are forms which suggest invulnerability) marks himself as a member of the male community and is esteemed by other men. Consequently, the maintenance of that demeanor contributes to the man's self-esteem. It is felt as good, and he can feel good about himself. The way this restriction fits into the structures of men's lives is as one of the socially required behaviors which, if carried off, contribute to their acceptance and respect by significant others and to their own self-esteem. It is to their benefit to practice this discipline.

Consider, by comparison, the discipline of women's cramped physical postures and attenuated stride. This discipline can be relaxed in the company of women; it generally is at its most strenuous in the company of men.[5] Like men's emotional restraint, women's physical restraint is required by men. But unlike the case of men's emotional restraint, women's physical restraint is not rewarded. What do we get for it? Respect and esteem and acceptance? No. They mock us and parody our mincing steps. We look silly, incompetent, weak and generally contemptible. Our exercise of this discipline tends to low esteem and low self-esteem. It does not benefit us. It fits in a network of behaviors through which we constantly announce to others our membership in a lower caste and our unwillingness and/or inability to defend our bodily or moral integrity. It is degrading and part of a pattern of degradation.

Acceptable behavior for both groups, men and women, involves a required restraint that seems in itself silly and perhaps damaging. But the social effect is drastically different. The woman's restraint is part of a structure oppressive to women; the man's restraint is part of a structure oppressive to women.

V

One is marked for application of oppressive pressures by one's membership in some group or category. Much of one's suffering and frustration befalls one partly or largely because one is a member of that category. In the case at hand, it is the category, *woman*. Being a woman is a major factor in my not having a better job than I do; being a woman selects me as a likely victim of sexual assault or harassment; it is my being a woman that reduces the power of my anger to a proof of my insanity. If a woman has little or no economic or political power, or achieves little of what she wants to achieve, a major causal factor in this is that she is a woman. For any woman of any race or economic class, being a woman is significantly attached to whatever disadvantages and deprivations she suffers, be they great or small.

None of this is the case with respect to a person's being a man. Simply being a man is not what stands between him and a better job; whatever assaults and harassments he is subject to, being male is not what selects him for victimization; being male is not a factor which would make his anger impotent—quite the opposite. If a man has little or no material or political power, or achieves little of what he wants to achieve, his being male is no part of the explanation. Being male is something he has going *for* him, even if race or class or age or disability is going against him.

Women are oppressed, *as women*. Members of certain racial and/or economic groups and classes, both the males and the females, are oppressed *as* members of those races and/or classes. But men are not oppressed *as men*.

. . . and isn't it strange that any of us should have been confused and mystified about such a simple thing?

NOTES

1. This example is derived from *Daddy Was A Number Runner*, by Louise Meriwether (Prentice-Hall, Englewood Cliffs, New Jersey, 1970), p. 144.

2. Coerced assimilation is in fact one of the *policies* available to an oppressing group in its effort to reduce and/or annihilate another group. This tactic is used by the U.S. government, for instance, on the American Indians.

3. At higher class levels women may not *do* all these kinds of work, but are generally still responsible for hiring and supervising those who do it. These services are still, in these cases, women's responsibility.

4. Of course this is complicated by race and class. Machismo and "Black manhood" politics seem to help keep Latin or Black men in control of

more cash than Latin or Black women control; but these politics seem to me also to ultimately help keep the larger economy in *white* male control.

5. Cf. *Let's Take Back Our Space: "Female" and "Male" Body Language as a Result of Patriarchal Structures,* by Marianne Wex (Frauenliterature-verlag Hermine Fees, West Germany 1979), especially p. 173. This remarkable book presents literally thousands of candid photographs of woman and men, in public, seated, standing and lying down. It vividly demonstrates the very systematic differences in women's and men's postures and gestures.

Questions

1. What are some of the connotations of the word "oppression"? Why does Frye believe that "oppression" is an important word, one that should be defined and used precisely?
2. What metaphors does Frye employ to convey the complicated nature of oppression? What is a "double-bind" and how does it illustrate oppression?
3. How does Frye distinguish between suffering and oppression? Why is this difference significant? What is the difference between barriers experienced by individuals and barriers experienced because of individual membership in a group? What does Frye mean when she argues that women are oppressed *as women,* but men are not oppressed *as men*? Do this mean that no men are ever oppressed?
4. How do differences among women complicate the issue of considering women as an oppressed group? Does Frye address diversity among women in her essay, explicitly or implicitly?
5. How does Frye's essay reflect the time period in which she wrote? Can you think of some contemporary examples of oppression?

White Privilege: Unpacking the Invisible Knapsack (1989)

Peggy McIntosh

This well-known consciousness-raising essay, written in 1988, examines the advantages that can come from being white in U.S. society. Although often unrecognized or unacknowledged, these advantages have a direct relationship to the disadvantages and oppression people of color face. McIntosh pinpoints concrete examples from her own experience that illustrate how even daily activities of white people reflect invisible privileges upon which other racial groups cannot depend. Peggy McIntosh, an educator and activist, is the Associate Director of the Center for Research on Women at Wellesley College.

Through work to bring materials from women's studies into the rest of the curriculum, I have often noticed men's unwillingness to grant that they are overprivileged, even though they may grant that women are disadvantaged. They may say they will work to improve women's status, in the society, the university, or the

"White Privilege: Unpacking the Invisible Knapsack," by Peggy McIntosh, reprinted from *Independent School*, Winter, 1990.

curriculum, but they can't or won't support the idea of lessening men's. Denials that amount to taboos surround the subject of advantages that men gain from women's disadvantages. These denials protect male privilege from being fully acknowledged, lessened, or ended.

Thinking through unacknowledged male privilege as a phenomenon, I realized that, since hierarchies in our society are interlocking, there was most likely a phenomenon of white privilege that was similarly denied and protected. As a white person, I realized I had been taught about racism as something that puts others at a disadvantage, but had been taught not to see one of its corollary aspects, white privilege, which puts me at an advantage.

I think whites are carefully taught not to recognize white privilege, as males are taught not to recognize male privilege. So I have begun in an untutored way to ask what it is like to have white privilege. I have come to see white privilege as an invisible package of unearned assets that I can count on cashing in each day, but about which I was "meant" to remain oblivious. White privilege is like an invisible weightless knapsack of special provisions, maps, passports, codebooks, visas, clothes, tools, and blank checks.

Describing white privilege makes one newly accountable. As we in women's studies work to reveal male privilege and ask men to give up some of their power, so one who writes about having white privilege must ask. "Having described it, what will I do to lessen or end it?"

After I realized the extent to which men work from a base of unacknowledged privilege, I understood that much of their oppressiveness was unconscious. Then I remembered the frequent charges from women of color that white women whom they encounter are oppressive. I began to understand why we are justly seen as oppressive, even when we don't see ourselves that way. I began to count the ways in which I enjoy unearned skin privilege and have been conditioned into oblivion about its existence.

My schooling gave me no training in seeing myself as an oppressor, as an unfairly advantaged person, or as a participant in a damaged culture. I was taught to see myself as an individual whose moral state depended on her individual moral will. My schooling followed the pattern my colleague Elizabeth Minnich has pointed out: whites are taught to think of their lives as morally neutral, normative, and average, and also ideal, so that when we work to benefit others, this is seen as work that will allow "them" to be more like "us."

DAILY EFFECTS OF WHITE PRIVILEGE

I decided to try to work on myself at least by identifying some of the daily effects of white privilege in my life. I have chosen those conditions that I think in my case *attach somewhat more to skin-color privilege* than to class, religion, ethnic status, or geographic location, though of course all these other factors are intricately intertwined. As far as I can tell, my African American coworkers, friends, and acquaintances with whom I come into daily or frequent contact in this particular time, place, and line of work cannot count on most of these conditions.

1. I can, if I wish, arrange to be in the company of people of my race most of the time.
2. If I should need to move, I can be pretty sure of renting or purchasing housing in an area that I can afford and in which I would want to live.
3. I can be pretty sure that my neighbors in such a location will be neutral or pleasant to me.
4. I can go shopping alone most of the time, pretty well assured that I will not be followed or harassed.
5. I can turn on the television or open to the front page of the paper and see people of my race widely represented.
6. When I am told about our national heritage or about "civilization," I am shown that people of my color made it what it is.
7. I can be sure that my children will be given curricular materials that testify to the existence of their race.
8. If I want to, I can be pretty sure of finding a publisher for this piece on white privilege.

9. I can go into a music shop and count on finding the music of my race represented, into a supermarket and find the staple foods that fit with my cultural traditions, into a hairdresser's shop and find someone who can deal with my hair.

10. Whether I use checks, credit cards, or cash, I can count on my skin color not to work against the appearance of financial reliability.

11. I can arrange to protect my children most of the time from people who might not like them.

12. I can swear, or dress in second-hand clothes, or not answer letters without having people attribute these choices to the bad morals, the poverty, or the illiteracy of my race.

13. I can speak in public to a powerful male group without putting my race on trial.

14. I can do well in a challenging situation without being called a credit to my race.

15. I am never asked to speak for all the people of my racial group.

16. I can remain oblivious of the language and customs of persons of color, who constitute the world's majority, without feeling in my culture any penalty for such oblivion.

17. I can criticize our government and talk about how much I fear its policies and behavior without being seen as a cultural outsider.

18. I can be pretty sure that if I ask to talk to "the person in charge" I will be facing a person of my race.

19. If a traffic cop pulls me over, or if the IRS audits my tax return, I can be sure I haven't been singled out because of my race.

20. I can easily buy posters, postcards, picture books, greeting cards, dolls, toys, and children's magazines featuring people of my race.

21. I can go home from most meetings of organizations I belong to feeling somewhat tied in rather than isolated, out

of place, outnumbered, unheard, held at a distance, or feared.

22. I can take a job with an affirmative action employer without having coworkers on the job suspect that I got it because of race.
23. I can choose public accommodation without fearing that people of my race cannot get in or will be mistreated in the places I have chosen.
24. I can be sure that if I need legal or medical help my race will not work against me.
25. If my day, week, or year is going badly, I need not ask of each negative episode or situation whether it has racial overtones.
26. I can choose blemish cover or bandages in "flesh" color that more or less match my skin.

ELUSIVE AND FUGITIVE

I repeatedly forgot each of the realizations on this list until I wrote it down. For me white privilege has turned out to be an elusive and fugitive subject. The pressure to avoid it is great, for in facing it I must give up the myth of meritocracy. If these things are true, this is not such a free country; one's life is not what one makes it; many doors open for certain people through no virtues of their own.

In unpacking this invisible knapsack of white privilege, I have listed conditions of daily experience that I once took for granted. Nor did I think of any of these perquisites as bad for the holder. I now think that we need a more finely differentiated taxonomy of privilege, for some of these varieties are only what one would want for everyone in a just society, and others give license to be ignorant, oblivious, arrogant, and destructive.

I see a pattern running through the matrix of white privilege, a pattern of assumptions that were passed on to me as a white person. There was one main piece of cultural turf; it was my own turf, and I was among those who could control the turf. *My skin color was an asset for any move I was educated to want to make.* I could think of myself as belonging in major ways and of making social systems work for me. I could freely disparage, fear, neglect, or be oblivious to anything outside of the dominant cultural forms. Being of the main culture, I could also criticize it fairly freely.

In proportion as my racial group was being made confident, comfortable, and oblivious, other groups were likely being made unconfident, uncomfortable, and alienated. Whiteness protected me from many kinds of hostility, distress, and violence, which I was being subtly trained to visit, in turn, upon people of color.

For this reason, the word "privilege" now seems to me misleading. We usually think of privilege as being a favored state, whether earned or conferred by birth or luck. Yet some of the conditions I have described here work systematically to overempower certain groups. Such privilege simply *confers dominance* because of one's race or sex.

Earned strength, unearned power

I want, then, to distinguish between earned strength and unearned power conferred systemically. Power from unearned privilege can look like strength when it is in fact permission to escape or to dominate. But not all of the privileges on my list are inevitably damaging. Some, like the expectation that neighbors will be decent to you, or that your race will not count against you in court, should be the norm in a just society. Others, like the privilege to ignore less powerful people, distort the humanity of the holders as well as the ignored groups.

We might at least start by distinguishing between positive advantages, which we can work to spread, and negative types of advantage, which unless rejected will always reinforce our present hierarchies. For example, the feeling that one belongs within the human circle, as Native Americans say, should not be seen as privilege for a few. Ideally it is an *unearned entitlement*. At present, since only a few have it, it is an *unearned advantage* for them. This paper results from a process of coming to see that some of the power that I originally saw as attendant on being a human being in the United States consisted in *unearned advantage* and *conferred dominance*.

I have met very few men who are truly distressed about systemic, unearned male advantage and conferred dominance. And so one question for me and others like me is whether we will be like them, or whether we will get truly distressed, even outraged, about unearned race advantage and conferred dominance, and, if so, what we will do to lessen them. In any case, we need to do more work in identifying how they actually affect our daily lives. Many, perhaps most, of our white students in the United States think that racism doesn't affect them because they are not people of color; they do not see "whiteness" as a racial identity. In addition, since race and sex are not the only advantaging systems at work, we need similarly to examine the daily experience of having age advantage, or ethnic advantage, or physical ability, or advantage related to nationality, religion, or sexual orientation.

Difficulties and dangers surrounding the task of finding parallels are many. Since racism, sexism, and heterosexism are not the same, the advantages associated with them should not be seen as the same. In addition, it is hard to disentangle aspects of unearned advantage that rest more on social class, economic class, race, religion, sex, and ethnic identity than on other factors. Still, all of the oppressions are interlocking, as the members of the Combahee River collective pointed out in their "Black Feminist Statement" of 1977.

One factor seems clear about all of the interlocking oppressions. They take both active forms, which we can see, and embedded forms, which as a member of the dominant group one is taught not to see. In my class and place, I did not see myself as a racist because I was taught to recognize racism only in individual acts of meanness by members of my group, never in invisible systems conferring unsought racial dominance on my group from birth.

Disapproving of the systems won't be enough to change them. I was taught to think that racism could end if white individuals changed their attitudes. But a "white" skin in the United States opens many doors for whites whether or not we approve of the way dominance has been conferred on us. Individual acts can palliate, but cannot end, these problems.

To redesign social systems we need first to acknowledge their colossal unseen dimensions. The silences and denials surrounding privilege are the key political tool here. They keep the thinking about equality or equity incomplete, protecting unearned advantage and conferred dominance by making these subjects taboo. Most talk by whites about equal opportunity seems to me now to be about equal opportunity to try to get into a position of dominance while denying that *systems* of dominance exist.

It seems to me that obliviousness about white advantage, like obliviousness about male advantage, is kept strongly inculturated in the United States so as to maintain the myth of meritocracy, the myth that democratic choice is equally available to all. Keeping most people unaware that freedom of confident action is there for just a small number of people props up those in power and serves to keep power in the hands of the same groups that have most of it already.

Although systemic change takes many decades, there are pressing questions for me and, I imagine, for some others like me if we raise our daily consciousness on the perquisites of being light-skinned. What will we do with such knowledge? As we know from watching men, it is an open question whether we will choose to use unearned advantage to weaken hidden systems of advantage, and whether we will use any of our arbitrarily awarded power to try to reconstruct power systems on a broader base.

QUESTIONS

1. What is "white privilege"? How is white privilege connected to the disadvantages and oppression people of color face? What distinction does McIntosh make between "positive" and "negative" advantages?

2. How do racism and white privilege differ? How do individual and institutional racism differ?

3. Why is whiteness, and the advantages that come from being white, so often unrecognized? What examples does McIntosh offer that resonate with your experience?

X: A FABULOUS CHILD'S STORY (1972)

Lois Gould

Lois Gould is a writer and journalist whose novels include Necessary Objects *(1972),* La Presidenta *(1981) and* Subject to Change *(1988). This short story about "X" explores our culture's obsession with gender. Suggesting that rigid gender norms constrain behavior and limit human development, Gould hints at the creative potential possible in a less gender-focused environment.*

Once upon a time, a baby named X was born. This baby was named X so that nobody could tell whether it was a boy or a girl. Its parents could tell, of course, but they couldn't tell anybody else. They couldn't even tell Baby X, at first.

You see, it was all part of a very important Secret Scientific Xperiment, known officially as Project Baby X. The smartest scientists had set up this Xperiment at a cost of Xactly 23 billion dollars and 72 cents, which might seem like a lot for just one baby, even a very important Xperimental baby. But when you remember the prices of things like strained carrots and stuffed bunnies, and pop-

---

corn for the movies and booster shots for camp, let alone 28 shiny quarters from the tooth fairy, you begin to see how it adds up.

Also, long before Baby X was born, all those scientists had to be paid to work out the details of the Xperiment, and to write the *Official Instruction Manual* for Baby X's parents and, most important of all, to find the right set of parents to bring up Baby X. These parents had to be selected very carefully. Thousands of volunteers had to take thousands of tests and answer thousands of tricky questions. Almost everybody failed because, it turned out, almost everybody really wanted either a baby boy or a baby girl, and not Baby X at all. Also, almost everybody was afraid that a Baby X would be a lot more trouble than a boy or a girl. (They were probably right, the scientists admitted, but Baby X needed parents who wouldn't *mind* the Xtra trouble.)

There were families with grandparents named Milton and Agatha, who didn't see why the baby couldn't be named Milton or Agatha instead of X, even if it *was* an X. There were families with aunts who insisted on knitting tiny dresses and uncles who insisted on sending tiny baseball mitts. Worst of all, there were families that already had other children who couldn't be trusted to keep the secret. Certainly not if they knew the secret was worth 23 billion dollars and 72 cents—and all you had to do was take one little peek at Baby X in the bathtub to know if it was a boy or a girl.

But, finally, the scientists found the Joneses, who really wanted to raise an X more than any other kind of baby—no matter how much trouble it would be. Ms. and Mr. Jones had to promise they would take equal turns caring for X, and feeding it, and singing it lullabies. And they had to promise never to hire any baby-sitters. The government scientists knew perfectly well that a baby-sitter would probably peek at X in the bathtub, too.

The day the Joneses brought their baby home, lots of friends and relatives came over to see it. None of them knew about the secret Xperiment, though. So the first thing they asked was what kind of a baby X was. When the Joneses smiled and said, "It's an X!" nobody knew what to say. They couldn't say, "Look at her cute little dimples!" And they couldn't say, "Look at his husky little biceps!" And they couldn't even say just plain "kitchy-coo." In fact, they all thought the Joneses were playing some kind of rude joke.

But, of course, the Joneses were not joking. "It's an X" was absolutely all they would say. And that made the friends and relatives very angry. The relatives all felt embarrassed about having an X in the family. "People will think there's something wrong with it!" some of them whispered. "There *is* something wrong with it!" others whispered back.

"Nonsense!" the Joneses told them all cheerfully. "What could possibly be wrong with this perfectly adorable X?"

Nobody could answer that, except Baby X, who had just finished its bottle. Baby X's answer was a loud, satisfied burp.

Clearly, nothing at all was wrong. Nevertheless, none of the relatives felt comfortable about buying a present for a Baby X. The cousins who sent the baby a tiny football helmet would not come and visit any more. And the neighbors who sent a pink-flowered romper suit pulled their shades down when the Joneses passed their house.

The *Official Instruction Manual* had warned the new parents that this would happen, so they didn't fret about it. Besides, they were too busy with Baby X and the hundreds of different Xercises for treating it properly.

Ms. and Mr. Jones had to be Xtra careful about how they played with little X. They knew if they kept bouncing it up in the air and saying how *strong* and *active* it was, they'd be treating it more like a boy than an X. But if all they did was cuddle it and kiss it and tell it how *sweet* and *dainty* it was, they'd be treating it more like a girl than an X.

On page 1,654 of the *Official Instruction Manual*, the scientists prescribed: "plenty of bouncing and plenty of cuddling, *both*. X ought to be strong and sweet and active. Forget about *dainty* altogether."

Meanwhile, the Joneses were worrying about other problems. Toys, for instance. And clothes. On his first shopping trip, Mr. Jones told the store clerk, "I need some clothes and toys for my new baby." The clerk smiled and said, "Well, now, is it a boy or a girl?" "It's an X," Mr. Jones said, smiling back. But the clerk got all red in the face and said huffily, "In *that* case, I'm afraid I can't help you, sir." So Mr. Jones wandered helplessly up and down the aisles trying to find what X needed. But everything in the store was piled up in sections marked "Boys" or "Girls." There were "Boys' Pajamas" and "Girls' Underwear" and "Boys' Fire Engines" and "Girls' Housekeeping Sets." Mr. Jones went home without buying anything for X. That night he and Ms. Jones consulted page 2,326 of the *Official Instruction Manual*. "Buy plenty of everything!" it said firmly.

So they bought plenty of sturdy blue pajamas in the Boys' Department and cheerful flowered underwear in the Girls' Department. And they bought all kinds of toys. A boy doll that made pee-pee and cried, "Pa-pa." And a girl doll that talked in three languages and said, "I am the Pres-i-dent of Gen-er-al Mo-tors." They also bought a storybook about a brave princess who rescued a handsome prince from his ivory tower, and another one about a sister and brother who grew up to be a baseball star and a ballet star, and you had to guess which was which.

The head scientists of Project Baby X checked all their purchases and told them to keep up the good work. They also reminded the Joneses to see page 4,629 of the *Manual*, where it said, "Never make Baby X feel *embarrassed* or *ashamed* about what it wants to play with. And if X gets dirty climbing rocks, never say 'Nice little Xes don't get dirty climbing rocks.'"

Likewise, it said, "If X falls down and cries, never say 'Brave little Xes don't cry.' Because, of course, nice little Xes *do* get dirty, and brave little Xes do cry. No matter how dirty X gets, or how hard it cries, don't worry. It's all part of the Xperiment."

Whenever the Joneses pushed Baby X's stroller in the park, smiling strangers would come over and coo: "Is that a boy or a girl?" The Joneses would smile back and say, "It's an X." The strangers would stop smiling then, and often snarl something nasty—as if the Joneses had snarled at *them*.

By the time X grew big enough to play with other children, the Joneses' troubles had grown bigger, too. Once a little girl grabbed X's shovel in the sandbox, and zonked X on the head with it. "Now, now, Tracy," the little girl's mother began to scold, "little girls mustn't hit little—" and she turned to ask X, "Are you a little boy or a little girl, dear?"

Mr. Jones who was sitting near the sandbox, held his breath and crossed his fingers.

X smiled politely at the lady, even though X's head had never been zonked so hard in its life. "I'm a little X," X replied.

"You're a *what*?" the lady exclaimed angrily. "You're a little b-r-a-t, you mean!"

"But little girls mustn't hit little Xes, either!" said X, retrieving the shovel with another polite smile. "What good does hitting do, anyway?"

X's father, who was still holding his breath, finally let it out, uncrossed his fingers, and grinned back at X.

And at their next secret Project Baby X meeting, the scientists grinned, too. Baby X was doing fine.

But then it was time for X to start school. The Joneses were really worried about this, because school was even more full of rules for boys and girls, and there were no rules for Xes. The teacher would tell boys to form one line, and girls to form another line. There would be boys' games and girls' games, and boys' secrets and girls' secrets. The school library would have a list of recommended books for girls, and a different list of recommended books for boys. There would even be a bathroom marked BOYS and another one marked GIRLS. Pretty soon boys and girls would hardly talk to each other. What would happen to poor little X?

The Joneses spent weeks consulting their *Instruction Manual* (there were 249 1/2 pages of advice under "First Day of School"), and attending urgent special conferences with the smart scientists of Project Baby X.

The scientists had to make sure that X's mother had taught X how to throw and catch a ball properly, and that X's father had been sure to teach X what to serve at a doll's tea party. X had to know how to shoot marbles and how to jump rope and, most of all, what to say when the Other Children asked whether X was a Boy or a Girl.

Finally, X was ready. The Joneses helped X button on a nice new pair of red-and-white checked overalls, and sharpened six pencils for X's nice new pencil box, and marked X's name clearly on all the books in its nice new book bag. X brushed its teeth and combed its hair, which just about covered its ears, and remembered to put a napkin in its lunchbox.

The Joneses had asked X's teacher if the class could line up alphabetically, instead of forming separate lines for boys and girls. And they had asked if X could use the principal's bathroom, because it wasn't marked anything except BATHROOM. X's teacher promised to take care of all those problems. But nobody could help X with the biggest problem of all—Other Children.

Nobody in X's class had ever known an X before. What would they think? How would X make friends?

You couldn't tell what X was by studying its clothes—overalls don't even button right-to-left, like girls' clothes, or left-to-right, like boys' clothes. And you couldn't guess whether X had a girl's short haircut or a boy's long haircut. And it was very hard to tell by the games X liked to play. Either X played ball very well for a girl, or else X played house very well for a boy.

Some of the children tried to find out by asking X tricky questions, like "Who's your favorite sports star?" That was easy. X had two favorite sports stars: a girl jockey named Robyn Smith and a boy archery champion named Robin Hood. Then they asked, "What's your favorite TV program?" And that was even easier. X's favorite TV program was "Lassie," which stars a girl dog played by a boy dog.

When X said that its favorite toy was a doll, everyone decided that X must be a girl. But then X said that the doll was really a robot, and that X had computerized it, and that it was programmed to bake fudge brownies and then clean up the kitchen. After X told them that, the other children gave up guessing what X was. All they knew was they'd sure like to see X's doll.

After school, X wanted to play with the other children. "How about shooting some baskets in the gym?" X asked the girls. But all they did was make faces and giggle behind X's back.

"How about weaving some baskets in the arts and crafts room?" X asked the boys. But they all made faces and giggled behind X's back too.

That night, Ms. and Mr. Jones asked X how things had gone at school. X told them sadly that the lessons were okay, but otherwise school was a terrible place for an X. It seemed as if Other Children would never want an X for a friend.

Once more, the Joneses reached for their *Instruction Manual.* Under "Other Children," they found the following message: "What did you Xpect? *Other Children* have to obey all the silly boy-girl rules, because their parents taught them to. Lucky X—you don't have to stick to the rules at all! All you have to do is be yourself. P.S. We're not saying it'll be easy."

X liked being itself. But X cried a lot that night, partly because it felt afraid. So X's father held X tight, and cuddled it, and couldn't help crying a little, too. And X's mother cheered them both up by reading an Xciting story about an enchanted prince called Sleeping Handsome, who woke up when Princess Charming kissed him.

The next morning, they all felt much better, and little X went back to school with a brave smile and a clean pair of red-and-white checked overalls.

There was a seven-letter-word spelling bee in class that day. And a seven-lap boys' relay race in the gym. And a seven-layer-cake baking contest in the girls' kitchen corner. X won the spelling bee. X also won the relay race. And X almost won the baking contest, except it forgot to light the oven. Which only proves that nobody's perfect.

One of the Other Children noticed something else, too. He said: "Winning or losing doesn't seem to count to X. X seems to have fun being good at boys' skills *and* girls' skills."

"Come to think of it," said another one of the Other Children, "maybe X is having twice as much fun as we are!"

So after school that day, the girl who beat X at the baking contest gave X a big slice of her prize winning cake. And the boy X beat in the relay race asked X to race him home.

From then on, some really funny things began to happen. Susie, who sat next to X in class, suddenly refused to wear pink dresses to school any more. She insisted on wearing red-and-white checked overalls—just like X's. Overalls, she told her parents, were much better for climbing monkey bars.

Then Jim, the class football nut, started wheeling his little sister's doll carriage around the football field. He'd put on his entire football uniform, except for the helmet. Then he'd put the helmet *in* the carriage, lovingly tucked under an old set of shoulder pads. Then he'd start jogging around the field, pushing the carriage and singing "Rock-a-bye Baby" to his football helmet. He told his family that X did the same thing, so it must be okay. After all X was now the team's star quarterback.

Susie's parents were horrified by her behavior, and Jim's parents were worried sick about his. But the worst came when the twins, Joe and Peggy, decided to share everything with each other. Peggy used Joe's hockey skates, and his microscope, and took half his newspaper route. Joe used Peggy's needlepoint kit, and her cookbooks, and took two of her three baby-sitting jobs. Peggy started running the lawn mower, and Joe started running the vacuum cleaner.

Their parents weren't one bit pleased with Peggy's wonderful biology experiments, or with Joe's terrific needlepoint pillows. They didn't care that Peggy mowed the lawn better, and that Joe vacuumed the carpet better. In fact, they were furious. It's all that little X's fault, they agreed. Just because X doesn't know what it is, or what it's supposed to be, it wants to get everybody *else* mixed up, too!

Peggy and Joe were forbidden to play with X any more. So was Susie, and then Jim, and then *all* the Other Children. But it was too late; the Other Children stayed mixed up and happy and free, and refused to go back to the way they'd been before X.

Finally, Joe and Peggy's parents decided to call an emergency meeting of the school's Parents' Association, to discuss "The X Problem." They sent a report to the principal stating that X was a "disruptive influence." They demanded immediate action. The Joneses, they said, should be *forced* to tell whether X was a boy or a girl. And then X should be *forced* to behave like whichever it was. If the Joneses refused to tell, the Parents' Association said, then X must take an Xamination. The school psychiatrist must Xamine it physically and mentally, and issue a full report. If X's test showed it was a boy, it would have to obey all the boys' rules. If it proved to be a girl, X would have to obey all the girls' rules.

And if X turned out to be some kind of mixed-up misfit, then X should be Xpelled from the school. Immediately!

The principal was very upset. Disruptive influence? Mixed-up misfit? But X was an Xcellent student. All the teachers said it was a delight to have X in their classes. X was president of the student council. X had won first prize in the talent show, and second prize in the art show, and honorable mention in the science fair, and six athletic events on field day, including the potato race.

Nevertheless, insisted the Parents' Association, X is a Problem Child. X is the Biggest Problem Child we have ever seen!

So the principal reluctantly notified X's parents that numerous complaints about X's behavior had come to the school's attention. And that after the psychiatrist's Xamination, the school would decide what to do about X.

The Joneses reported this at once to the scientists, who referred them to page 85,759 of the *Instruction Manual*. "Sooner or later," it said, "X will have to be Xamined by a psychiatrist. This may be the only way any of us will know for sure whether X is mixed up—or whether everyone else is."

The night before X was to be Xamined, the Joneses tried not to let X see how worried they were. "What if—?" Mr. Jones would say. And Ms. Jones would reply, "No use worrying." Then a few minutes later, Ms. Jones would say, "What if—?" and Mr. Jones would reply, "No use worrying."

X just smiled at them both, and hugged them hard and didn't say much of anything. X was thinking. What if—? And then X thought: No use worrying.

At Xactly 9 o'clock the next day, X reported to the school psychiatrist's office. The principal, along with a committee from the Parents' Association, X's teacher, X's classmates, and Ms. and Mr. Jones, waited in the hall outside. Nobody knew the details of the tests X was to be given, but everybody knew they'd be *very* hard, and that they'd reveal Xactly what everyone wanted to know about X, but were afraid to ask.

It was terribly quiet in the hall. Almost spooky. Once in a while, they would hear a strange noise inside the room. There were buzzes. And a beep or two. And several bells. An occasional light would flash under the door. The Joneses thought it was a white light, but the principal thought it was blue. Two or three children swore it was either yellow or green. And the Parents' Committee missed it completely.

Through it all, you could hear the psychiatrist's low voice, asking hundreds of questions, and X's higher voice, answering hundreds of answers.

The whole thing took so long that everyone knew it must be the most complete Xamination anyone had ever had to take. Poor X, the Joneses thought. Serves X right, the Parents' Committee thought. I wouldn't like to be in X's overalls right now, the children thought.

At last, the door opened. Everyone crowded around to hear the results. X didn't look any different; in fact, X was smiling. But the psychiatrist looked terrible. He look as if he was crying! "What happened?" everyone began shouting. Had X done something disgraceful? "I wouldn't be a bit surprised!" muttered Peggy and Joe's parents. "Did X flunk the *whole* test?" cried Susie's parents. "Or just the most important part?" yelled Jim's parents.

"Oh, dear," sighed Mr. Jones.

"Oh, dear," sighed Ms. Jones.

"*Sssh,*" ssshed the principal. "The psychiatrist is trying to speak."

Wiping, his eyes and clearing his throat, the psychiatrist began, in a hoarse whisper. "In my opinion," he whispered—you could tell he must be very upset—"in my opinion, young X here—"

"Yes? Yes?" shouted a parent impatiently.

"*Sssh!*" ssshed the principal.

"Young *Sssh* here, I mean young X," said the doctor, frowning, "is just about—"

"Just about *what*? Let's have it!" shouted another parent.

". . . just about the *least* mixed-up child I've ever Xamined!" said the psychiatrist.

"Yay for X!" yelled one of the children. And then the others began yelling, too. Clapping and cheering and jumping up and down.

"*SSSH!*" SSShed the principal, but nobody did.

The Parents' Committee was angry and bewildered. How *could* X have passed the whole Xamination? Didn't X have an *identity* problem? Wasn't X mixed up at *all*? Wasn't X *any* kind of a misfit? How could it *not* be, when it didn't even *know* what it was? And why was the psychiatrist crying?

Actually, he had stopped crying and was smiling politely through his tears. "Don't you see?" he said. "I'm crying because it's wonderful! X has absolutely no identity problem! X isn't one bit mixed up! As for being a misfit—ridiculous! X knows perfectly well what it is! Don't you, X?" The doctor winked, X winked back.

"But what *is* X?" shrieked Peggy and Joe's parents. "*We* still want to know what it is!"

"Ah, yes," said the doctor, winking again. "Well, don't worry. You'll all know one of these days. And you won't need me to tell you."

"What? What does he mean?" some of the parents grumbled suspiciously.

Susie and Peggy and Joe all answered at once. "He means that by the time X's sex matters, it won't be a secret any more!"

With that, the doctor began to push through the crowd toward X's parents. "How do you do," he said, somewhat stiffly. And then he reached out to hug them both. "If I ever have an X of my own," he whispered, "I sure hope you'll lend me your instruction manual."

Needless to say, the Joneses were very happy. The Project Baby X scientists were rather pleased, too. So were Susie, Jim, Peggy, Joe, and all the Other Children. The Parents' Association wasn't, but they had promised to accept the psychiatrist's report, and not make any more trouble. They even invited Ms. and Mr. Jones to become honorary members, which they did.

Later that day, all X's friends put on their red-and-white checked overalls and went over to see X. They found X in the back yard, playing with a very tiny baby that none of them had ever seen before. The baby was wearing very tiny red-and-white checked overalls.

"How do you like our new baby?" X asked the Other Children proudly.

"It's got cute dimples," said Jim.

"It's got husky biceps, too," said Susie.

"What kind of baby is it?" asked Joe and Peggy.

X frowned at them. "Can't you tell?" Then X broke into a big, mischievous grin. *"It's a Y!"*

Questions

1. What are Gould's goals in this story? What issues does the story introduce? Why do many of the story's characters react negatively to X and X's parents? Why is it important for the characters to know X's gender?
2. What obstacles do X and X's parents encounter in their gender-specific world? How do they deal with these obstacles? What advantages does X's mixed-gender upbringing offer?
3. Why is gender such an important category in our culture? How does it limit us?

On Campus, Rethinking Biology 101 (2004)

Fred A. Bernstein

Fred A. Bernstein holds degrees in both architecture and law. A writer on various subjects, Bernstein has been published in The New York Times, The Wall Street Journal, *and* The Washington Post, *as well as numerous other newspapers, magazines, and journals. Bernstein writes articles on the diverse topics of architecture, law, real estate, travel, and art, among others.*

Arriving in Providence last fall to begin his senior year at Brown University, Luke Woodward didn't have to tell friends what he had done on his summer vacation.

They could tell with one glance. Before the summer Luke had had the body of a woman. Now Luke's breasts were gone, leaving a chest more compatible with Luke's close-cropped hair, baggy jeans and hooded sweatshirts. Some classmates had chipped in to pay for the surgery; to cover the rest, Luke took out loans.

Thanks to the "chest surgery," Luke said, "my quality of life is better." Before, if Luke entered a women's bathroom on campus,

---

"someone might yell, 'Oh my God, there's a man here' and call security," he said. "In men's bathrooms I'd have to fold my arms over my chest and hope that no one would notice." Now he and several other Brown students are pressing the university to create more single-stall bathrooms, so students who don't look clearly male or female can avoid harassment.

Luke, a 23-year-old international-relations major, is at the cutting edge of a new kind of campus activism: transgender students and their allies who are convincing colleges to meet needs that include private bathrooms and showers, specialized housing and sports teams on which students who don't identify themselves as either male or female can play. In the last year, transgender students have won accommodations from four East Coast colleges, including Wesleyan, Sarah Lawrence and Smith.

While it isn't clear if the number of students who consider themselves transgender is increasing, their openness—a generation after gay and lesbian students began identifying themselves on campuses—clearly is. Zachary Strassburger, a sophomore at Wesleyan University, in Middletown, Conn., said he "came out" to his parents as "trans" in the 10th grade. (Luke and Zachary, who were born female, asked to be referred to with male pronouns.)

Transgender is a term that describes, and unites, a broad category of people who are uncomfortable in the gender of their birth, said Dr. Ken Zucker, a psychologist who heads a child and adolescent gender-identity clinic in Toronto. Transgender students may also be transsexual—moving from male to female, or female to male with the help of surgery or hormones. (Luke considers himself a "female-to-male trans," no longer fully female but not yet fully male.)

Some transgender students aren't moving between sexes; they're parked somewhere in the middle and prefer to describe themselves as "gender queer"—signifying that they reject the either-or male-female system.

Dr. Zucker said young people claiming a transgender identity "vary in the degree to which they want physical intervention." He added: "Gender identity is distinct from sexual orientation. Gender identity pertains to how a person feels about being male or female; sexual orientation pertains to who are you attracted to sexually."

Zachary, 19, said, "Some people think it's important to be seen as a specific gender; that's not me." There are several dozen "gender queers" among Wesleyan's 2,700 students, said Zachary, who changed his name at 18 and asked that his original first name not be published.

Brown and Sarah Lawrence, in Yonkers, will offer housing for the first time this fall to accommodate transgender students. Wesleyan has assigned a hallway for students who choose to live without designating their gender. A Wesleyan student who was born female but now looks and acts more male than female can have a male roommate. The Wesleyan campus health services clinic no longer requires students to check off "M" or "F" when coming in for a "wellness and sexual health visit." Instead, they are asked on a form to "describe your gender identity history." And this year, the former women's rugby team eliminated "women's" from its name, so that Zachary and several other transgender students would feel comfortable playing. "We don't want people yelling, 'Go, girls!'" from the sidelines, Zachary explained.

Mark Nickel, a spokesman for Brown, said members of its incoming freshman class will "fill out a housing questionnaire that will allow them to elect a gender-neutral option." He said the policy "would give transgender students the option to live with other transgender students." And they will be in dorms where there are "lockable bathrooms for use by one person."

At Sarah Lawrence, the assistant dean for residential life, Sarah Cardwell, said the university planned to allow upper-class students to live with students regardless of their sex, and to designate certain bathrooms as "all gender."

"We have a small population of transgender students," Ms. Cardwell said, "and we decided to be proactive, rather than reactive." One of the residents of Wesleyan's transgender hallway, Paige Kruza, is biologically female but looks androgynous. Paige's roommate is male and is extremely respectful, Paige said. When referring to Paige, he uses pronouns that have evolved in the transgender community: "ze" instead of "he" or "she"; "hir" instead of "him" or "her."

Zachary began thinking about the housing issue when he was a senior at a high school in Pittsburgh, where he was harassed because of his masculine appearance. "I ended up threatening to sue the school for not protecting me," he said.

He wanted college to be better. During visits to colleges, he made a point of identifying himself as transgender and asking the schools where he would live as a freshman. "Harvard was the most confused," Zachary said. "They sent me from office to office, not knowing how to react. But I didn't get in anyway."

Wesleyan, by contrast, was the most responsive, Zachary said, adding, "I wanted to come to a college where I'd feel safe."

In his freshman year, he chose to live alone—many Wesleyan freshmen have singles, so not having a roommate didn't stigmatize him. And then he began lobbying for the special hallway. Under existing university policy, a student who was biologically female but dressed and looked male would have to live with another female student. But that could make the female roommate uncomfortable. A male roommate, or another transgender roommate, were better options, Zachary argued.

"Every college student, of any gender, should be able to have the experience of living with a roommate," Zachary said. Now in its first year, 12 students have chosen to live on the freshman hallway, though it's unclear how many identify themselves as transgender.

Zachary himself, now a sophomore, has chosen to room with mostly Jewish students, in one of a number of upper-class residences based around common interests. He also devotes much time to rugby—"my favorite part of college." He said the team had been completely supportive, even paying to replace sweatshirts that said "Women's Rugby" with ones that say "Rugby."

On a sunny afternoon at Wesleyan, Zachary sat on the library steps, chatting with friends who are male, female and transgender. Although transgender people around the country have been victims of hate crimes, students like Zachary say they do not feel discrimination or fear on campus; they know they are lucky to live in environments—small private colleges—with traditions of tolerance.

"It's a very small campus, and everyone knows everyone," Zachary said. "It helps to have a sense of humor if you're trans," he added.

Dr. Davis Smith, the medical director at Wesleyan's student health services, said about a dozen transgender students have identified themselves to him, and the administration, he added, "encouraged me to use a lot of my administrative time" to look at transgender health issues.

"For purposes of sexual health, it doesn't matter if you call yourself male or female," said Dr. Smith, an affable 35-year-old with photos of his wife and daughter in his office. He said that what matters is what a person is doing with his sexual partners.

Dr. Smith added that the transgender students have an influence larger than their numbers. "On this campus," he said, "transgender students are real opinion leaders." He said that as far as he could tell, "there hasn't been any backlash."

At Brown, Sarah Lawrence and Wesleyan, most of the transgender students appear to be women who are fully or partially male-appearing. "I think it's a lot harder if you're male-assigned to come out as transgender," Zachary said. At Hunter College in Manhattan, Dr. Gerald Mallon, a professor in the school of social work and the author of a book on social services for transgender youths, said he knows a number of male-to-female transgender students.

"The transgender community is becoming more vocal and more visible," Dr. Mallon said. "Some are asking for accommodations; others don't need accommodations, but just want to be respected for the gender that they are. I think it may be where the gay movement was 10 or 15 years ago."

At Smith, the women's college in Northampton, Mass., students voted last year to eliminate female pronouns from the student constitution at the request of transgender students. "She" and "her" were replaced with the phrase "the student."

Laurie Fenlason, a college spokeswoman, said that "the vote was undertaken by the students as a gesture of good will toward a handful of fellow students."

But the change was not without controversy. "It contradicts the whole point of having a women's college," said Esi Cleland, a Smith sophomore. "I am opposed to it, because there's something to be said for a women's college, and a lot of us come here because we choose to be in an environment where women are the primary focus."

Students at Barnard have also been grappling with the implications of the fact that some students at a women's college don't identify themselves as women. A recent article in The Columbia Spectator about transgender activism was headlined "Can a Man Attend Barnard College?" "Trans issues," the article reported, "are gaining traction at Barnard."

"We are a women's college," said Suzanne Trimel, the director of public affairs at Barnard. "But if a student began here as a woman and then wanted to change her gender, does that mean we would kick her out of college? No, it doesn't. We are a sensitive and caring community."

"That said, the question has not arisen," Ms. Trimel added. "To the best of our knowledge, no Barnard student has changed gender."

To parents, the phenomenon may be unsettling. Luke says his father's reaction was, "I got married at 25, and that was too young." His point was that changing genders is a big decision for a young person to make, Luke explained. But Luke said he isn't worried that his chest surgery may be irreversible. "I don't know who I'm going to be," he said, "but I can integrate the decisions I make into the person I become."

Luke said that when he arrived at Brown, he was a masculine-appearing lesbian, but had no plans to change sex. "I had questioned my sexuality, but not my gender," Luke said. Then he spent a year studying in Cuba, where people "were genuinely shocked when I said I was a woman. It was disorienting and scary. And I had to really think about it: am I a woman?" After returning from Cuba, he said, "I took more and more pains to hide my breasts and to pass as male." After meeting several female-to-male transsexuals, he said, "I realized I had options."

Luke said the reaction of "my immediate family has been awesome," though "my extended family is having a harder time. My grandparents still refer to me as 'she.'"

Some parents might think that gender experimentation in college is just a phase. "So what if it is a phase—why is that a value judgment?" asked Daniel Bassichis, a Brown sophomore who is a friend of Luke's. "And if something goes wrong for Luke," Daniel said, "his friends will be here to support him."

But there are still issues for transgender students. Luke's voice sounds female, which makes him reluctant to "assert myself vocally." He is considering taking testosterone, which would lower his voice (as well as create facial hair and redistribute muscle), but hasn't been able to afford the hormone treatment. (At Smith, a therapist the college hired to serve as a transgender specialist told The Daily Hampshire Gazette last year that a small number of students there were taking testosterone to acquire male characteristics.)

As to whether he will have further surgery, Luke said he hasn't decided. "This is often the first thing people ask me—about whether I'll get surgery 'down there,' and I think it is really weird," Luke wrote in an e-mail message.

Most doctors require patients hoping for gender-reassignment surgery to live as a member of the opposite gender for a full year. Luke and others see that standard as unreasonable—"for a guy who's 6-foot-2 to use ladies' rooms for a year is a recipe for disaster," he said.

Besides, the protocol negates the experience of students who don't want to be one gender or another, but something in between, Luke said. "It erases the space between male and female," he said. In an ideal world, he wouldn't have to conceal his female past in order to achieve a more male persona, he said. "I wouldn't be seen as male or female," he said, "but a female-to-male trans."

Luke will graduate this spring, but his effects on Brown may only be beginning. Some students predict that when Brown's new policies become known, more transgender students will want to apply. And if they do, "they can't just be plopped down," Daniel Bassichis said. "We have to make sure they feel safe here and can live the way they want to live."

Dr. Smith of Wesleyan said: "It takes a lot of courage to be out as a transgender person. I hope they'll be able to do it in the outside world the way they can in college."

Questions

1. What is the distinction between gender identity and sexual orientation? How does one's identity as "transgender" or "gender queer" impact one's sexuality?
2. What changes are college campuses making to facilitate those who identify as transgender? Do you see changes on your own campus?
3. According to the article, are there transgender issues that are particular to college campuses or is the larger transgender activism influencing campus changes?

Confessions of a Recovering Misogynist (2000)

Kevin Powell

Kevin Powell takes an honest, critical look at his own upbringing as a sexist male. His education, his family, his church and his peers all played roles in training him to act aggressively and disdainfully toward women until a traumatic event forced him to take a hard look at his behavior. Powell's narrative reflects the power of male gender socialization and the particular vulnerability of black men in our racist culture. Men can play significant roles in the feminist movement by facing their own complicity in the system of sexism and by publicly acknowledging their struggles and reaching out to other men.

I AM A SEXIST MALE. I take no great pride in saying this, I am merely stating a fact. It is not that I was born this way—rather, I was born into this male-dominated society, and consequently, from the very moment I began forming thoughts, they formed in a

"Confessions of a Recovering Misogynist," by Kevin Powell. Reprinted from *Ms.* Magazine,, April/May 2000, pp. 72–77

decidedly male-centered way. My "education" at home with my mother, at school, on my neighborhood playgrounds, and at church, all placed males in the middle of the universe. My digestion of 1970s American popular culture in the form of television, film, ads, and music only added to my training, so that by as early as age nine or ten I saw females, including my mother, as nothing more than the servants of males. Indeed, like the Fonz, I thought I could snap my fingers and girls would come running.

My mother, working-poor and a product of the conservative and patriarchal South, simply raised me as most women are taught to raise boys: the world was mine; there were no chores to speak of; and my aggressions were considered somewhat normal, something that we boys carry out as a rite of passage. Those "rites" included me routinely squeezing girls' butts on the playground. And it was at school that boys were encouraged to do "boy" things: work and build with our hands, fight each other, and participate in the most daring activities during our gym time. Meanwhile, the girls were relegated to home economics, drawing cute pictures, and singing in the school choir. Now that I think about it, school was the place that spearheaded the omission of women from my world view. Save Betsy Ross (whom I remember chiefly for sewing a flag), I recall virtually no women making appearances in my American history classes.

The church my mother and I attended, like most black churches, was peopled mainly by black women, most of them single parents, who dragged their children along for the ride. Not once did I see a preacher who was anything other than an articulate, emotionally charged, well-coiffed, impeccably suited black man running this church and, truly, these women. And behind the pulpit of this black man, where he convinced us we were doomed to hell if we did not get right with God, was the image of our savior, a male, always white, named Jesus Christ.

Not surprisingly, the "savior" I wanted in my life was my father. Ten years her senior, my father met my mother, my father wooed my mother, my father impregnated my mother, and then my father—as per his socialization—moved on to the next mating call. Responsibility was about as real to him as a three-dollar bill. When I was eight, my father flatly told my mother, via a payphone, that he felt she had lied, that I was not his child, and that he would never give her money for me again. The one remotely tangible image of maleness in my life was gone for good.

Both my mother and I were devastated, albeit for different reasons. I longed for my father's affections. And my mother longed to be married. Silently, I began to blame my mother for my father's disappearance. Reacting to my increasingly bad behavior, my mother turned resentful and her beatings became more frequent, more charged. I grew to hate her and all females, for I felt it was women who made men act as we do.

At the same time, my mother, a fiercely independent and outspoken woman despite having only a grade-school education and being poor, planted within me the seeds of self-criticism, of shame for wrongful behavior—and, ultimately, of feminism. Clear that she alone would have to shape me, my mother spoke pointedly about my father for many years after that call, demanding that I not grow up to "be like him." And I noted the number of times my mother rejected low-life male suitors, particularly the ones who wanted to live with us free of charge. I can see now that my mother is a feminist, although she is not readily familiar with the term. Like many women before and since, she fell hard for my father, and only through enduring immense pain did she realize the power she had within herself.

I ONCE HATED WOMEN, AND I TAKE NO PRIDE IN THIS CONFESSION. I entered Rutgers University in the mid-1980s and my mama's-boy demeanor advanced to that of pimp. I learned quickly that most males in college are some variety of pimp. Today I lecture regularly, from campus to campus, all over the country, and I see that not much has changed. For college is simply a place where we men, irrespective of race or class, can—and do—act out the sexist attitudes entrenched since boyhood. Rape, infidelity, girlfriend beat downs, and emotional abuse are common, and pimpdom reigns supreme. There is the athlete-pimp, the fratboy-pimp, the independent-pimp, and the college-professor-pimp. Buoyed by the anti apartheid movement and the presidential bids of Jesse Jackson, my social consciousness blossomed along racial lines and, behold, the student-leader-pimp was born.

Blessed with a gift for gab, a poet's sensibility, and an acute memory for historical facts, I baited women with my self-righteousness by quoting Malcolm X, Fratz Fanon, Machiavelli, and any other figure I was sure they had not studied. It was a polite form of sexism, for I was always certain to say "My sister" when I addressed women at Rutgers. But my politeness did not lend me tolerance for women's issues, nor did my affiliation with a variety of black nationalist organizations, especially the Nation of Islam. Indeed, whenever women in our African Student Congress would question the behavior and attitudes of men, I would scream, "We don't have time for them damn lesbian issues!" My scream was violent, mean-spirited, made with the intention to wound. I don't think it is any coincidence that during my four years in college I did not have one relationship with a woman that lasted more than three or four months. For every friend or girlfriend who would dare question my behavior, there were literally hundreds of others who acquiesced to the ways of us men, making it easy for me to ignore the legitimate cries of the feminists. Besides, I had taken on the demanding role of pimp, of conqueror, of campus revolutionary, and there was little time, or room, for real intimacy, and even less time for self-reflection.

CONFESSIONS ARE DIFFICULT BECAUSE THEY FORCE ME TO VISIT GHETTOES IN THE MIND I THOUGHT I HAD LONG ESCAPED. I was kicked out of college at the end of my fourth year because I drew a knife on a female student. We were both members of the African Student Congress and she was one of the many "subversive" female leaders I had sought to purge from the organization. She had left but for some reason was in our office a few days after we had brought Louis Farrakhan to speak at Rutgers. Made tense by her presence, I ignored her and turned to a male student asking him, as she stood there, to ask her to jet. As she was leaving, she turned and charged toward me. My instincts nurtured by my inner-city upbringing and several months of receiving anonymous threats as the Farrakhan talk neared, caused me to reach inside my pocket and pull out a knife.

My intent was to scare her into submission. The male student panicked and knocked the knife from my hand, believing I was going to stab this woman. I would like to believe that that is not the case. It does not matter. This woman pressed charges on and off campus, and my college career, the one I took on for myself, my undereducated mother, and my illiterate grandparents, came to a screeching halt.

IT IS NOT EASY FOR ME TO ADMIT I HAVE A PROBLEM. Before I could be readmitted to school I had to see a therapist. I went, grudgingly, and agonized over my violent childhood, my hatred of my mother, my many problems with women, and the nauseating torment of poverty and instability. But then it was done. I did not bother to try to return to college, and I found myself again using women for money, for sex, for entertainment. When I moved to New York City in August of 1990, my predator mentality was still in full effect. I met a woman, persuaded her to allow me to live with her, and then mentally abused her for nearly a year, cutting off her friends, her peace of mind, her spirit, and eventually pushing her into a bathroom door when she blew up my spot, challenging me and my manhood.

I do not want to recount the details of "the incident" here. What I will say is that I, like most black men I know, have spent much of my life living in fear. Fear of white racism, fear of the circumstances that gave birth to me, fear of walking out my door wondering what humiliation will be mine today. Fear of black women—of their mouths, of their bodies, of their attitudes, of their hurts, of their fear of us black men. I felt fragile, as fragile as a bird with clipped wings, that day my ex-girlfriend stepped up her game and spoke back to me. Nothing in my world, nothing in my self-definition prepared me for dealing with a woman as an equal. My world said women were inferior, that they must, at all costs, be put in their place, and my instant reaction was to do that. When it was over, I found myself dripping with sweat, staring at her back as she ran barefoot out of the apartment.

Guilt consumed me after the incident. The women I knew through my circle of poet and writer friends begged me to talk through what I had done, to get counseling, to read the books of bell hooks, Pearl Cleage's tiny tome, *Mad at Miles*, the poetry of Audre Lorde, the many meditations of Gloria Steinem. I resisted at first, but eventually I began to listen and read, feeling electric shocks running through my body when I realized these women, in describing abusive, oppressive men, were talking about me. Me, who thought I was progressive. Me, who claimed to be a revolutionary. Me, who still felt women were on the planet to take care of men.

During this time I did restart therapy sessions. I did, also, spend a good deal of time talking with young feminist women—some friends, some not. Some were soothing and understanding, some berated me and all men. I also spent a great deal of time alone, replaying my life in my mind: my relationship with my mother, how my mother responded to my father's behavior, how I responded to my mother's response to my father. I thought of my education, of the absence of women in it. How I managed to attend a major university affiliated with one of the oldest women's college in America, Douglass College, and visit that campus only in pursuit of sex. I thought of the older men I had encountered in my life—the ministers, the high school track coach, the street hustlers, the local businessmen, the college professors—and realized that many of the ways I learned to relate to women came from listening to and observing those men. Yeah, I grew up after women's studies classes had appeared in most of the major colleges in America, but that does not mean that feminism actually reached the people it really needed to reach: average, everyday American males.

The incident, and the remorse that followed, brought about something akin to a spiritual epiphany. I struggled, mightily, to rethink the context that created my mother. And my aunts. And my grandmother. And all the women I had been intimate with, either physically or emotionally or both. I struggled to understand terms like "patriarchy," "misogyny," "gender oppression." A year after the incident I penned a short essay for *Essence* magazine called simply, "The Sexist in Me," because I wanted to be honest in the most public forum possible, and because I wanted to reach some men, some young black men, who needed to hear from another male that sexism is as oppressive as racism. And at times, worse.

I AM NO HERO. I AM NO SAINT. I REMAIN A SEXIST MALE. But one who is now conscious of it and who has been waging an internal war for several years. Some days I am incredibly progressive, other days I regress. It is very lonely to swim against the stream of American male-centeredness, of black-man bravado and nut-grabbing. It is how I was molded, it is what I know, and in rejecting it I often feel mad naked and isolated. For example, when I publicly opposed the blatantly sexist and patriarchal rhetoric and atmosphere of the Million Man March, I was attacked by black men, some questioning my sanity, some accusing me of being a dupe for the white man, and some wondering if I was just "trying' to get some pussy from black women."

Likewise, I am a hip-hop head. Since adolescence I have been involved in rap culture as a dancer, a graffiti writer, an activist, a concert organizer, and most prominently, a hip-hop journalist. Indeed, as a journalist at *Vibe* magazine, I found myself interviewing rap icons like Dr. Dre, Snoop Dogg, and the late Tupac Shakur. And although I did ask Snoop and Tupac some pointed questions about their sexism, I still feel I dropped the ball. We black men often feel so powerless, so sure the world—politically, economically, spiritually, and psychologically—is aligned against us. The last thing any of us want is for another man to question how we treat women. Aren't we, black men, the endangered species anyhow? This is how many of us think.

While I do not think hip-hop is any more sexist or misogynist than other forms of American culture, I do think it is the most explicit form of misogyny around today. It is also a form of sexism that gets more than its share of attention, because hip-hop—now a billion-dollar industry—is the soundtrack for young America, regardless of race or class. What folks don't understand is that hip-hop was created on the heels of the civil rights era by impoverished black men and Latinos, who literally made something out of nothing. But in making that something out of nothing, many of us men of color have held tightly to white patriarchal notions of manhood—that is, the way to be a man is to have power. Within hip-hop culture, in our lyrics, in our videos, and on our tours, that power translates into material possessions, provocative and often foul language, flashes of violence, and blatant objectification of and disrespect for women. Patriarchy, as manifested in hip-hop, is where we can have our version of power within this very oppressive society. Who would want to even consider giving that up?

Well, I have, to a large extent, and these days I am a hip-hopper-in-exile. I dress, talk, and walk like a hip-hopper, yet I cannot listen to rap radio or digest music videos without commenting on the pervasive sexism. Moreover, I try to drop seeds, as we say, about sexism, whenever and wherever I can, be it a community forum or on a college campus. Some men, young and old alike, simply cannot deal with it and walk out. Or there is the nervous shifting in seats, the uneasy comments during the question-and-answer sessions, generally in the form of "Why you gotta pick on the men, man?" I constantly "pick on the men" and myself, because I truly wonder how many men actually listen to the concerns of women. Just as I feel it is whites who need to be more vociferous about racism in their communities, I feel it is men who need to speak long and loud about sexism among each other.

I AM A RECOVERING MISOGYNIST. I do not say this with pride. Like a recovering alcoholic or a crack fiend who has righted her on his ways, I am merely cognizant of the fact that I have had some serious problems in my life with and in regard to women. I am also aware of the fact that I can lapse backward—and have—at any time. My relationship with my mother is better than it has ever been, though there are days when speaking with her turns me back into that little boy, cowering beneath the belt and tongue of a woman deeply wounded by my father, by poverty, by her childhood, by the sexism that had dominated her life. My relationships since the incident with my ex-girlfriend have been better, no doubt, but not the bomb.

So I flow solo, and have done so for some time. For sure, I now count among my friends, peers, and mentors feminist women like bell hooks and Johnnetta B. Cole, and young feminists like Nikki Stewart, a girls' rights advocate in Washington, D.C., and Aishah Simmons, who is currently putting together a documentary on rape within the black community. I do not always agree with these women, but I also know that if I do not struggle, hard and constantly, backsliding is real. This is made worse by the fact that outside of a handful of male friends, there are no young men I know—and I know many people around the country—who I can speak with regarding sexism as easily as I do with women. So few of us actually believe there is a problem.

The fact is there was a blueprint handed to me in childhood telling me this is the way a man should behave, and I unwittingly followed the script verbatim. There was no blueprint handed to me about how to begin to wind myself out of sexism as an adult, but maybe there should have been. Everyday I struggle within myself not to use the language of gender oppression, to see the sexism inherent in every aspect of America, to challenge all injustices, not just those that are convenient for me. I am ashamed of my ridiculously sexist life, of raising my hand to my girlfriend. But with that shame has come a consciousness and, as the activists said during the civil rights movement, this consciousness, this knowing, is a river of no return. I have finally learned how to swim, I have finally learned how to push forward. I may become tired, I may lose my breath, I may hit a rock from time to time and become cynical, but I am not going to drown this time around.

QUESTIONS

1. What does Powell mean by "misogynist"? What sort of "training" did he receive to become this way? What type of behavior and feelings does Powell characterize as sexist or misogynistic? Give examples from the selection.
2. Why does he use the language of misogynist "in recovery"? What does it mean to be in "recovery"?
3. What events and feelings led Powell to face his issues with women and sexism? How was feminism helpful to him in thinking about his own gender socialization?
4. According to Powell, how can sexism be as oppressive as racism? How does the particular position of black men complicate the issue of living in a sexist culture?
5. How does Powell address his sexism? How does he recommend other men deal with their sexism? What obstacles exist in our culture to the honest discussion of masculinity, sexism and gender socialization issues among men?
6. Do you think Powell is overstating men's sexism in our culture? Why or why not?

When Dreams Differ: Male-Female Relations on Campuses (1999)

Barbara Kerr

Gender roles and women's opportunities have changed dramatically in the last 30 years, yet male and female students continue to have strikingly different expectations for their personal relationships. Barbara Kerr, professor of counseling psychology at Arizona State University, explains that American social change has left students with insufficient role models for how to have healthy, equitable relationships, share family responsibilities and balance multiple careers. Academics can play a crucial role in this issue by increasing research and offering more courses on the hopes and possibilities of modern personal relationships.

Over the past three decades, women have made great educational and social progress. Significant numbers of women are now active

"When Dreams Differ: Male-Female Relations on Campuses" by Barbara Kerr reprinted from *The Chronicle of Higher Education*, March 5, 1999.

in professions that were traditionally dominated by men, such as medicine, law, and business. Most female undergraduates expect to have a career after marriage. Yet many male students think they will marry women who will stay at home. What can we—as researchers, teachers, and mentors—do to help our students be more realistic about their futures? Can we do anything to change the social patterns on college campuses that foster conflicting expectations for men and women?

My research concerns the ways in which talented young women and men fulfill—or fail to fulfill—their promise. For 20 years, I have observed groups of students as they discussed their dreams and goals with their counselors and their peers. My favorite technique for assessing students' expectations about their futures is an exercise called "The Perfect Future Day Fantasy." In this fantasy, students imagine a day in their lives, 10 years in the future.

A typical college male's fantasy goes something like this: "I wake up and get in my car—a really nice, rebuilt '67 Mustang—and then I go to work—I think I'm some kind of a manager of a computer firm—and then I go home, and when I get there, my wife is there at the door (she has a really nice figure), she has a drink for me, and she's made a great meal. We watch TV or maybe play with the kids." Here is the typical college female's fantasy: "I wake up, and my husband and I get in our twin Jettas, and I go to the law firm where I work. Then after work, I go home, and he's pulling up in the driveway at the same time. We go in and have a glass of wine, and we make an omelet together and eat by candlelight. Then the nanny brings the children in, and we play with them until bedtime."

Additional evidence of the different expectations of men and women comes from Alexander Astin's analysis of trends in the attitudes of college freshmen from 1966 to 1996, which he published in *The Review of Higher Education* in 1998. The proportion of female college freshmen who agree with the statement "The activities of married women are best confined to the home and family" has dropped to 19 per cent from 44.3 per cent. Male college freshmen are now also less likely to agree with the statement—30.8 per cent in 1996, as opposed to 66.5 per cent in 1966. But the figures show that three out of every 10 male undergraduates whom a college woman meets probably expect that, after marriage, their wives will "confine" themselves to caring for them and their children. In fact, it is likely that even more men who publicly endorse equitable relationships secretly wish for a more-traditional life style.

The old-fashioned dating system that still holds sway on most campuses contributes to the problem. In the archetypal date, the man invites the woman out, picks her up, and pays for all the expenses of the date, while the woman decides what kinds of intimacies she will allow. As the psychologists Suzanna Rose and Irene Frieze wrote in a 1993 article in *Sex Roles*, dating relationships follow a script that clearly perpetuates traditional, inequitable gender roles—even when students claim that they are behaving equitably.

In *Educated in Romance: Women, Achievement, and College Culture*, the anthropologists Dorothy C. Holland and Margaret A. Eisenhart rather baldly describe the model that men and women take for granted as follows: A man and a woman meet and are attracted to one another. The man shows his attraction by treating the woman well, paying attention to her, buying her things, taking her places, and showing that he appreciates her special qualities. She in turn shows her admiration and affection for him by allowing the relationship to become intimate. If a woman is unattractive, she can only win a man by accepting bad treatment. If the woman is more attractive than the man, then he usually compensates by treating her especially well.

A "culture of romance" on college campuses, Holland and Eisenhart say, continues to force women onto the sexual auction block, and to trap men into competing for them. Based on in-depth interviews with 23 college women and surveys of 362 other female students at a large, predominantly white state university and a large, predominantly black university, the researchers found that women put an extraordinary amount of time into grooming, talking about dates and relationships, and participating in dating and events to attract dates. Additionally, women show their interest in men by compromising their own goals in order to support the men's goals.

Holland and Eisenhart comment that such behavior may make sense, because our culture measures men's achievement by their accomplishments as well as their relationships, but assesses women only in terms of their relationships with men. The researchers found considerable dissatisfaction with the culture of romance among the students they interviewed, but little support for those women and men who chose to resist that culture.

The kind of work done by Rose and Frieze, and by Holland and Eisenhart—work that examines everyday social relationships of men and women—is quite rare. A review of the research on social relationships of college men and women shows that the vast majority of published studies in this area pertains to dating violence or date rape. Is this because of the morbid interest of social scientists in the pathologies of human relationships, or because dating truly is in deep trouble? Whatever the cause of this bias in the research, there is precious little scholarship on positive models of male-female interaction, and virtually none on alternatives to dating.

In spite of the sizable proportion of men who expect their wives not to work, most students are eager for guidance on how to meet possible mates outside of a bar or a blind date, how to create an equitable relationship, and how to plan for dual careers and shared family responsibilities. It seems to me that when students flock to courses on human sexuality, it is not simply for the fun of talking about sex, but because they hope the courses might include some pointers about how to have a happy and supportive relationship.

Students often do not consider their parents' marriages—a high percentage of which have been unhappy—as good models. Nor do the media give many examples of the kinds of relationships students hope to have (I heard the commentator Elvis Mitchell opine on National Public Radio that the success of *The X-Files* could be at least partly attributed to the fact that Fox Mulder and Dana Scully represent the first truly equal, romantically attracted male and female in television history). In the absence of any popular literature based on sound scholarship about male and female relationships, students turn to *Men Are from Mars, Women Are from Venus, The Rules,* and other pop-psychology books. Those works perpetuate the myth that men and women are so alien to one another that they can get along only by using intricate strategies of manipulation.

Although students may enjoy the amusing simplicities of such books, they quickly learn that the authors provide few answers to practical questions such as: "Should we go to graduate school at Purdue together or have a commuter relationship between Purdue and Indiana University?" "How do you decide whose job is most important?" "How do you balance family responsibilities with your career?" "How can a guy help with a newborn baby if his wife decides to breast-feed?"

Only a few well-written books by scholars provide an alternative vision of male-female relationships—Carol Tavris's *The Mismeasure of Woman* and Pepper Schwartz's *Peer Marriage: How Love Between Equals Really Works* come to mind—but those books lack the visibility of less scholarly works.

Another disturbing trend that seems to be emerging in gender relations is the disengagement of young men from leadership positions in organizations dominated by women, and men's apparent flight from college majors once dominated by males that now attract large numbers of women. The disengagement of young men from leadership was first called to my attention by Lyn Fiscus of the National Association of Secondary School Principals, whose research for the association shows that girls now hold about two-thirds of the leadership positions in high schools. On college campuses as well, women are surging into leadership positions in student government, college newspapers, and social-service organizations. What often happens is that the males simply begin to drop out when the proportion of females to males becomes high. As a young man said to me when I asked him why he wasn't involved in student government, "It's just a bunch of girls playing politics."

College majors are showing some interesting shifts as well. Biology is becoming a female ghetto, as undergraduate women pour into the one natural science that they perceive as friendly to them. Prelaw classes have shifted since 1990 from predominantly male to predominantly female. Astin's study of trends from 1966 to 1996 shows that when women's interest in a scholarly field grows, men's interest in that field declines.

As females broaden their choices, males may be narrowing theirs. In our studies of honors students, using data from American College Testing, Nicholas Colangelo, a professor of counselor education at the University of Iowa, and I found that bright males are crowding into the few majors—including business, engineering, and computer science—that they deem appropriate to both their intelligence and their gender. As women enter traditional male careers in ever-larger numbers over the next decades, men may find themselves increasingly disengaged from those pursuits, unless they can recast their definition of masculinity so that they are less threatened by association with women.

Conflicts among races and classes obscure the immensity of the gap between the sexes. Rita J. Simon, a law professor at American University, argued in an opinion article in *The Chronicle* (October 2, 1998) that "Race and Class Drive Most Conflict Now" in our society, and that gender issues are the province of white professional women who are concerned about equal pay. But if racism decreases and more of the poor join the middle class, gender may emerge as a major issue for people of color as well. Many of the acclaimed works of creative fiction by people of color deal with the troubled relationships between men and women. Isabel Allende, Louise Erdrich, Toni Morrison, and Amy Tan all have shown how race, class, and gender roles interact to limit the choices and dreams of both women and men. Given the magnitude of the changes under way in our society, I think our gender problems have just begun.

As academics, we can help men and women address these issues. First, we need to do fewer studies of date rape, and more studies of alternatives to dating. We need more research on how men and women can work toward their goals, based on their own deeply held values rather than on traditional gender roles. The creative ways in which some women and men have built truly equitable relationships outside of the culture of romance also need to be investigated. And we need to make sure that the results of those studies are clearly written, so that they enter the mainstream of social-science research, as well as the popular media.

Second, we need to offer our students more courses on personal relationships, in such departments as psychology, education, and family studies. We need to examine gender relations in the classroom, and confront the culture of romance directly. That means showing our students how the traditional dating system has made it harder for them to have open, friendly, and satisfying relationships. Faculty members need to share information about their own successful egalitarian relationships, as well as talk openly about marriage, family, and dual-career issues.

Third, in our one-on-one relationships with students—as their advisers and mentors—we should not consider their career and relationship goals separately. We should encourage men and women to discuss the ways in which those goals interact. All too often, I have seen counselors subtly lead female clients into a discussion focusing on relationship issues, and male clients into a discussion of career issues.

Fourth, we need to realize that gender equity in our relationships with our colleagues is not merely a matter of preventing sexual harassment and attaining equality in terms of pay and promotion. True equity is far broader and affects how we work together. We need to focus on the details that make equality between the sexes possible, such as not expecting young parents to teach courses or attend meetings that take place late in the day, and monitoring interactions in meetings to make sure that men don't constantly interrupt women.

We enter the new millennium with young women and men in an uncomfortable dance of courtship for which the old rules are sadly inadequate, and no new rules yet exist. No amount of nostalgic return to swing dancing and romantic comedy will bring back the old gender roles. Many faculty members may feel inadequate to speak to students about such matters, given their own awkward attempts to adjust to new roles and their difficulties in intimate relationships. In our reluctance, we are missing an opportunity to participate positively in what could be the greatest transition in history in the relationships between women and men. We all must help each other change.

QUESTIONS

1. What changes have occurred in the last 30 years that make the "old scripts" insufficient for modern relationships, according to Kerr? Why might men and women have such different expectations for their personal relationships?

2. What are the "sexual auction block" and the "culture of romance?" How do these phenomenon affect women's educational pursuits? How has the distribution of men and women in the workforce changed in the last 30 years? In what fields are men working? How might these changes affect relationships?

3. Why might heterosexual men and women who fully support social efforts to achieve equal rights choose to follow

"old scripts" in their relationships? Are equitable personal relationships less desirable to achieve? Are they more challenging? Why or why not?

4. Is a classroom setting an appropriate place to discuss relationship issues? Why or why not? Why does Kerr believe academics should become involved in these types of discussions? What specific suggestions does she offer to academics?

Age, Race, Class, and Sex: Women Redefining Difference (1984)

Audre Lorde

An African-American feminist poet, theorist, and activist, Audre Lorde is the author of 12 collections of poetry and 6 works of prose, including Coal, Sister Outsider, Cables to Rage, Use of the Erotic: The Erotic as Power, *and a memoir about her battle with breast cancer entitled* The Cancer Journals. *She is also credited with co-founding Kitchen Table: Women of Color Press with Barbara Smith. In this 1984 essay, Lorde conveys the difficulties of African American women active in a movement dominated by white women, and a civil rights movement dominated by African American men. Urging the acknowledgment of differences both within and across categories of age, race, class and sex, Lorde emphasizes human diversity as a force to seize and utilize, rather than as an obstacle to unity.*

Much of Western European history conditions us to see human differences in simplistic opposition to each other: dominant/subordinate, good/bad, up/down, superior/inferior.[1,2] In a society where the good is defined in terms of profit rather than in terms of human need, there must always be some group of people who, through systematized oppression, can be made to feel surplus, to occupy the place of the dehumanized inferior. Within this society, that group is made up of Black and Third World people, working-class people, older people and women.

As a 49-year-old Black lesbian feminist socialist mother of two, including one boy, and a member of an interracial couple, I usually find myself a part of some group defined as other, deviant, inferior or just plain wrong. Traditionally, in American society, it is the members of oppressed, objectified groups who are expected to stretch out and bridge the gap between the actualities of our lives and the consciousness of our oppressor. For in order to survive, those of us for whom oppression is as American as apple pie have always had to be watchers, to become familiar with the language and manners of the oppressor, even sometimes adopting them for some illusion of protection. Whenever the need for some pretense of communication arises, those who profit from our oppression call upon us to share our knowledge with them. In other words, it is the responsibility of the oppressed to teach the oppressors their mistakes. I am responsible for educating teachers who dismiss my children's culture in school. Black and Third World people are expected to educate white people as to our humanity. Women are expected to educate men. Lesbians and gay men are expected to educate the heterosexual world. The oppressors maintain their position and evade responsibility for their own actions. There is a constant drain of energy which might be better used in redefining ourselves and devising realistic scenarios for altering the present and constructing the future.

Institutionalized rejection of difference is an absolute necessity in a profit economy which needs outsiders as surplus people. As members of such an economy, we have *all* been programmed to respond to the human differences between us with fear and loathing and to handle that difference in one of three ways: ignore it, and if that is not possible, copy it if we think it is dominant, or destroy it if we think it is subordinate. But we have no patterns for relating across our human differences as equals. As a result, those differences have been misnamed and misused in the service of separation and confusion.

Certainly there are very real differences between us of race, age, and sex. But it is not those differences between us that are separating us. It is rather our refusal to recognize those differences, and to examine the distortions which result from our misnaming them and their effects upon human behavior and expectation.

Racism, the belief in the inherent superiority of one race over all others and thereby the right to dominance. Sexism, the belief in the inherent superiority of one sex over the other and thereby the right to dominance. Ageism. Heterosexism. Elitism. Classism.

It is a lifetime pursuit for each one of us to extract these distortions from our living at the same time as we recognize, reclaim and define those differences upon which they are imposed. For we have all been raised in a society where those distortions were endemic within our living. Too often, we pour the energy needed for recognizing and exploring difference into pretending those differences are insurmountable barriers, or that they do not exist at all. This results in a voluntary isolation, or false and treacherous connections. Either way, we do not develop tools for using human difference as a springboard for creative change within our lives. We speak not of human difference, but of human deviance.

Somewhere, on the edge of consciousness, there is what I call a *mythical norm*, which each one of us within our hearts knows "that is not me." In America, this norm is usually defined as white, thin, male, young, heterosexual, christian and financially secure. It is with this mythical norm that the trappings of power reside within this society. Those of us who stand outside that power often identify one way in which we are different, and we assume that to be the primary cause of all oppression, forgetting other distortions around difference, some of which we ourselves may be practicing. By and large within the woman's movement today, white women focus upon their oppression as women and ignore differences of race, sexual preference, class and age. There is a pretense to a homogeneity of experience covered by the word *sisterhood* that does not in fact exist.

Unacknowledged class differences rob women of each other's energy and creative insight. Recently a women's magazine collective made the decision for one issue to print only prose, saying poetry was a less "rigorous" or "serious" art form. Yet even the form our creativity takes is often a class issue. Of all the art forms, poetry is the most economical. It is the one which is the most secret, which requires the least physical labor, the least material, and the one which can be done between shifts, in the hospital pantry, on the subway, and on scraps of surplus paper. Over the last few years, writing a novel on tight finances, I came to appreciate the enormous differences in the material demands between poetry and prose. As we reclaim our literature, poetry has been the major voice of poor, working-class and Colored women. A room of one's own may be a necessity for writing prose, but so are reams of paper, a typewriter and plenty of time. The actual requirements to produce the visual arts also help determine, along class lines, whose art is whose. In this day of inflated prices for material, who are our sculptors, our painters, our photographers? When we speak of a broadly based women's culture, we need to be aware of the effect of class and economic differences on the supplies available for producing art.

As we move toward creating a society within which we can each flourish, ageism is another distortion of relationship which interferes without vision. By ignoring the past, we are encouraged to repeat its mistakes. The "generation gap" is an important social tool for any repressive society. If the younger members of a community view the older members as contemptible or suspect or excess, they will never be able to join hands and examine the living memories of the community, nor ask the all important question, "Why?" This gives rise to a historical amnesia that keeps us working to invent the wheel every time we have to go to the store for bread.

We find ourselves having to repeat and relearn the same old lessons over and over that our mothers did because we do not pass on what we have learned, or because we are unable to listen. For instance, how many times has this all been said before? For another, who would have believed that once again our daughters are allowing their bodies to be hampered and purgatoried by girdles and high heels and hobble skirts?

Ignoring the differences of race between women and the implications of those differences presents the most serious threat to the mobilization of women's joint power.

As white women ignore their built-in privilege of whiteness and define *woman* in terms of their own experience alone, then women of Color become "other," the outsider whose experience and tradition is too "alien" to comprehend. An example of this is the signal absence of the experience of women of Color as a resource for women's studies courses. The literature of women of Color is seldom included in women's literature courses and almost never in other literature courses, nor in women's studies as a whole. All too often, the excuse given is that the literatures of women of Color can only be taught by Colored women, or that they are too difficult to understand, or that classes cannot "get into" them because they come out of experiences that are "too different." I have heard this argument presented by white women of otherwise quite clear intelligence, women who seem to have no trouble at all teaching and reviewing work that comes out of the vastly different experiences of Shakespeare, Molière, Dostoyevsky and Aristophanes. Surely there must be some other explanation.

This is a very complex question, but I believe one of the reasons white women have such difficulty reading Black women's work is because of their reluctance to see Black women as women and different from themselves. To examine Black women's literature effectively requires that we be seen as whole people in our actual complexities—as individuals, as women, as human—rather than as one of those problematic but familiar stereotypes provided in this society in place of genuine images of Black women. And I believe this holds true for the literatures of other women of Color who are not Black.

The literatures of all women of Color recreate the textures of our lives, and many white women are heavily invested in ignoring the real differences. For as long as any difference between us means one of us must be inferior, then the recognition of any difference must be fraught with guilt. To allow women of Color to step out of stereotypes is too guilt provoking, for it threatens the complacency of those women who view oppression only in terms of sex.

Refusing to recognize difference makes it impossible to see the different problems and pitfalls facing us as women.

Thus, in a patriarchal power system where white skin privilege is a major prop, the entrapments used to neutralize Black women and white women are not the same. For example, it is easy for Black women to be used by the power structure against Black men, not because they are men, but because they are Black. Therefore, for Black women, it is necessary at all times to separate the needs of the oppressor from our own legitimate conflicts within our communities. This same problem does not exist for white women. Black women and men have shared racist oppression and still share it, although in different ways. Out of that shared oppression we have developed joint defenses and joint vulnerabilities to each other that are not duplicated in the white community, with the exception of the relationship between Jewish women and Jewish men.

On the other hand, white women face the pitfall of being seduced into joining the oppressor under the pretense of sharing power. This possibility does not exist in the same way for women of Color. The tokenism that is sometimes extended to us is not an invitation to join power; our racial "otherness" is a visible reality that makes that quite clear. For white women there is a wider range of pretended choices and rewards for identifying with patriarchal power and its tools.

Today, with the defeat of ERA, the tightening economy and increased conservatism, it is easier once again for white women to believe the dangerous fantasy that if you are good enough, pretty enough, sweet enough, quiet enough, teach the children to behave, hate the right people, and marry the right men, then you will be allowed to co-exist with patriarchy in relative peace, at least until a man needs your job or the neighborhood rapist happens along. And true, unless one lives and loves in the trenches it is difficult to remember that the war against dehumanization is ceaseless.

But Black women and our children know the fabric of our lives is stitched with violence and with hatred, that there is no rest. We do not deal with it only on the picket lines, or in the dark midnight alleys, or in the places where we dare to verbalize our resistance. For us, increasingly, violence weaves through the daily tissues of our living—in the supermarket, in the classroom, in the elevator, in the clinic and the schoolyard, from the plumber, the baker, the sales woman, the bus driver, the bank teller, the waitress who does not serve us.

Some problems we share as women, some we do not. You fear your children will grow up to join the patriarchy and testify against you, we fear our children will be dragged from a car and shot down in the street, and you will turn your backs upon the reasons they are dying.

The threat of difference has been no less blinding to people of Color. Those of us who are Black must see that the reality of our lives and our struggle does not make us immune to the errors of ignoring and misnaming difference. Within Black communities where racism is a living reality; differences among us often seem dangerous and suspect. The need for unity is often misnamed as a need for homogeneity, and a Black feminist vision mistaken for betrayal of our common interests as a people. Because of the continuous battle against racial erasure that Black women and Black men share, some Black women still refuse to recognize that we are also oppressed as women, and that sexual hostility against Black women is practiced not only by the white racist society, but implemented within our Black communities as well. It is a disease striking the heart of Black nationhood, and silence will not make it disappear. Exacerbated by racism and the pressures of powerlessness, violence against Black women and children often becomes a standard within our communities, one by which manliness can be measured. But these women-hating acts are rarely discussed as crimes against Black women.

As a group, women of Color are the lowest-paid wage earners in America. We are the primary targets of abortion and sterilization abuse, here and abroad. In certain parts of Africa, small girls are still being sewed shut between their legs to keep them docile and for men's pleasure. This is known as female circumcision, and it is not a cultural affair as the late Jomo Kenyatta insisted, it is a crime against Black women.

Black women's literature is full of the pain of frequent assault, not only by racist patriarchy, but also by Black men. Yet the necessity for and history of shared battle have made us, Black women, particularly vulnerable to the false accusation that anti-sexist is anti-Black. Meanwhile, womanhating as a recourse of the powerless is sapping strength from Black communities, and our very lives. Rape is on the increase, reported and unreported, and rape is not aggressive sexuality, it is sexualized aggression. As Kalamu ya Salaam, a Black male writer, points out, "As long as male domination exists, rape will exist. Only women revolting and men made conscious of their responsibility to fight sexism can collectively stop rape."[3]

Differences between ourselves as Black women are also being misnamed and used to separate us from one another. As a Black lesbian feminist comfortable with the many different ingredients of my identity, and a woman committed to racial and sexual freedom from oppression, I find I am constantly being encouraged to pluck out some one aspect of myself and present this as the meaningful whole, eclipsing or denying the other parts of self. But this is a destructive and fragmenting way to live. My fullest concentration of energy is available to me only when I integrate all the parts of who I am, openly, allowing power from particular sources of my living to flow back and forth freely through all my different selves, without the restrictions of externally imposed definition. Only then can I bring myself and my energies as a whole to the service of those struggles which I embrace as part of my living.

A fear of lesbians, or of being accused of being a lesbian, has led many Black women into testifying against themselves. It has led some of us into destructive alliances, and others into despair and isolation. In the white women's communities, heterosexism is sometimes a result of identifying with the white patriarchy, a rejection of that interdependence between women-identified women which allows the self to be, rather than to be used in the service of men. Sometimes it reflects a die-hard belief in the protective coloration of heterosexual relationships, sometimes a self-hate which all women have to fight against, taught us from birth.

Although elements of these attitudes exist for all women, there are particular resonances of heterosexism and homophobia among Black women. Despite the fact that woman-bonding has a long and honorable history in the African and African-American communities, and despite the knowledge and accomplishments of many strong and creative women-identified Black women in the political, social and cultural fields, heterosexual Black women often tend to ignore or discount the existence and work of Black lesbians. Part of this attitude has come from an understandable terror of Black male attack within the close confines of Black society, where the punishment for any female self-assertion is still to be accused of being a lesbian and therefore unworthy of the attention or support of the scarce Black male. But part of this need to misname and ignore Black lesbians comes from a very real fear that openly women-identified Black women who are no longer dependent upon men for their self-definition may well reorder our whole concept of social relationships.

Black women who once insisted that lesbianism was a white woman's problem now insist that Black lesbians are a threat to Black nationhood, are consorting with the enemy, are basically un-Black. These accusations, coming from the very women to whom we look for deep and real understanding, have served to keep many Black lesbians in hiding, caught between the racism of white women and the homophobia of their sisters. Often, their work has been ignored, trivialized or misnamed, as with the work of Angelina Grimké, Alice Dunbar-Nelson, Lorraine Hansberry. Yet women-bonded women have always been some part of the power of Black communities, from our unmarried aunts to the amazons of Dahomey.

And it is certainly not Black lesbians who are assaulting women and raping children and grandmothers on the streets of our communities.

Across this country, as in Boston during the spring of 1979 following the unsolved murders of 12 Black women, Black lesbians are spearheading movements against violence against Black women.

What are the particular details within each of our lives that can be scrutinized and altered to help bring about change? How do we redefine difference for all women? It is not our differences which separate women, but our reluctance to recognize those differences and to deal effectively with the distortions which have resulted from the ignoring and misnaming of those differences.

As a tool of social control, women have been encouraged to recognize only one area of human difference as legitimate, those differences which exist between women and men. And we have learned to deal across those differences with the urgency of all oppressed subordinates. All of us have had to learn to live or work or co-exist with men, from our fathers on. We have recognized and negotiated these differences, even when this recognition only continued the old dominant/subordinate mode of human relationship, where the oppressed must recognize the masters' difference in order to survive.

But our future survival is predicated upon our ability to relate within equality. As women, we must root out internalized patterns of oppression within ourselves if we are to move beyond the most superficial aspects of social change. Now we must recognize differences among women who are our equals, neither inferior nor superior, and devise ways to use each other's difference to enrich our visions and our joint struggles.

The future of our earth may depend upon the ability of all women to identify and develop new definitions of power and new patterns of relating across difference. The old definitions have not served us, nor the earth that supports us. The old patterns, no matter how cleverly rearranged to imitate progress, still condemn us to cosmetically altered repetitions of the same old exchanges, the same old guilt, hatred, recrimination, lamentation and suspicion.

For we have, built into all of us, old blueprints of expectation and response, old structures of oppression, and these must be altered at the same time as we alter the living conditions which are a result of those structures. For the master's tools will never dismantle the master's house.

As Paulo Freire shows so well in *The Pedagogy of the Oppressed,*[4] the true focus of revolutionary change is never merely the oppressive situations which we seek to escape, but that piece of the oppressor which is planted deep within each of us, and which knows only the oppressors' tactics, the oppressors' relationships.

Change means growth, and growth can be painful. But we sharpen self-definition by exposing the self in work and struggle together with those whom we define as different from ourselves, although sharing the same goals. For Black and white, old and young, lesbian and heterosexual women alike, this can mean new paths to our survival.

We have chosen each other
and the edge of each others battles
the war is the same
if we lose
someday women's blood will congeal
upon a dead planet
if we win
there is no telling
we seek beyond history
for a new and more possible meeting.[5]

NOTES

1. The editors and publishers gratefully acknowledge permission of Crossing Press © 1984 and Audre Lorde to reproduce "Age, Race, Class, and Sex: Women Redefining Difference" from *Sister Outsider.*

2. This paper was delivered at the Copeland Colloquium, Amherst College, April 1980.

3. From "Rape: A Radical Analysis, An African-American Perspective" by Kalamu ya Salaam in *Black Books Bulletin*, Vol. 6, no. 4 (1980).

4. Seabury Press: New York, 1970.
5. From "Outlines," unpublished poem.

QUESTIONS

1. What is the tone of Lorde's writing in this essay? How does she feel about her argument? What textual evidence can you offer for your assessment?
2. What does Lorde mean by a mythical norm? How does this norm work in our society? What are the three most common ways to deal with difference, according to Lorde? Why are these problematic?
3. Why does Lorde focus so much on "difference" in this piece? Why does she urge us to acknowledge differences among people? What are the consequences for African American women if differences get obscured, or if a "homogeneity of experience" among women is assumed?
4. What concrete differences does Lorde pinpoint between women of color and white women's experiences?

From "Kike" to "JAP": How Misogyny, Anti-Semitism, and Racism Construct the "Jewish American Princess" (1988)

Evelyn Torton Beck

Professor Evelyn Torton Beck explores how the stereotype of the "Jewish American Princess" is constructed and perpetrated. Demonstrating how the "JAP" ethnic epithet legitimizes the economic and violent exploitation of Jewish women, Beck offers an historical perspective documenting forces that create and maintain categories of difference in the United States, including language use as a tool of social control. Beck, director of the Women's Studies Program at the University of Maryland-College Park, is the

"From 'Kike' to 'Jap': How Misogyny, Anti-Semitism, and Racism Construct the 'Jewish American Princess,'" by Evelyn Torton Beck, reprinted from the September 1988 issue of *Sojourner: The Women's Forum*.

author of a number of texts in Jewish Studies, including Nice Jewish Girls: A Lesbian Anthology *(1982).*

The stereotyping of the Jewish American woman as the JAP, which stands for Jewish American Princess, is an insult, an injury, and violence that is done to Jewish women. The term is used widely by both men and women, by both Jews and non-Jews. When gentiles use it, it is a form of anti-Semitism. When Jews use it, it is a form of self-hating or internalized anti-Semitism. It is a way of thinking that allows some Jewish women to harm other Jewish women who are just like them except for the fact that one is okay—she's *not* a JAP. The other is not okay—she's too JAPie. The seriousness of this term becomes evident when we substitute the words "too Jewish" for "too JAPie" and feel ourselves becoming considerably less comfortable.

When I speak on college campuses, young women frequently tell me that when someone calls them a Jew they are insulted because they know it's being said with a kind of hostility, but if someone calls them a JAP they don't mind because they frequently use this term themselves. They think the "J" in JAP really doesn't mean anything—it's just there. While everyone seems to know what the characteristics of a "Jewish American Princess" are, no one ever seems to think about what they are saying when they use the term. How is it that you don't have to be Jewish to be a JAP? If this is so, why is the word "Jewish" in the acronym at all? Words are not meaningless unless we choose to close our ears and pretend not to hear.

This subject is frequently trivialized, but when it is not, when we take it seriously, it makes us extremely tense. Why is that? I think it's because it takes us into several "war zones": It brings us in touch with Jew-hating, or anti-Semitism. It brings us in touch with misogyny, or woman-hating. And it brings us in touch with class-hatred, old money vs. nouveau riche. (Jews have classically been seen as intruders in the United States and have been resented for "making it.") It also puts us strongly in touch with racism. It is no accident that the acronym JAP is also the word used for our worst enemies in World War II—who were known as "the Japs." During World War II, posters and slogans saying "Kill Japs" were everywhere. It was a period in which slang terms were readily used in a pejorative way to identify many different minorities: "Japs," "Kikes" "Spics," "Wops," "Chinks" were commonplace terms used unthinkingly. And women were—and, unfortunately, still are—easily named "bitches," "sluts," and "cunts."

In such a climate, negative stereotypes easily overlap and elide. For example, in the popular imagination, Jews, "Japs," women and homosexuals have all been viewed as devious, unreliable, and power hungry. What has happened in the decades following World War II is that the "Japs," whom we dehumanized when we dropped our atom bomb on them, have subliminally merged in the popular imagination with "kikes" and other foreign undesirables. (The fact that in the 1980s Japan poses a serious economic threat to the United States should not be overlooked either.) While efforts to eradicate slurs against ethnic minorities have made it not okay to use explicitly ethnic epithets, women still provide an acceptable target, especially when the misogyny is disguised as supposedly "good-natured" humor. In this insidious and circuitous way, the Jewish American woman carries the stigmas of the "kikes" and "Japs" of a previous era. And that is very serious.

The woman, the Jewish woman as JAP, has replaced the male Jew as the scapegoat, and the Jewish male has not only participated, but has, in fact, been instrumental in creating and perpetuating that image. I want to show how some of the images of Jewish women created in American culture by Jewish men provided the roots of the "Jewish American Princess." But first I want to provide a context for understanding the development of this image. I want to look at anti-Semitism in the United States, and at misogyny, and show how the merging of anti-Semitism and misogyny creates the Jewish American Princess.

Between 1986 and 1987 there was a 17 percent rise in anti-Semitic incidents in this country. Of these incidents, 48 percent occurred in the Northeast, and the highest rates of increase were in New York State; California, particularly Los Angeles; and Florida. These are all areas where there are high concentrations of Jews. On November 9 and 10, 1987, the anniversary of *Kristalnacht,* the Night of Broken Crystal, when Goebbels staged a mass "spontaneous pogrom" in Austria and Germany in 1938, swastikas were painted on entrances to synagogues in a number of different cities in the United States: Chicago, Yonkers, and others dotted across the country. Windows were smashed—not simply of Jewish-owned stores, but of identifiably Jewish businesses such as kosher meat markets, a kosher fish store, a Jewish book store—in five different neighborhoods, particularly in a Chicago suburb largely populated by Holocaust survivors. Having grown up in Vienna and having lived under the Nazis, the horror of that night resonated for me in a way that it might not for those who are much younger. But that these pogrom-like episodes happened on the eve of *Kristalnacht* cannot have been an accident, and the timing of these incidents should not be lost upon us.

In response to these attacks many members of the Jewish community wanted to hide the facts, and one member of the Jewish community in Chicago actually said, "The swastikas could have meant general white supremacy; they were not necessarily aimed at Jews." They just "happened" to be placed on synagogues, right? In the same way, it just "happens" that the word "Jewish" is lodged in the very negative image of this hideous creature known as the Jewish American Princess. Anyone who is aware of Jewish history and knows about the ridicule, defamation, and violence to which Jews have been subject will not be able to write this off so easily.

The Jewish American Princess phenomenon is not new; I (as well as other Jewish feminists) have been talking about it for at least ten years now, but only recently has it been given wide public attention. One reason for this is that it is beginning to be seen in the light of increased anti-Semitism and racism, particularly on college campuses. Dr. Gary Spencer, who is a *male* professor of sociology at Syracuse University (and it is unfortunate that his being male gives him credibility over women saying the same things) closely examined the library and bathroom graffiti of his school and interviewed hundreds of students on his campus and has concluded that "JAP"-baiting is widespread, virulent, and threatening to all Jews, not "just" Jewish women (which we gather might have been okay or certainly considerably less serious).

Spencer discovered that nasty comments about "JAPS" led to more generally anti-Semitic graffiti that said among other slogans, "Hitler was right!" "Give Hitler a second chance!" and "I hate Jews." He also discovered that there were certain places in which Jewish women—JAPS—were not welcome: for example, certain cafes where Jewish women were hassled if they entered. He also found that certain areas of the university were considered "JAP-free zones" and other areas (particularly dorms) were called "Jew havens." At The American University in Washington, D.C., largely Jewish residence halls are called "Tokyo Towers," making the racial overtones of "JAP" explicit. But let the parallels to Nazi-occupied Europe not be lost upon us. Under the Nazis, movements of the Jews were sharply restricted: there were many areas which Jews could not enter, and others (like ghettos and concentration camps) that they could not leave.

What I want to do now is to show how characteristics that have historically been attributed to Jews, primarily Jewish men, have been reinterpreted in terms of women: how misogyny combined with Jew-hating creates the Jewish American Princess. And I want you to remember that Jewish men have not only participated in this trashing, but they have not protected Jewish women when other men and women have talked about JAPS in this way. And this fact, I think, has made this an arena into which anyone can step—an arena that becomes a minefield when Jews step into it.

Jews have been said to be materialistic, money-grabbing, greedy, and ostentatious. Women have been said to be vain, trivial and shallow; they're only interested in clothing, in show. When you put these together you get the Jewish-woman type who's only interested in designer clothes and sees her children only as extensions of herself. The Jew has been seen as manipulative, crafty, untrustworthy, unreliable, calculating, controlling, and malevolent. The Jewish Princess is seen as manipulative, particularly of the men in her life, her husband, her boyfriend, her father. And what does she want? Their *money!* In addition, she's lazy—she doesn't work inside or outside the home. She is the female version of the Jew who, according to anti-Semitic lore, is a parasite on society; contradictorily, the Jew has been viewed both as dangerous "communist" as well as non-productive "capitalist." The cartoon vision of the Jewish American Princess is someone who sucks men dry: she is an "unnatural mother" who refuses to nurture her children (the very opposite of the "Jewish mother" whose willingness to martyr herself makes *her* ludicrous). And she doesn't "put out" except in return for goods; she isn't really interested in either sexuality or lovingness. We live in a world climate and culture in which materialism is rampant, and Jewish women are taking the rap for it. The irony is they are taking the rap from non-Jews and Jewish men alike—even from some Jewish women.

Another way in which women are carrying the anti-Semitism that was directed in previous eras at Jewish men is in the arena of sexuality. Jews have been said to be sexually strange, exotic. There are many stereotypes of Jewish men as lechers. The Jewish American Princess is portrayed as both sexually frigid (withholding) and as a nymphomaniac. Here we again see the familiar anti-Semitic figure of the Jew as controlling and insatiably greedy, always wanting more, combining with the misogynist stereotype of the insatiable woman, the woman who is infinitely orgasmic, who will destroy men with her desire. Like the Jew of old, the Jewish woman will suck men dry. But she is worse than "the Jew"—she will also turn on her own kind.

There are physical stereotypes as well: the Jew with the big hook nose, thick lips, and frizzy hair. The Jewish American Princess has had a nose job and her hair has been straightened, but she too has large lips (an image we immediately recognize as racist). Jews are supposed to be loud, pushy, and speak with unrefined accents. Jewish American Princesses are said to come from Long Island and speak with funny accents: "Oh my Gawd!" The accent has changed from the lampooned immigrant speech of previous generations, but assimilation into the middle class hasn't helped the Jewish American Princess get rid of her accent. It doesn't matter how she speaks, because if it's Eastern and recognizably Jewish, it's not okay.

I also want to give you some idea of how widespread and what a money-making industry the Jewish American Princess phenomenon has become. There are greeting cards about the "JAP Olympics," with the JAP doing things like "bank-vaulting" instead of pole-vaulting. Or cross-country *"kvetching"* instead of skiing. In this card the definition of the Yiddish term *kvetch* reads: "an irritable whine made by a three-year-old child or a JAP at any age." So in addition to the all-powerful monster you also have the infantilization of the Jewish woman. And there are the Bunny Bagelman greeting cards: Bunny has frizzy hair, big lips, is wearing ostentatious jewelry—and is always marked as a Jew in some way. One of her cards reads, "May God Bless you and keep you . . . rich!" Or Bunny Bagelman is a professional, dressed in a suit carrying a briefcase, but this image is undermined by the little crown she incongruously wears on her head bearing the initials "JAP." There is also a Halloween card with a grotesque female figure; the card reads, "Is it a vicious vampire? No, it's Bunny Bagelman with PM syndrome!" In analyzing these kinds of cartoons, you begin to see how sexism is absolutely intertwined with anti-Semitism.

Such attacks devalue Jewish women and keep them in line. An incident reported by Professor Spencer at Syracuse University makes this quite evident. At a basketball game, when women who were presumed to be "JAPs" stood up and walked across the floor at half-time (and it happened to Jewish and non-Jewish women), 2,000 students stood up, accusingly pointed their fingers at them, and repeatedly yelled, "JAP, JAP, JAP, JAP, JAP" in a loud chorus. This was so humiliating and frightening that women no longer got out of their seats to go to the bathroom or to get a soda. This is a form of public harassment that is guaranteed to control behavior and parallels a phenomenon called "punching" at the University of Dar El Salaam, Tanzania. Here, when women were "uppity" or otherwise stepped out of line, huge posters with their pictures on them were put all over campus, and no one was to speak to them. If you spoke to these women, you were considered to be like them. This is a very effective way of controlling people.

The threat of physical violence against Jewish women (in the form of "Slap-a-JAP" T-shirts and contests at bars) is evident on many Eastern college campuses. A disc jockey at The American University went so far as to sponsor a "fattest JAP-on-campus" contest. That this kind of unchecked verbal violence can lead to murder is demonstrated by lawyer Shirley Frondorf in a recent book entitled *Death of a "Jewish American Princess": The True Story of a Victim on Trial* (Villard Books, 1988). Frondorf shows how the murder of a Jewish woman by her husband was exonerated and the victim placed on trial because she was someone who was described by her husband as "materialistic, who shopped and spent, nagged shrilly and bothered her husband at work"—in other words, she was a "JAP" and therefore deserved what she got. This account demonstrates the dangers inherent in stereotyping and the inevitable dehumanization that follows.

One of the most aggressively sexual forms of harassment of Jewish women, which amounted to verbal rape, were signs posted at a college fair booth at Cornell University that read, "Make her prove she's not a JAP, make her swallow." Part of the mythology is that the Jewish woman will suck, but she won't swallow. So you see that as the degradation of woman *as woman* escalates, the anti-Semitism also gets increasingly louder. In a recent Cornell University student newspaper, a cartoon offered advice on how to "exterminate" JAPS by setting up a truck offering bargains, collecting the JAPS as they scurried in, and dropping them over a cliff. While the word "Jew" was not specifically mentioned, the parallels to the historical "rounding up" of Jews and herding them into trucks to be exterminated in the camps during World War II can hardly be ignored. This cartoon was created by a Jewish man.

This leads me directly to the third thing I want to discuss, namely, how and why Jewish men have participated in constructing and perpetuating the image of the Jewish American Princess as monster. How is it that the Jewish Mother (a mildly derogatory stereotype that nonetheless contained some warmth) has become the grotesque that is the Jewish American Princess, who, unlike the Jewish Mother, has absolutely no redeeming features? Exactly how the Jewish Mother (created entirely by second generation American men who had begun to mock the very nurturance they had relied upon for their success) gave birth to the Jewish American Princess is a long and complex story. This story is intertwined with the overall economic success of Jews as a class in the United States, the jealousy others have felt over this success, and the discomfort this success creates in Jews who are fearful of living out the stereotype of the "rich Jew." It is also a likely conjecture that middle-class American Jewish men view the large numbers of Jewish women who have successfully entered the work force as professionals as a serious economic and ego threat.

We find the origins of the Jewish American Princess in the fiction of American Jewish males of the last three decades. In the '50s, Herman Wouk's *Marjory Morningstar* (nee Morgenstern) leaves behind her immigrant background, takes a new name (one that is less recognizably Jewish), manipulates men, has no talent, and is only interested in expensive clothing. The postwar Jewish male, who is rapidly assimilating into American middle-class culture and leaving behind traditional Jewish values, is creating the Jewish woman—the materialistic, empty, manipulative Jewish woman, the Americanized daughter who fulfills the American Dream for her parents but is, at the same time, punished for it. It looks as if the Jewish woman was created in the image of the postwar Jewish male but viewed by her creator as grotesque. All the characteristics he cannot stand in himself are displaced onto the Jewish woman.

In the '60s, Philip Roth created the spoiled and whiny Brenda Potemkin in *Goodbye, Columbus* at the same time that Shel Silverstein created his image of the perfect Jewish mother as martyr. Some of you may remember this popular story from your childhood. A synopsis goes something like this: "Once there was a tree and she loved the little boy. And he slept in her branches, and loved the tree and the tree was happy. And as the boy grew older, he needed things from her. He needed apples, so she gave him apples, and she was happy. Then she cut off her branches because the boy needed them to build a house. And she was happy. Then finally he needed her trunk because he wanted to build a big boat for himself. And she was happy. The tree gave and gave of herself, and finally the tree was alone and old when the boy returned one more time. By now, the tree had nothing to give. But the boy/man is himself old now, and he doesn't need much except a place on which to sit. And the tree said, 'An old stump is good for sitting and resting on. Come boy and sit and rest on me.' And the boy did, and the tree was happy." This "positive" entirely self-*less* mother, created as a positive wish fantasy by a Jewish man, very easily tips over into its opposite, the monstrous woman, the self-absorbed "JAP" who is negatively self-less. She has no center. She *is* only clothes, money, and show.

In concluding, I want to bring these strands together and raise some questions. Obviously Jews need to be as thoughtful about consumerism as others, but we need to ask why the Jewish woman is taking the rap for the consumerism which is rampant in our highly materialistic culture in general. We need to think about the image of the Jewish American Princess and the father she tries to manipulate. What has happened to the Jewish Mother? Why has she dropped out of the picture? If (as is likely true of all groups) some middle-class Jewish women (and men) are overly focused on material things, what is the other side of that? What about the middle-class fathers who measure their own success by what material goods they are able to provide to their wives and children and who don't know how to show love in any other way? Someone who doesn't know how to give except through material goods could easily create a child who comes to expect material goods as a proof of love and self-worth, especially if sexist gender expectations limit the options for women. We need to look more closely at the relationship between the "monster" daughter and the father who helped create her. . . .

Last, I want to say that we have many false images of Jewish families. There *is* violence in Jewish families, just as there is violence in families of all groups. It is time to put the whole question of the Jewish American Princess into the context of doing away with myths of all kinds. The Jewish family is no more nor less cohesive than other families, although there is great pressure on Jewish families to pretend they are. Not all Jewish families are non-alcoholic; not all Jewish families are heterosexual; not all Jews are upper or middle class; and not all are urban or Eastern. It's important that the truth of Jewish women's (and also Jewish men's) lives be spoken. Beginning to take apart this image of the Jewish American Princess can make us look more closely at what it is that we, in all of our diversity as Jews, are; what we are striving toward; and what we hope to become.

QUESTIONS

1. What contemporary issues and historical practices are highlighted when "Jewish American Princess" is examined as an ethnic epithet?
2. What parallels does the author draw between contemporary use of the term "JAP" and the Nazi persecution of Jewish people? Why are these parallels important in Beck's suggestion that "JAP" is a dangerous and harmful construction of difference?
3. How does the incident at the Syracuse University basketball game illustrate the ways constructions of difference can be used as tools of social control?
4. How does the economic exploitation of the "JAP" image provide evidence that supports Beck's argument?
5. Why would some Jewish men and women use the "JAP" image? What does this usage imply about the power of stereotypes to influence Jewish women's developing ethnic and self-identity?

FROM *LOVING IN THE WAR YEARS* (1983)

Cherríe Moraga

Cherríe Moraga was born in California in 1952. A writer and poet, Moraga has co-edited two collections of writing by women of color: This Bridge Called My Back *(1981) and* Cuentos: Stories by Latinas *(1983). In this passage from her collection of prose and journal selections entitled* Loving in the War Years *(1983), Moraga claims the race of her mother. The daughter of a Chicana mother and Anglo father, Moraga explains that her love for her mother is inextricably tied to her identity as a "brown" woman.*

para Gloria Anzaldúa, in gratitude

Sueño: 15 de julio 1982

During the long difficult night that sent my lover and I to separate beds, I dreamed of church and cunt. I put it this way because that is how it came to me. The suffering and the thick musty mysticism of the catholic church fused with the sensation of entering the vagina—like that of a colored woman's—dark, rica, full-bodied. The heavy sensation of complexity. A journey I must unravel, work out for myself.

I long to enter you like a temple.

My Brother's Sex Was White. Mine, Brown

If somebody would have asked me when I was a teenager what it means to be Chicana, I would probably have listed the grievances done me. When my sister and I were fifteen and fourteen, respectively, and my brother a few years older, we were still waiting on him. I write "were" as if now, nearly two decades later, it were over. But that would be a lie. To this day in my mother's home, my brother and father are waited on, including by me. I do this now out of respect for my mother and her wishes. In those early years, however, it was mainly in relation to my brother that I resented providing such service. For unlike my father, who sometimes worked as much as seventy hours a week to feed my face every day, the only thing that earned my brother my servitude was his maleness.

It was Saturday afternoon. My brother, then seventeen-years-old, came into the house with a pile of friends. I remember Fernie, the two Steves, and Roberto. They were hot, sweaty, and exhausted from an afternoon's basketball and plopped themselves down in the front room, my brother demanding, "Girls, bring us something to drink."

"Get it yourself, pig," I thought, but held those words from ever forming inside my mouth. My brother had the disgusting habit on these occasions of collapsing my sister, JoAnn's and my name when referring to us as a unit: his sisters. "Cher'ann," he would say. "We're really thirsty." I'm sure it took everything in his power *not* to snap his fingers. But my mother was out in the yard working and to refuse him would have brought her into the house with a scene before these boys' eyes which would have made it impossible for us to show our faces at school that following Monday. We had been through that before.

When my mother had been our age, over forty years earlier, she had waited on her brothers and their friends. And it was no mere lemonade. They'd come in from work or a day's drinking. And las mujeres, often just in from the fields themselves, would

---

Reprinted from *Loving in the War Years,* by Cherríe Moraga, 1983, with permission from the publisher, South End Press, 116 Saint Botolph Street, Boston, MA 02115.

already be in the kitchen making tortillas, warming frijoles or pigs feet, albóndigas soup, what-have-you. And the men would get a clean white tablecloth and a spread of food laid out before their eyes and not a word of resentment from the women.

The men watched the women—my aunts and mother moving with the grace and speed of girls who were cooking before they could barely see over the top of the stove. Elvira, my mother, knew she was being watched by the men and loved it. Her slim hips moved patiently beneath the apron. Her deep thick-lidded eyes never caught theirs as she was swept back into the kitchen by my abuelita's call of "Elvirita," her brown hands deepening in color as they dropped back into the pan of flour.

I suppose my mother imagined that Joe's friends watched us like that, too. But we knew different. We were not blonde or particularly long-legged or "available" because we were "Joe's sisters." This meant no boy could "make" us, which meant no boy would bother asking us out. Roberto, the Guatemalan, was the only one among my brother's friends who seemed at all sensitive to how awkward JoAnn and I felt in our role. He would smile at us nervously, taking the lemonade, feeling embarassed being waited on by people he considered peers. He knew the anglo girls they visited would never have succumbed to such a task.

Roberto was the only recompense.

As I stopped to wait on their yearning throats, "jock itch" was all that came to my mind. Their cocks became animated in my head, for that was all that seemed to arbitrarily set us apart from each other and put me in the position of the servant and they, the served.

I wanted to machine-gun them all down, but swallowed that fantasy as I swallowed making the boy's bed every day, cleaning his room each week, shining his shoes and ironing his shirts before dates with girls, some of whom *I* had crushes on. I would lend him the money I had earned house-cleaning for twelve hours, so he could blow it on one night with a girl because he seldom had enough money because he seldom had a job because there was always some kind of ball practice to go to. As I pressed the bills into his hand, the car honking outside in the driveway, his double-date waiting, I knew I would never see that money again.

Years later, after I began to make political the fact of my being a Chicana, I remember my brother saying to me, *"I've* never felt 'culturally deprived'," which I guess is the term "white" people use to describe Third World people being denied access to *their* culture. At the time, I wasn't exactly sure what he meant, but I remember in re-telling the story to my sister, she responded, "Of course, he didn't. He grew up male in our house. He got the best of both worlds." And yes, I can see now that that's true. *Male in a man's world. Light-skinned in a white world. Why change?*

The pull to identify with the oppressor was never as great in me as it was in my brother. For unlike him, I could never have *become* the white man, only the white man's *woman.*

The first time I began to recognize clearly my alliances on the basis of race and sex was when my mother was in the hospital, extremely ill. I was eight years old. During my mother's stay in the hospital, my tía Eva took my sister and me into her care; my brother stayed with my abuela; and my father stayed by himself in our home. During this time, my father came to visit me and my sister only once. (I don't know if he ever visited my brother.) The strange thing was I didn't really miss his visits, although I sometimes fantasized some imaginary father, dark and benevolent, who might come and remind us that we still *were* a family.

I have always had a talent for seeing things I don't particularly want to see and the one day my father did come to visit us with his wife/our mother physically dying in a hospital some ten miles away, I saw that he couldn't love us—not in the way we so desperately needed. I saw that he didn't know how and he came into my tía's house like a large lumbering child—awkward and embarassed out of his league—trying to play a parent when he needed our mother back as much as we did just to keep him eating and protected. I hated and pitied him that day. I knew how he was letting us all down, visiting my mother daily, like a dead man, unable to say, "The children, honey, I held them. They love you. They think of you." Giving my mother *something.*

Years later, my mother spoke of his visits to the hospital. How from behind the bars of her bed and through the tubes in her nose, she watched this timid man come and go daily—going through the "motions" of being a husband. "I knew I had to live," she told us. "I knew he could never take care of you."

In contrast to the seeming lack of feeling I held for my father, my longings for my mother and fear of her dying were the most passionate feelings that had ever lived inside my young heart.

> We are riding the elevator. My sister and I pressed up against one wall, holding hands. After months of separation, we are going to

visit mamá in the hospital. Mi tía me dice, "Whatever you do, no llores, Cherríe. It's too hard on your mother when you cry." I nod, taking long deep breaths, trying to control my quivering lip.

As we travel up floor by floor, all I can think about is not crying, breathing, holding my breath. "¿Me prometes?" she asks. I nod again, afraid to speak fearing my voice will crack into tears. My sister's nervous hand around mine, sweating too. We are going to see my mamá, mamá, after so long. She didn't die after all. She didn't die.

The elevator doors open. We walk down the corridor, my heart pounding My eyes are darting in and out of each room as we pass them, fearing/anticipating my mamá's face. Then as we turn around the corner into a kind of lobby, I hear my tía say to an older woman—skin and bones. *An Indian,* I think, straight black and grey hair pulled back. I hear my tía say, "Elvira."

I don't recognize her. This is not the woman I knew, so round and made-up with her hair always a wavy jet black! I stay back until she opens her arms to me—this strange and familiar woman—her voice hoarse, "¡Ay mi'jita! " Instinctively, I run into her arms, still holding back my insides—"Don't cry. Don't cry." I remember. "Whatever you do, no llores." But my tía had not warned me about the smell, the unmistakable smell of the woman, mi mamá—el olor de aceite y jabón and comfort and home. "Mi mamá. " And when I catch the smell I am lost in tears, deep long tears that come when you have held your breath for centuries.

There was something I knew at that eight-year-old moment that I vowed never to forget—the smell of a woman who is life and home to me at once. The woman in whose arms I am uplifted, sustained. Since then, it is as if I have spent the rest of my years driven by this scent toward la mujer.

when her india makes love
it is with the greatest reverence
to color, texture, smell

by now she knew the scent of earth
could call it up
even between the cracks
in sidewalks
steaming dry
from midday summer
rain

With this knowledge so deeply emblazed upon my heart, how then was I supposed to turn away from La Madre, La Chicana? If I were to build my womanhood on this self-evident truth, it is the love of the Chicana, the love of myself as a Chicana I had to embrace, no white man. Maybe this ultimately was the cutting difference between my brother and me. To be a woman fully necessitated my claiming the race of my mother. My brother's sex was white. Mine, brown.

Questions

1. Why does Moraga "wait on" her brother, father, and brother's friends? Why did Moraga's brother have "the best of both worlds"?
2. How does Moraga describe her mother? Why did Moraga's mother's body in the hospital exude "home" to her? Why does she choose to claim her mother's race? What hope does it offer her? Why did her mother's hospitalization clarify Moraga's alliances?
3. Moraga states, "My brother's sex was white. Mine brown." What does this mean? How can sex be "brown" or "white"? How can Moraga's race as a woman differ from her brother's race as a man? Why does Moraga think her sex and race are inextricably tied together? How does Moraga connect her identity with the color of her mother's skin?

Rebecca Adamson
For helping indigenous people claim their rights and preserve their wisdom (1997)

Gloria Steinem

Prominent activist, author, and founder of Ms., a feminist magazine, Gloria Steinem presents Rebecca Adamson, one of the magazine's 'Women of the Year" for 1997. This brief biography of Adamson introduces readers to a woman whose life has been dedicated to fighting invisibility and discrimination. Adamson's efforts to resist the colonization of indigenous cultures in the United States and elsewhere demonstrates the power of feminist organizing. This selection offers an opportunity to explore how individual differences can create personal understanding and collective activism.

Every once in a while, there is someone who has a gift not only for bringing people together, but for bringing worlds together. Both despite and because of her quiet, unassuming manner, Rebecca Adamson is one of those rare leaders. A feminist, a philosopher, and an innovative organizer, she takes on the whole process, from inspiring those around her with a future vision to calculating the budget; from making a ten-year plan to strategizing in emergencies. Most of all, this Cherokee woman brings a deep knowledge of ancient cultures into the modern world, and knowledge of how to survive the modern world to those cultures. As she says, "There are indigenous cultures that offer ways of living and sharing power and sharing wealth and building communities that the rest of the world needs to learn." Last year, First Nations Development Institute, the group she started with an unemployment check and a dream in 1980, celebrated its sixteenth anniversary of nurturing culturally appropriate economic enterprises in Indian country. It now has an operating budget of $1.4 million, a revolving loan fund of nearly $1 million, and a fund that provides approximately $1 million in grants yearly. First Nations, which responded to more than 1,000 requests for technical assistance last year, is beginning to see more pride in native values and less dependency on the handouts and top-down policies of Washington. And last year, Adamson's quiet leadership also took root in other indigenous struggles in the world, among groups whose survival despite centuries of genocide is a miracle in itself. They are threatened by the loss of natural resources, the dumping of hazardous and nuclear waste, and other forces ranging from old racism to new biopiracy. In the late 1980s, she became a United States representative to the drafting of the Indigenous and Tribal Peoples' Convention. Unlike a United Nations human rights draft document on indigenous people on which she also consulted, this statement by the International Labor Organization has been adopted and is being enforced by the governments of nine countries so far. It became a lightening rod for indigenous hopes, but also for resistance from national governments and multinational corporations. As a result of her work with native groups from Canada to Australia, helping to get their concerns about land rights and self-governance into the convention, Adamson's name began to be passed from one activist to the next.

One result was an emergency request from the Khwe and San people of southern Africa—also called the Bushpeople—whose

---

long history as hunter-gatherers in the Kalahari was about to end with a forced removal by the Bostwana government. In response, Adamson took a small group of activists and foundation people to the Bushpeople's remote homeland to help publicize their plight, and to answer their questions about land rights and the experiences of other native peoples. To further diminish Botswana's appetite for this forced removal, she organized a tour in the U.S. and Europe for two Khwe representatives, thus putting them in a media and U.N. spotlight. Though the problem is far from solved—the Botswana government is still trying to move the last 3,000 Bushpeople into settlements—Adamson was one of many people who promised to help, and one of the few who delivered. This year, she also traveled to the Australian outback to consult with aboriginal groups about cultural tourism as a way of increasing jobs, pride, and international understanding. "After all," as she explained, "if France can invite people from all over the world to experience its culture, why can't indigenous nations do the same?"

Rebecca Adamson's ability to sense what others need stems in part from her long struggle against invisibility as a Native American woman.

Growing up near Akron, Ohio, Adamson was a pretty, silent, honey-skinned child who felt odd and isolated among her white classmates. Born in 1949 to a Cherokee mother and a Swedish father who was a policeman, she wasn't exposed to her Indian culture at home. But during summers spent in rural North Carolina with her maternal grandparents, she discovered their deep Native American values. She remembers walking through the woods with her grandfather and sitting silently for hours. "He gave me a kind of calm, concentrated understanding of nature," she says. "He passed on his love of silence." It was also in North Carolina that her sense of injustice began to take hold as she noticed how her Cherokee cousins were economically and educationally deprived. Yet the community to which she returned each fall didn't seem to include her either.

In high school, she was quizzed by a psychologist assigned to figure out why this obviously bright student wasn't participating in class. She remembers sitting rigidly, trying to calculate what he wanted, what was required, what was "normal." That feeling grew into a lasting realization that she saw the world differently from most of her peers, and gave her an enduring empathy with anyone engulfed by a culture not their own.

As a student at the University of Akron, she was drawn to philosophy by her love of conceptual thinking, and to psychology by her continuing need to figure out what was "normal." After transferring to Piedmont College in Georgia, she took courses in law and economics. Whenever she read books or listened to lectures that interpreted progress as the domination of nature, or scarcity and accumulation as the basis of economics, or the adversarial system as the only way to reach justice, she remembers hearing a voice deep within her saying, "I don't think so."

At 20, she dropped out of college and hitchhiked to the West Coast. Once there, she was drawn to reservations where urban, politicized Indians were beginning to work in coalition with rural traditionalists who had guarded the old ways of life. It was a time of discovering a way of living that made sense to her: reciprocity with the community and with nature, sharing and sustainability as economic values, reaching justice by consensus, and a history that not only included women but was as old as the land itself.

It was also a time of learning what centuries of genocide, economic dependency, isolation, and cultural shaming had done. Adamson saw the living examples of statistics that give Native Americans the most or least of many things: the lowest employment and life expectancy; the highest rates of poverty, death by homocide, and diseases like tuberculosis and diabetes; plus a death rate from alcoholism almost six times the national norm. She also saw social experiments conducted with impunity on reservations: children removed from their families and culture, sterilizations and contraceptive testing performed on women, and people being exposed to a range of environmental hazards. It was like being in a Third World country locked inside the U.S., a special kind of colonialism that surrounded and rendered the colonized invisible.

Soon, she was working in the Indian-controlled school movement that galvanized people in much the same way that sit-ins and voter registration drives had fueled the civil rights movement. For more than a century, the U.S. government had been contracting Indian boarding schools to Christian religious groups, and children had been taken from their parents, forbidden to speak their own languages or learn their cultures, and denied the right to their own religious beliefs. Given the isolation, bias, and extreme power differences in those schools, it's not surprising that they often became places of emotional and physical cruelty, including sexual abuse. (In the 1980s, Native American groups in the U.S. and Canada would trace their cycles of child sexual abuse to such boarding schools.) Even children who went to day schools were generally kept from honoring their culture, history, language, and spiritual practices.

Working in the movement, Adamson found a place where the definition of "normal" honored interdependence as well as independence, and nature as well as invention. In 1972, she became the director of the Coalition of Indian Controlled School Boards. She traveled the country, helping communities gain control of their own schools, and was arrested three times for this peaceful organizing. She also helped restore the teaching of native languages by using bilingual education laws initiated on behalf of Latino groups: a lesson in how empowering one group empowers others. The school movement led to the founding of tribal colleges and the passage of the Indian Self-Determination and Education Assistance Act, which allowed Native Americans to run their own schools, law enforcement, environmental protection, welfare, and other programs.

During those years, she met and married a Native American activist and gave birth to a daughter, Neva (which means snowbird in Cree). In 1976, she took her baby with her as she began to consult with tribes on how to take control of reservation economics as well as schools. Adamson had become convinced that self-sufficiency and local control were the solution. Successful enterprise had to be based on the unique potential of each reservation. By 1979, two years after her marriage ended, she had created a proposal that reflected her dream of a place where the talents of Indian professionals and the ideas of grassroots reservation people could be combined with outside capital and technical help. In 1980, this single mother cashed her unemployment check, and went to New York City to brave the world of foundations and fund-raising. Within a year, while in the midst of struggling to overcome uterine cancer, she had taught herself the basics of running an organization and opened an office in Fredericksburg, Virginia; close enough to Washington to educate Congress, far enough away to stay clear of the bureaucracy. By slowly building a staff as devoted as she was and staying true to the problems on reservations, she came to be trusted in both the foundation world and Indian country.

Now, she can look with pride on results that First Nations has helped nurture, from the Saginaw Chippewa construction company that builds homes on the Isabella Reservation in Michigan, to the Ramah Navajo women weavers in New Mexico and the Umatilla Tribes' rebuilding of a land base in Oregon. In what Adamson calls "indigenous economics—economics with values added," instead of a single financial solution, many different solutions are woven together.

She has no illusions about the monumental task ahead. "Of the top 100 economies in the world," she points out, "47 are corporations, yet they have no responsibility for education and social welfare, nor do they have any commitment to place." Those are the kinds of forces working through governments to displace indigenous people. But Rebecca Adamson already has a new proposal and an expanded dream: First Peoples Worldwide, a bottom-up network of indigenous activists. People who know her say that the multinationals had better watch out.

"We are the canaries in the mine," Adamson warns. "If we go, the last ecosystems go. So does the wisdom of how to sustain resources, live in balance with nature, and create communities based on cooperation, not competition. I think the rest of the world is searching for these values. I know we're here to share them. But we can only share them if we're here.

Gloria Steinem is consulting editor and cofounder of *Ms.* magazine. She went to the Kalahari with Adamson, and plans to write about traditions of equality in indigenous cultures.

QUESTIONS

1. Who is Rebecca Adamson? How did her childhood experiences help shape her activism and understanding as an adult?

2. What characteristics of an "Indian way of life" were a source of self-empowerment for Adamson? How do these characteristics contrast with the realities Indians face as a "colonized" culture? What does it mean for a culture to be "colonized"?

3. What efforts has Adamson made to fight the "colonized" status of indigenous people, both in the U.S. and elsewhere? What are "indigenous economies"?

4. How would you describe Steinem's tone in this piece? Why was Rebecca Adamson selected as one of the "Women of the Year"? Why is this representation of Adamson's life a valuable source of knowledge? What does Adamson's life reveal about the nature of differences and the role they can play in maintaining and challenging inequity?

The Gap Between Striving and Achieving: The Case of Asian American Women (1989)

Deborah Woo

Sociologist Deborah Woo examines the concept of the "model minority" and its relationship to the gap she observes between Asian American women's efforts and their occupational and financial rewards. By assessing the structural factors that impact different groups of Asian-American women, Woo challenges the tendency to consider Asian-Americans as all alike, rather than as individuals with geographic, ethnic, and cultural differences.

Much academic research on Asian Americans tends to underscore their success, a success which is attributed almost always to a cultural emphasis on education, hard work, and thrift. Less familiar is the story of potential not fully realized. For example, despite the appearance of being successful and highly educated, Asian American women do not necessarily gain the kind of recognition or rewards they deserve.

The story of unfulfilled dreams remains unwritten for many Asian Americans. It is specifically this story about the gap between striving and achieving that I am concerned with here. Conventional wisdom obscures the discrepancy by looking primarily at whether society is adequately rewarding individuals. By comparing how minorities as disadvantaged groups are doing relative to each other, the tendency is to view Asian Americans as a "model minority." This practice programs us to ignore structural barriers and inequities and to insist that any problems are simply due to different cultural values or failure of individual effort.

Myths about the Asian American community derive from many sources. All ethnic groups develop their own cultural myths. Sometimes, however, they create myths out of historical necessity, as a matter of subterfuge and survival. Chinese Americans, for example, were motivated to create new myths because institutional opportunities were closed off to them. Succeeding in America meant they had to invent fake aspects of an "Oriental culture," which became the beginning of the Chinatown tourist industry.

What has been referred to as the "model minority myth," however, essentially originated from without. The idea that Asian Americans have been a successful group has been a popular news media theme for the last twenty years. It has become a basis for cutbacks in governmental support for all ethnic minorities—for Asian Americans because they apparently are already successful as a group; for other ethnic minorities because they are presumably not working as hard as Asian Americans or they would not need assistance. Critics of this view argue that the portrayal of Asian Americans as socially and economically successful ignores fundamental inequities. That is, the question "Why have Asians been successful vis-à-vis other minorities?" has been asked at the expense of another equally important question: "What has kept Asians from *fully* reaping the fruits of their education and hard work?"

The achievements of Asian Americans are part reality, part myth. Part of the reality is that a highly visible group of Asian Americans are college-educated, occupationally well-situated, and earning relatively high incomes. The myth, however, is that hard work reaps commensurate rewards. This essay documents the gap between the level of education and subsequent occupational or income gains.

The Roots and Contours of the "Model Minority" Concept

Since World War II, social researchers and news media personnel have been quick to assert that Asian Americans excel over other ethnic groups in terms of earnings, education, and occupation. Asian Americans are said to save more, study more, work more, and so achieve more. The reason given: a cultural emphasis on education and hard work. Implicit in this view is a social judgment and moral injunction: if Asian Americans can make it on their own, why can't other minorities?

While the story of Asian American women workers is only beginning to be pieced together, the success theme is already being sung. The image prevails that despite cultural and racial oppression, they are somehow rapidly assimilating into the mainstream. As workers, they participate in the labor force at rates higher than all others, including Anglo women. Those Asian American women who pursue higher education surpass other women, and even men, in this respect. Moreover, they have acquired a reputation for not only being conscientious and industrious but docile, compliant, and uncomplaining as well.

In the last few decades American women in general have been demanding "equal pay for equal work," the legitimation of housework as work that needs to be recompensed, and greater representation in the professional fields. These demands, however, have not usually come from Asian American women. From the perspective of those in power, this reluctance to complain is another feature of the "model minority." But for those who seek to uncover employment abuses, the unwillingness to talk about problems on the job is itself a problem. The garment industry, for example, is a major area of exploitation, yet it is also one that is difficult to investigate and control. In a 1983 report on the Concentrated Employment Program of the California Department of Industrial Relations, it was noted:

> The major problem for investigators in San Francisco is that the Chinese community is very close-knit, and employers and employees cooperate in refusing to speak to investigators. In two years of enforcing the Garment Registration Act, the CEP has never received a complaint from an Asian employee. The few complaints received have been from Anglo or Latin workers.[1]

While many have argued vociferously either for or against the model minority concept, Asian Americans in general have been ambivalent in this regard. Asian Americans experience pride in achievement born of hard work and self-sacrifice, but at the same time, they resist the implication that all is well. Data provided here indicate that Asian Americans have not been successful in terms of benefitting fully (i.e., monetarily) from their education. It is a myth that Asian Americans have proven the American Dream. How does this myth develop?

The working consumer: income and cost of living. One striking feature about Asian Americans is that they are geographically concentrated in areas where both income and cost of living are very high. In 1970, 80 percent of the total Asian American population resided in five states—California, Hawaii, Illinois, New York, and Washington. Furthermore, 59 percent of Chinese, Filipino, and Japanese Americans were concentrated in only 5 of the 243 Standard Metropolitan Statistical Areas (SMSA) in the United States—Chicago, Honolulu, Los Angeles/Long Beach, New York, and San Francisco/Oakland.[2] The 1980 census shows that immigration during the intervening decade has not only produced dramatic increases, especially in the Filipino and Chinese populations, but has also continued the overwhelming tendency, for these groups to concentrate in the same geographical areas, especially those in California.[3] Interestingly enough, the very existence of large Asian communities in the West has stimulated among more recent refugee populations what is now officially referred to as "secondary migration," that is, the movement of refugees away, from their sponsoring communities (usually places where there was no sizable Asian population prior to their own arrival) to those areas where there are well-established Asian communities.[4]

This residential pattern means that while Asian Americans may earn more by living in high income areas, they also pay more as consumers. The additional earning power gained from living in

San Francisco or Los Angeles, say, is absorbed by the high cost of living in such cities. National income averages which compare the income of Asian American women with that of the more broadly dispersed Anglo women systematically distort the picture. Indeed, if we compare women within the same area, Asian American women are frequently less well-off than Anglo American females, and the difference between women pales when compared with Anglo males, whose mean income is much higher than that of any group of women.[5]

When we consider the large immigrant Asian population and the language barriers that restrict women to menial or entry-level jobs, we are talking about a group that not only earns minimum wage or less, but one whose purchasing power is substantially undermined by living in metropolitan areas of states where the cost of living is unusually high.

Another striking pattern about Asian American female employment is the high rate of labor force participation. Asian American women are more likely than Anglo American women to work full time and year round. The model minority interpretation tends to assume that mere high labor force participation is a sign of successful employment. One important factor motivating minority women to enter the work force, however, is the need to supplement family resources. For Anglo American women some of the necessity for working is partly offset by the fact that they often share in the higher incomes of Anglo males, who tend not only to earn more than all other groups but, as noted earlier, also tend to receive higher returns on their education. Moreover, once regional variation is adjusted for, Filipino and Chinese Americans had a median annual income equivalent to black males in four mainland SMSAs—Chicago, Los Angeles/Long Beach, New York, San Francisco/Oakland.[6] Census statistics point to the relatively lower earning capacity of Asian males compared to Anglo males, suggesting that Asian American women enter the work force to help compensate for this inequality. Thus, the mere fact of high employment must be read cautiously and analyzed within a larger context.

The different faces of immigration. Over the last decade immigration has expanded the Chinese population by 85.3 percent, making it the largest Asian group in the country at 806,027, and has swelled the Filipino population by 125.8 percent, making it the second largest at 774,640. Hence at present the majority of

Chinese American and Filipino American women are foreign-born. In addition the Asian American "success story" is misleading in part because of a select group of these immigrants: foreign-educated professionals.

Since 1965 U.S. immigration laws have given priority to seven categories of individuals. Two of the seven allow admittance of people with special occupational skills or services needed in the United States. Four categories facilitate family reunification, and the last applies only to refugees. While occupation is estimated to account for no more than 20 percent of all visas, professionals are not precluded from entering under other preference categories. Yet this select group is frequently offered as evidence of the upward mobility possible in America, when Asian Americans who are born and raised in the United States are far less likely to reach the doctoral level in their education. Over two-thirds of Asians with doctorates in the United States are trained and educated abroad.[7]

Also overlooked in some analyses is a great deal of downward mobility among the foreign-born. For example, while foreign-educated health professionals are given preferential status for entry into this country, restrictive licensing requirements deny them the opportunity to practice or utilize their special skills. They are told that their educational credentials, experience, and certifications are inadequate. Consequently, for many the only alternatives are menial labor or unemployment.[8] Other highly educated immigrants become owner/managers of Asian businesses, which also suggests downward mobility and an inability to find jobs in their field of expertise.

"Professional" obscures more than it reveals. Another major reason for the perception of "model minority" is that the census categories implying success, "professional-managerial" or "executive, administrative, managerial," frequently camouflage important inconsistencies with this image of success. As managers, Asian Americans, usually male, are concentrated in certain occupations. They tend to be self-employed in small-scale wholesale and retail trade and manufacturing. They are rarely buyers, sales managers, administrators, or salaried managers in large-scale retail trade, communications, or public utilities. Among foreign-born Asian women, executive-managerial status is limited primarily to auditors and accountants.[9]

In general, Asian American women with a college education are concentrated in narrow and select, usually less prestigious, rungs of the "professional-managerial" class. In 1970, 27 percent of native-born Japanese women were either elementary or secondary school teachers. Registered nurses made up the next largest group. Foreign-born Filipino women found this to be their single most important area of employment, with 19 percent being nurses. They were least represented in the more prestigious professions—physicians, judges, dentists, law professors, and lawyers.[10] In 1980 foreign-born Asian women with four or more years of college were most likely to find jobs in administrative support or clerical occupations.

Self-help through "taking care of one's own." Much of what is considered ideal or model behavior in American society is based on Anglo-Saxon, Protestant values. Chief among them is an ethic of individual self-help, of doing without outside assistance or governmental support. On the other hand, Asian Americans have historically relied to a large extent on family or community resources. Their tightly-knit communities tend to be fairly closed to the outside world, even when under economic hardship. Many below the poverty level do not receive any form of public assistance.[11] Even if we include social security benefits as a form of supplementary income, the proportion of Asian Americans who use them is again very low, much lower than that for Anglo Americans.[12] Asian American families, in fact, are more likely than Anglo American families to bear economic hardships on their own.

While Asian Americans appear to have been self-sufficient as communities, we need to ask, at what personal cost? Moreover, have they as a group reaped rewards commensurate with their efforts? The following section presents data which document that while Asian American women may be motivated to achieve through education, monetary returns for them are less than for other groups.

The Nature of Inequality

The decision to use white males as the predominant reference group within the United States is a politically charged issue.

When women raise and push the issue of "comparable worth," of "equal pay for equal work," they argue that women frequently do work equivalent to men's, but are paid far less for it.

The same argument can be made for Asian American women, and the evidence of inequality is staggering. For example, after adjustments are made for occupational prestige, age, education, weeks worked, hours worked each week, and state of residence in 1975, Chinese American women could be expected to earn only 70 percent of the majority male income. Even among the college-educated, Chinese American women fared least well, making only 42 percent of what majority males earned. As we noted earlier, the mean income of all women, Anglo and Asian, was far below that of Anglo males in 1970 and 1980. This was true for both native-born and foreign-born Asians. In 1970 Anglo women earned only 54 percent of what their male counterparts did. Native-born Asian American women, depending on the particular ethnic group, earned anywhere from 49 to 57 percent of what Anglo males earned. In 1980, this inequity persisted.

Another way of thinking about comparable worth is not to focus only on what individuals do on the job, but on what they bring to the job as well. Because formal education is one measure of merit in American society and because it is most frequently perceived as the means to upward mobility, we would expect greater education to have greater payoffs.

Asian American women tend to be extraordinarily successful in terms of attaining higher education. Filipino American women have the highest college completion rate of all women and graduate at a rate 50 percent greater than that of majority males. Chinese American and Japanese American women follow closely behind, exceeding both the majority male and female rate of college completion.[13] Higher levels of education, however, bring lower returns for Asian American women than they do for other groups.

While education enhances earnings capability, the return on education for Asian American women is not as great as that for other women, and is well below parity with white males. Data on Asian American women in the five SMSAs where they are concentrated bear this out.[14] In 1980 all these women fell far behind Anglo males in what they earned in relation to their college education. Between 8 and 16 percent of native-born women earned $21,200 compared to 50 percent of Anglo males. Similar patterns were found among college-educated foreign-born women.

The fact that Asian American women do not reap the income benefits one might expect given their high levels of educational achievement raises questions about the reasons for such inequality. To what extent is this discrepancy based on outright discrimination? On self-imposed limitations related to cultural modesty? The absence of certain social or interpersonal skills required for upper managerial positions? Or institutional factors beyond their control? It is beyond the scope of this paper to address such concerns. However, the fact of inequality is itself noteworthy and poorly appreciated.

In general, Asian American women usually are over represented in clerical or administrative support jobs. While there is a somewhat greater tendency for foreign-born college-educated Asian women to find clerical-related jobs, both native- and foreign-born women have learned that clerical work is the area where they are most easily employed. In fact, in 1970 a third of native-born Chinese women were doing clerical work. A decade later Filipino women were concentrated there. In addition Asian American women tend to be over-represented as cashiers, file clerks, office machine operators, and typists. They are less likely to get jobs as secretaries or receptionists. The former occupations not only carry less prestige but generally have "little or no decision-making authority, low mobility and low public contact."[15]

In short, education may improve one's chances for success, but it cannot promise the American Dream. For Asian American women education seems to serve less as an opportunity for upward mobility than as protection against jobs as service or assembly workers, or as machine operatives—all areas where foreign-born Asian women are far more likely to find themselves.

Conclusion

In this essay I have attempted to direct our attention on the gap between achievement and reward, specifically the failure to reward monetarily those who have demonstrated competence. Asian American women, like Asian American men, have been touted as "model minorities," praised for their outstanding achievements. The concept of model minority, however, obscures the fact that one's accomplishments are not adequately recognized in terms of commensurate income or choice of occupation. By focusing on the achievements of one minority in relation to another, our attention is diverted from larger institutional and historical factors which influence a group's success. Each ethnic group has a different history, and a simplistic method of modeling which assumes the experience of all immigrants is the same ignores the sociostructural context in which a certain kind of achievement occurred. For example, World War II enabled many Asian Americans who were technically trained and highly educated to move into lucrative war-related industries.[16] More recently, Korean immigrants during the 1960s were able to capitalize on the fast-growing demand for wigs in the United States. It was not simply cultural ingenuity or individual hard work which made them successful in this enterprise, but the fact that Korean immigrants were in the unique position of being able to import cheap hair products from their mother country.[17]

Just as there are structural opportunities, so there are structural barriers. However, the persistent emphasis in American society on individual effort deflects attention away from such barriers and creates self-doubt among those who have not "made it." The myth that Asian Americans have succeeded as a group, when in actuality there are serious discrepancies between effort and achievement, and between achievement and reward, adds still further to this self-doubt.

While others have also pointed out the myth of the model minority, I want to add that myths do have social functions. It would be a mistake to dismiss the model minority concept as merely a myth. Asian Americans are—however inappropriately—thrust into the role of being models for other minorities.

A closer look at the images associated with Asians as a model minority group suggests competing or contradictory themes. One image is that Asian Americans exemplify a competitive spirit enabling them to overcome structural barriers through perseverance and ingenuity. On the other hand, they are also seen as complacent, content with their social lot, and expecting little in the way of outside help. A third image is that Asian Americans are experts at assimilation, demonstrating that this society still functions as a melting pot. Their values are sometimes equated with white, middle-class, Protestant values of hard work, determination, and thrift. Opposing this image, however, is still another, namely that Asian Americans have succeeded because they possess cultural values unique to them as a group—their family-centeredness and long tradition of reverence for scholarly achievement, for example.

Perhaps, then, this is why so many readily accept the myth, whose tenacity is due to its being vague and broad enough to appeal to a variety of different groups. Yet to the extent that the myth is based on misconceptions, we are called upon to reexamine it more closely in an effort to narrow the gap between striving and achieving.[18]

NOTES

1. Ted Bell, "Quiet Loyalty Keeps Shops Running," *Sacramento Bee*, 11 February 1985.
2. Amado Y. Cabezas and Pauline L. Fong, "Economic and Employment Status of Asian-Pacific Women" (Background paper; San Francisco: ASIAN, Inc., 1976).
3. U.S. Bureau of the Census, *Race of the Population by States* (Washington, D.C., 1980). According to the census, 40 percent of all Chinese in America live in California, as well as 46 percent of all Filipinos, and 37 percent of all Japanese. New York ranks second for the number of Chinese residing there, and Hawaii is the second most populated state for Filipinos and Japanese.
4. Tricia Knoll, *Becoming Americans: Asian Sojourners, Immigrants, and Refugees in the Western United States* (Portland, Oreg.: Coast to Coast Books, 1982), 152.
5. U.S. Commission on Civil Rights, *Social Indicators of Equality for Minorities and Women* (Washington, D.C., 1978), 24, 50, 54, 58, 62.
6. David M. Moulton, "The Socioeconomic Status of Asian American Families in Five Major SMSAs" (Paper prepared for the Conference of Pacific and Asian American Families and HEW-related Issues, San Francisco, 1978). No comparative data were available on blacks for the fifth SMSA, Honolulu.
7. James E. Blackwell, *Mainstreaming Outsiders* (New York: General Hall, Inc., 1981), 306; and Commission on Civil Rights, *Social Indicators*, 9.
8. California Advisory Committee, "A Dream Unfulfilled: Korean and Filipino Health Professionals in California" (Report prepared for submission to U.S. Commission on Civil Rights, May 1975), iii.

9. See Amado Y. Cabezas, "A View of Poor Linkages between Education, Occupation and Earnings for Asian Americans" (Paper presented at the Third National Forum on Education and Work, San Francisco, 1977), 17; and Census of the Population, PUS, 1980.

10. Census of the Population, PUS, 1970, 1980.

11. A 1977 report on California families showed that an average of 9.3 percent of Japanese, Chinese, and Filipino families were below the poverty level, but that only 5.4 percent of these families received public assistance. The corresponding figures for Anglos were 6.3 percent and 5.9 percent. From Harold T. Yee, "The General Level of Well-Being of Asian Americans" (Paper presented to U.S. government officials in partial response to Justice Department amicus).

12. Moulton, "Socioeconomic Status," 70–71.

13. Commission on Civil Rights, *Social Indicators*, 54.

14. The few exceptions occur in Honolulu with women who had more than a high school education and in Chicago with women who had a high school education or three years of college. Even these women fared poorly when compared to men, however.

15. Bob H. Suzuki, "Education and the Socialization of Asian Americans: A Revisionist Analysis of the 'Model Minority' Thesis," *Amerasia Journal* 4:2 (1977): 43. See also Cabezas and Fong, "Economic and Employment Status," 48–49; and Commission on Civil Rights, *Social Indicators*, 97–98.

16. U. S. Commission on Civil Rights, "Education Issues" in *Civil Rights Issues of Asian and Pacific Americans: Myths and Realities* (Washington, DC, 1979), 370–376. This material was presented by Ling-chi Wang, University of California, Berkeley.

17. Illsoo Kim, *New Urban Immigrants: The Korean Community in New York* (Princeton, N.J.: Princeton University Press, 1981).

18. For further discussion of the model minority myth and interpretation of census data, see Deborah Woo, "The Socioeconomic Status of Asian American Women in the Labor Force: An Alternative Views" *Sociological Perspectives* 28:3 (July 1985): 307–338.

QUESTIONS

1. What is the myth of the "model minority"? What is the social function of this concept? How does it affect other minority groups? Why has it been an appealing concept? Why does it persist?
2. What are the contradictions and inadequacies of the "model minority" concept? Does this concept apply to both men and women in the same way? What does the concept obscure about Asian-Americans?
3. What are some of the structural factors that create the gap between the efforts and rewards of Asian-American women? What relationship does education have to individual financial success?
4. What examples of the varying positions of different Asian-American groups does Woo offer? How do these examples help deconstruct the category of "Asian" and the myth of the "model minority"?

Coming Out (1991)

Linda Villarosa and Clara Villarosa

Linda Villarosa is the author of Body & Soul: The Black Woman's Guide to Physical Health and Emotional Well-Being, *and the co-author of* Finding Our Way: The Teen Girls' Survival Guide *(1995). She is also the executive editor of* Essence, *the first general magazine directed at African-American women, which as been in circulation since 1970. In this 1991 Mother's Day special edition essay, Linda and her mother Clara, a Denver bookstore owner, share their feelings about Linda's lesbian identity. Mother and daughter describe the coming out process and the effects it has had on their relationship.*

The Model Daughter

Linda—Growing up, I was what you'd call a "good girl." I minded my parents, sent Hallmark cards to all my great-aunts on

"Coming Out," by Linda Villarosa and Clara Villarosa, reprinted from *Essence*, Vol. 22, No. 1, May 1991. Reprinted by permission of Linda Villarosa.

their birthdays, said the Pledge of Allegiance and never got into trouble. Other kids probably thought I was nauseating.

In high school I was a cheerleader, the president of the senior class, captain of the track team, an honor student and a prom-queen candidate, and I still managed to work evenings and weekends. I had a nice boyfriend, and I wanted to marry him, have two children, live near my parents and have a career as a lawyer or writer, or maybe even a social worker like my mother.

I seemed just like all the other girls I knew who were my age—only more of a goody-goody. But somehow deep inside I suspected I was different.

Becoming a Mother

Clara—At 3 P.M. on January 9, 1959, the doctor smiled at me and said, "You have a beautiful baby girl." And beautiful my baby was, dainty and small, a cute little thing I could dress up, play with and read to. Her father and I named her Linda, which in Spanish means pretty. In my life, all was well. I had completed my master's in psychiatric social work. I had worked for five years before having the baby, so that I could stay at home with her once I had her. Three years later, just as we'd planned, I had another baby.

As Linda grew up she remained petite and feminine. Whenever we went out, people remarked on her beauty and grace. She had large hazel eyes that stared both knowingly and inquisitively, and I enjoyed dressing her up in frilly dresses and fixing her hair in two bouncy ponytails. She loved little-girl activities, like having tea parties and playing house with real chores. When she was older she modeled in fashion shows, demonstrating poise and confidence.

Linda dated in high school, and by that time I was back at work, surrounded by friends. The highlight of those years for me was Linda's senior prom. I made her a beautiful peach-colored dress, and that prom night, when her steady boyfriend picked her up, I was so proud of my beautiful daughter. As I watched her leave, I fantasized about her being happily married, a mother, with me a happy grandmother.

I used to think of Linda as my "normal" child. That turned out to be totally unrealistic, because all the other parents were having problems with their adolescents. But Linda was so good.

Facing Up to It

Linda—Even in high school I was attracted to other girls. I loved slumber parties, cheerleading practice, basketball and track workouts and other all-girl activities. Sometimes I assumed my feelings were normal, just another one of those adolescent things you don't really understand, you're ashamed of and don't tell a soul.

By the time I reached my sophomore year in college, my high-school boyfriend and I had broken up. It was very difficult for me for a few months because he had been my first love, and we had been—and remain—good friends. We had also fumbled through losing our virginity together, and he was a loving, caring and creative sexual partner and I liked having sex with him. I continued to date men. The men I dated were handsome and outgoing and my parents approved of them. I felt that I was sleepwalking, though, going through the motions. One of my boyfriends was really cute but he was boring. All he talked about was his fraternity. But I wanted to have a boyfriend so I could be like everybody else. I wasn't very attentive, I didn't dress up or wear makeup and I wasn't particularly excited about sex. And of course this lackadaisical attitude made me more attractive because guys thought I was a challenge.

Then everything changed. I became increasingly attracted to Laura, one of my female instructors. She was bright and funny and she listened with interest to everything I said. Eventually I admitted to myself that I was attracted to this woman. Finally, after I had spent five months worshiping her in the classroom, we spent a day together. After that I realized I was in love. That realization was all at once frightening, horrifying, gratifying and relieving. At that point I began to think of myself as bisexual, something that seemed cool and hip. I didn't think about what this might mean to my life, I didn't wonder why I was this way, I didn't contemplate whether gay people were good or bad or would go to heaven or be sweating it out in hell. All I could think of was how nice it felt to truly love someone and admit it.

Suspicion

Clara—Once Linda got to college, I began to notice that she didn't have much romantic interest in men. I would frequently ask about any man that she mentioned even casually, but she never really seemed to care. Nor did she seem to care about clothes and makeup. I tried not to get upset, thinking that she didn't have much time to date or worry about her appearance because she was too busy with her classes and her job.

By her second year in college, I had gone from being quietly worried to being truly panicked about Linda. She spoke about men only in platonic ways, and I noticed that an inordinate amount of her conversation focused on one of her female instructors, Laura. Linda brought Laura to dinner, and my suspicions were heightened because Laura appeared more "butch" than feminine. The way the two interacted and the things they talked about made it clear to me that they were spending a lot of time together. My husband and I exchanged looks across the dinner table. After they left, I just had to say it. I turned to my husband and asked, "Did you see it?" He said yes. I said, "Do you think Laura is gay?" He did. Finally we spoke the unspeakable: Could our daughter be a lesbian?

The Confrontation

Linda—Eventually Laura and I became lovers. I was happy, but too afraid to tell a soul what was going on. We went on a trip to San Francisco together, which was exciting and freeing to the sheltered 19-year-old that I was. Afterward I called my mother from the airport to tell her that I'd be home for a couple of days and that I had so much to tell her about my trip. "That's fine, honey," she said with a strange catch in her voice. "Your dad and I have something to talk to you about."

Still riding high from my trip, I was completely unprepared for the confrontation that was to follow. Both my parents were in their bedroom, sitting on the edge of the bed and looking very solemn. My mother turned to me and without missing a beat she asked, "Are you a lesbian?"

Laura had coached me about what to do in the event that my parents asked me anything about being gay. "Lie at all costs. You aren't ready to deal with this yet, and neither are they," she had warned me. But when they confronted me, I was too stunned. "Yes, I think so," I stuttered.

My mother just looked sick and my father's eyes filled with tears. This news really broke him, destroying the perfect image that he had of me. He was afraid that I didn't like men and that I didn't love him. My mother, an adolescent therapist at the time, took a more practical tack: She thought I could be fixed. She told me that I *would* go to therapy. During the whole ordeal, I had been crying and feeling guilty, apologetic, confused and upset, but at that point something snapped. "I don't need to go to therapy. I'm really happy now," I told my parents.

I'm not really a crier, but this confrontation was just so hard. I felt that I'd let my parents down and that doing so was the worst thing. I was always so good, I took pride in that. We all stared at one another without speaking, letting the silence absorb the very strong emotions we each felt. The scene was over, at least for the moment. Finally my mother told me to tell my sister. I went downstairs, crying. My sister was lying on the couch watching TV and I blurted out, "I'm gay." She asked, "Am I?" I said no. Then, like the typical 16-year-old she was, she asked me if I wanted to go shopping.

Clara—The day we confronted Linda was so painful for me that I have blanked it out of my mind; I can't remember anything about it. I couldn't accept the fact that my daughter was a lesbian—I just couldn't believe it. I assumed it was a phase she was going through and that it would go away like an unpleasant dream. This was the seventies, when homosexuals were thought of as sick. I was a child therapist, and I'd been dealing with parents who took the blame for their kids' problems. I figured it would go away faster if she would just get help and if I could get her away from that horrible woman.

I placed all the blame on Laura. I couldn't even bear to hear her name. It was projection, pure and simple. It was easier to focus on this other person whom I didn't really know than to let myself believe that my daughter, whom I loved so much, could do something I found so disgusting.

With all my anger focused on Laura, I thought of confronting her and telling her to stay away from my child. I considered reporting her to the university, to get her fired and sent out of town. But, I worried, then everyone would know. I really didn't know what to do. I decided just to lie low, to think things over until I could figure out how to approach this situation, how to make everything right in my life. My career was going well, but my marriage had begun to fall apart. In the meantime, I avoided my daughter. When she called me, I would contain my anger and disappointment, and we would never bring up *that* subject.

Trying to Come Out of Hiding

Linda—It was a relief to have told my parents the truth and to have stopped hiding from them. My mother wasn't taking it well, but I thought I'd give her time. Clearly she was disappointed and upset, but I knew eventually she'd come to understand. At that point my bigger worry was learning to accept myself.

After I realized I was gay, I had to reinvent myself and the image of my life. I had to let go of everything I thought I was supposed to have, such as a beautiful wedding. I had to figure out who I was apart from the straight world I no longer felt I belonged in. This was a very difficult and lonely period because I couldn't tell anyone. Finally, after two years, I told my best friend.

I didn't know any other gay women besides my lover and a few of her friends. And like everybody else I had been brought up on a steady diet of antigay stereotypes. I felt like one of society's outcasts. I no longer fit into heterosexual society, and I didn't want to fit into the gay community—whatever and wherever it was. I assumed there were only a handful of other lesbians in the world, all short, fat, unattractive women with bad haircuts. All they did was play softball and go to feminist group meetings and try to hide who they were from their coworkers, friends and family. It went without saying that they all hated men. There was a reason these girls didn't have a man. Because I wasn't like this, I wasn't too sure who I was.

So unsure of myself, I was deathly afraid of rejection. I just kept my mouth shut about my sexuality and quietly locked myself away in the closet. I tried to straddle both worlds, happy with my lover and pretending to be accepting of my new life, but secretly scared and insecure. Like one of those tragic mulattos of the past, I was passing but always petrified that someone would uncover my secret. I didn't stop hanging with my friends, I simply stopped talking about myself and steered clear of any personal questions. I listened to dyke and fag jokes and sometimes even laughed along. I went to weddings and would cry, always attributing it to happiness, not loss.

Feeling the Pain

Clara—Despite my hopes, the nightmare was not ending. And the more Linda began to try to explore herself and identify as a lesbian, the angrier I got, and now not at Laura anymore, but at her. How could my daughter do this to me? I was so embarrassed. I was paranoid, thinking that everyone in my community knew and that they were laughing at me, at my failure as a parent. It was doubly humiliating for me—trained as an adolescent therapist—to have raised a daughter who had "gone wrong."

I was devastated and blamed myself. I searched through the past to determine what I had done to make this happen to her. At this point I was in the middle of a divorce. I was also searching for my purpose in life, but I wasn't finding it. People had said I have an aggressive personality, and I wondered if Linda was a lesbian because of my behavior. Maybe I gave her the impression that I hated men. I felt my whole world collapsing.

Resolution and Acceptance

Linda—After college, I moved to New York. As the years went by I began to develop a circle of lesbian friends, women a lot like me who were happy and well adjusted and fun. I started to accept myself and my life and stop worrying that being gay was some kind of punishment or a horrible mistake I could change. Or that it was a phase, a political choice, a form of rebellion or something to be ashamed of.

It has been important for me, too, to realize that being gay is not a curse; in fact, it's been an awakening. I've become more introspective and tolerant of people who are different. Before I "came out," I had always tried to do everything right, everything according to plan—society's plan and my parents' plan—but not my own plan because I didn't really have one. And that behavior—be a good girl, go to college, get married, have a child—was valued by society. So when I turned out to be different, I assumed something was wrong with me. I had no reason to question the world I was brought up in, much less to try to understand anyone who wasn't thinking and behaving exactly the way I was. When I realized I wasn't going to live in the suburbs, I was free to forge my own path and not get stuck in a Black society thing—wearing nice shoes and going to club meetings.

But having felt like an outcast, separate from everyone Black and white, has made me empathize with others who have felt the same way for whatever reason.

Most important, I've also stopped being so afraid of being rejected by people who find out I'm gay. The closet is dark and lonely and not somewhere I plan to hide away. The most important people in my life already know, and they still accept me. No matter how disappointed and angry my mother felt, she never stopped loving me. She and the rest of my family made it okay for me to be me.

Resolution

Clara—After Linda moved to New York, the distance and time gave me the opportunity to be more reflective and less emotional. I asked myself, *Who is my daughter?*

She is still pretty and funny and bright and well regarded. She is kind and cares about other people. She remembers Mother's Day, sends me birthday presents and listens when I need to talk to her. I am proud of her and I love her.

The only difference is her sexual preference. But then I thought, *So what?* She's not on drugs, or harming anyone, or in jail or involved in any of the other terrible scenarios I could imagine. So eventually I was able to let go of my disappointment. I also stopped trying to figure out why she is gay and I stopped blaming myself. Scientists don't know why some people are heterosexual and some homosexual. Psychiatrists don't know, I don't know and no one knows.

Now Linda and I have a close relationship; what we've been through has brought us closer as mother and daughter and as friends. She's a writer and now I own a bookstore, so we have much in common. Sometimes she calls to ask my advice. I remember once she wanted to talk about a problem with her lover. As she started to tell me the situation, I could feel myself say, "Oh, no, I don't want to hear about this." But then I forced myself to listen and I began to relax. What she was going through was no different from things heterosexual couples have to deal with—honesty, communication and patience. I helped her work through her problem and felt happy that she trusted me and could confide in me.

Even though having a lesbian daughter is not what I would have chosen, I've learned to accept Linda for who she is, not what I wanted her to be. Now I can look at my daughter with a sense of pride and a sense of peace.

Questions

1. What are Linda and Clara trying to accomplish in this essay? Is their style of expression effective for accomplishing their goals? What is significant about Linda's choice of *Essence* as a vehicle for sharing her experiences?
2. What issues are involved in the coming out process, both from Linda's perspective and from Clara's? What feelings do the authors express? What issues did they each struggle with individually?
3. What were Linda's motivations in telling her mother? How did they resolve the issue? What stereotypes does this essay contradict?

Sexual Dissent and the Family: The Sharon Kowalski Case (1991)

Nan D. Hunter

In the context of heterosexual marriage, participants typically enjoy an array of rights and privileges granted and reinforced by the legal marriage contract. Whether these rights, and the rights to rear children and form families, should be extended to gays and lesbians is often a controversial issue. Legal activist Nan Hunter uses the Kowalski case to explore the emotional effects that the legally sanctioned withholding of rights and privileges can have upon same-sex couples.

In the effort to end second-class citizenship for lesbian and gay Americans, no obstacle has proved tougher to surmount than the cluster of issues surrounding "the family." The concept of family functions as a giant cultural screen. Projected onto it, contests over race, gender, sexuality and a range of other "domestic" issues from crime to taxes constantly create and recreate a newly identified zone of social combat, the politics of the family. Activists of all persuasions eagerly seek to enter the discursive field, ever ready to debate and discuss: Who counts as a family? Which "family values" are the authentic ones? Is there a place in the family for queers? As battles are won and lost in this cultural war, progressives and conservatives agree on at least one thing—the family is highly politicized terrain.

For lesbians and gays, these debates have dramatic real-life consequences, probably more so than with any other legal issue. Relationship questions touch almost every person's life at some point, in a way that military issues, for example, do not. Further, the unequal treatment is blatant, *de jure* and universal, as compared with the employment arena, where discrimination may be more subtle and variable. No state allows a lesbian or gay couple to marry. No state recognizes (although a number of counties and cities do) domestic partnership systems under which unmarried couples (gay or straight) can become eligible for certain benefits usually available only to spouses. The fundamental inequity is that, barring mental incompetence or consanguinity, virtually any straight couple has the option to marry and thus establish a next-of-kin relationship that the state will enforce. No lesbian or gay couple can. Under the law, two women or two men are forever strangers, regardless of their relationship.

One result is that every lesbian or gay man's nightmare is to be cut off from one's primary other, physically incapacitated, stranded, unable to make contact, without legal recourse. It is a nightmare that could not happen to a married couple. But it did happen to two Minnesota women, Sharon Kowalski and Karen Thompson, in a remarkable case that threaded its way through the courts for seven years.

Sharon Kowalski, notwithstanding the Minnesota State District Court's characterization of her as a "child of divorce," is an adult with both a committed life partner and parents who bitterly refuse to acknowledge either her lesbianism or her lover. Kowalski is a former physical education teacher and amateur athlete, whose Minnesota women's high school shot-put record still stands. In 1983, she was living with her lover, Thompson, in the home they had jointly purchased in St. Cloud. Both women were deeply closeted; they exchanged rings with each other but told virtually no one of their relationship. That November, Kowalski suffered devastating injuries in a car accident, which left her unable to speak or walk, with arms deformed and with major brain damage, including seriously impaired short-term memory.

After the accident, both Thompson and Kowalski's father petitioned to be appointed Sharon's guardian; initially, an agreement was entered that the father would become guardian on the condition that Thompson retain equal rights to visit and consult with doctors. By the summer of 1985, after growing hostilities, the father refused to continue the arrangement, and persuaded a local court that Thompson's visits caused Kowalski to feel depressed. One doctor hired by the father wrote a letter stating that Kowalski was in danger of sexual abuse. Within twenty-four hours after being named sole guardian, the father cut off all contact between Thompson and Kowalski, including mail. By this time, Kowalski had been moved to a nursing home near the small town where she grew up in the Iron Range, a rural mining area in northern Minnesota.

Surely one reason the Kowalski case is so compelling is that, for millions of parents, learning that one's son is gay or daughter is lesbian would be *their* worst nightmare. That is all the more true in small-town America, among people who are religiously observant and whose expectations for a daughter are primarily marriage and motherhood. "The good Lord put us here for reproduction, not that kind of way," Donald Kowalski told the *Los Angeles Times* in 1988. "It's just not a normal life style. The Bible will tell you that." Karen Thompson, he told other reporters, was "an animal" and was lying about his daughter's life. "I've never seen anything that would make me believe" that his daughter is lesbian, he said to the *New York Times* in 1989. How much less painful it must be to explain a lesbian daughter's life as seduction, rather than to experience it as betrayal.

In 1988, Thompson's stubborn struggle to "bring Sharon home" entered a new stage. A different judge, sitting in Duluth, ordered Kowalski moved to a new facility for medical evaluation. Soon thereafter, based on staff recommendations from the second nursing facility, the court ordered that Thompson be allowed to visit. The two women saw each other again in the spring of 1989, after three and a half years of forced separation. Kowalski, who can communicate by typing on a special keyboard, said that she wanted to live in "St. Cloud with Karen."

In May 1990, citing a heart condition for which he had been hospitalized, Donald Kowalski resigned as his daughter's guardian. This resignation set the stage for Thompson to file a renewed petition for appointment as guardian, which she did. But in an April 1991 ruling, Minnesota State District Court judge Robert Campbell selected as guardian Karen Tomberlin—a friend of both Kowalski and her parents, who supported Tomberlin's request. On the surface, the court sought balance. The judge characterized the Kowalski parents and Karen Thompson as the "two wings" of Sharon Kowalski's family. He repeatedly asserted that both must have ample access to visitation with Kowalski. He described Tomberlin as a neutral third party who would not exclude either side. But the biggest single reason behind the decision, the one that he characterized as "instrumental," seemed to be the judge's anger at Thompson for ever telling Kowalski's parents (in a private letter), and then the world at large, that she and Kowalski were lovers.

The court condemned Thompson's revelation of her own relationship as the "outing" of Sharon Kowalski. Thompson did write the letter to Kowalski's parents without telling Kowalski (who was at the time just emerging from a three-month coma after the accident) and did build on her own an active political organization around the case, composed chiefly of disability and lesbian and gay rights groups. Of course, for most of that period, she could not have consulted Kowalski because the two were cut off from each other.

In truth, though, the judge's concern seemed to be more for the outing of Kowalski's parents. He describes the Kowalskis as "outraged and hurt by the public invasion of Sharon's privacy and their privacy," and he blames this outing for the bitterness between Thompson and the parents. Had Thompson simply kept this to herself, the court implies, none of these nasty facts would ever have had to be discussed. The cost, of course, would have been the forfeiture of Thompson's relationship with her lover.

An openly stated preference for ignorance over knowledge is remarkable in a judicial opinion. One imagines the judge silently cursing Thompson for her arrogance in claiming the role of spouse, and for her insistence on shattering the polite fiction of two gym teachers living and buying a house together as just good friends. Women, especially, aren't supposed to be so stubborn or uppity. One can sense the court's empathetic response of shared embarrassment with the parents, of the desire not to be told and thus not to be forced to speak on this subject.

The final chapter in the Kowalski case vindicated Karen Thompson's long struggle. The Minnesota Court of Appeals granted Thompson's guardianship petition in December 1991, reversing the trial judge on every point.

The conflict in the Kowalski case illustrates one of the prime contradictions underlying all the cases seeking legal protection for lesbian and gay couples. This culture is deeply invested with a notion of the ideal family as not only a zone of privacy and a structure of authority (preferably male in the conservative view) but also as a barrier against sexuality unlicensed by the state. Even many leftists and progressives, who actively contest male authority and at least some of the assumptions behind privacy, are queasy about constructing a family politics with queerness on the inside rather than the outside.

When such sexuality is culturally recognized *within* family bounds, "the family" ceases to function as an enforcer of sexual norms. That is why the moms and dads in groups like P-FLAG, an organization primarily of parents supportive of their lesbian and gay children, make such emotionally powerful spokespersons for the cause of civil rights. Parents who welcome sexual dissenters within the family undermine the notion that such dissent is intrinsically antithetical to deep human connection.

The theme of cultural anxiety about forms of sexuality not bounded and controlled by the family runs through a series of recent judicial decisions. In each case, the threat to norms did not come from an assault on the prerogatives of family by libertarian outsiders, a prospect often cited by the right wing to trigger social anxieties. Instead, each court faced the dilemma of how to repress, at least in the law, the anomaly of unsanctioned sexuality within the family.

In a stunning decision in 1989, the Supreme Court ruled in *Michael H. v. Gerald D.* that a biological father had no constitutionally protected right to a relationship with his daughter, despite both paternity (which was not disputed) and a psychological bond that the two had formed. Instead, the court upheld the rule that because the child's mother—who had had an affair with the child's biological father—was married to another man, the girl would be presumed to be the husband's child. It was more important, the court declared, to protect the "unitary family," that is, the marriage, than to subject anyone to "embarrassment" by letting the child and her father continue to see each other. The court ruled that a state could properly force the termination of that bond rather than "disrupt an otherwise harmonious and apparently exclusive marital relationship." We are not bound, the court said, to protect what it repeatedly described as "adulterous fathers."

In *Hodgson v. Minnesota,* the Supreme Court upheld a Minnesota requirement that a pregnant teenager had to notify both of her parents—even if they were divorced or if there was a threat of violence from her family—prior to obtaining an abortion, so long as she had the alternative option to petition a court. The decision was read primarily as an abortion decision and a ruling on the extent of privacy protection that will be accorded a minor who decides to have an abortion. But the case was also, at its core, about sex in the family and specifically about whether parents could rely on the state for assistance in learning whether a daughter is sexually active.

In two very similar cases in 1991, appellate courts in New York and California ruled that a lesbian partner who had co-parented a child with the biological mother for some years had no standing to seek visitation after the couple split up. Both courts acknowledged that the best interests of the child would be served by allowing a parental relationship to continue, but both also ruled that the law would not recognize what the New York court called "a biological stranger." Such a person could be a parent only if there had been a marriage or an adoption.

Indeed, perhaps the most important point in either decision was the footnote in the California ruling that invited lesbian and gay couples to adopt children jointly: "We see nothing in these [statutory] provisions that would preclude a child from being jointly adopted by someone of the same sex as the natural parent." This opens the door for many more such adoptions, at least in California, which is one of six states where lesbian- or gay-couple adoption has occurred, although rarely. The New York court made no such overture.

The effort to legalize gay marriage will almost certainly emerge as a major issue in the next decade. Lawsuits seeking a right to marry have been filed in the District of Columbia and Hawaii, and activists in other states are contemplating litigation. In 1989, the Conference of Delegates of the State Bar of California endorsed an amendment of that state's law to permit lesbian and gay couples to marry.

The law's changes to protect sexual dissent within the family will occur at different speeds in different places, which might not be so bad. Family law has always been a province primarily of state rather than federal regulation, and often has varied from state to state; grounds for divorce, for example, used to differ dramatically depending on geography. What seems likely to occur in the next wave of family cases is the same kind of variability in the legal definition of the family itself. Those very discrepancies may help to denaturalize concepts like "marriage" and "parent," and to expose the utter contingency of the sexual conventions that, in part, construct the family.

Questions

1. According to Hunter, what does the Sharon Kowalski case imply for our understanding of "family values" in the United States?
2. Why does Hunter argue that "sexual dissidents create anxiety in popular culture"? What significance does this anxiety have for individual rights?
3. Explain Hunter's argument that "family" functions as a "giant cultural screen."

The Athletic Esthetic (1996)

Holly Brubach

In her analysis of several recent trends in the representation of "ideal femininity," Holly Brubach emphasizes that the definition of what is "beautiful" varies across cultures and historical periods. The means women employ to modify their bodies vary as well—fashion might be the method in one historical period, and athletics, dieting, piercing, or cosmetic surgery might be prevalent in another. Focusing on the current ideal of female athleticism in this article from the New York Times Magazine, *Brubach discusses the anxiety that often accompanies cultural changes.*

A woman might train her body to excel in an astonishing variety of sports, to be precise and fast, to run with longer strides and to reach with her legs for the finish line, bettering her personal record by precious seconds, until eventually she wins three Olympic medals and commands such widespread admiration that she is called "the greatest athlete of all mankind for all time." But could she find a husband? That was the question with which the

---

"The Athletic Esthetic," by Holly Brubach, reprinted from *The New York Times Magazine*, June 23, 1996.

press confronted Mildred (Babe) Didrikson after her triumph in the track and field events at the Los Angeles games in 1932.

A single woman, Didrikson was upheld as an example of the miserable fate that could befall young girls who grew too muscular. If the natural order decreed that women were "the weaker sex," then the woman who became strong disqualified herself from the attentions of the average man, who would no longer feel superior in her presence. In 1938, Didrikson set the matter to rest once and for all when she married George Zaharias, a 300-pound wrestler.

Hindsight enables us to see that Didrikson was the harbinger of a new ideal, and that most people at the time were simply not fitted to appreciate the beauty of a strong woman's body. Her glory, it seems, posed a threat to the existing order. Other women, for their part, were apparently content to aspire to the prevailing notions of the ideal female body. Those notions, reiterated and updated, persist in the images that surround us, and women persist in transforming their bodies accordingly, in an effort to endear themselves to the world.

But before setting out in pursuit of beauty, a woman must decide which—or rather, whose—idea of beauty she wants to pursue. Until recently, there were only two options. The first—the body custom-built for clothes—is an image of women as they would like to see themselves. The second ideal—the body custom-built for sex—is a vision of women as men would like to see them. The end dictates the means, dividing women into separate camps. Some diet, in order to approximate the models in *Vogue*. Some get breast implants, in the hope of looking like the women featured in the *Victoria's Secret* catalogue.

It is only in the last few years, in ads for sneakers and sports clothes, in fitness magazines with circulations a fraction the size of *Vogue*'s, that a third ideal has begun to emerge: the body custom-built for athletics. It is an ideal whose consequences are still unsettling and far-reaching. But at this point our fascination outweighs our trepidation. We made our way through *Terminator 2*, riveted by the sight of Linda Hamilton's biceps. On Sunday nights, an audience of young girls tunes in to a television show whose host is their heroine, the pro volleyball star Gabrielle Reece. Condé Nast, the publishing empire whose titles include *Vogue, Mademoiselle* and *Glamour*, has announced its plans to introduce a new magazine about women and sports next spring. A woman—the basketball star Sheryl Swoopes—has, like Michael Jordan, had a sneaker named after her. Didrikson was simply born too soon. The ideal she represented was dismissed in her day, but it will not be put off any longer.

Back in the 1970s, at the onset of the so-called fitness craze, women's magazines that had been turning out perfunctory articles on calisthenics and spot-reducing, timed to coincide with the onset of bathing suit season, began directing their attention to the science of aerobics. Readers were exhorted to work up a sweat. Weight loss and muscle tone would follow. The argument for regular, vigorous exercise was not only esthetic but also medical, buttressed by quotations from doctors. Not that it needed buttressing—the women's movement and sexual liberation had predisposed women to the idea of taking responsibility for their bodies. Clothes and makeup were considered not for the trends they represented but as tools to be deployed at will, in the service of the magazines' larger subject: a woman's self-image. If the models pictured in these fitness articles weren't appreciably different from the models pictured in the fashion pages—if, in fact, at times they were the *same* models—the magazines could be forgiven: the women in aerobics classes at the time, even the diehards, were mostly taut and lean, with muscles that weren't especially pronounced.

Since then, the glamour of fashion and the culture of fitness have pretty much parted company. As research has come out in favor of strength training, with weights or some other form of resistance as a supplement to cardiovascular workouts, bodies have changed, and women have acquired muscles that their mothers never had. Meanwhile, the narrow standard for the bodies that populate the pages of the fashion magazines remains unchanged. After a brief—and highly touted—moment a few years ago, when women who looked more ample and somewhat fleshier were being admitted to the ranks of the top models, the norm has reverted to the emaciated type that has predominated since Twiggy's heyday in the late '60s. In fact, the new generation of so-called supermodels—Kirsty Hume, Kate Moss, Shalom Harlow, Trish Goff, Amber Valletta—is stick-thin. Even Cindy Crawford and Claudia Schiffer, who star in their own exercise videos, look more toned than strong, their muscles lacking definition.

The fashion magazines have abdicated any responsibility for women's fitness. The exhortations are gone; the articles on the physiological benefits of exercise are brief and infrequent, eclipsed if not replaced by first-person accounts of liposuction and other cosmetic surgery in keeping with the ideal body shown in the fashion pages. When, in 1979, Condé Nast inaugurated a magazine by the name of *Self*, to be devoted in large part to exercise and health, it cleaved the two ideals, freeing each to pursue its own course. From then on, *Vogue* could concentrate on the body best suited to the latest clothes, and women hungry for serious information about exercise were obliged to turn to special-interest magazines (of which *Self* is today only one of a dozen or so).

It's instructive to contemplate the differences between the various ideals for women and how the corresponding physiques are acquired. The fashion body is an achievement, arrived at by means of renunciation; it is the paradigm for an esthetic of purity, for a nunlike dedication to the cult of appearances and a capacity to forgo the sensual pleasure that food has to offer. In fashion photographs, the women who have attained this ideal strike aggressive poses, their limbs attenuated, angular and linear. Their faces, innocent and flawless, convey a certain smugness; their looks are outward evidence not of what they've done but of what they *haven't* done. They have risen above their bodies, subjugated them, pared them down to their essence of skin and bones. A tendency to appear frail and brittle lends these women an air of feminine helplessness; they must be handled with care. In a train station at rush hour, men would stop and offer to carry their suitcases.

Offers of another kind undoubtedly come the way of the odalisques in the *Victoria's Secret* catalogue, who are seen reclining, in various states of dishabille. Their attitude is languorous, passive and complacent, as if they were waiting for something to happen or for a man to come along. Their proportions are improbable, if not as preposterous as those of the women in *Playboy* and in pornographic magazines. Still, the *Victoria's Secret* types look like cartoon versions of real women, their bustlines selectively exaggerated to an extent that occurs rarely, if ever, in nature. (Because breast tissue is composed mostly of fat, a woman that bosomy would be fuller in the hips and thighs as well.) It seems safe to assume that this ideal, as embodied by these women, is the result not of what they've done but of what has been done to—or for—them: breast implants and, in some cases, liposuction. Even so, their legs and arms are never scrawny. Unlike fashion models, these women look as if they have an extra layer of upholstery gently cushioning the sharp corners of their joints.

These privileged glimpses of a life set in the boudoir are in stark contrast to the scenes in *Women's Sports and Fitness*, in which athletes streak across sunlit, wide-open landscapes. Caught in the act of biking, rowing, jogging, training for a triathlon, they look as if they refused to stop long enough to have their pictures taken. These women exude competence; they can carry their own suitcases. Their muscles, like the fashion models' slenderness, are hard-earned, but here the means is not abstinence but exertion. Though their bodies have been meticulously cultivated, their bodies aren't the point: the point is their ability to perform. What is most striking, given that it's the other two ideals that are calculated to please—to win the admiration of women or the affection of men—is the fact that these athletes seem content in a way that the other women don't.

And so, if the women in our society are confused about what's required of them in order to qualify as beautiful, it's no wonder.

The progress of women in sports has been, admittedly, somewhat fitful, and the image of a muscular woman has been particularly slow to gain currency—perhaps to some degree because, deep down, our attitudes toward women's physical strength are conflicted. We applaud the notion of women at long last coming into their own. And yet, we wonder whether their achievement, by encroaching on what has traditionally been a man's prerogative, might in some way skew the balance between the sexes: women's gain is suspected of being men's loss.

Worse, women who have muscles are regarded by some people—men and women alike—as traitors to their sex, guilty of trying to become men. (Female body builders are widely regarded as the prime offenders. The trouble with this argument, and with this example, is that female body builders look not so much like men in general but like male body builders—their fellow subscribers to an esthetic that many, if not most, of the rest of us find grotesque.)

There is no underestimating the anxieties triggered by the prospect of women's physical strength. Will women, having laid claim to attributes we think of as manly, eventually usurp the positions that men have been occupying? What if women injure themselves by trying to do what nature, in its almighty wisdom, never intended them to do? By inviting comparisons (if not competing directly) with men, who are biologically better equipped for most sports, are women setting themselves up for humiliation and defeat? Will muscles do away with the last trace of women's vulnerability—a quality that men have traditionally found attractive and touching?

And yet, muscles on women seem to serve a purpose. Anne Hollander believes that they are a way for women to take up space, as men do—to add physical substance, which, she says, "makes everyone take notice and listen to what you have to say and pay attention to your existence." A critic whose first book, *Seeing Through Clothes*, traced the parallels between artists' depiction of the nude body and fashionable dress, Hollander notes that, in other centuries, substance was something women achieved by means of the clothes they wore. "Queen Elizabeth I was a skinny little thing with a flat chest," she explains. "In order to make her presence felt, she had to wear pounds of padded stuff that expanded her torso at the sides, giving her the force she needed. It was absolutely not an option where she was concerned to have that narrow nymph's body, which was much admired in the love poetry of the time. That sort of woman had only indirect power."

At 6 foot 3 and 172 pounds, Gabrielle Reece commands respect and attention, too, but she's wearing a sports bra and briefs. The techniques available to Elizabeth I for colonizing the space around her would be impractical today, as would the avoirdupois of the imposing Victorian matron. We wear clothes that expose our bodies, and so the only acceptable way for us to add mass is to add muscle.

What is especially striking about the images of women we see in Nike ads or in the sports pages of the newspapers is that they come to us with so few precedents. From classical antiquity right up to our century, painters and sculptors have rendered women without muscles. (Michelangelo was one of the few exceptions.) Even Amazons, on the basis of their bodies alone, are indistinguishable from the goddesses of love; we recognize them by their short, one-sided tunics. The men in art, in a tradition descended from the Greeks, wear their muscles like a suit of armor just beneath the skin; no insult, physical or otherwise, could penetrate their strength. Their bodies are faceted, the surface subdivided into planes, like a Cubist painting. The women, however, tend to be enveloped in a blanket of fat. The transition from their ankles to their calves, from their calves to their knees, is made smoothly, uninterrupted by bones and tendons. Their thighs are lush. Their breasts are like peaches.

Judging from this calvacade of inherited images, we might easily conclude that the guys in ads for Calvin Klein underwear look enough like the men we see in Poussin's paintings to be directly descended from them; it's the women today who look as if they're no relation to their predecessors. Along the road to independence, which has spanned the better part of our century, changes in the way women look and dress have ratified the changes in their lives. First, they cut their hair; then they seized on articles of clothing from men's wardrobes—trousers, shirts, hats, coats, even neckties and boxer shorts. Now women are appropriating the muscles in which men have outfitted themselves for so long. Hollander envisions a day in the not-too-distant future when men and women will look reasonably similar, meeting on some androgynous middle ground, with muscles on women much more commonplace. Then the woman's hairstyle will be different from the man's; her tattoos will be in different places; she'll pierce a different part of her body. Both may wear high heels; he still won't wear skirts. The process by which we alter our appearances in some ways and not in others is "irrational, the way it's supposed to be," Hollander says. "What looks right undergoes a change."

The course of fashion in the 20th century has been a long, slow striptease: first, the ankles came out from under long skirts; then the calves and the knees; the midriff; the thighs; the breasts. The vestiges of shame linger for a short time after the initial exposure, until eventually the sight of what had been hidden becomes familiar. Women's legs, when we first get a glimpse of them in photographs from the late teens and early '20s, in dresses that abruptly stop short at the knee, look awkward and hesitant at first, then energized, charged with a new awareness. With time, they grow confident and aggressive, accustomed to the attention of strangers.

As bodies, like other means of transportation—automobiles, trains and airplanes—have become increasingly streamlined, hips have been eliminated (in principle, if not in fact). Hips now strike us as excess baggage, slowing our pace, lowering our center of gravity, making us earthbound. Hollander notes that our three current notions of the ideal female body, as disparate as they may be, have this in common: none of them, not even the curvaceous one that incites men to sex, have hips. Hips are part of the equipment with which nature outfits women for motherhood, and motherhood these days is optional.

As the century has gone on, we have stripped women's bodies of anything extraneous—any padding, any surplus flesh, which in another era might have been considered decorative. In the process of lightening the load, bones have come into play. We now delight in watching the levers and pistons and hinges of the human machines in motion.

Will the tyranny of the body built for sports be any less punishing—or any healthier—than the tyranny of the body built for fashion? There is no reason to imagine that it will. Already, there is alarming evidence of eating disorders among female athletes, and the hormonal ramifications of rigorous training are yet to be defined. Like models, athletes have been genetically ordained. The 12-year-old who wants to grow up to look just like her heroine stands no more chance of turning out like Gabrielle Reece than she does of becoming the next Shalom Harlow, no matter how much time she puts in at the gym. As it turns out, the athletic ideal, like the others, is beyond the grasp of all but a few. Even so, it seems reasonable to think that in the process of emulating her favorite sports star, a girl might gain a sense of pride in her body and its accomplishments. Which, in any case, is a far better hope than can be held out for those young girls who strive to resemble their role models by starving themselves.

It's one thing to allow that the muscular body constitutes a new ideal for women—that it is in fact beautiful. But the truth is that, despite the anxieties it provokes, it's also sexy. Muscles bestow on a woman a grace in motion that is absent from fashion photographs and other images in which the impact resides in a carefully orchestrated, static pose. Muscles also impart a sense of self-possession—a quality that is unfailingly attractive. This is not sex appeal conferred on a woman, as it's conferred on supermodels and sex goddesses. The athlete has come by her powers of attraction honestly. Other women's valiant attempts to make themselves beautiful—even when they succeed—are no match for the athlete's evident pleasure in her own articulate body.

It is a kind of fetishism—albeit a healthy one—that has taught us to appreciate women's bodies in detail. Our education has been gradual, requiring the better part of the last hundred years. Fashion designers, models and movie stars have been our tutors. We have learned to love a woman's pelvis, her hipbones jutting out through a bias-cut satin gown. We have come to admire the clavicle in its role as a coat hanger from which clothes are suspended. And, more recently, we have discovered elegance in the swell of a woman's quads, in the tapering form of her lats, in the way her delts square the line of her shoulders. Women, as they have gradually come into their own, have at last begun to feel at home in their bodies, which previously they were only renting. In athletes, we recognize women who own their bodies, inhabiting every inch of them, and the sight of their vitality is exhilarating. Our own potential has become apparent, thanks to their example. We want to be like them—alive all over.

QUESTIONS

1. Why does the article suggest that images of muscular women have been so slow to gain appreciation? Are women's gains suspected of being men's losses?
2. Are women's bodies built for sport, tending toward an "androgynous middle ground"? Why have changes in how women look or dress been linked to their social "independence"? Will changes in appearance "skew the balance between the sexes," as this article suggests?
3. Why does the author pose the question, "Will the tyranny of the body built for sports be any less punishing—or any healthier—than the tyranny of the body built for fashion?" How would you answer it?

Straightening Our Hair (1989)

bell hooks

bell hooks is a well-known African-American scholar and Distinguished Professor of English at City College of New York. She has been a long time activist in the feminist movement and has written extensively on feminist and racial issues, including Black Looks: Race and Representation *(1992),* Teaching to Transgress: Education as the Practice of Freedom *(1994) and* Bone Black: Memories of Girlhood *(1996). In this selection, hooks describes the cultural politics embedded in what at surface glance seems to be a relatively innocent cosmetic practice—hair straightening.*

On Saturday mornings we would gather in the kitchen to get our hair fixed, that is straightened. Smells of burning grease and hair, mingled with the scent of our freshly washed bodies, with collard greens cooking on the stove, with fried fish. We did not go to the hairdresser. Mama fixed our hair. Six daughters—there was no way we could have afforded hairdressers. In those days, this process of straightening black women's hair with a hot comb

"Straightening Our Hair" by bell hooks. Reprinted from *Zeta Magazine* Sept. 1988. pp.33–37.

(invented by Madame C. J. Walker) was not connected in my mind with the effort to look white, to live out standards of beauty set by white supremacy. It was connected solely with rites of initiation into womanhood. To arrive at that point where one's hair could be straightened was to move from being perceived as child (whose hair could be neatly combed and braided) to being almost a woman. It was this moment of transition my sisters and I longed for.

Hair pressing was a ritual of black women's culture—of intimacy. It was an exclusive moment when black women (even those who did not know one another well) might meet at home or in the beauty parlor to talk with one another, to listen to the talk. It was as important a world as that of the male barber shop—mysterious, secret. It was a world where the images constructed as barriers between one's self and the world were briefly let go, before they were made again. It was a moment of creativity, a moment of change.

I wanted this change even though I had been told all my life that I was one of the "lucky" ones because I had been born with "good hair"—hair that was fine, almost straight—not good enough but still good. Hair that had no nappy edges, no "kitchen," that area close to the neck that the hot comb could not reach. This "good hair" meant nothing to me when it stood as a barrier to my entering this secret black woman world. I was overjoyed when mama finally agreed that I could join the Saturday ritual, no longer looking on but patiently waiting my turn. I have written of this ritual: "For each of us getting our hair pressed is an important ritual. It is not a sign of our longing to be white. There are no white people in our intimate world. It is a sign of our desire to be women. It is a gesture that says we are approaching womanhood. . . Before we reach the appropriate age we wear braids, plaits that are symbols of our innocence, our youth, our childhood. Then, we are comforted by the parting hands that comb and braid, comforted by the intimacy and bliss. There is a deeper intimacy in the kitchen on Saturdays when hair is pressed, when fish is fried, when sodas are passed around, when soul music drifts over the talk. It is a time without men. It is a time when we work as women to meet each other's needs, to make each other feel good inside, a time of laughter and outrageous talk."

Since the world we lived in was racially segregated, it was easy to overlook the relationship between white supremacy and our obsession with hair. Even though black women with straight hair were perceived to be more beautiful than those with thick, frizzy hair, it was not overtly related to a notion that white women were a more appealing female group or that their straight hair set a beauty standard black women were struggling to live out. While this was probably the ideological framework from which the process of straightening black women's hair emerged, it was expanded so that it became a real space of black woman bonding through ritualized, shared experience. The beauty parlor was a space of consciousness raising, a space where black women shared life stories—hardship, trials, gossip; a place where one could be comforted and one's spirit renewed. It was for some women a place of rest where one did not need to meet the demands of children or men. It was the one hour some folk would spend "off their feet," a soothing, restful time of meditation and silence. These positive empowering implications of the ritual of hair pressing mediate but do not change negative implications. They exist alongside all that is negative.

Within white supremacist capitalist patriarchy, the social and political context in which the custom of black folks straightening our hair emerges, it represents an imitation of the dominant white group's appearance and often indicates internalized racism, self-hatred, and/or low self-esteem. During the 1960s black people who actively worked to critique, challenge, and change white racism pointed to the way in which black people's obsession with straight hair reflected a colonized mentality. It was at this time that the natural hairdo, the "afro," became fashionable as a sign of cultural resistance to racist oppression and as a celebration of blackness. Naturals were equated with political militancy. Many young black folks found just how much political value was placed on straightened hair as a sign of respectability and conformity to societal expectations when they ceased to straighten their hair. When black liberation struggles did not lead to revolutionary change in society the focus on the political relationship between appearance and complicity with white racism ceased and folks who had once sported afros began to straighten their hair.

In keeping with the move to suppress black consciousness and efforts to be self-defining, white corporations began to acknowledge black people and most especially black women as potential consumers of products they could provide, including hair-care products. Permanents specially designed for black women eliminated the need for hair pressing and the hot comb. They not only cost more but they also took much of the economy and profit out of black communities, out of the pockets of black women who had previously reaped the material benefits (see Manning Marable's *How Capitalism Underdeveloped Black America,* South End Press). Gone was the context of ritual, of black woman bonding. Seated under noisy hair dryers black women lost a space for dialogue, for creative talk.

Stripped of the positive binding rituals that traditionally surrounded the experience, black women straightening our hair seemed more and more to be exclusively a signifier of white supremacist oppression and exploitation. It was clearly a process that was about black women changing their appearance to imitate white people's looks. This need to look as much like white people as possible, to look safe, is related to a desire to succeed in the white world. Before desegregation black people could worry less about what white folks thought about their hair. In a discussion with black women about beauty at Spelman College, students talked about the importance of wearing straight hair when seeking jobs. They were convinced and probably rightly so that their chances of finding good jobs would be enhanced if they had straight hair. When asked to elaborate they focused on the connection between radical politics and natural hairdos, whether natural or braided. One woman wearing a short natural told of purchasing a straight wig for her job search. No one in the discussion felt black women were free to wear our hair in natural styles without reflecting on the possible negative consequences. Often older black adults, especially parents, respond quite negatively to natural hairdos. I shared with the group that when I arrived home with my hair in braids shortly after accepting my job at Yale my parents told me I looked disgusting.

Despite many changes in racial politics, black women continue to obsess about their hair, and straightening hair continues to be serious business. It continues to tap into the insecurity black women feel about our value in this white supremacist society. Talking with groups of women at various college campuses and with black women in our communities there seems to be general consensus that our obsession with hair in general reflects continued struggles with self-esteem and self-actualization. We talk about the extent to which black women perceive our hair as the enemy, as a problem we must solve, a territory we must conquer. Above all it is a part of our black female body that must be controlled. Most of us were not raised in environments where we learned to regard our hair as sensual or beautiful in an unprocessed state. Many of us talk about situations where white people ask to touch our hair when it is unprocessed then show surprise that the texture is soft or feels good. In the eyes of many white folks and other non-black folks, the natural afro looks like steel wool or a helmet. Responses to natural hairstyles worn by black women usually reveal the extent to which our natural hair is perceived in white supremacist culture as not only ugly but frightening. We also internalize that fear. The extent to which we are comfortable with our hair usually reflects on our overall feelings about our bodies. In our black women's support group, *Sisters of the Yam,* we talk about the ways we don't like our bodies, especially our hair. I suggested to the group that we regard our hair as though it is not part of our body but something quite separate—again a territory to be controlled. To me it was important for us to link this need to control with sexuality, with sexual repression. Curious about what black women who had hot-combed or had permanents felt about the relationship between straightened hair and sexual practice I asked whether people worried about their hairdo, whether they feared partners touching their hair. Straightened hair has always seemed to me to call attention to the desire for hair to stay in place. Not surprisingly many black women responded that they felt uncomfortable if too much attention was focused on their hair, if it seemed to be too messy. Those of us who have liberated our hair and let it go in whatever direction it seems fit often receive negative comments.

Looking at photographs of myself and my sisters when we had straightened hair in high school I noticed how much older we looked than when our hair was not processed. It is ironic that we live in a culture that places so much emphasis on women looking young, yet black women are encouraged to change our hair in ways that make us appear older. This past semester we read Toni Morrison's *The Bluest Eye* in a black women's fiction class. I ask students to write autobiographical statements which reflect their thoughts about the connection between race and physical beauty. A vast majority of black women wrote about their hair. When I asked individual women outside class why they continued to straighten their hair, many asserted that naturals don't look good on them, or that they required too much work. Emily, a favorite student with very short hair, always straightened it and I would tease and challenge her. She explained to me convincingly that a natural hairdo would look horrible with her face, that she did not have the appropriate forehead or bone structure. Later she shared that during spring break she had gone to the beauty parlor to have her perm and as she sat there waiting, thinking about class reading and discussion, it came to her that she was really frightened that no one else would think she was attractive if she did not straighten her hair. She acknowledged that this fear was rooted in feelings of low self-esteem. She decided to make a change. Her new look surprised her because it was so appealing. We talked afterwards about her earlier denial and justification for wearing straightened hair. We talked about the way it hurts to realize connection between racist oppression and the arguments we use to convince ourselves and others that we are not beautiful or acceptable as we are.

In numerous discussions with black women about hair one of the strongest factors that prevent black women from wearing unprocessed hairstyles is the fear of losing other people's approval and regard. Heterosexual black women talked about the extent to which black men respond more favorably to women with straight or straightened hair. Lesbian women point to the fact that many of them do not straighten their hair, raising the question of whether or not this gesture is fundamentally linked to heterosexism and a longing for male approval. I recall visiting a woman friend and her black male companion in New York years ago and having an intense discussion about hair. He took it upon himself to share with me that I could be a fine sister if I would do something about my hair (secretly I thought mama must have hired him). What I remember is his shock when I calmly and happily asserted that I like the touch and feel of unprocessed hair.

When students read about race and physical beauty, several black women describe periods of childhood when they were overcome with longing for straight hair as it was so associated with desirability, with being loved. Few women had received affirmation from family, friends, or lovers when choosing not to straighten their hair and we have many stories to tell about advice we receive from everyone, including total strangers, urging to understand how much more attractive we would be if we would fix (straighten) our hair. When I interviewed for my job at Yale, white female advisers who had never before commented on my hair encouraged me not to wear braids or a large natural to the interview. Although they did not say straighten your hair, they were suggesting that I change my hairstyle so that it would most resemble theirs, so that it would indicate a certain conformity. I wore braids and no one seemed to notice. When I was offered the job I did not ask if it mattered whether or not I wore braids. I tell this story to my students so that they will know by this one experience that we do not always need to surrender our power to be self-defining to succeed in an endeavor. Yet I have found the issue of hairstyle comes up again and again with students when I give lectures. At one conference on black women and leadership I walked into a packed auditorium, my hair unprocessed wild and all over the place. The vast majority of black women seated there had straightened hair. Many of them looked at me with hostile contemptuous stares. I felt as though I was being judged on the spot as someone out on the fringe, an undesirable. Such judgments are made particularly about black women in the United States who choose to wear dreadlocks. They are seen and rightly so as the total antithesis of straightening one's hair, as a political statement. Often black women express contempt for those of us who choose this look.

Ironically, just as the natural unprocessed hair of black women is the subject of disregard and disdain we are witnessing return of the long dyed, blonde look. In their writing my black women students described wearing yellow mops on their heads as children to pretend they had long blonde hair. Recently black women singers who are working to appeal to white audiences, to be seen as crossovers, use hair implanting and hair weaving to have long straight hair. There seems to be a definite connection between a black female entertainer's popularity with white audiences and the degree to which she works to appear white, or to embody aspects of white style. Tina Turner and Aretha Franklin were trend setters; both dyed their hair blonde. In everyday life we see more and more black women using chemicals to be blonde. At one of my talks focusing on the social construction of black female identity within a sexist and racist society, a black woman came to me at the end of the discussion and shared that her seven-year-old daughter was obsessed with blonde hair, so much so that she had made a wig to imitate long blonde curls. This mother wanted to know what she was doing wrong in her parenting. She asserted that their home was a place where blackness was affirmed and celebrated. Yet she had not considered that her processed straightened hair was a message to her daughter that black women are not acceptable unless we alter our appearance or hair texture. Recently I talked with one of my younger sisters about her hair. She uses bright colored dyes, various shades of red. Her skin is very dark. She has a broad nose and short hair. For her these choices of straightened dyed hair were directly related to feelings of low self-esteem. She does not like her features and feels that the hairstyle transforms her. My perception was that her choice of red straightened hair actually called attention to the features she was trying to mask. When she commented that this look receives more attention and compliments, I suggested that the positive feedback might be a direct response to her own projection of a higher level of self-satisfaction. Folk may be responding to that and not her altered looks. We talked about the messages she is sending her dark-skinned daughters—that they will be most attractive if they straighten their hair.

A number of black women have argued that straightened hair is not necessarily a signifier of low self-esteem. They argue that it is a survival strategy; it is easier to function in this society with straightened hair. There are fewer hassles. Or as some folk stated, straightened hair is easier to manage, takes less time. When I responded to this argument in our discussion at Spelman by suggesting that perhaps the unwillingness to spend time on ourselves, caring for our bodies, is also a reflection of a sense that this is not important or that we do not deserve such care. In this group and others, black women talked about being raised in households where spending too much time on appearance was ridiculed or considered vanity. Irrespective of the way individual black women choose to do their hair, it is evident that the extent to which we suffer from racist and sexist oppression and exploitation affects the degree to which we feel capable of both selflove and asserting an autonomous presence that is acceptable and pleasing to ourselves. Individual preferences (whether rooted in self-hate or not) cannot negate the reality that our collective obsession with straightening black hair reflects the psychology of oppression and the impact of racist colonization. Together racism and sexism daily reinforce to all black females via the media, advertising, etc. that we will not be considered beautiful or desirable if we do not change ourselves, especially our hair. We cannot resist this socialization if we deny that white supremacy informs our efforts to construct self and identity.

Without organized struggles like the ones that happened in the 1960s and early 1970s, individual black women must struggle alone to acquire the critical consciousness that would enable us to examine issues of race and beauty, our personal choices, from a political standpoint. There are times when I think of straightening my hair just to change my style, just for fun. Then I remind myself that even though such a gesture could be simply playful on my part, an individual expression of desire, I know that such a gesture would carry other implications beyond my control. The reality is: straightened hair is linked historically and currently to a system of racial domination that impresses upon black people, and especially black women, that we are not acceptable as we are, that we are not beautiful. To make such a gesture as an expression of individual freedom and choice would make me complicit with a politic of domination that hurts us. It is easy to surrender this freedom. It is more important that black women resist racism and sexism in every way; that every aspect of our self-representation be a fierce resistance, a radical celebration of our care and respect for ourselves.

Even though I have not had straightened hair for a long time, this did not mean that I am able to really enjoy or appreciate my hair in its natural state. For years I still considered it a problem. (It wasn't naturally nappy enough to make a decent interesting afro. It was too thin.) These complaints expressed my continued dissatisfaction. True liberation of my hair came when I stopped trying to control it in any state and just accepted it as it is. It has been only in recent years that I have ceased to worry about what other people would say about my hair. It has been only in recent years that I could feel consistent pleasure washing, combing, and caring for my hair. These feelings remind me of the pleasure and comfort I felt as a child sitting between my mother's legs feeling the warmth of her body and being as she combed and braided my hair. In a culture of domination, one that is essentially anti-intimacy, we must struggle daily to remain in touch with ourselves and our bodies, with one another. Especially black women and men, as it is our bodies that have been so often devalued, burdened, wounded in alienated labor. Celebrating our bodies, we participate in a liberatory struggle that frees mind and heart.

Questions

1. What did the ritual of hair straightening mean to hooks and the other females in her family when she was a child? What tone does she use to describe her memories of this time? Refer to specific words or phrases in the text. What did having "good" hair mean?
2. How did cultural politics change the meaning of hair straightening? How does hooks see hair straightening and lightening linked to racist oppression, low self-esteem and fear? How can it reflect internalized racism? How is it tied to issues of control?
3. Why does hooks believe that men and white women are uncomfortable when African-American women wear their hair naturally? What are the possible negative economic and personal consequences of going "natural"? What are the possible benefits?
4. What political statement does your hair make? What cultural or political meanings do weaves, extensions and dreadlocks have among African-Americans today? Do hip-hop hairstyles have any particular meanings? What might it mean for a white person to wear dreadlocks? Or for a man to wear long hair? Can a hairstyle ever be just a hairstyle?

The Good, the Bad, and the Ugly: From *Buffy the Vampire Slayer* to *Dr. 90210* (2006)

Heather Hendershot

Heather Hendershot is an associate professor of media studies at Queens College and at the CUNY Graduate Center. She is the editor of Nickelodeon Nation: The History, Politics, and Economics of America's Only TV Channel for Kids *(2004) and is the author of* Saturday Morning Censors: Television Regulation before the V-Chip *(1998) and* Shaking the World for Jesus: Media and Conservative Evangelical Culture *(2004).*

Any picture of the future tells us mostly about the present. For years, Disney's Tomorrowland offered a wonderful snapshot of the 1950s; *Soylent Green* (dir. Richard Fleischer, US, 1973) and other futuristic dystopic films of the 1970s provided potent images of disillusionment in the post-Watergate years. Faced, then, with the question of what the future holds for feminism, culture, and media studies, I can only truthfully discuss what I am most concerned about right now, with some expectation (indeed, hope) that in ten years my concerns will seem as ridiculously dated as today's pierced tongues and artfully exposed high-riding underpants doubtlessly will.

When I watch TV as a feminist media critic, I am frequently alarmed, and I would like to call for more outrage from my compatriots. To feel alarm is not to be an alarmist. For a good twenty years, feminist television-studies scholars have been fighting against panicked declarations that soap operas make women stupid, that cartoons make children violent, that TV can only be reformed with highbrow, upscale programming. Instead of accepting these so-called common sense declarations, we have tried to decipher the subtle ways in which viewers understand television. The title of Ellen Seiter et al.'s breakthrough essay on soap opera viewers kind of says it all: "Don't Treat Us Like We're So Stupid and Naïve."[1] As we continue to respect the intelligence and resourcefulness of many TV viewers, however, we also need to look at the television landscape and, with righteous feminist indignation, to examine what has gone wrong.

Before I get too melodramatic, I will turn to what has gone right. First and foremost, there is the *Dallas* legacy. Soap opera plotting strategies found their way into prime-time programming in the 1980s, and character development over the lifetime of programs has since led to the evolution of some of the best female TV characters ever created. Looking back on earlier programs like *Mary Tyler Moore*, one is startled by the relative stasis of characters. Any number of shows from the past ten years—*The Larry Sanders Show, Daria, Buffy the Vampire Slayer, Alias* (sometimes), and the short-lived *Freaks and Geeks*—have showcased brilliant characters and writing. And *Chappelle's Show, The Daily Show*, and *Mr. Show* offer exhilarating social satire—without extensive character development (though also, unfortunately, with uneven insights on gender issues).

Thirty years ago, feminists were concerned about increasing the number of "positive" female characters on television. Now we have had some fantastic bitches such as Kim (Busy Phillips) on *Freaks and Geeks* and Cordelia (Charisma Carpenter) on *Buffy*. When I met *Buffy* writer Jane Espenson at a conference on gender and television, she told me that one of the lines she was most proud of having written was when Cordelia reveals that she does well on standardized tests, and the Scoobies look at her in disbelief. "What, I can't have layers?" she responds. On the surface, it's not one of the most clever lines ever spoken on the show, but it is important because it points to complexity in a TV character who, in the past, simply would not have had layers.

So what am I upset about? Simply put, I think that the proliferation of cheap, improvisational, or underwritten "nonfiction" shows like *Growing Up Gotti and EX-treme Dating* has changed programming and the industry for the worse. By reducing or eliminating writing staff and using as much nonunion acting talent as possible, these mind-numbingly dull programs have devastating economic consequences for Hollywood labor. Furthermore, many reality shows are designed to cruelly humiliate their willing participants. I don't want to sound like Steve Allen here. It's not that this stuff is "destroying Western civilization." But much of it is mean-spirited and voyeuristic. Am I the only person who squirmed watching drunk-off-her-ass Anna Nicole Smith eating an entire bag of Cheetos and lamenting her sad sex life? Or watching Verne Troyer, drunk and naked, peeing on himself on *The Surreal Life*?

Unlike most American reality shows, complex narrative programs offer characters with subjectivity and nuance that viewers can identify with. The confirmed bachelor Squidward (*Sponge-Bob SquarePants*) and queer couples like Willow and Tara (*Buffy*), for example, demand empathic connection. Reality shows, on the other hand, are more likely to assume a disengaged, ironic viewer. This is not to say that ironic viewing should be off limits. It's one thing when disengagement is fun, but quite another when it is simply the only way to cope with watching a nauseating program like *The Simple Life*. Perhaps the best model for both ironic and sincere viewing is offered by *The Gilmore Girls*; the eponymous girls enjoy the *Brady Bunch Variety Hour* as much as they enjoy *Grey Gardens*. But it's hard to imagine them giving the time of day to a reality show about a woman explaining why her self-confidence will be improved by getting buttock implants.

The growing number of misogynist plastic surgery reality shows is particularly dispiriting. Though generally designed to be uplifting rather than nasty, *Dr. 90210, Body Work*, and *Plastic Surgery: Before and After* are antithetical to any feminist visions of the world: a woman with C cup-sized breast implants feels her breasts are too small and upgrades to a double D; a woman suffering from botched liposuction gets more, better liposuction; a woman gets a chemical peel, her face red and raw and wrapped in antibiotic ointment and bandages after acid is poured on it—she is getting married soon and, she explains, wants to be "a trophy wife." Each woman says she feels confident and empowered by her procedures. There are no negatives in sight, though we do occasionally witness patients vomiting from general anesthesia.

Like the majority of reality TV programs, these shows mostly star nonunion labor and are barely written, which means less and less work for writers. The characters are gone by the next program, so there is little possible development over time, though we do learn a bit about the doctors' personal lives. The main protagonist of *Dr. 90210*, Dr. Rey, is adept at inserting breast implants through belly buttons; he spends all day empowering women but ignores his own wife. Therein lies the central dramatic tension of the program, though the doctor does occasionally encounter conflict with his patients: one woman demands a B cup implant, even though Dr. Rey insists that bigger breasts are better.

There are certainly comic elements on these programs, such as when women toss around plastic bags of saline and chat about how much fun their new boobies will be, but the programs remain depressing. I am tempted to say that they make me despair that feminism never happened, but that would be all wrong. Feminism has provided the language of female empowerment used on the programs. Empowerment used to mean better jobs, better pay, a better division of domestic labor, and better sex. On these shows it now only means better sex, implicitly achieved by having huge knockers. The images of plastic surgery programs remind me of Mary Ann Doane's analysis of women's films.[2] These women are represented as so close to themselves that there is nothing outside. It's like what Groucho Marx famously said to Margaret Dumont in *A Day at the Races* (dir. Sam Wood, US, 1937): "If I hold you any closer, I'll be in back of you." Female characters on plastic surgery reality shows have folded into themselves so far that they are in back of themselves. They have put themselves inside the saline sacks instead of the reverse.

I fear that, like an errant student, I have not really done the right assignment here. I think I was supposed to discuss historiography and methodology, to synthesize where we feminist media scholars are and where we are going. Instead, I have tried to show by example that there is still value in analyzing important, progressive shows like *Buffy*, while also getting really pissed off about the misogyny that persists on television. Is anyone else out there mad as hell and not going to take it anymore?

Notes

1. Ellen Seiter, H. Borchers, G. Kreutzner, and E. M. Warth, "'Don't Treat Us Like We're So Stupid and Naïve': Towards an Ethnography of Soap Opera Viewers," in *Remote Control: Television, Audiences, and Cultural Power*, ed. Seiter et al. (London: Routledge, 1989), 223–47.
2. Mary Ann Doane, *The Desire to Desire: The Woman's Film of the 1940s* (Bloomington: Indiana University Press, 1987).

QUESTIONS

1. What does Hendershot praise about contemporary media? Do you agree? Can you offer further examples?
2. What does Hendershot critique? Do you agree? Why or why not? Can you offer further examples?
3. What action does Hendershot want her readers to take? What kind of media analysis is she encouraging?

THE BODY POLITIC (1995)

Abra Fortune Chernik

Body hatred is something many women share in what Abra Chernik terms a "diet culture," but the life-threatening aspects of anorexia and bulimia are sometimes dismissed. In the following narrative from Listen Up! Voices From the Next Feminist Generation, *screenwriter and activist Abra Chernik describes her hospitalization for anorexia and her struggle to overcome the illusion of power and control that she felt in her anorexic world.*

My body possesses solidness and curve, like the ocean. My weight mingles with Earth's pull, drawing me onto the sand. I have not always sent waves into the world. I flew off once, for five years, and swirled madly like a cracking brown leaf in the salty autumn wind. I wafted, dried out, apathetic.

I had no weight in the world during my years of anorexia. Curled up inside my thinness, a refugee in a cocoon of hunger, I lost the capacity to care about myself or others. I starved my body and twitched in place as those around me danced in the energy of shared existence and progressed in their lives. When I graduated from college crowned with academic honors, professors praised my potential. I wanted only to vanish.

It took three months of hospitalization and two years of outpatient psychotherapy for me to learn to nourish myself and to live in a body that expresses strength and honesty in its shape. I accepted my right and my obligation to take up room with my figure, voice and spirit. I remembered how to tumble forward and touch the world that holds me. I chose the ocean as my guide.

Who disputes the ocean's fullness?

Growing up in New York City, I did not care about the feminist movement. Although I attended an all-girls high school, we read mostly male authors and studied the history of men. Embracing mainstream culture without question, I learned about womanhood from fashion magazines, Madison Avenue and Hollywood. I dismissed feminist alternatives as foreign and offensive, swathed as they were in stereotypes that threatened my adolescent need for conformity.

Puberty hit late; I did not complain. I enjoyed living in the lanky body of a tall child and insisted on the title of "girl." If anyone referred to me as a "young woman," I would cry out, horrified, "Do not call me the W word!" But at sixteen years old, I could no longer deny my fate. My stomach and breasts rounded. Curly black hair sprouted in the most embarrassing places. Hips swelled from a once-flat plane. Interpreting maturation as an unacceptable lapse into fleshiness, I resolved to eradicate the physical symptoms of my impending womanhood.

Magazine articles, television commercials, lunchroom conversation, gymnastics coaches and write-ups on models had saturated me with diet savvy. Once I decided to lose weight, I quickly turned expert. I dropped hot chocolate from my regular breakfast order at the Skyline Diner. I replaced lunches of peanut butter and Marshmallow Fluff sandwiches with small platters of cottage cheese and cantaloupe. I eliminated dinner altogether and blunted my appetite with Tab, Camel Lights, and Carefree bubble gum. When furious craving overwhelmed my resolve and I swallowed an extra something, I would flee to the nearest bathroom to purge my mistake.

Within three months, I had returned my body to its preadolescent proportions and had manipulated my monthly period into drying up. Over the next five years, I devoted my life to losing my weight. I came to resent the body in which I lived, the body that threatened to develop, the body whose hunger I despised but could not extinguish. If I neglected a workout or added a pound or ate a bite too many, I would stare in the mirror and drown myself in a tidal wave of criticism. Hatred of my body generalized to hatred of myself as a person, and self-referential labels such as "pig," "failure" and "glutton" allowed me to believe that I deserved punishment. My self-hatred became fuel for the self-mutilating behaviors of the eating disorder.

As my body shrank, so did my world. I starved away my power and vision, my energy and inclinations. Obsessed with dieting, I allowed relationships, passions and identity to wither. I pulled back from the world, off of the beach, out of the sand. The waves of my existence ceased to roll beyond the inside of my skin.

And society applauded my shrinking. Pound after pound the applause continued, like the pounding ocean outside the door of my beach house.

The word "anorexia" literally means "loss of appetite." But as an anorexic, I felt hunger thrashing inside my body. I denied my appetite, ignored it, but never lost it. Sometimes the pangs twisted so sharply, I feared they would consume the meat of my heart. On desperate nights I rose in a flannel nightgown and allowed myself to eat an unplanned something.

No matter how much I ate, I could not soothe the pangs. Standing in the kitchen at midnight, spotlighted by the blue-white light of the open refrigerator, I would frantically feed my neglected appetite: the Chinese food I had not touched at dinner; ice cream and whipped cream; microwaved bread; cereal and chocolate milk; doughnuts and bananas. Then, solid sadness inside my gut, swelling agitation, a too-big meal I would not digest. In the bathroom I would rip off my shirt, tie up my hair, and prepare to execute the desperate ritual, again. I would ram the back of my throat with a toothbrush handle, crying, impatient, until the food rushed up. I would vomit until the toilet filled and I emptied, until I forgave myself, until I felt ready to try my life again. Standing up from my position over the toilet, wiping my mouth, I would believe that I was safe. Looking in the mirror through puffy eyes in a tumescent face, I would promise to take care of myself. Kept awake by the fast, confused beating of my heart and the ache in my chest, I would swear I did not miss the world outside. Lost within myself, I almost died.

By the time I entered the hospital, a mess of protruding bones defined my body, and the bones of my emaciated life rattled me crazy. I carried a pillow around because it hurt to sit down, and I shivered with cold in sultry July. Clumps of brittle hair clogged the drain when I showered, and blackened eyes appeared to sink into my head. My vision of reality wrinkled and my disposition turned mercurial as I slipped into starvation psychosis, a condition associated with severe malnutrition. People told me that I resembled a concentration camp prisoner, a chemotherapy patient, a famine victim or a fashion model.

In the hospital, I examined my eating disorder under the lenses of various therapies. I dissected my childhood, my family structure, my intimate relationships, my belief systems. I participated in experiential therapies of movement, art and psychodrama. I learned to use words instead of eating patterns to communicate my feelings. And still I refused to gain more than a minimal amount of weight.

I felt powerful as an anorexic. Controlling my body yielded an illusion of control over my life; I received incessant praise for my figure despite my sickly mien, and my frailty manipulated family and friends into protecting me from conflict. I had reduced my world to a plate of steamed carrots, and over this tiny kingdom I proudly crowned myself queen.

I sat cross-legged on my hospital bed for nearly two months before I earned an afternoon pass to go to the mall with my mother. The privilege came just in time; I felt unbearably large and desperately wanted a new outfit under which to hide gained weight. At the mall, I searched for two hours before finally discovering, in the maternity section at Macy's, a shirt large enough to cover what I perceived as my enormous body.

With an hour left on my pass, I spotted a sign on a shop window: "Body Fat Testing, $3.00." I suggested to my mother that we split up for ten minutes; she headed to Barnes & Noble, and I snuck into the fitness store.

I sat down in front of a machine hooked up to a computer, and a burly young body builder fired questions at me:

"Age?"

"Twenty-one."

"Height?"
"Five nine."
"Weight?"
"Ninety-nine."

The young man punched my statistics into his keyboard and pinched my arm with clippers wired to the testing machine. In a moment, the computer spit out my results. "Only ten percent body fat! Unbelievably healthy. The average for a woman your age is twenty-five percent. Fantastic! You're this week's blue ribbon winner."

I stared at him in disbelief. *Winner? Healthy? Fantastic?* I glanced around at the other customers in the store, some of whom had congregated to watch my testing, and I felt embarrassed by his praise. And then I felt furious. Furious at this man and at the society that programmed him for their ignorant approbation of my illness and my suffering.

"I am dying of anorexia," I whispered. "Don't congratulate me."

I spent my remaining month in the hospital supplementing psychotherapy with an independent examination of eating disorders from a social and political point of view. I needed to understand why society would reward my starvation and encourage my vanishing. In the bathroom, a mirror on the open door behind me reflected my backside in a mirror over the sink. Vertebrae poked at my skin, ribs hung like wings over chiseled hip bones, the two sides of my buttocks did not touch. I had not seen this view of myself before.

In writing, I recorded instances in which my eating disorder had tangled the progress of my life and thwarted my relationships. I filled three and a half Mead marble notebooks. Five years' worth of: *I wouldn't sit with Daddy when he was alone in the hospital because I needed to go jogging; I told Derek not to visit me because I couldn't throw up when he was there; I almost failed my comprehensive exams because I was so hungry; I spent my year at Oxford with my head in the toilet bowl; I wouldn't eat the dinner my friends cooked me for my nineteenth birthday because I knew they had used oil in the recipe; I told my family not to come to my college graduation because I didn't want to miss a day at the gym or have to eat a restaurant meal.* And on and on for hundreds of pages.

This honest account of my life dissolved the illusion of

anorexic power. I saw myself naked in the truth of my pain, my loneliness, my obsessions, my craziness, my selfishness, my defeat. I also recognized the social and political implications of consuming myself with the trivialities of calories and weight. At college, I had watched as classmates involved themselves in extracurricular clubs, volunteer work, politics and applications for jobs and graduate schools. Obsessed with exercising and exhausted by starvation, I did not even consider joining in such pursuits. Despite my love of writing and painting and literature, despite ranking at the top of my class, I wanted only to teach aerobics. Despite my adolescent days as a loud-mouthed, rambunctious class leader, I had grown into a silent, hungry young woman.

And society preferred me this way: hungry, fragile, crazy. *Winner! Healthy! Fantastic!* I began reading feminist literature to further understand the disempowerment of women in our culture. I digested the connection between a nation of starving, self-obsessed women and the continued success of the patriarchy. I also cultivated an awareness of alternative models of womanhood. In the stillness of the hospital library, new voices in my life rose from printed pages to echo my rage and provide the conception of my feminist consciousness.

I had been willing to accept self-sabotage, but now I refused to sacrifice myself to a society that profited from my pain. I finally understood that my eating disorder symbolized more than "personal psychodynamic trauma." Gazing in the mirror at my emaciated body, I observed a woman held up by her culture as the physical ideal because she was starving, self-obsessed and powerless, a woman called beautiful because she threatened no one except herself. Despite my intelligence, my education, and my supposed Manhattan sophistication, I had believed all the lies; I had almost given my life in order to achieve the sickly impotence that this culture aggressively links with female happiness, love and success. And everything I had to offer to the world, every tumbling wave, every thought and every passion, nearly died inside me.

As long as society resists female power, fashion will call healthy women physically flawed. As long as society accepts the physical, sexual and economic abuse of women, popular culture will prefer women who resemble little girls. Sitting in the hospital the summer after my college graduation, I grasped the absurdity of a nation of adult women dying to grow small.

Armed with this insight, I loosened the grip of the starvation disease on my body. I determined to recreate myself based on an image of a woman warrior. I remembered my ocean, and I took my first bite.

Gaining weight and getting my head out of the toilet bowl was the most political act I have ever committed.

I left the hospital and returned home to Fire Island. Living at the shore in those wintry days of my new life, I wrapped myself in feminism as I hunted sea shells and role models. I wanted to feel proud of my womanhood. I longed to accept and honor my body's fullness.

During the process of my healing, I had hoped that I would be able to skip the memory of anorexia like a cold pebble into the dark winter sea. I had dreamed that in relinquishing my obsessive chase after a smaller body, I would be able to come home to rejoin those whom I had left in order to starve, rejoin them to live together as healthy, powerful women. But as my body has grown full, I have sensed a hollowness in the lives of women all around me that I had not noticed when I myself stood hollow. I have made it home only to find myself alone.

Out in the world again, I hear the furious thumping dance of body hatred echoing every place I go. Friends who once appeared wonderfully carefree in ordering late-night french fries turn out not to eat breakfast or lunch. Smart, talented, creative women talk about dieting and overeating and hating the beach because they look terrible in bathing suits. Famous women give interviews insulting their bodies and bragging about bicycling twenty-four miles the day they gave birth.

I had looked forward to rejoining society after my years of anorexic exile. Ironically, in order to preserve my health, my recovery has included the development of a consciousness that actively challenges the images and ideas that define this culture. Walking down Madison Avenue and passing emaciated women, I say to myself, *those women are sick*. When smacked with a diet commercial, I remind myself, *I don't do that anymore*. I decline invitations to movies that feature anorexic actors, I will not participate in discussions about dieting, and I refuse to shop in stores that cater to women with eating-disordered figures.

Though I am critical of diet culture, I find it nearly impossible to escape. Eating disorders have woven their way into the fabric of my society. On television, in print, on food packaging, in casual conversation and in windows of clothing stores populated by ridiculously gaunt mannequins, messages to lose my weight and control my appetite challenge my recovered fullness. Finally at home in my body, I recognize myself as an island in a sea of eating disorders, a sea populated predominantly by young women.

A perversion of nature by society has resulted in a phenomenon whereby women feel safer when starving than when eating. Losing our weight boosts self-esteem, while nourishing our bodies evokes feelings of self-doubt and self-loathing.

When our bodies take up more space than a size eight (as most of our bodies do), we say, *too big*. When our appetites demand more than a Lean Cuisine, we say, *too much*. When we want a piece of a friend's birthday cake, we say, *too bad*. Don't eat too much, don't talk too loudly, don't take up too much space, don't take from the world. Be pleasant or crazy, but don't seem hungry. Remember, a new study shows that men prefer women who eat salad for dinner over women who eat burgers and fries.

So we keep on shrinking, starving away our wildness, our power, our truth.

Hiding our curves under long T-shirts at the beach, sitting silently and fidgeting while others eat dessert, sneaking back into the kitchen late at night to binge and hating ourselves the next day, skipping breakfast, existing on diet soda and cigarettes, adding up calories and subtracting everything else. We accept what is horribly wrong in our lives and fight what is beautiful and right.

Over the past three years, feminism has taught me to honor the fullness of my womanhood and the solidness of the body that hosts my life. In feminist circles I have found mentors, strong women who live with power, passion and purpose. And yet, even in groups of feminists, my love and acceptance of my body remains unusual.

Eating disorders affect us all on both a personal and a political level. The majority of my peers—including my feminist peers—still measure their beauty against anorexic ideals. Even among feminists, body hatred and chronic dieting continue to consume lives. Friends of anorexics beg them to please start eating; then these friends go home and continue their own diets. Who can deny that the millions of young women caught in the net of disordered eating will frustrate the potential of the next wave of feminism?

Sometimes my empathy dissolves into frustration and rage at our situation. For the first time in history, young women have the opportunity to create a world in our image. But many of us concentrate instead on recreating the shape of our thighs.

As young feminists, we must place unconditional acceptance of our bodies at the top of our political agenda. We must claim our bodies as our own to love and honor in their infinite shapes and sizes. Fat, thin, soft, hard, puckered, smooth, our bodies are our homes. By nourishing our bodies, we care for and love ourselves on the most basic level. When we deny ourselves physical food, we go hungry emotionally, psychologically, spiritually and politically. We must challenge ourselves to eat and digest, and allow society to call us too big. We will understand their message to mean too powerful.

Time goes by quickly. One day we will blink and open our eyes as old women. If we spend all our energy keeping our bodies small, what will we have to show for our lives when we reach the end? I hope we have more than a group of fashionably skinny figures.

QUESTIONS

1. How can individual eating problems actually be considered political problems? What factors contribute to the existence of eating problems?
2. What is the meaning and significance of "body hatred"? What are the effects of body hatred for both the individual and society?
3. How does Chernik change through the course of her narrative? What issues does Chernik face in her struggle for personal growth as a woman? How does she feel about her experiences?

Keeping the Forces of Decrepitude at Bay (2004)

Daphne Merkin

A critic, essayist and novelist, Daphne Merkin is a regular contributor to The New York Times Book Review. *Many of her essays address the issue of the body, gender, and aging. She has written a novel,* Enchantment, *and a collection of essays,* Dreaming of Hitler. *She is currently at work on a cultural and personal memoir of depression,* Melancholy Baby.

I am lying in bed, reading Dr. Gerald Imber's "Youth Corridor," a friendly and sagacious book with helpful drawings and a clearly laid-out text, about the whys and wherefores of plastic surgery. I am reading this book because in another minute I'll be—but can this be?—50. It's actually more a matter of weeks than minutes, and yes, I'm keeping count, but the particulars don't make much difference because it's clear to me that whenever 50 shows up—it could be tomorrow or two years from now—it comes as a blow to one's perennially youthful psyche, as impossible to grasp about one's own sprightly self as it seems perfectly plausible when it comes to other people.

Reaching one's 50th birthday is no longer a feat the way it was in, say, Montaigne's time, when the odds were against reaching 60 (Montaigne didn't) and "death of old age" was "a rare, singular and extraordinary death." Although it pains me to my contrarian core to have to admit to being part of a national trend (or, as some view it, an epidemic), my birth date marks me inescapably as part of the graying herd. I am just another face in a crowd of aging baby boomers, demanding the best golden years money and a well-developed sense of entitlement can buy. It may be true, as Francis Bacon observed, that age will not be defied, but that doesn't mean we're prepared to yield to its advance either. Who, I might ask, ever feels 50 inside? Like the proverbial thin person stuck inside every fat person, inside every 50-year-old is nestled a 30- or 25-year-old—if not an even younger ghostly self, an adolescent habitué of dreams and fantasies who haunts the sites of ancient traumas, replaying juvenile regrets or hopes, failing the chemistry final or bedding the crush-object who never gave you a second look back then.

Here I am, for instance, still discussing the scars of my childhood in therapy, trying to undo (or, failing that, come to terms with) the forces that have warped my character so that I am a person who is always late, rarely returns phone calls and never feels sufficiently appreciated; meanwhile, mortality is about to appear in my doorway in a graceless flurry of American Association of Retired Persons information and exhortations to sign up for something that is advertised on late-night TV as the "silver care" insurance policy. How is it that my alma mater, Barnard College, has tracked me down just in time for my birthday at the end of May with an invitation to attend a meeting of Project Continuum, which solemnly describes itself as addressing "the needs of alumnae who are 50 and older," said needs having been adduced to include "navigating the health care system" and "memory training." Oh, the indignity of it all. Never mind that I have hardly decided whether a writer is what I really want to be, much less whether I'm ready to retire from the profession. Or that the prospect of receiving discounts on wheelchairs isn't one to fill me with joy. Indeed, as far as I can tell, this milestone—one that most of the population had little hope of reaching until the beginning of the 20th century brought with it a dazzling advance in life expectancy—doesn't call out for celebration, unless you happen to be Oprah and merrily confuse your own birthday with the nation's.

Why the big rush, may I ask? What's to get hepped up and festive about when all I can see in front of me is a decades-long campaign of vigilantly keeping the forces of decrepitude at bay as I totter forward over the next 15 years into first the demographic embrace of the "young old" (the oxymoronic term coined by the gerontologist Bernice Neugarten to demarcate the age group from 65 to 74); then into the trembling clutches of the "old old" (the over-75's); and then, if the fates and my genes are so inclined, finally into the frail company of the "oldest old." One doesn't need to have "mortuary inclinations," like the death-fixated Alice James, the younger sister of William and Henry, to get a bit grim around the mouth at the prospect. At what point do I let my hair go gray? Cease apologizing for my lapses in memory? Allow myself to huff and puff after climbing half a flight of stairs? Is there any moment when it becomes O.K. for a woman to stop sucking in her stomach and holding her wobbly chins up—when you get, that is, to acknowledge that you have now earned the right to act piteously hunched over and enfeebled?

The paradox of it is that while our culture increasingly treats growing old as a malady, women are increasingly pressured to treat aging as a pesky inconvenience best not acknowledged. Of course, lying about one's age is second nature for most women. Aging, like gender, is a social construction, shaped by the forces of culture more than by the imperatives of biology, and there is much to be said for fighting artifice with artifice. All the same, few of us have the wit—or the aristocratic temerity—to pick a number, like the great hostess and horsewoman Nancy Astor did, and stoutly stick with it, creating havoc as we go along: "I refuse to admit that I am more than 52," she declared, "even if that does make my sons illegitimate." Most of us are more conveniently vague in our strategies, like the friend of mine who paused when I asked her how old she was, answering that she had been lying so long about her age that she couldn't remember her real one. Or we are touchingly modest in our self-fabrications, chopping off a year or two at an opportune moment. When I joined a dating service some years back, for instance, it seemed important to me, notwithstanding my ambivalence about the whole enterprise, to bill myself as a year younger than I actually was, as if those paltry 12 months would make the difference between finding or not finding a man. Oscar Wilde, who understood the importance of social masks as well as anyone, considered women who didn't lie about their age to be suspect: "One should never trust a woman who tells one her real age," he opined. "A woman who would tell one that would tell one anything."

So call me brave or call me foolhardy for announcing the advent of my sixth decade in this bald and inelegant way, but I must confess I do so more in a spirit of defeat than liberation. I wish I could say that I thought committing this wince-inducing truth to print would free me to age gracefully, much less daringly—to accept my crow's feet and sagging muscle tone as signs of having endured, of having lived to tell the tale of life as I know it to those who come after me, like some massively wrinkled tribal woman with a pair of proudly bared drooping breasts. But the reality is that I consider myself to be a hostage to an age-phobic culture, one that fears the inevitability of aging the way earlier cultures once feared death.

Back in bed, my head propped against the pillows, I read "The Youth Corridor" into the early morning with steadily mounting anxiety, in spite of Dr. Imber's insistence that the subject of how we age "is not nearly as terrifying as it sounds." Who's the man kidding? Here he has just spelled out the appalling situation wrinkles are forever. What it comes down to is this: You're born; you get about three decades to prance around looking fresh as a daisy before the inexorable forces of gravity, the sun, free radicals and pesky emotions like sadness and happiness put the shiv in; and, eventually, after looking haggard for the next umpteen years, you die. If you're 23 and a model who exercises and diets rigorously, you're not treading dangerous water yet, but you should, according to Imber, already be buoying yourself with time-consuming and deeply boring preventive care. By the time you've passed 40, you would do well to be looking beyond the wonders of Retin-A, Vitamin C, alpha hydroxy and other topical applications and into the claustrophobic vista of the operating room. If you haven't gone under the surgeon's knife by 50, it seems, yours is the face nature meant you to have—the face, that is, of an incipient hag. At some point, I bound up in a state of real terror and lean over the bathroom sink the better to examine my face in the mirror. Here, staring back at me, are all the "stigmata of aging," as Imber calls them, a map of ruin delineating the erosions left by time, sun and life experience: laugh lines, worry lines, furrows, nasolabial folds, hooded upper eyelid skin, decreased firmness in the jaw line and—God help me—the neck. Best face up to the stark reality, I tell myself, and don't shoot the messenger. I will call a plastic surgeon, perhaps Imber himself, tomorrow, today, yesterday. I will begin by scheduling appointments for Botox and collagen, although more drastic measures are probably called for. It may already be too late to undo the damage, for ideally I should have been vigilantly proactive since about the age of 13. How have I let myself slip over the boundary into the dreaded category of the discernibly aging woman?

So that's how I found myself one December morning in the waiting room of Gerald H. Pitman, an Upper East Side plastic surgeon who wrote the standard medical textbook on liposuction and aesthetic surgery. Pitman is a relative veteran, having been in the business since the days when face and body work were the exclusive province of ladies who lunched and Brazilian heiresses—before, that is, the second coming of Goldie Hawn's lips and the advent of nip-'n'-tuck reality shows. While I wait to see him, I am given a form to fill out; unlike the ones that go into anthropological detail, his questionnaire is relatively brisk, pausing mainly to ask whether I am under psychiatric care.

By the time Pitman is ready to see me in his examining room, I have had a chance to study the truly staggering number of cosmetic options that fill a matte silver wall file. My anxiety is percolating (if you're not seeing a shrink before you enter a plastic surgeon's office, trust me, you will be afterward), and I am pondering whether an inner-thigh lift—something I had never considered before—might not be more conducive to restoring a sense of lost youth than the less esoteric measures available, like doing away with those periorbital lines (crow's feet). But the idea of tackling my slackened waistline or any other part of my gravity-challenged corpus is not one I am prepared to confront today, in spite of Pitman's assurance that trimming one's middle is akin to a face lift for the body.

The doctor, who looks fit and somewhere on the late end of his 50's, barks out the particular ignominies of my facial appearance—"laxity of lids," "early wobbling" and the number of c.c.'s of fat that would need to be taken from my jaw line to restore its crisp profile—to a decorative young nurse who notes it all down. Pitman is fairly easy to talk to; none of the surgeons or dermatologists I meet in the course of my research could be accused of being of a remotely Aristotelian bent, but there is something pleasingly straightforward and unembossed about his approach. When I ask whether he thinks cosmetic surgery is addictive, he stares at me as if I were obtuse. "Is alcohol addictive," he replies; it is an assertion, not a question.

We discuss the ever-younger age at which women feel pressured to seek out surgery, beginning usually with their eyes in their mid- or late 30's (the eyelids are the first to go), as opposed to a decade or so ago when they generally waited until their late 40's or 50's to begin. Going a bit further back in cosmetic-surgery prehistory, one comes upon those unfazed Park Avenue matrons who were content to cool their heels until they turned 65 and went in for the "big overhaul," as one surgeon put it. But in what is either an objective instance of the aesthetic end justifying the means or just better business, this all-or-nothing approach is generally advised against nowadays in favor of working your way over a period of, say, 30 years through what one surgeon describes as "a lot of little surgeries."

I leave Pitman's office after airing on his pretty and bored-looking office manager my hastily formulated plan to schedule surgery immediately, within days, before I change my mind and he goes away over the Christmas holidays. We discuss fees and recovery time; Pitman has said it'll take six weeks, "every minute of it," but she breezily suggests that I'll be out and about much sooner. When I assure her I'll be back in touch the next day, she looks as if she doesn't believe a word of it. And right she is, too. I'm far too scared, for starters.

Of course, there's nothing more guaranteed to make a woman feel not only ancient but also mentally unhinged than seeing a cosmetic surgeon appreciably younger than herself, as I found out when I sought advice from a much-touted 37-year-old colleague of Pitman's named Robert Silich. Silich, who comes from a family of doctors, seems to live and breathe his work and has no less than 14 diplomas hanging on his office wall. He expertly analyzes the pros and cons of the various kinds of face lifts—the "classic," the "S" or "limited incision" face lift (which eliminates the scar behind the ear and on the hairline), and the newest kid on the block, the midface lift, which many of the tonier surgeons consider to be of dubious value. (Pitman, in his pithy fashion, describes it as "more sizzle than steak.") He also fills me in on recent changes in the overall aesthetic approach, away from brow lifts (think Jocelyn Wildenstein) and from pulling and tightening the skin to restoring volume in the face. He goes on to note the all-important geographical factor. "You get a totally different face in Dallas than you do in Beverly Hills or Miami," he points out. I nod, knowingly. But beneath my journalistic immersion, I am beginning to feel slightly disoriented, as if it has finally been convincingly demonstrated that the existentialists were wrong and the French semioticians were right all along: that life as we now know it adds up to no more than a magazine photo shoot, the reproduction and manipulation of visual images, and either your particular style of face fits into the overall scheme or you're out of the picture. Perhaps this accounts for the strange sense of relief that comes over me when I leave Silich's office, as if I had just stepped out of a transparent universe that has succeeded in bypassing the problem of meaning altogether into a slightly more complex one that can be prodded into showing traces of authenticity.

Later, when I hear of Olivia Goldsmith's untoward end while undergoing cosmetic surgery, Pitman's gift for concise phrase-making comes back to haunt me: "The three most dangerous words in plastic surgery? 'It's only liposuction.'"

Improved longevity may sound like a wonderful thing in the abstract, a testament to medical advances and human ingenuity, providing chunks of extra time in which to take up a second career, read Milton or start on a new and improved family. And there is no doubt that, in the West, at least, we have triumphed over many of the forces that assail us from within: historically people died of infectious diseases that are now largely treatable or curable. But the hard truth of the matter is that, in spite of the fact that the geriatric population is the fastest growing, the science of aging is still a fairly new discipline, no more than 25 years old at most, and the biology of aging—including the basic fact that our bodies are wired for something called apoptosis, or preprogrammed cell death, which in turn ensures that our various systems will break down and that our tissues will get thinner and hang on the bones more as we grow older—is only beginning to be understood. For all the breakthroughs and advances in cosmetic rejuvenation—the latest injectable dermafillers based on the use of hyaluronic acid are Restylane and Hylaform, both of which received F.D.A. approval in the last five months; a new form of Botox called Dysport is hovering on the horizon; and there are newer fillers like Artecoll being tested all the time—there are still things that even the most cutting-edge plastic-surgery technique can't do anything about: our eye sockets, for example, are a cruel indicator of age, especially if you know how to look out for a "senile" shape to the orbit. As is the "turgor," or level of elasticity, in the skin on the back of the hand—how quickly it bounces back after you pluck it.

It is hard, moreover, to think of growing older as an unadulterated triumph in a world where "ageism" thrives and the elderly are routinely treated as comically dependent on the good graces of the young. In her excellent book, "Learning to Be Old: Gender, Culture and Aging," Margaret Cruikshank compares the aged to a "colonized people," suggesting that ageism goes beyond dehumanization into actual scapegoating of the old. We have always had mixed feelings about the mental and physical decline that comes with living longer, but for women, especially, who in America outlive men by six years on average (the nerve of us!), visible signs of aging are treated as profound insults to one's physical and psychological well-being. Thomas R. Cole, in his cultural history of American aging, "The Journey of Life," observes that our society's "intractable hostility" to growing old is "imposed with particular vengeance on older women." And here I must admit that I have been taking a degree of comfort all along in the assumption that men have begun to fret more about "turkey-gobbler neck" and faltering elastin. What goes around comes around and all that. But when I check this out with Pitman, he informs me of the astonishing fact—proof positive that men grow more distinguished with age while women grow more desperate—that the relative percentage of male patients has remained unchanged over the past two decades. Jonathan Swift was obviously on to something when he has Gulliver pronounce the Struldbruggs, who are frozen in old age and doomed never to die, "the most horrifying sight I ever beheld; and the Women are more horrible than the Men."

How is it, really, that American women have been so successfully terrorized by the thought of showing their age—of becoming what even the fiercely independent-minded lesbian writer May Sarton described as "an old woman, a grotesque miserable animal"—that they will spend enormous amounts of money and time in the effort to stave off a process that was once considered to be a natural, even revered one by any means, ranging from the patently ludicrous to the purportedly scientific to the bloodily effective?

My fear of the scalpel may have kept me from rushing on to the operating table, but the cosmeceutical industry has invaded and conquered my bathroom cabinet, which is a veritable triage center of anti-aging creams and potions and serums (similar to creams, but more costly), with a special emphasis on products for the eyes and ones that magically claim to "lift" or "tighten" the skin. Among the more plebeian and reasonably priced items from Neutrogena and L'Oréal there is a jar of Cellular Revitalization Age Renewal, the ingredients of which take up nine lines of tiny print, from the dermatologist Howard Sobel's DDF line (which carries more than 100 exhaustively calibrated products in all); a tiny silvery jar of Awake eye cream on which I have spent a cool $95; and a firming serum from the cult facialist Tracie Martyn that goes for a whopping $165.

When does it start, this feeling that you have a week—two weeks uppermost—before you become irreversibly old and crepey, before you become all but invisible, the sort of woman no man will ever look at again and think: I want her. Forty-one? Thirty-eight? Twenty-nine? "In another minute I'll be 30," Zelda Fitzgerald is supposed to have said, by way of explaining her decision to take up grueling training as a ballerina in her late 20's. Zelda's burst of dedicated professionalism—in the year or so that was left to her before she had a series of nervous breakdowns and became a lifelong mental patient, she practiced from 8 to 10 hours a day—would eventually be held against her as yet another indication of her eccentricity and problematic competitiveness with her acclaimed spouse, the writer F. Scott Fitzgerald. But it has always seemed to me that along with Zelda's whim of iron came a shatteringly clear sense of reality. Who better than a woman married to a man who never met a beautiful young girl whose dewy looks he didn't try to immortalize in a gleaming phrase—Fitzgerald kept a section in his notebooks titled "Descriptions of Girls"—to be keenly conscious of the brief life of a woman's amorous desirability? Along with Nabokov's Humbert Humbert, whose "fancy prose style" is a besotted witness to the rosebud charms of Lolita's pubescence, there is no more painstaking annotator of the cosmetic sheen provided by youth than Fitzgerald. Here, for instance, is Description No. 475, exacting and chilling as a steel instrument: "She was a stalk of ripe corn, but bound not as cereals are but as a rare first edition, with all the binder's art. She was lovely and expensive, and about 19."

Was there ever a time before Fear of Aging, a time when the lines in a woman's face attested to her character rather than to her lack of allure? The Chinese are known for honoring their elderly, and college anthropology courses abound in descriptions of cultures—albeit mostly primitive tribes or altogether vanished ones—that cherished rather than disdained their grandmothers and great-grandmothers. It is with some relief, then, that I fall into the waiting room of Ellen Gendler, a dermatologist whose expertise and no-nonsense style have earned her a six-month waiting list and countless mentions in glossy magazines. There on the wall hangs a Shelby Lee Adams photo of an antediluvian Appalachian woman, her face a map of Cy Twombly-esque scrawls. "She's younger than you think she is," Dr. Gendler says cheerfully. "You know she smokes and hasn't had dental care. Her teeth are long gone." Gendler's tone strikes me as a sophisticated mixture of common sense and commercial savvy, as if she were acknowledging in one and the same breath the worthy ideal of aging graciously and the remunerative reality that there is no such thing anymore. "Plastic surgery attacks a face as a project," she points out, "as something to be fixed. There are a lot of things you can fix on a face. But aging is not stoppable. At best you can slow it down." So she plays all the angles: providing services like laser resurfacing while pooh-poohing the search-for-eternal-youth, "hope in a bottle" approach while conceding the panic that accompanies catching sight of your aging reflection in the mirror: "It happens one day. You're fine until a certain point because you can't see what happens inside your body, and then one day you see signs of aging in your face. It's a sharp reminder of mortality."

It all goes back to that, of course, as simple a fact of life as it is profound: the dying of the light that leads to the pitch-darkness at the end of the tunnel. Out, out, brief flame. "Aging," declares Dr. Marianne Legato, a leading medical researcher who founded the Partnership for Gender-Specific Medicine at Columbia University, "is nature's way of preparing us for death. That's why we hate old people." I suppose the one good thing to be said about having already aged is that it gives you the upper hand in a strange, secretive sort of way. I mean you can look at young girls in their barely-there whiffs of clothes—their abbreviated tank tops or skirts that stop just below the pelvis, strutting their juicy stuff, and think: Just you wait, just you wait. Your spring-chicken days are numbered, all you fine-feathered chickadees. We may live in postfeminist times, but the unspoken cutoff point for women as far as their desirability as females goes still pretty much revolves around their reproductive capacity. "In the mind of the public, we literally go overnight from being an object of desire to being discardable," observes Legato, a slim and elegantly dressed 68-year-old with a perfectly coifed grayish-blond pageboy and ram-rod-straight posture. "There's a switch that goes from 'on' to 'off.' 'On' is premenopausal and 'off' is postmenopausal."

But then what solace, when you come right down to it, is there in the bitter irony that youth is fleeting, the average onset of menopause is 51 and life is becoming ever more prolonged—the average life expectancy of an infant girl born today is 86 years, and estimates are that this number will reach 120 by the middle of the century—other than the dubious one of Schadenfreude?

I wish I were more like Marianne Legato, who identifies strongly with the physician father who nurtured her curiosity and is firmly convinced that women are "a gift to man" and refuses to have plastic surgery. In the end, though, I am only me, a 49-year-old mother of a 14-year-old daughter whose skin—especially, as Nabokov wrote, "that silky shimmer above her temple"—would make any "Lolita" lover weep. My father was radically inattentive (one of those childhood scars), and never having been endowed with any great faith in my own irresistible allure when I was young, I am fairly sure that I am getting easier to resist with each passing year.

In the end, then, I caved in and fell into the arms of Fredric Brandt, cosmetic dermatologist extraordinaire. Brandt, along with the dermatologists Nicolas Perricone and Dennis Gross, has his own eponymous line of age-retarding products and is purportedly the single biggest user of Botox in the world. An eccentric man who sings while he injects—he has written songs for a musical in his head called "Botox Nation"—Brandt looks younger than his own 54 years and readily admits to trying his procedures, some of them unconventional, on himself. There is something of the miracle worker about him, having less to do with any swaggering air he conveys (he doesn't) than with a sense one gets that he sees the you that has become obscured under the passage of time—and, perhaps most important of all, that he will redress nature's injuries without inserting a knife and with minimal investment of that bugaboo known as "down time."

On a Friday afternoon in March, I made my way to the nondescript building on 34th Street that houses Brandt's suite of offices. In one long session that stretched over two hours, he addressed the areas of my face—around my eyes and cheekbones and under my chin—that he said would most benefit from his help. One of his bevy of perky young nurses applied a thick white numbing cream to my face, which left me looking like a Kabuki actress; during the half-hour it took for it to work, I considered leaping up and running for my life and alternately pondered why I, who sent my daughter to an all-girls school in the hope that it would help her to prize her intellect and worry less about looking like Britney Spears, had succumbed to the decadent blandishments of a narcissistic, Extreme Makeover culture while a war is raging in Iraq and across the globe terrorist cells are trying to figure out how to blast Western civilization off the map. Then Brandt entered the room and began to work, pumping me full of Restylane and eventually a smaller amount of Botox, one precisely inserted syringe after another, causing pinpricks of pain through the anesthetic. He paused frequently to step back and assess the results, smiling at his handiwork, and every once in a while asked for an ice pack to be placed over an area he had just treated. When he was done, everyone told me that the results were amazing. I studied myself in a hand mirror: the face that looked back at me was the face of a mugged person—swollen and bruised and dotted with dried-up specks of blood. After Brandt and his nurses assured me that I would like what I saw better within a few days, I was sent home with a prescription for an anti-inflammatory cream and a flesh-toned cream to disguise the black-and-blue marks. Even before I gave the cabdriver my address, my face had begun throbbing in protest.

What can i say? The swelling went down, the bruising disappeared and no one noticed a thing. The money, the pain, the guilt—all were in vain, or so it seemed. I pressed several of my friends: didn't they see something different about me? One ventured that my face looked a little thinner, another that my hair looked good. My daughter, who was privy to the day-by-dayness of the post-procedural process, hazarded that she could see as how I maybe looked a tiny bit younger, but she sounded dubious behind her reassurances. But perhaps this was as it was meant to be, an infinitely subtle Mies van der Rohe aesthetic of rejuvenation. Less is more even when it looks like less. Or perhaps I had expected too much, in the way of constitutionally skeptical or rejection-sensitive people who arm themselves for disappointment but secretly harbor the most unrealistic of hopes.

Except the truth is that I noticed, and that's—or so I tell myself—what really matters. I can see it, a slight freshening of my expression, a less haggard look around the eyes, a greater definition around the jaw line, the general suggestion of a less worn-out contour. Dr. Brandt's newest cream, Crease Release, which is sold out wherever it's carried, might add to the effect if only I weren't too lazy to apply it and then wait two minutes to reapply it for the proper lifting effect. Meanwhile, I've been doing a lot of thinking about the future, anticipating my 60th birthday, which, given the way time speeds up once you've hit 30, is just around the corner. And here's what I'm working toward: forget the apologies and the cringing. I plan on borrowing from a little-known Nepalese ceremony that calls for me to be carried aloft on a palanquin for all the world to see. Since I live on the Upper East Side and not in a tiny prelapsarian village, this celebratory rite of passage will have to take place squarely on Madison Avenue. I can just see the faces of the toned and implausibly tight-faced women out walking their dogs as I am carried past first Dean & DeLuca and then Schweitzer Linen, where featured in the window is a boudoir pillow inscribed with the saying "Age is a number and mine is unlisted." Just the thought of it makes me smile, adding a crease or two in the process. But what the hell. By then I hope to be well on my way to aging dangerously.

QUESTIONS

1. Do you agree with the author that we live in an age-phobic culture? What social pressures and cultural practices are often associated with the largely stigmatized aging process?

2. In what ways is aging a gendered process? Why does the author find herself in the office of plastic surgeons on the eve of her fiftieth birthday? What does she try to tell us about women's experience of growing old in the current youth-centered culture?

3. What role is played by the cosmetic industry in the anti-aging culture? What kind of social values and norms are promoted by the industry? How does it impact women's aging experience?
4. How does the author feel about the results of her own facial surgery? What critiques of ageism and mockeries against the practice of "cosmetic rejuvenation" are embedded in her personal story?

The Little Law that Could (2001)

Denise Kiernan

Title IX of the Educational Amendment Acts of 1972 has had dramatic effects on women's opportunities in education—but there is much work yet to do. A law usually associated with women's increased participation in sports, Title IX originally was created to address broader issues of discrimination in educational institutions such as employment and admissions. This essay from Ms. *magazine explains the history of the bill we have come to know as Title IX and the breadth—and limits—of its impact.*

Angela was home for the summer and wanted to play a little pick-up hockey at her local rink. "No women," said the woman guarding the entrance.

"I can really play," she said, assuming the attendant was concerned for her safety on the ice.

"No women."

The place: Saint Clair Shores, Michigan.

The year: 1999.

"The Little Law That Could," by Denise Kiernan, reprinted from *Ms.*, February/March 2001, pp. 19–25.

The player: Angela Ruggiero, 1998 Olympic hockey gold medalist.

Ruggerio is one of thousands of women athletes who benefited from Title IX of the Education Amendments of 1972, the federal law that prohibits discrimination in federally funded educational programs. That Ruggiero played on an Olympic ice hockey team is evidence of how far women have come since Title IX. That she was turned away from her hometown rink is a sign of how far we still have to go—not just in the courts but in a culture that still resists women's evolving roles.

Perhaps no other legislative act has had a greater impact on the lives of girls and women in the United States, yet remains so misunderstood. Its original purpose has been clouded by media squabbles and misinformation campaigns and has been overshadowed by highly publicized events that have lulled us into a false sense of security.

Although Title IX is now synonymous with equality in women's sports, it originally had nothing to do with athletics. In order to look at where the legislation is headed, it's helpful to glance back at where it started—not with soccer and basketball players but with Ivy League students and college professors.

As a schoolgirl in the 1930s and '40s, Bernice Sandler wanted to do three things: change the inkwells, operate the slide projectors, and be a school crossing guard. But girls weren't allowed to do any of these things, and at that time, there was no word to explain this inequity.

By 1969, when Sandler was turned down three times for three different jobs as a professor, the word "sexism" was still only rarely used. "Too strong for a woman" was part of the justification for one of the rejections. The assumption that she would miss work if her children were sick was another.

Now 72, Sandler says that she knew what happened to her was immoral and suspected it could be illegal. She was right about the former but wrong about the latter. While there were laws against various types of discrimination, there were loopholes that failed to protect women at educational institutions.

- Title VII of the Civil Rights Act prohibited discrimination in employment on the basis of race, color, religion, national origin, and sex but excluded educational institutions.

- Title VI of the Civil Rights Act prohibited discrimination in federally assisted programs—which could include educational institutions—but only on the basis of race, color, and national origin, not sex.
- The Equal Pay Act prohibited salary discrimination on the basis of sex, but not for professional and administrative employees, which included professors.

Sandler was curious about what African Americans had done in terms of desegregation in education. Her curiosity led her to a report by the U.S. Commission on Civil Rights, which mentioned Executive Order 11246, prohibiting federal contractors from discrimination in employment based on race, color, religion, and national origin. But there was a footnote: President Lyndon Johnson had amended this executive order to include discrimination based on sex. Sandler reasoned that the amendment gave women who were fighting discrimination at educational institutions that received federal funds a legal leg to stand on.

To confirm her suspicion, she called the Department of Labor's Office of Federal Contract Compliance and met with a higher-up, who assured her she was right but asked her not to disclose his name. Though he couldn't publicly support her, he helped her file a complaint, and a secret alliance was forged. "He was essentially telling me how to put pressure on his office," Sandler says. "I knew very little about legislation and lobbying, and he taught me."

Sandler found an ad in the newspaper that put her in touch with the Women's Equity Action League (WEAL) and together they filed a class-action complaint against all colleges and universities with federal contracts and then launched a nationwide campaign inviting women to share their stories. Since Sandler alone was named in the subsequent complaints, women could gather evidence about discrimination and file charges without being named.

Sandler sent copies of all complaints that WEAL received to Representative Edith Green (D.-Oreg.), chair of the special subcommittee on education and a WEAL advisory board member. For seven days during the summer of 1970, Green held the first ever congressional hearing on women's education and employment. The bill that would become Title IX was born. It reads: "No person in the United States shall, on the basis of sex, be excluded from participation in, be denied the benefits of, or be subjected to discrimination under any educational program or activity receiving federal financial assistance."

The testimonies heard by Congress—or "horror stories," as Sandler describes them—focused on higher education. One woman professor said she taught at a university for free because the school told her that her husband worked there and they could afford to pay only one of them. More than one woman was told that she would not get tenure because, well, she was a woman.

There were complaints that many want ads were still segregated according to sex and that there were strict quotas limiting the number of women students allowed into universities in general—and medical and law programs in particular. Women said they were often required to have higher test scores than men. And it was reported that over one three-year period in the 1960s, the state of Virginia refused 21,000 women admission to state institutions. During the same period, Sandler says, "not one male student was rejected."

Green dissuaded Sandler and others from lobbying prior to the final passage of the House bill, reasoning that the less attention drawn to it the better. She was right. Indiana's Democratic Senator Birch Bayh ushered the bill through the Senate—where athletics were mentioned for the first time. The concern was that under the bill, women would be allowed to play football, and so a colloquy was added stating that they would not. (Green also snuck in an amendment to the Equal Pay Act to include administrators and executives, which helped professors.) Congress passed Title IX on June 23, 1972, and on July 1, President Richard Nixon signed it into law. "He's not thinking Title IX is a big deal," Sandler says. "It's lust a little thing that's in there."

Sexual harassment was not originally discussed during the drafting of the legislation. The phrase "sexual harassment" didn't even exist until around 1975. But in 1976, a federal case held that sexual harassment was a form of sexual discrimination in the workplace, and in 1977, the first sexual harassment charges against an educational institution (Yale) were filed under Title IX. The case was lost, but, the judge made clear that sexual harassment was a form of discrimination. And in 1992, the Supreme

Court ruled that monetary damages can be awarded under Title IX.

During the same year, ten-year-old LaShonda Davis told her mother, Aurelia, about the fifth-grade boy who kept rubbing against her and telling her that he wanted to have sex with her. Five months of repeated complaints to all the right authorities had little result. LaShonda's grades dropped, and she eventually wrote a suicide note. A criminal complaint was filed, and the boy pled guilty to sexual battery. Aurelia Davis then sued the Monroe County school board under Title IX. In June of 1999, the Supreme Court ruled in favor of the Davises. Verna Williams, lead counsel on the case, says the decision "is making schools reevaluate how they deal with sexual harassment."

And they'd better. Statistics gathered by the American Association of University Women show that 81 percent of students surveyed (85 percent of girls, 76 percent of boys) have experienced sexual harassment. Williams says the Davis case also offsets some of the backlash caused by highly publicized incidents that portray sexual harassment cases as political correctness run amok, like the boy who made the papers after kissing a fellow pupil. "It makes sexual harassment appear to be a joke," says Williams. "That the gender police are out to get boys." Compare that to a call Williams got about second-grade boys pretending to rape a girl. "That kind of stuff doesn't get attention," she says.

But one of Title IX's most significant developments came about two years after its passage when the National Collegiate Athletic Association (NCAA) inquired whether this new law applied to athletics.

"Slowly but surely the implications became apparent," says Donna Lopiano, now executive director of the Women's Sports Foundation, and a former championship softball player. This aspect of education suddenly presented very quantifiable inequities.

"All hell broke loose," says Lopiano.

Growing up in the 1950s and '60s, Lopiano, like Sandler, wanted to be on safety patrol. She also wanted to take wood shop, be an altar girl—and play in Little League.

Lopiano was so good that at ten, when she tried out for Little League, she was drafted first. She was waiting for her uniform when a father walked up to her with the Little League rule book that clearly stated girls were not allowed to play. She went home and cried. Girls wouldn't be allowed to play in Little League until around the same time that a grown-up Lopiano and the Association for Intercollegiate Athletics for Women sat across the table from representatives of the NCAA—which at that time did not govern women's sports—and the American Football Coaches Association to iron out the regulations for Title IX.

The women said to "'split the pie down the middle,' and the guys fell off their chairs," Lopiano laughs. What the football coaches and NCAA came back with was the now highly contested three-pronged test. Only one prong must be met for an institution to be in compliance: 1. "Substantial proportionality"—the percentage of female undergrads must be roughly equal to the percentage of female athletes; 2. Proof of "fully and effectively accommodating the interests and abilities of women"; 3. "A history and continuing practice of adding teams."

Lopiano believed the three-pronged test was a way for the football folks to maintain the status quo, and a glance at 1973 stats supports that. With 60 percent of college students being male, men would have the financial upper hand in proportionality. There was an assumption that women weren't interested in sports, so item 2 wasn't a problem. And item 3 looked like it gave colleges a never-ending period to achieve compliance.

The football coaches and NCAA walked away with what they considered to be a win over the women, and at that time no one had any idea what an impact Title IX would have on athletics. The issue of sports was so important, says Lopiano, because "it was a highly visible cultural institution that was previously all male. It's sex-separate, in-your-face discrimination. And it played into the press coverage beautifully."

Nearly 30 years after it was devised, the three-pronged test remains controversial. And, with women making up more than 50 percent of college enrollment and women's sports more popular than ever, Title IX itself has come under fire from school administrators who don't want to pay for women's teams.

In 1984, a court decision known as *Grove City* v. *Bell* limited the jurisdiction of Title IX to specific *programs* that received federal funding, such as financial aid, rather than to *institutions* that received federal funds. This decision exempted almost all athletic programs from Title IX compliance from 1984 to 1988.

But the most visible legal decision regarding athletics and

Title IX came in 1996—*Cohen* v. *Brown University*—in which a federal appeals court upheld a 1993 district court ruling that Brown illegally discriminated against its female athletes. (*Ms.*, January/February 1998) Brown gymnast Amy Cohen, in response to her squad being cut from the varsity program, hoped that the threat of a lawsuit would get the school to comply. Instead, the school retaliated, curtailing the women's use of the locker rooms and failing to provide them with athletic trainers. In the end, Brown's legal fees far surpassed the $64,000 that would have been required to keep both the women's gymnastics and volleyball teams on the varsity roster.

Cohen, meanwhile, had become a poster girl for Title IX, riding a wave of media attention paid to women athletes. The late 1990s was a watershed: U.S. women competed for the first time in Olympic soccer and won the gold; ditto for the first U.S. women's Olympic ice hockey team. There was the birth of the Women's National Basketball Association (WNBA). The 1999 Women's World Cup soccer competition proved that not only could women play sports, but hundreds of thousands of people would pay to watch them do it. With all this, it's easy to overlook the onset of backlash. As Lopiano says, "A singular event gives the impression that the problem is over with."

And with the backlash centering around the *Q* word—quotas—Title IX has come full circle. In 1972, *proponents* of Title IX wanted to eliminate quotas since they were being used to limit the number of women allowed into colleges. Now it's the *opponents* of Title IX who want to eliminate what they consider a gender quota—the proportionality aspect of Title IX compliance in athletics.

College wrestling, more than any other college sport, has undergone a decline in recent years, and Title IX apparently presented a convenient scapegoat when wrestling coaches started looking for a reason for the decline. Anti-Title IX groups like Americans Against Quotas and the Independent Women's Forum point to a high number of cancelled wrestling programs—evidence, they say, that opportunities are being wrenched from boys and foisted on girls who are not even interested. Indeed, when money is tight, school administrators often *do* cut minor men's teams, such as wrestling, in order to add women's teams and thus comply with Title IX. This gives athletic directors an opportunity to say that Title IX is the reason they don't have money for minor mens' sports instead of looking at funding for major sports, like football or basketball. Speaker of the House and former wrestling coach Dennis Hastert has backed efforts to change Title IX enforcement.

Says Lopiano: "People don't realize that the regs the wrestling coaches are now trying to change—proportionality and the rest—was the position of the NCAA and the American Football Coaches Association—not the women."

But Title IX is an easy target compared to the behemoth budgets of football and basketball, which take up 69 percent of the men's athletic operating budgets of Division I-A schools. In 1997, the average Division I school spent $576,000 on men's football compared with the $478,000 it spent on *all* its women's sports programs. "The football coaches are keeping their mouths shut, trying to let the wrestling coaches fight their battle for them," says Lopiano. "The wrestling coaches are being duped."

In fact, if the coaches look at the numbers, they'd see that most schools have a long way to go before women's sports outspend men's. Women receive only 38 percent of all athletic scholarship money, 27 percent of recruiting money, and 23 percent of overall athletic budgets. Between 1992 and 1997, men's athletic operating budgets increased 139 percent, women's increased 89 percent. For every new dollar spent on women, three were spent on men.

And while many wrestling advocates point to Title IX as the reason for the sport's decline, it was during the four years that *Grove City* was in effect (1984–88) and Title IX was benched that wrestling experienced a decline of 18.3 percent. That's greater than the 15.6 percent decline it experienced in the ten years after Title IX's jurisdiction over athletics was reinstated.

While sports gets the lion's share of Title IX play, with sexual harassment a close second, the issue looming on the horizon is one that hearkens back to inequities commonplace in Title IX's infancy: career and vocational education.

Carpentry, auto mechanics. It's déjà vu all over again in middle and high schools where girls tend not to get the kind of training that translates into high pay. Thirty years ago girls weren't even allowed in most wood shop or auto mechanics classes. Now, there are other concerns, such as counselors who hand out pamphlets about careers in construction to males but not to females and teachers who pay less attention to girls in their shop classes.

In 1997, when the National Coalition for Women and Girls in Education published its report card on gender equity for Title IX's twenty-fifth anniversary, the organization gave career education a C, noting that "sex segregation persists in vocational education—men are clustered in high-skill, high-wage job tracks, women in the low-wage, traditionally female tracks." The report further noted that the new programs that came out of Congress's School-to-Work Opportunities Act of 1994 "are also segregated by sex."

Vocational education "is going to be an emerging issue," says Verna Williams. "These are avenues that girls typically don't go into, or if they do, they're finding it really hard to stick it out." While no cases are currently being argued, Williams has received anecdotal evidence of problems. "So, for example," Williams says, "a female student in a carpentry class is assigned to sweeping up after the boys while the boys are learning how to make cabinets."

The potential damage is even greater in areas where technology is making vocational education a lucrative option. Auto mechanics, in particular, focuses on technological advances that provide students with training that enables them to earn as much as $80,000 a year, right out of high school. "This will be an avenue for kids who may not go to college," says Williams. "It's like a digital divide issue, with a gender spin."

So, where does that leave Title IX? Although women's sports may seem to draw too much attention from Title IX's other aspects, sports remains an appropriate arena in which to fight the gender equity battle. Last year was the first year women competed in Olympic pole vaulting. A new professional women's soccer league is set to launch. The Little League reject who made a gas mask instead of an Easter bonnet in art class because she wasn't allowed to take shop, sat at her brother's wedding and laughed to herself at the sight of an altar girl whose Adidas peeked out from under her robe. Lopiano described it as "the perfect snapshot of change."

So after 28 years, it's part celebration, part wake-up call. The Independent Women's Forum wants to dismantle Title IX, while athletic girls and their families fight to preserve it. And no sane politician wants to ostracize the female voter in what's odiously come to be known as the era of the "soccer mom."

But a gold medal still doesn't get a gal on the ice at her

hometown rink. "People recognize we're not just talking about jobs," Sandler says. "It's about changing the world, and that makes people very scared."

QUESTIONS

1. What is the intention of Title IX? What does it address specifically? How does it differ from other gender equity legislation? Give examples.
2. How did the original Title IX bill come into formation?
3. Why has the bill come to be primarily associated with sports?
4. Why is proportionality in sports important? Does proportionality insure equity? Why or why not?
5. Why might sports be such a prominent arena for working out tension over Title IX? Why does such resistance exist to full implementation of Title IX, particularly in sports?
6. What examples of inequity in sports funding, participation and support have you experienced or witnessed in the world around you?

SOMETHING IS WRONG HERE AND IT'S NOT ME: CHALLENGING THE DILEMMAS THAT BLOCK GIRLS' SUCCESS (1989)

Lee Ann Bell

As part of a larger project, Lee Ann Bell interviews 26 girls between third and sixth grade to explore the internal messages that can interfere with young girls' achievement drive. Exploring five "core dilemmas" confronting girls in competitive situations, Bell clarifies how gender shapes the way events are experienced and interpreted.

"I bet all you do is study. You probably never have fun."
"I was just lucky. I'm sure yours was just as good."

These quotes are taken from a discussion with a group of third and fourth grade girls in Project REACH, a project designed to explore internal barriers to girls' achievement.[1] Two students

"Something Is Wrong Here and It's Not Me: Challenging the Dilemmas that Block Girls' Success," by Lee Ann Bell, reprinted from *Journal for the Education of the Gifted*, Vol. 12, No. 2, 1989.

were comparing their achievement on a project for which one of them has received an award. In the initial role play of this incident, the girl who did not win was envious and responded by teasing the other girl. The other girl, in an attempt to minimize the differences between them, downplayed her achievement. This taunt and the response to it encapsulate a core dilemma girls experience in school, the perceived disjunction between achievement and affiliation.

Something *is* wrong here. Each girl ends up feeling bad about herself. The "winner" at best feels uncomfortable and at worst undeserving. The "loser" feels inadequate, jealous and guilty for her reaction. Yet, this discomfort with competitive achievement situations is not uncommon among girls (Dweck, et al., 1978; Horner, 1972; Nicholls, 1975; Stein & Bailey, 1973.) Suggested interventions often seek to raise female aspirations and self-esteem (Kerr, 1983; Wilson, 1982) but whether intentional or not, present the problem as something *in* girls that needs to be fixed.

Girls who exhibit outstanding academic ability, intense commitment to their chosen interests, leadership and critical judgment are at risk in public schools today (Callahan, 1980; Rodenstein, Pfleger & Colangelo, 1977). By fourth grade, they begin to lose self-confidence, become extremely self-critical, and often lower their effort and aspirations in order to conform to gender stereotyped social expectations (Entwisle & Baker, 1983; Robinson-Awana, Kehle & Jenson, 1986). Underachievement among girls with high potential begins to emerge by fourth or fifth grade and becomes widespread by junior high school (Fitzpatrick, 1978; Olshen & Matthews, 1987; Callahan, 1980). As girls pull back from achieving to their fullest they drastically reduce their options for the future.

Project REACH sought to understand the core dilemmas girls experience in school from the perspective of the girls themselves. We identified a pool of high potential girls in one urban elementary school. From this pool, we randomly selected a group of 26 girls within racial/ethnic and economic categories which matched the diversity of the district as a whole (15% Hispanic, 28% Black, 57% White, 39% eligible for free or reduced lunch). Thirteen were in third and fourth grade and thirteen in fifth and sixth grade.[2] We met weekly for one hour with each group for fourteen weeks to explore achievement-related issues identified in educational and psychological literature as problematic for females. The dilemmas posed in this paper came from discussions with this diverse group of eight to eleven year old girls.

Dilemma #1: Smart vs. Social

The segment of dialogue quoted at the beginning of this article illustrates one core dilemma girls experience, the perception that achievement and affiliation are mutually exclusive. We asked the girls to examine the science contest situation more closely and think of alternatives that would enable both girls to feel good about themselves *and* get what they want; to feel good about achieving *and* get the friendship and support they value. The girls eagerly engaged in a discussion which yielded the following options: "tear the trophy in half," "give it to the teacher," "leave it in school," "give half to the other girls," "give the trophy away, it's just a piece of metal." All of the suggested options sacrificed achievement in order to preserve the relationship.

We reiterated our challenge to the group to find a solution that would affirm both girls. They struggled and seemed stuck until Hadley, a fourth grader, offered:

> When they [the judges] pick, probably a lot of people *could* have gotten first place, but they can only pick one. She wasn't there [to hear the judging process], she could have won too.

The sense of breakthrough was palpable. Immediately several new solutions emerged. All aimed at restructuring the situation to allow many people to do creative, high quality projects by working together cooperatively. The problem was externalized onto the system of judging rather than internalized as defects in individual girls. By expanding the problem to the larger context, in this case the competitive structure of the situation, the girls broke through the either/or dilemma and generated new options for confronting competitive situations. This process was used to examine additional dilemmas presented below.

Dilemma #2: Silence vs. Bragging

Success is a loaded experience for females that incorporates a myriad of conflicting feelings, values and cultural messages about femininity. Girls receive contradictory messages about success from a competitively-oriented society that on the one hand claims females can be and do anything, but on the other promotes the belief that females should be "feminine" (e.g., passive and protected from risk) (Chodorow, 1974). The literature on achievement often claims that females avoid success because it conflicts with the feminine role (Horner, 1972), but discussions with Project REACH girls revealed just how complicated this issue is. The girls expressed pride in success but did not want to achieve it at the expense of others. Their responses support Sassen's (1980) assertion that females don't fear success itself so much as the social isolation with which they associate success.

This theme of hiding success for fear of seeming to put oneself above others was prevalent among all the girls in our sample regardless of grade. The student who won the science prize grappled with the dilemma in the following way:[3]

> *Jane:* (after receiving a compliment on her prize): Well, I don't feel that great when you say that to me because I feel like everybody's equal and everybody should have gotten a prize no matter what they did. I think Chris should've gotten it.
>
> *Myra:* OK, Jane, tell the group why you didn't say "I feel good about winning this prize."
>
> *Jane:* Well, because I feel like um, like everybody's looking at me and um saying "Oh, she shouldn't have won that prize, I should have won," and everybody's gonna be mad at me because, um, I won and they didn't.
>
> *Myra:* Is there any situation that you could think of where you won an honor that you were deserving of and feel good about it?
>
> *Jane:* If other people won also.

While Jane feels uncomfortable about acknowledging her success publicly, she does feel good about her accomplishment.

Myra: When you said you didn't want to accept a compliment and thought other people should win, did you also really think you deserved it deep down? Just within yourself, not worrying about other people?

Jane: Yeah, I thought I deserved it but I didn't want to say it because then other people might think I was bragging.

Betsy: Jane, when you got the part of [a lead in the school play] and people said like congratulations and stuff, what did you do?

Jane: Well, I tried not to talk about it too much. I talked about it sometimes but you know, like with Tommy. You know I always eat with Melissa, Linda and Tommy. Well, um, he really wanted that part so I tried not to talk about it cuz I didn't want to make anyone feel bad.

The literature on achievement motivation indicates that girls are more likely to attribute success to external causes such as luck, timing or the help of others while boys are more likely to take credit for success by attributing it to ability or effort (Dweck, et al., 1978; Maehr & Nicholls, 1980). Our research found that girls learn to muffle acknowledgement of their successes in order to avoid the appearance of "bragging."

The term "bragging" was brought up so repeatedly by girls in both groups that we began to see it as symbolizing a core issue. This issue has at least two aspects. First, girls do not like to place themselves above others, partly because they fear ostracism but also because they value social solidarity. Second, girls may see more clearly the actual conditions that govern success in a competitive system.

Black and Hispanic children evidence similar conflicts with success (Lindstrom & Van Sant, 1986). Marginality provides insight into the unspoken norms governing social situations, norms that are often invisible to those who benefit from and thus have no reason to question the status quo (Miller, 1986). As members of subordinate groups, perhaps girls and minority boys experience a value conflict that the dominant group does not. Part of the difficulty they have in taking credit for success may be the result of perceptive insight into a competitive system that mystifies the conditions for success. That is, although the system purports that individual effort alone is necessary, in fact, social class, race, status and opportunity have a great deal to do with actual achievement.

To the extent that girls do not become conscious of the conflicting values embedded in their reaction to success, they internalize the problem. Their ambivalence about success can lead to failure to own their achievements, an unwillingness to take risks in order to achieve, and ultimately an avoidance of success situations. When girls learn to publicly affirm their achievements and at the same time take seriously their aversion to competitive structures, they can then consider more than an either/or option to this dilemma.

Dilemma #3: Failure vs. Perfection

Girls also receive conflicting messages about failure. The literature suggests that girls are more likely to internalize failure while boys are more likely to externalize it (Frieze, 1980). Boys' ability to more easily accept and learn from failure is attributed to their wider experience with competitive team sports and the greater amount of critical, academic feedback they receive from teachers (Sadker & Sadker, 1982). The failure dilemma for girls is further confounded by race since many teachers give less attention and hold lower expectations for Black students (Rubovitz & Maehr, 1973); reward nonacademic, custodial behaviors in Black girls (Scott-Jones & Clark, 1986; Grant, 1984) and give Black girls fewer opportunities to respond in the classroom than they do boys and White girls (Irvine, 1986).

We asked each of our girls to tell about a time when she did poorly or failed. Many described athletic or academic situations. One fourth grader, gives this representative example:

> *Alexis:* I was at baseball and we were losing the game. I was the last person to bat and I had to not get out. And I got out and they all said, "You're no good."
>
> *Evy:* How did that make you feel?
>
> *Alexis:* Like a basket case!

The result of doing poorly or failing was embarrassment and humiliation. We asked, "When you make a mistake or fail like everyone does, what do you do to make yourself feel better?"

Their responses were to withdraw from the situation and to express or avoid feelings. None focused on ways to improve their performance or challenge the dynamics of the situation itself.

Anika: I lie to myself and say I don't care.

Judith: I turn my head away from everyone till everyone stops laughing. When they try to act nice, I'll be cheered up by them.

Rosa: I call my friend up and talk for two or three hours.

Celeste: I write something on notes then I hide them away in my treasure box.

We asked them to consider how they might respond differently. They struggled to move beyond the all or nothing dilemma of performing with perfection or withdrawing, but no other alternatives emerged until we suggested the possibility of asserting their feelings and ideas for change within the situation itself. We described a formula used in assertiveness training for learning to make an assertive statement:

"I feel __________ when you __________ because __________." The girls rehearsed this statement in response to the failure situations they had recounted previously:

Kamillah: I feel angry when you say that I can't act because I study a lot and I learn my lines.

Amy: I feel insulted when you say I should give up on math because it's not fair. I could just work harder and I could try to do it.

Dilemma #4: Media "Beauty" vs. Marginality

The girls were extremely self-conscious about how they looked on the videotapes. This led us to explore the role physical appearance plays in girls' attitudes toward success. We asked them to list the media messages females receive about how we should look in order to be successful. The following list (a composite of both groups) was generated:

tall
thin
beautiful
pretty
long, wavy hair
dainty personality
matching clothes
look neat and in place, even with babies
blonde
rich
skinny
popular
fur coats
nice figure
accessories (extra stuff)
blue-eyed
long hair
good looking
famous
wear makeup
nice smile
clothes and dress for every occasion

We then displayed a collection of pictures we had assembled on three walls of the room. These pictures included girls and women of all sizes, shapes, races, ages, and social classes doing a variety of interesting things. We asked the girls to examine the pictures and make a list of all the ways in which they contradicted the media messages. Their new list said: "You can be successful and look . . .

fat
old
poor
dressy
handicapped
wrinkly
many different ways
lots of different shades and colors
skinny
black
rich

Spanish
not rich
beautiful or not beautiful
doing different things
young
white
sloppy
in the middle
tough
boyish or feminine
old, young, and in-between

The girls discussed the differences between the two lists and then worked together on a definition of beauty that would include all the females in the pictures:

Beauty is . . . doing your own thing
having lots of interests
believing in yourself
looking how you want to . . .

Through this activity the girls challenged the "Success = Beauty" dilemma and created new options for themselves. This proved to be a powerful session having a lasting impact as evidenced by their continual references to it. At the beginning of this session one third grade Black girl whispered to me, "I really want to be white. I told my parents and that's what I want." At the end of the session we asked each girl to write an essay entitled: "Ways in which I am beautiful." This girl then wrote, "I am beautiful because I am proud of my race, I'm smart and I have pretty brown eyes." Another girl who had initially stated that she wanted to look like Vanna White, a stereotypic blonde, blue-eyed television game show hostess, later wrote, "I am beautiful because I'm good in school, I'm Puerto Rican and Dominican, and I'm good at sports."

Dilemma #5: Passive vs. Aggressive

Research indicates that boys, especially White boys, demand and receive more attention from teachers than girls (Grant, 1984; Irvine,

1986). Our girls expressed annoyance with the greater attention boys receive and with their method of getting this attention.

> *Judith:* Sometimes, when the boys are uh with us they always misbehave and make the teachers scream and I hate it. I hate to hear people scream.

In addition to giving boys more attention, teachers often reward passivity and punish assertiveness in girls as well (Sadker & Sadker, 1982).

For our girls the alternatives to competing with boys for teacher attention were either to withdraw and be passive ("I just won't raise my hand anymore") or fight back ("I'll punch him out"). In this dilemma, clear racial differences emerged, with White and Hispanic girls more likely to withdraw and Black girls more likely to fight back. Either way, boys' behavior defines the situation and the girls are left to react.

The consequences are often negative for girls. Those girls who withdraw in response to boys' behavior lose opportunities to respond in class, to verbally explore their ideas, to actively shape the classroom, and to meet their own needs and desires. Those girls who fight back also receive more teacher disapproval and punishment for their assertiveness. This dilemma is especially damaging for Black girls whose resistance becomes a source of teacher hostility and disciplinary action.

We explored this dilemma by asking the girls to describe various situations in school that bothered them and develop alternative responses. Those girls who tended to withdraw or avoid expressing their needs were encouraged to respond actively. Those girls who tended to fight back in self-defeating or ineffective ways practiced asserting themselves more effectively, assertively rather than aggressively.

An interesting outcome of one discussion was observed in one fourth grade classroom following this session. The teacher was working with a small reading group and, as we had noticed repeatedly in our classroom observations, boys dominated the group by raising their hands more, calling out for the teacher's attention and misbehaving. One of our girls, small for her age and usually quiet, turned to a boy next to her who was pounding the table to get the teacher's attention and said, "When you do that it annoys me. Please control yourself. I want a chance to answer the question."

Group support for such endeavors is crucial. Students, especially girls, who respond assertively to authority figures run a high risk of punishment. Group support may increase the likelihood of being taken seriously.

Until adults change, however, girls are caught in the bind of conforming or being punished. Educators and counselors concerned about girls' achievement must work to challenge and change adult attitudes, behaviors and classroom structures that block girls' potential. Without such changes girls' resistance will continue to be met with individual and structural, conscious and unconscious barriers that undermine their attempts to participate fully and successfully in all areas of school.

Conclusion

Discussing dilemmas about achievement in a supportive environment with others can be a powerful form of consciousness raising for girls. The group context counteracts isolation by showing us that the problems we experience as "mine alone" are in fact shared by many others.

Group discussion and support also provide a way to analyze the social messages and behaviors that reinforce feelings of inadequacy and fears about achievement. Girls can help each other understand and critique the situations that create achievement-related conflicts and explore alternatives that would allow for achievement and connection to others. By defining the problem collectively, girls can then brainstorm ways to change the situation. Finally, females of all ages can organize to implement changes in the oppressive structures and situations that devalue female capacities and choices. Like consciousness raising for adults, these groups help their participants to stop asking "What's wrong with me?" and instead learn to say "What's wrong out there and what can we do collectively to change it for the better?"[4]

[1992]

NOTES

1. The research for Project REACH was conducted during the 1987–1988 school year. Methods included ethnographic observations in classrooms, interviews with teachers and fourteen one hour sessions with third/fourth and fifth/sixth grade groups. This article draws upon only one portion of the data collected, the transcripts of the videotapes of the sessions with the girls.
2. The pool from which sample girls were drawn was established in cooperation with already established procedures of the gifted/talented program in the district. These procedures focused on academic ability and included IQ scores and parent and teacher nomination. Additional methods to identify athletic, artistic, creative and social ability were added to the criteria used by the district in developing the pool from which our sample was drawn.
3. Fictitious names were used for all the girls quoted in this article.
4. The Coopersmith Self-Esteem Inventory was administered as a pre/post test but these data have not yet been analyzed. Anecdotal comments from the principal, teachers and parents suggest that the program had a positive effect in raising the confidence of the girls in the sample group. We have also received letters from parents requesting that their daughters be allowed to continue with the program.

REFERENCES

Callahan, C. (1980). The gifted girl: An anomaly? *Roeper Review*, Vol. 2, No. 3, Feb–Mar.

Chodorow, N. (1974). Family structure and feminine personality. In M. Rosaldo and L. Lamphere (Eds.). *Women, Culture and Society*. Stanford, CA: Stanford University Press.

Dweck, C., Davidson, W., Nelson, S., and Enna, B. (1978). Sex differences in learned helplessness: II. The contingencies of evaluative feedback in the classroom and III. An experimental analysis. *Developmental Psychology*, Vol. 14, No. 3, 268–276.

Entwisle, D., and Baker, D. (1983). Gender and young children's expectations for performance in arithmetic. *Developmental Psychology*, 19, 200–209.

Fitzpatrick, J. (1978). Academic achievement, other-directedness and attitudes toward women's roles in bright adolescent females. *Journal of Educational Psychology*, Vol. 70, No. 4, 650–654.

Frieze, I. (1980). Beliefs about success and failure in the classroom. In J. H. McMillen (Ed.), *The social psychology of school learning*. New York: Academic Press.

Grant, L. (1984). Black females' "place" in desegregated classrooms. *Sociology of Education*. Vol. 57 (April): 98–111.

Horner, M. (1972). Toward an understanding of achievement-related conflicts in women. *Journal of Social Issues*. Vol. 28, 157–175.

Irvine, J. (1986). Teacher-student interactions: Effects of student race, sex and grade level. *Journal of Educational Psychology*, Vol. 78, No. 1, 14–21.

Kerr, B. (1983). Raising the career aspirations of gifted girls. *Vocational Guidance Quarterly*, Vol. 32, 37–43.

Lindstrom, R., and Van Sant, S. (1986). Special issues in working with gifted minority adolescents. *Journal of Counseling and Development*. Vol. 64, May, 583–586.

Maehr, M. and Nicholls, J. (1980). Culture and achievement motivation: A second look. In N. Warren (Ed.), *Studies in Cross-Cultural Psychology Vol 2*. New York: Academic Press.

Miller, J. B. (1986). *Toward a New Psychology of Women*. Boston: Beacon Press.

Nicholls, J. (1975). Causal attributions and other achievement-related cognitions: Effects of task outcomes, attainment value and sex. *Journal of Personality and Social Psychology*. Vol. 31, 379–389.

Olshen, S., and Matthews, D. (1987). The disappearance of giftedness in girls: An intervention strategy. *Roeper Review*. Vol. 9, No. 4, 251–254.

Robinson-Awana, P., Kehle, T., and Jenson, W. (1986). But what about smart girls? Adolescent self-esteem and sex role perceptions as a function of academic achievement. *Journal of Educational Psychology*. Vol. 78, No. 3, 179–183.

Rodenstein, J., Pfleger, L., and Colangelo, N. (1977). Career development of gifted women. *The Gifted Child Quarterly*, 21, 340–347.

Rubovitz, P. and Maehr, M. (1973). Pygmalion, black and white. *Journal of Personality and Social Psychology*. Vol. 25, 210–218.

Sadker, M., and Sadker, D. (1982). *Sex Equity Handbook for Schools*. New York: Longman.

Sassen, G. (1980). Success anxiety in women: A constructivist interpretation of its sources and significance. *Harvard Educational Review, 50,* 13–25.

Scott-Jones, D., and Clark, M. (March 1986). The school experience of black girls: The interaction of gender, race, and socioeconomic status. *Phi Delta Kappa,* 520–526.

Stein, A., and Bailey, N. (1973). The socialization of achievement orientation in females. *Psychological Bulletin, 80,* 345–366.

Wilson, S. (1982). A new decade: The gifted and career choice. *Vocational Guidance Quarterly, 31,* 53–59.

Questions

1. When do girls begin to lose confidence in themselves? What do researchers attribute this to? What factors interfere with girls' achievement drive?
2. What dilemmas does Bell explore in this essay? How do girls cope with these dilemmas? What feminine gender messages are evident in these dilemmas? How do these messages intensify the struggles of young girls in competitive situations? Does race make a difference in the way girls respond? Why don't young boys experience the same dilemmas?
3. What is the significance of the ages of the girls in this research? What implications do Bell's findings have for the achievement of females in later years?
4. Do teachers contribute to these dilemmas in girls? Whose responsibility is it to address the issue of girls' underachievement?

Gender Equity in the Classroom: The Unfinished Agenda (1994)

Myra Sadker, David Sadker, Lynn Fox, and Melinda Salata

Equal access to schools and colleges does not necessarily mean equal educational opportunities for women. In 1972, Congress passed Title IX of the Education Amendment Act, banning sex discrimination in education at all levels. Advocates for women had to lobby and file lawsuits to ensure enforcement of the sex discrimination ban. Yet recent research by a group of education professors at American University, presented in the following 1993 selection, reveals that women still do not enjoy educational equity.

In my science class the teacher never calls on me, and I feel like I don't exist. The other night I had a dream that I vanished.

"Gender Equity in the Classroom: The Unfinished Agenda," by Myra Sadker, David Sadker, Lynn Fox, and Melinda Salata, reprinted by permission from *The College Board Review*, No. 170, Winter 1993–1994.

Our interviews with female students have taught us that it is not just in science class that girls report the "disappearing syndrome." Female voices are also less likely to be heard in history and math classes, girls' names are less likely to be seen on lists of national merit finalists, and women's contributions infrequently appear in school textbooks. Twenty years after the passage of Title IX, the law prohibiting gender discrimination in U.S. schools, it is clear that most girls continue to receive a second-class education.

The very notion that women should be educated at all is a relatively recent development in U.S. history. It was not until late in the last century that the concept of educating girls beyond elementary school took hold. Even as women were gradually allowed to enter high school and college, the guiding principle in education was separate and unequal. Well into the twentieth century, boys and girls were assigned to sex-segregated classes and prepared for very different roles in life.

In 1833 Oberlin became the first college in the United States to admit women; but these early female college students were offered less rigorous courses and required to wait on male students and wash their clothes. Over the next several decades, only a few colleges followed suit in opening their doors to women. During the nineteenth century, a number of forward-thinking philanthropists and educators founded postsecondary schools for women—Mount Holyoke, Vassar, and the other seven-sister colleges. It was only in the aftermath of the Civil War that coeducation became more prevalent on campuses across the country, but even here economics and not equity was the driving force. Since the casualties of war meant the loss of male students and their tuition dollars, many universities turned to women to fill classrooms and replace lost revenues. In 1870 two-thirds of all universities still barred women. By 1900 more than two-thirds admitted them. But the spread of coeducation did not occur without a struggle. Consider that as late as the 1970s the all-male Ivy League colleges did not admit women, and even now state-supported Virginia Military Institute fights to maintain both its all-male status and its state funding.

Cycle of Loss

Today, most female and male students attend the same schools, sit in the same classrooms, and read the same books; but the legacy of inequity continues beneath the veneer of equal access. Although the school door is finally open and girls are inside the building, they remain second-class citizens.

In the early elementary school years, girls are ahead of boys academically, achieving higher standardized test scores in every area but science. By middle school, however, the test scores of female students begin a downward spiral that continues through high school, college, and even graduate school. Women consistently score lower than men on the Graduate Record Exams as well as on entrance tests for law, business, and medical schools. As a group, women are the only students who actually lose ground the longer they stay in school.

Ironically, falling female performance on tests is not mirrored by lower grades. Some have argued that women's grade-point averages are inflated because they tend not to take the allegedly more rigorous courses, such as advanced mathematics and physics. Another hypothesis suggests that female students get better grades in secondary school and college as a reward for effort and better behavior rather than a mastery of the material. Another possibility is that the standardized tests do not adequately measure what female students know and what they are really able to do. Whatever the reason, course grades and test grades paint very different academic pictures.

Lower test scores handicap girls in the competition for places at elite colleges. On average, girls score 50 to 60 points less than boys on the Scholastic Aptitude Test (SAT), recently renamed the Scholastic Assessment Test, which is required for admission to most colleges. Test scores also unlock scholarship money at 85 percent of private colleges and 90 percent of the public ones. For example, in 1991 boys scored so much higher on the Preliminary SAT/National Merit Scholarship Qualifying Test (PSAT/NMSQT) that they were nominated for two-thirds of the Merit Scholarships®—18,000 boys compared to 8,000 girls.[2]

The drop in test scores begins around the same time that another deeply troubling loss occurs in the lives of girls: self-esteem. There is a precipitous decline from elementary school to high school. Entering middle school, girls begin what is often the most turbulent period in their young lives. According to a national survey sponsored by the American Association of University Women, 60 percent of elementary school girls agreed with the statement "I'm happy the way I am," while only 37 percent still agreed in middle school. By high school, the level had dropped an astonishing 31 points to 29 percent, with fewer than three out of every 10 girls feeling good about themselves. According to the survey, the decline is far less dramatic for boys; 67 percent report being happy with themselves in elementary school, and this drops to 46 percent in high school.[3]

Recent research points to the relationship between academic achievement and self-esteem. Students who do well in school feel better about themselves; and in turn, they then feel more capable. For most female students, this connection has a negative twist and a cycle of loss is put into motion. As girls feel less good about themselves, their academic performance declines, and this poor performance further erodes their confidence. This pattern is particularly powerful in math and science classes, with only 18 percent of middle school girls describing themselves as good in these subjects, down from 31 percent in elementary school. It is not surprising that the testing gap between boys and girls is particularly wide in math and science.[3]

Inequity in Instruction

During the past decade, Myra and David Sadker have investigated verbal interaction patterns in elementary, secondary, and college classrooms in a variety of settings and subject areas. In addition, they have interviewed students and teachers across the country. In their new book, *Failing at Fairness: How America's Schools Cheat Girls*, they expose the microinequities that occur daily in classrooms across the United States—and they show how this imbalance in attention results in the lowering of girls' achievement and self-esteem.[1] Consider the following:

- From grade school to graduate school, girls receive less teacher attention and less useful teacher feedback.

- Girls talk significantly less than boys do in class. In elementary and secondary school, they are eight times less likely to call out comments. When they do, they are often reminded to raise their hands while similar behavior by boys is accepted.
- Girls rarely see mention of the contributions of women in the curricula; most textbooks continue to report male worlds.
- Too frequently female students become targets of unwanted sexual attention from male peers and sometimes even from administrators and teachers.

From omission in textbooks to inappropriate sexual comments to bias in teaching behavior, girls experience a powerful and often disabling education climate. A high school student from an affluent northeastern high school describes her own painful experience:

> My English teacher asks the class, "What is the purpose of the visit to Johannesburg?" . . . I know the answer, but I contemplate whether I should answer the question. The boys in the back are going to tease me like they harass all the other girls in our class . . . I want to tell them to shut up. But I stand alone. All of the other girls don't even let themselves be bold. Perhaps they are all content to be molded into society's image of what a girl should be like—submissive, sweet, feminine . . . In my ninth period class, I am actually afraid—of what [the boys] might say. . . . As my frustration builds, I promise myself that I will yell back at them. I say that everyday . . . and I never do it.[4]

Teachers not only call on male students more frequently than on females; they also allow boys to call out more often. This imbalance in instructional attention is greatest at the college level. Our research shows that approximately one-half of the students in college classrooms are silent, having no interaction whatsoever with the professor. Two-thirds of these silent students are women. This verbal domination is further heightened by the gender segregation of many of today's classes. Sometimes teachers seat girls and boys in different sections of the room, but more often students segregate themselves. Approximately one-half of the elementary and high school classrooms and one-third of the coeducational college classrooms that the Sadkers visited are sex-segregated. As male students talk and call out more, teachers are drawn to the noisier male sections of the class, a development that further silences girls.

Not only do male students interact more with the teacher but at all levels of schooling they receive a higher quality of interaction. Using four categories of teacher responses to student participation—praise, acceptance, remediation, and criticism—the Sadkers' studies found that more than 50 percent of all teacher responses are mere acceptances, such as "O.K." and "uh huh." These nonspecific reactions offer little instructional feedback. Teachers use remediation more than 30 percent of the time, helping students correct or improve answers by asking probing questions or by phrases such as "Try again." Only 10 percent of the time do teachers actually praise students, and they criticize them even less. Although praise, remediation, and criticism provide more useful information to students than the neutral acknowledgment of an "O.K." these clearer, more precise teacher comments are more often directed to boys.

Who gets taught—and how—has profound consequences. Student participation in the classroom enhances learning and self-esteem. Thus, boys gain an educational advantage over girls by claiming a greater share of the teacher's time and attention. This is particularly noteworthy in science classes, where, according to the AAUW report *How Schools Shortchange Girls*, boys perform 79 percent of all student-assisted demonstrations. When girls talk less and do less, it is little wonder that they learn less.[5] Even when directing their attention to girls, teachers sometimes short-circuit the learning process. For example, teachers frequently explain how to focus a microscope to boys but simply adjust the microscope for the girls. Boys learn the skill; girls learn to ask for assistance.

When female students do speak in class, they often preface their statements with self-deprecating remarks such as, "I'm not sure this is right," or "This probably isn't what you're looking for." Even when offering excellent responses, female students may begin with this self-criticism. Such tentative forms of speech project a sense of academic uncertainty and self-doubt—almost a tacit admission of lesser status in the classroom.

Women are not only quiet in classrooms; they are also missing from the pages of textbooks. For example, history textbooks currently in use at middle and high schools offer little more than 2 percent of their space to women. Studies of music textbooks have found that 70 percent of the figures shown are male. A recent content analysis of five secondary school science textbooks revealed that more than two-thirds of all drawings were of male figures and that not a single female scientist was depicted. Furthermore, all five books used the male body as the model for the human body, a practice that continues even in medical school texts.[6] At the college level, too, women rarely see themselves reflected in what they study. For example, the two-volume *Norton Anthology of English Literature* devotes less than 15 percent of its pages to the works of women. Interestingly, there was greater representation of women in the first edition of the anthology in 1962 than in the fifth edition, published in 1986.[7]

Presence and Power

Not only are women hidden in the curriculum and quiet in the classroom, they are also less visible in other school locations. Even as early as the elementary grades, considered by some to be a distinctly feminine environment, boys tend to take over the territory. At recess time on playgrounds across the country, boys grab bats and balls as they fan out over the schoolyard for their games. Girls are likely to be left on the sideline—watching. In secondary school, male students become an even more powerful presence. In *Failing at Fairness*, high school teachers and students tell these stories:

> A rural school district in Wisconsin still has the practice of having the cheerleaders (all girls, of course) clean the mats for the wrestling team before each meet. They are called the "Mat Maidens."
>
> In our local high school, boys' sports teams received much more support from the school system and the community. The boys' teams got shoes, jackets, and played on the best-maintained grounds. The girls' softball team received no clothes and nobody took care of our fields. Cheerleaders did not cheer for us. When we played, the bleachers were mostly empty.

Sports are not the only fields where women lose ground. In many secondary schools, mathematics, science, and computer technology remain male domains. In the past, girls were actively discouraged or even prohibited from taking the advanced courses in these fields. One woman, now a college professor, recalls her high school physics class:

> I was the only girl in the class. The teacher often told off-color jokes and when he did he would tell me to leave the room. My great regret today is that I actually did it.

Today, we hope such explicitly offensive behavior is rare, yet counselors and teachers continue to harbor lower expectations for girls and are less likely to encourage them to take advanced classes in math and science. It is only later in life that women realize the price they paid for avoiding these courses as they are screened out of lucrative careers in science and technology.

By the time they reach college, male students' control of the environment is visible. Male students are more likely to hold positions of student leadership on campus and to play in heavily funded sports programs. College presidents and deans are usually men, as are most tenured professors. In a sense, a "glass wall" divides today's college campus. On one side of the glass wall are men, comprising 70 percent of all students majoring in chemistry, physics, and computer science. The percentage is even higher in engineering. While the "hard sciences" flourish on the men's side of the campus, the women's side of the glass wall is where education, psychology, and foreign languages are taught. These gender walls not only separate programs, they also indicate social standing. Departments with higher male enrollment carry greater campus prestige and their faculty are often paid higher salaries.

These gender differences can be seen outside academic programs, in peer relationships both at college and in high school. In 1993 a national survey sponsored by the AAUW and reported in *Hostile Hallways* found that 76 percent of male students and 85 percent of female students in the typical high school had experienced sexual harassment.[8] What differed dramatically for girls and boys was not the occurrence of unwanted touching or profane remarks but their reaction to them. Only 28 percent of the boys, compared to 70 percent of the girls, said they were upset by these experiences. For 33 percent of the girls, the encounters were so troubling that they did not want to talk in class or even go to school. On college campuses problems range from sexist comments and sexual propositions to physical assault. Consider the following incidents:

- A UCLA fraternity manual found its way into a campus magazine. Along with the history and bylaws were the songs the pledges were supposed to memorize. The lyrics described sexual scenes that were bizarre, graphic, and sadistic.[9]
- One fraternity on a New England campus hosted "pig parties" where the man bringing the female date voted the ugliest wins.[1]
- A toga party on the campus of another elite liberal arts college used for decoration the torso of a female mannequin hung from the balcony and splattered with paint to look like blood. A sign below suggested the female body was available for sex.[10]

When one gender is consistently treated as less important and less valuable, the seeds of contempt take root and violence can be the result.

Strategies for Change

One of the ironies of gender bias in schools is that so much of it goes unnoticed by educators. While personally committed to fairness, many are unable to see the microinequities that surround them. The research on student-teacher interactions led the Sadkers to develop training programs to enable teachers and administrators to detect this bias and create equitable teaching methods. Program evaluations indicate that biased teaching patterns can be changed, and teachers can achieve equity in verbal interactions with their students. Research shows that for elementary and secondary school teachers, as well as college professors, this training leads not only to more equitable teaching but to more effective teaching as well.

During the 1970s, content analysis research showed women missing from schoolbooks. Publishers issued guidelines for equity and vowed to reform. But recent studies show that not all publishing companies have lived up to the promise of their guidelines. The curriculum continues to present a predominately male model of the world. Once again publishers and authors must be urged to incorporate women into school texts. Teachers and students need to become aware of the vast amount of excellent children's literature, including biographies that feature resourceful girls and strong women. *Failing at Fairness*[1] includes an extensive list of these resources for both elementary and secondary schools.

In postsecondary education, faculty members typically select instructional materials on the basis of individual preference. Many instructors would benefit from programs that alert them to well-written, gender-fair books in their academic fields. And individual professors can enhance their own lectures and discussions by including works by and about women.

Education institutions at every level have a responsibility to create comfortable and safe learning environments for students in and beyond the classroom. Harassing and intimidating behaviors that formerly might have been excused with the comment "boys will be boys" are now often seen as less excusable and less acceptable. Many schools offer workshops for students and faculty to help eliminate sexual harassment. While controversy surrounds the exact definition of sexual harassment, the education community must take this issue seriously and devise strategies to keep the learning environment open to all.

After centuries of struggle, women have finally made their way into our colleges and graduate schools, only to discover that access does not guarantee equity. Walls of subtle bias continue to create different education environments, channeling women and men toward separate and unequal futures. To complete the agenda for equity, we must transform our education institutions and empower female students for full participation in society.

NOTES

1. M. Sadker and D. Sadker, *Failing at Fairness: How America's Schools Cheat Girls* (New York: Charles Scribner's Sons, 1994). The research for this article as well as the anecdotes are drawn from this book.
2. Test data were obtained from Educational Testing Service.
3. The Analysis Group, Greenberg-Lake, *Shortchanging Girls, Shortchanging America* (Washington, D.C.; American Association of University Women, 1990).

4. L. Kim, "Boys Will Be Boys . . . Right?" *The Lance*, Livingston High School (June 1993) 32:5.

5. The Wellesley College Center for Research on Women, *How Schools Shortchange Girls: The AAUW Report* (Washington, D.C.: American Association of University Women Educational Foundation, 1992).

6. J. Bazler and D. Simonis, "Are Women Out of the Picture?" *Science Teacher 57* (December 1990):9.

7. W. Sullivan, "*The Norton Anthology* and the Canon of English Literature." Paper presented at the Annual Meeting of the College English Association, San Antonio, Texas, 1991.

8. Louis Harris and Associates, *Hostile Hallways: The AAUW Survey on Sexual Harassment in America's Schools* (Washington, D.C.: American Association of University Women, 1993).

9. J. O'Gorman and B. Sandler, *Peer Harassment: Hassles for Women on Campus* (Washington, D.C.: Project on the Status and Education of Women, Association of American Colleges, 1988).

10. B. A. Crier, "Frat Row," *Los Angeles Times* (February 9, 1990).

QUESTIONS

1. What is the "disappearing syndrome"? What measures indicate the existence of this syndrome? Why is the syndrome significant?

2. How do teacher attitudes and behavior discourage women in the classroom? How do the attitudes and behaviors of male students affect female participation in the classroom? What is the "cycle of loss"? How do external influences affect the cycle of loss? What are the long-term consequences of educational inequity for women?

3. What strategies for change are offered by the authors? How might these strategies affect the disappearing syndrome and the cycle of loss?

Left at the Starting Gate: Gender Inequality in Education (1997)

Lori Murray

Lori Murray, a teacher and contributor to Columbus Parent, *briefly discusses Myra and David Sadker's research on gender inequity in elementary and secondary school classrooms. Suggesting ways for both parents and teachers to address classroom practices that routinely shortchange girls, this selection provides a foundation for exploring the impact of gender on the educational possibilities for female students. Murray also demonstrates how theoretical observations can be transformed into practical solutions.*

What are little boys made of? Snakes and snails and puppy dogs' tails; and that's what little boys are made of.

What are little girls made of? Sugar and spice and all that's nice; And that's what little girls are made of.

(*The Illustrated Treasury of Children's Literature*, Grosset and Dunlap Publishers, 1955.)

At least at the starting gate, that's how we sum up life for little boys and girls. When children enroll for kindergarten, girls exhibit more of the strengths to succeed in school—being able to sit still, listen attentively and "act nice." Boys, on the other hand, demonstrate behaviors that include running, jumping and good spatial skills. Since today's kindergarten classrooms more closely resemble the first grades of yesteryear, parents of less mature five year old boys face the reality their sons will have less time to develop the necessary maturity. For this reason many boys are held back a year, beginning school at age six.

Ironically enough, the same characteristics that make it difficult for boys to adapt to early schooling are the very things that enable them to succeed later on. Well-meaning teachers who work hard to help boys adjust, overcompensate by giving them more attention than girls. Teachers often call on boys more frequently, allow them to talk out of turn and offer them more constructive criticism. Even when praising the boys, teachers many times supply them with more specific and useful feedback. In a study done by professors Myra and David Sadker at The American University, results showed even when girls did get the teacher's attention, they were often treated differently from boys in three ways: Girls were given less time to respond to questions; girls received far less praise and/or advice than their male counterparts, and, when all students were challenged with a difficult task, boys were encouraged to try harder to work out the problem for themselves.

In many instances, teachers simply provided the answer for the girls. The Sadkers' research uncovered the squeaky-wheel syndrome of the classroom—those running, jumping, loud, immature boys who demanded attention, got it. To further compound the problem, there are few female role models in school textbooks and literature. This translates into a shortage of good role models for girls, unfortunately leaving it up to television and the rest of the media. The consequences are somewhat devastating for girls. By the time children reach middle school, the boys have left the girls at the starting gate. In both academic achievement and self-esteem, girls lag behind.

Further research by the Sadkers indicates, many times, girls are discouraged in subtle ways from being successful academically. Along these same lines, girls are more frequently praised for qualities such as neatness and good manners—the "sugar-and-spice syndrome." By the time adolescence arrives, their intellect has developed to a point where they can now perceive the power in our society. Television heroes are male, the President is male, and most of the high-powered jobs are held by men. There is no female Ninja Turtle.

But there is hope. Young girls can benefit when the caring adults in their lives take the time to combat some of these negative stereotypes.

1. *Parents must show confidence in their daughter's abilities and intellect*. This will allow her to accomplish great things.

2. *Be cautious about the stories, textbooks, and classroom examples that are guiding girls.* Unfortunately, many of them send the message boys are bright and girls are passive or silent.

3. *Share stories about great women with your daughter.* They will serve as an inspiration for her own dreams and adventures.

4. *Give your child lots of opportunities to make choices.* Even very young children can develop anatomy by selecting their own clothing and feeding themselves.

5. *Expose your child to a wide range of experiences.* Take her with you on errands, travel together; purchase toys like trucks and dolls for both sexes.

6. *Watch TV with your child.* Instill your values by discussing what is being watched.

7. *Check your child's school textbooks and other curriculum materials for gender equity,* especially those published before 1970.

8. *Encourage your daughter's studies in math and science.* For both sexes, confidence in math and science skills is tied to overall self-esteem and ambition in career plans. According to studies done by the American Association of University Women, girls are much less confident about their math skills than boys, and they are less likely to believe they can pursue a math-related career. This decline in confidence is generally followed by a decline in ability.

9. *Insist girls speak up more frequently.* Parents can encourage this behavior at home while teachers can encourage it in the classroom.

10. *Give your daughter some adolescent responsibilities* such as handling her own money, running to the store or library and organizing her own school assignments.

11. *Teach your daughter how to handle stressful situations on her own.* Don't always come to her rescue; instead, let her speak up for herself.

As head of the Columbus School For Girls, Pat Hayot insists. "It's all about good communication. We need to counter some very negative stereotypes in our society." When much of the media is telling girls there's only one way to be (pretty, passive and often silent), girls are bombarded with a stereotypical message that is often defeating. By the time adolescence arrives, they often find themselves yearning to be someone else. Hayot offers tips to teachers. Parents need to make sure these strategies are being used in their child's classroom.

1. *Teachers should be aware of their own classroom behaviors.* Have a colleague observe them so they can begin to create a more equitable environment for girls and boys. When done properly, boys also become the winners as we no longer force them into a role where they are treated differently.

2. *Teachers should journal themselves.* Keep a record of daily classroom events and occurrence.

3. *Teachers can talk with the students about stereotypes* and how they are trying to combat them.

4. *Teachers can help girls move beyond tentative language* such as "Well, this might be stupid but. . . ."

5. *Teachers should understand techniques and strategies used by the media* and gain a working knowledge of media literacy.

The following are some additional tips for teachers and parents.

1. *Use equitable teaching techniques* such as cooperative learning, a method which makes use of student groups. Girls thrive in these situations because they feel more secure in this supportive environment.

2. *Change the style of teaching being used.* Less lecture and more hands-on learning is beneficial

3. *Take the emphasis off competition.* Reward children for personal progress instead.

4. *Encourage questioning in the classroom,* but make sure children are given a chance to figure things out themselves.

5. *Encouraging mentoring within the school.* Older children can be good role models and tutors for younger students.

6. *Look for school programs* that incorporate debate, voice training, performing, self-evaluation and conflict resolution.

7. *Encourage use of spatial skills* through activities like woodworking and ceramics.

Although the reality our education system is somehow shortchanging girls is alarming, parents and teachers can work together to promote change. Putting some of these tips into action insures a more equitable education for boys and girls. No one should be left at the starting gate.

Parents and teachers concerned about the issue of equity in education may want to read the book *Failing at Fairness—How America's Schools Cheat Girls*, by Myra and David Sadker.

Lori B. Murray is a teacher and frequent contributor to Columbus Parent.

QUESTIONS

1. What research results does Murray highlight? What do the results suggest about the impact of gender on the educational opportunities for female students?
2. What are Murray's suggestions for parents? How do these suggestions address the concerns identified by the Sadkers' research?
3. What are Murray's suggestions for teachers? Why would she offer two sets of suggestions, one for parents and one for teachers? Why make this distinction? What are the similarities and differences in the two sets of suggestions? Is education confined to the classroom? Why/why not?
4. What do you think about Murray's suggestions? Are they workable? Why/why not? Are there school systems or home environments where these suggestions might not work? Why?

NITZITAPI AND THE BLACKFEET COMMUNITY COLLEGE . . . A WOMAN AND SCHOOL IN PROCESS (1996)

Winona LaDuke

From the late 1870s through the early decades of the twentieth century, the U.S. government implemented a policy of off-reservation schooling. Native American children were forcibly taken from their parents and placed in boarding schools where they were required to speak English, wear European American clothing, and learn "white" culture. This policy made it difficult for adults to pass on their language and culture to the younger generation, which had a devastating impact on many tribes. The following article also focuses on Indian education, but chronicles a contemporary community college run by the Blackfeet Tribe designed to strengthen and help repair the community.

"NITZITAPI and the Blackfeet Community College . . . A Woman and School in Process," by Winona LaDuke, reprinted from *Indigenous Woman*, Vol. I, No. III, 1996.

Carol Murray, a graceful woman, mother and newly grandmother is the President of the Blackfeet Community College. This institution, like many other Native controlled colleges, is struggling to meet the growing needs of the community, and, through all the challenges, succeeding, remarkably. Drawn to her by the strength she shows in photographs, I pursued an interview with her about the College, her work, challenges, and some of the issues faced by Indian educators. She graciously agreed.

The beauty of the land is matched by that of the people. In my experience that is how it works, and the Nitzitapi people are no exception. Nitzitapi is the name the various members of the Blackfoot Confederacy have for themselves, and encompassing four bands of the Blackfeet Confederacy—the southern Peigan (in Montana), northern Peigan, Blood and Blackfoot in Alberta—somewhere around 50,000 people in total. "Nitzitapi" is defined as "people," in one characterization, but, perhaps more telling, is Carol's interpretation of the name: **". . . People who have to strive through their growth and development in their lives to become a person who is like a reflection of clear glass. Their thoughts are good, words are good, health is good. A pure person, one who does not have a bad thought. . . ."** Questioned further about the "transitional nature" of the self-definition, Carol laughs, and calls **Nitzitapi a name for "people in process".**

And that they are, as is the institution. Formed in 1976 as an extension of a two year state college, the Blackfeet Community College became a separate institution chartered under the Blackfeet tribe. A fully accredited institution as of 1985, the school offers two year programs in Blackfeet Studies, Human Services, Business Management, and other areas designed to empower local students. As well, the College works with other state institutions to allow Blackfeet to pursue Masters degrees, while they remain in their home community. There are five hundred students enrolled at the school, with 44 employees.

One of the biggest challenges Carol faces is to bring the college into most of the community. "One of the things I intend to do . . . is try and introduce higher education for adults to a member of every family on the reservation, in an attempt to assure equality of opportunity to everyone here. I'm trying to eliminate the 'haves and have nots,' here by making higher education accessible to everyone."

When the College started, "higher education" was not a common word in the households. "We came through an era where education was forced upon Indian people. A lot of Indian people resented that, and thought that you 'would get like the White man, if you got educated' . . . and now, that's starting to change." As she continues, "People didn't know what an associate degree or bachelor's degree was, and now that's getting to be a common word. Now people, parents, adults, uncles, aunts, and grandparents are coming home and doing their homework, with their kids around. That's a big step. Children are seeing that, and that begins to change things."

More than that, the College is integrally related to Blackfeet culture. "We'd like to develop a greater appreciation amongst the students of our own culture. We've been so separated by that imaginary line (Canada/US border) that one which divides us, that we're interested in becoming more familiar with ourselves. We're working, in some cases, with people who have no knowledge of what goes on in the north."

The need to rebuild the knowledge of the people is faced by many Native community colleges who teach general Native American studies, but often find that they need to attend to the culture of their specific community with more focus. "In 1985, I was involved with two of the societies of our tribe, at the same time, I was getting my college education, I was getting these instructions. In the societies, I was taught that there was a form of life we were to follow, and be guided in the development of our people. I was fortunate to have these teachings at the same time I was developing my career, and this [this need for our teachings] has played a big part in our focus on our own tradition—Blackfeet studies. The interest has picked up in many places, as now, curriculum material on Blackfeet culture is often provided for scholars and educators throughout the country, and many tribal members, living on or off the reservation request this information, as well as seek language instruction. Many people come back to the school from border towns, or off reservation, and they take our language as their language requirement. This is really picking up."

The inclusive nature of the programming is part of Blackfeet tradition. "In the ways of our tribe, we were all associated by clans and what we did traditionally. It seems to me that education being the most worthwhile avenue to benefit the most people, I think that all the families and clans should at least have access to that family and that world."

And, the school, like other Indian community colleges, faces financial constraints which make programming all the more challenging, yet important. There are 27 tribal colleges situated on or near reservations, which today reverse the national statistics on Indian education. Nine out of ten Indian students who go directly from high school into a mainstream college fail, yet nine out of ten who go to a tribal college succeed. They get jobs or continue their education.

Moreover, many tribal college graduates return to their reservations to serve as doctors, teachers, artists, and tribal administrators, and equally important, as role models for the next generation. The tribal colleges serve the poorest communities in North America, hold classes in trailers and dilapidated buildings, and, except in Minnesota and Nebraska, receive no state funds.

In 1978, Congress authorized an appropriation of $5288 in federal funds for every full time student, yet since that time, the government has earmarked only $1500 to $2000. Frankly, most Indian students can't afford to go to school. Most students who attend are extremely poor. The decision of whether to attend college might hinge upon a student having $50 or $75. "A typical profile of our student is a 35 year old female with two children, who is the head of household," says Gorden Belcourt, past president of the Blackfeet Community College. "That $75 could go for daycare or diapers." In short, a more generous Congress could do quite a bit.

On the other side, money from the private sector is being solicited by the American Indian College Fund, a three year old initiative modeled on the United Negro College Fund concept, with a motto, of ". . . The Past is in our Hearts. The Future is in our Minds. . . ." The Fund, headed by New York based Barbara Brantone, suggests recognition for the colleges, and $10 million to capitalize the growing number of colleges and students. Private funding, frankly, has been not much better than federal funding. A 1991 study released by Native Americans in Philanthropy found that .2 percent of the grants made by all foundations were to Indian people, and of that 40% went to non-Indian organizations and institutions working on Indian issues.

The American Indian College Fund, through an aggressive direct mail and advertising campaign (following on the heels of the *Dances with Wolves* publicity), has thus far raised $1 million towards their $10 million goal, and the tribal colleges are hopeful. That money will make a big difference in Native communities over the next fifty years of changes.

Meanwhile, back in Browning, Carol Murray carefully moves ahead with her plans to bring higher education into all of the community, and, preserve Blackfeet culture. Her 500 students are thankful for her work, and the 90% success rate of the College is something the Nitzitapi are counting on for their futures. It is, like their name, a process.

QUESTIONS

1. How does the Blackfeet Community College differ from "mainstream" community colleges? What accounts for these differences?
2. Why does Murray value education so highly?
3. How does LaDuke use a variety of voices to tell the story of Blackfeet Community College? Are different purposes served by the author's use of the first person, the voice of Carol Murray, and the third person? What evidence from the article can you offer to support your interpretation?

FEMINIST CLASS STRUGGLE (2000)

bell hooks

Activist bell hooks discusses the class politics of the feminist movement in this chapter from her book Feminism is For Everybody (2000). *The feminist movement ideally attempts to represent all women's interests but its inability to be sufficiently inclusive has been a steady source of conflict throughout the history of the movement. Women have bonded across class differences in resistance to economic discrimination, for instance, but class has also been a divisive force as privileged women began to make issues of gender equality with men central to the feminist cause at the expense of working-class women's concerns. Hooks, an African-American feminist activist who has been a leading figure in the women's movement, insists in this selection that challenging class elitism is essential to a true vision of feminist liberation.*

"Feminist Class Struggle," by bell hooks, reprinted from *Feminism is for Everyone: Passionate Politics*, 2000, South End Press. Pp. 37-43.

Class difference and the way in which it divides women was an issue women in feminist movement talked about long before race. In the mostly white circles of a newly formed women's liberation movement the most glaring separation between women was that of class. White working-class women recognized that class hierarchies were present in the movement. Conflict arose between the reformist vision of women's liberation which basically demanded equal rights for women within the existing class structure, and more radical and/or revolutionary models, which called for fundamental change in the existing structure so that models of mutuality and equality could replace the old paradigms. However, as feminist movement progressed and privileged groups of well-educated white women began to achieve equal access to class power with their male counterparts, feminist class struggle was no longer deemed important.

From the onset of the movement women from privileged classes were able to make their concerns "the" issues that should be focused on in part because they were the group of women who received public attention. They attracted mass media. The issues that were most relevant to working women or masses of women were never highlighted by mainstream mass media. Betty Friedan's *The Feminine Mystique* identified "the problem that has no name" as the dissatisfaction females felt about being confined and subordinated in the home as housewives. While this issue was presented as a crisis for women it really was only a crisis for a small group of well-educated white women. While they were complaining about the dangers of confinement in the home a huge majority of women in the nation were in the workforce. And many of these working women, who put in long hours for low wages while still doing all the work in the domestic household would have seen the right to stay home as "freedom."

It was not gender discrimination or sexist oppression that kept privileged women of all races from working outside the home, it was the fact that the jobs that would have been available to them would have been the same low-paying unskilled labor open to all working women. Elite groups of highly educated females stayed at home rather than do the type of work large numbers of lower-middle-class and working-class women were doing. Occasionally, a few of these women defied convention and worked outside the home performing tasks way below their educational skills and facing resistance from husbands and family. It was this resistance that turned the issue of their working outside the home into an issue of gender discrimination and made opposing patriarchy and seeking equal rights with men of their class the political platform that chose feminism rather than class struggle.

From the onset reformist white women with class privilege were well aware that the power and freedom they wanted was the freedom they perceived men of their class enjoying. Their resistance to patriarchal male domination in the domestic household provided them with a connection they could use to unite across class with other women who were weary of male domination. But only privileged women had the luxury to imagine working outside the home would actually provide them with an income which would enable them to be economically self-sufficient. Working-class women already knew that the wages they received would not liberate them.

Reformist efforts on the part of privileged groups of women to change the workforce so that women workers would be paid more and face less gender-based discrimination and harassment on the job had positive impact on the lives of all women. And these gains are important. Yet the fact that privileged gained in class power while masses of women still do not receive wage equity with men is an indication of the way in which class interests superceded feminist efforts to change the workforce so that women would receive equal pay for equal work.

Lesbian feminist thinkers were among the first activists to raise the issue of class in feminist movement expressing their viewpoints in an accessible language. They were a group of women who had not imagined they could depend on husbands to support them. And they were often much more aware than their straight counterpoints of the difficulties all women would face in the workforce. In the early '70s anthologies like *Class and Feminism,* edited by Charlotte Bunch and Nancy Myron, published work written by women from diverse class backgrounds who were confronting the issue in feminist circles. Each essay emphasized the fact that class was not simply a question of money. In "The Last Straw," Rita Mae Brown (who was not a famous writer at the time) clearly stated:

> Class is much more than Marx's definition of relationship to the means of production. Class involved your behavior, your basic

> assumptions, how you are taught to behave, what you expect from yourself and from others, your concept of a future, how you understand problems and solve them, how you think, feel, act.

These women who entered feminist groups made up of diverse classes were among the first to see that the vision of a politically based sisterhood where all females would unite together to fight patriarchy could not emerge until the issue of class was confronted.

Placing class on feminist agendas opened up the space where the intersections of class and race were made apparent. Within the institutionalized race, sex, class social system in our society black females were clearly at the bottom of the economic totem pole. Initially well-educated white women from working-class backgrounds were more visible than black females of all classes in feminist movement. They were a minority within the movement, but theirs was the voice of experience. They knew better than their privileged-class comrades of any race the costs of resisting race, class, and gender domination. They knew what it was like to struggle to change one's economic situation. Between them and their privileged-class comrades there were ongoing conflicts over appropriate behavior, over the issues that would be presented as fundamental feminist concerns. Within feminist movement women from privileged-class backgrounds who had never before been involved in leftist freedom fighting learned the concrete politics of class struggle, confronting challenges made by less privileged women, and also learning in the process assertiveness skills and constructive ways to cope with conflict. Despite constructive intervention many privileged white women continued to act as though feminism belonged to them, as though they were in charge.

Mainstream patriarchy reinforced the idea that the concerns of women from privileged-class groups were the only ones worthy of receiving attention. Feminist reform aimed to gain social equality for women within the existing structure. Privileged women wanted equality with men of their class. Despite sexism among their class they would not have wanted to have the lot of working class men. Feminist efforts to grant women social equality with men of their class neatly coincided with white supremacist capitalist patriarchal fears that white power would diminish if nonwhite people gained equal access to economic power and privilege. Supporting what in effect became white power reformist feminism enabled the mainstream white supremacist patriarchy to bolster its power while simultaneously undermining the radical politics of feminism.

Only revolutionary feminist thinkers expressed outrage at this co-optation of feminist movement. Our critique and outrage gained a hearing with the alternative press. In her collection of essays, *The Coming of Black Genocide,* radical white activist Mary Barfoot boldly stated:

> There are white women, hurt and angry, who believed that the '70s women's movement meant sisterhood, and who feel betrayed by escalator women. By women who went back home to the patriarchy. But the women's movement never left the father Dick's side. . . . There was no war. And there was no liberation. We got a share of genocide profits and we love it. We are Sisters of Patriarchy, and true supporters of national and class oppression, Patriarchy in its highest form is Euro-imperialism on a world scale. If we're Dick's sister and want what he has gotten, then in the end we support that system that he got it all from.

Indeed, many more feminist women found and find it easier to consider divesting of white supremacist thinking than of their class elitism.

As privileged women gained greater access to economic power with men of their class, feminist discussions of class were no longer commonplace. Instead, all women were encouraged to see the economic gains of affluent females as a positive sign for all women. In actuality, these gains rarely changed the lot of poor and working-class women. And since privileged men did not become equal caretakers in domestic households, the freedom of privileged-class women of all races has required the sustained subordination of working-class and poor women. In the '90s, collusion with the existing social structure was the price of "women's liberation." At the end of the day class power proved to be more important than feminism. And this collusion helped destabilize feminist movement.

When women acquired greater class status and power without conducting themselves differently from males feminist politics were undermined. Lots of women felt betrayed. Middle- and lower-middle-class women who were suddenly compelled by the ethos of feminism to enter the workforce did not feel liberated once they faced the hard truth that working outside the home did not mean work in the home would be equally shared with male partners. No-fault divorce proved to be more economically beneficial to men than women. As many black women/women of color saw white women from privileged classes benefiting economically more than other groups from reformist feminist gains, from gender being tacked on to racial affirmative action, it simply reaffirmed their fear that feminism was really about increasing white power. The most profound betrayal of feminist issues has been the lack of mass-based feminist protest challenging the government's assault on single mothers and the dismantling of the welfare system. Privileged women, many of whom call themselves feminists, have simply turned away from the "feminization of poverty."

The voices of "power feminism" tend to be highlighted in mass media far more than the voices of individual feminist women who have gained class power without betraying our solidarity towards those groups without class privilege. Being true to feminist politics, our goals were and are to become economically self-sufficient and to find ways to assist other women in their efforts to better themselves economically. Our experiences counter the assumption that women can only gain economically by acting in collusion with the existing capitalist patriarchy. All over this nation individual feminists with class power who support a revolutionary vision of social change share resources and use our power to aid reforms that will improve the lives of women irrespective of class.

The only genuine hope of feminist liberation lies with a vision of social change which challenges class elitism. Western women have gained class power and greater gender inequality because a global white supremacist patriarchy enslaves and/or subordinates masses of third world women. In this country the combined forces of a booming prison industry and workfare-oriented welfare in conjunction with conservative immigration policy create and condone the conditions for indentured slavery. Ending welfare will create a new underclass of women and children to be abused and exploited by the existing structures of domination.

Given the changing realities of class in our nation, widening gaps between the rich and poor, and the continued feminization of poverty, we desperately need a mass-based radical feminist movement that can build on the strength of the past, including the positive gains generated by reforms, while offering meaningful interrogation of existing feminist theory that was simply wrong-minded while offering us new strategies. Significantly a visionary movement would ground its work in the concrete conditions of working-class and poor women. That means creating a movement that begins education for critical consciousness where women, feminist women with class power, need to put in place low-income housing women can own. The creation of housing co-opts with feminist principles would show the ways feminist struggle is relevant to all women's lives.

When women with class power opportunistically use a feminist platform while undermining feminist politics that help keep in place a patriarchal system that will ultimately re-subordinate them, they do not just betray feminism; they betray themselves. Returning to a discussion of class, feminist women and men will restore the conditions needed for solidarity. We will then be better able to envision a world where resources are shared and opportunities for personal growth abound for everyone irrespective of their class.

QUESTIONS

1. What does hooks mean by "class"?
2. How have class divisions strengthened white power, according to hooks?
3. How have women worked across class differences to accomplish feminist goals? How have class issues interrupted feminist coalitions?
4. How might the issues and concerns of working-class women differ from those of more privileged women? How have privileged women put their own interests first at times in movement activities? Why do white privileged women receive more public attention than women of color?
5. What does hooks mean when she says, "women must conduct themselves differently from men to sustain feminist politics"?
6. Why is class a fundamental feminist issue? How must activists dedicated to the feminist cause keep the issue of class central?

WE ARE FAMILY (1996)

National Council for Research on Women

The Family and Medical Leave Act, signed into law in 1993, is a step toward increasing job security for those individuals—usually women—who must take time off from work to care for ill children. Yet, according to this brief article, FMLA does not go far enough.

What do you do? Your one-year-old daughter has meningitis; day care can't watch her in this condition; and family and friends are either working or too far away to help out. Someone has to stay home with the baby, and that someone is you.

You hesitate. In the last two years, you've been on maternity leave, missed work for a week to care for an elderly parent, and suffered a bout of the flu last winter. Will missing a few more days of work have repercussions? Will your job be waiting for you when your daughter is healthy enough to go back to the childcare center?

Under the Family Medical Leave Act (FMLA), signed into law by President Clinton in 1993, if you work for a company that employs 50 or more workers, you are entitled to up to 12 weeks of *unpaid, job-protected* leave to care for a newborn, a newly adopted

---

"We Are Family," by the National Council for Research on Women, from *Issues Quarterly*, Vol. 1, No. 4, 1996. Reprinted with permission of the National Council for Research on Women.

child, or a seriously ill child, spouse, or parent. FMLA also allows you to care for yourself if you are unable to work due to illness or temporary disability, including childbirth.[1]

On the face of it, FMLA is a good law for women. It allows them to care for their families and not only stay on the job but keep themselves moving on the fast track. According to the Washington, DC-based independent, nonprofit research center, the Institute for Women's Policy Research, "In the late 1980s about one-quarter of women who left jobs did so because of pregnancy or other family reasons."[2] Given that nationwide, working women give birth to more than 2 million babies each year and that the proposed cuts to Medicare threaten to greatly reduce the level of professional homecare available to a growing population of elderly Americans, the task of tending to the nation's families—its newest and oldest members—takes on Goliath proportions, especially for working women.[3] If it weren't for the FMLA, many families would be operating without a safety net.

That said, FMLA is not the be all and end all of family-leave policy. A year after FMLA became law, researchers at the University of California at Berkeley found that four in ten companies affected by FMLA were not adhering to its provisions.[4] Likewise, in an October 1994 telephone survey of nearly 700 workers, the Bureau of National Affairs found that 52 percent of those called knew little or nothing about the act.[5] Once briefed, most said they would hesitate to take advantage of FMLA because they could not afford to go on unpaid leave, even job-protected leave. Almost half of the employees with annual incomes between $15,000 and $20,000 expressed this concern, as did 40 percent of those with children under age 18.

Two studies conducted for the Commission on Family and Medical Leave at the US Department of Labor and released in October 1995 looked at the impact of FMLA on workers and their employers. Researchers found that most FMLA-covered companies report having incurred little or no costs due to the law and that only two to four percent of FMLA-covered employees have made use of the law since January 1994.[6] Like earlier studies, the employee survey also found that the majority of respondents who needed to take leave during this time period but didn't, said they couldn't afford to forgo their paychecks.[7]

Recognizing that unpaid leave means no leave for many workers, the Institute for Women's Policy Research (IWPR) would like to see FMLA expanded to include a paid-leave program modeled after the Temporary Disability Insurance (TDI) benefits currently available to workers in California, Hawaii, New Jersey, New York, Rhode Island, and Puerto Rico. If a worker must go on leave for a nonwork-related condition—including pregnancy, childbirth, automobile accidents, heart disease, or cancer—TDI partially replaces missed wages.

IWPR reports emphasize that "TDI is a pay-as-you-go system rather than a new entitlement paid out of general tax revenues."[8] Employers and employees pay for the benefit, not the general public. The distinction could make a world of difference in this era of federal-budget cutting and social-policy backpedaling. IWPR estimates the cost per worker for paid leave for both health- and family-care absences would range from $151 to $213 annually, well below the costs of government-run social security programs like Supplemental Security Income and Aid to Families with Dependent Children, and on par with the costs of Unemployment Insurance.[9]

IWPR projects that paid-family-medical leave would help women stay on the job longer, which is good news for women at the bottom and top of the income ladder. Research shows that women with paid maternity leaves are more likely to return to work and low-income women are more likely to stay off welfare. Given these outcomes, paid leave promises to yield high returns in the private and public sectors. Paid-family-medical leave is in the best interest of the government, business, and America's families: an opportunity whose time has come.

NOTES

1. In addition, to be eligible, employees must have worked for the employer for at least 12 months and for 1250 hours during the year preceding the leave. FMLA requires employers to maintain an employee's health benefits during the leave, and they may not require employees to forfeit any previously accrued seniority or benefits as a result of the leave. However, employers are not required to count the leave time as time accrued for purposes of seniority or other benefits.
2. Young-Hee Yoon, Heidi Hartmann, and Jill Braunstein, "Using Temporary Disability Insurance to Provide Paid Family Leave: A Com-

parison with the Family Medical Leave Act," (Washington, DC: Institute for Women's Policy Research, 1995). Pamphlet, 1.

3. Mike Meyers, "Taking Pregnancy Leaves," *Star Tribune* (February 6, 1995).
4. Julianne O'Gara, *Making Workplaces Work: Quality Work Policies for Small Business* (Washington, DC: Business and Professional Women's Foundation, 1995), 22.
5. Jeffrey Goldfarb, "Employment: Majority of US Workers Are Unaware of FMLA Provisions, BNA Survey Finds," *Analysis and Reports* (Washington, DC: Bureau of National Affairs, 1994), C1.
6. Commission on Family and Medical Leave, "New Studies Measure Impact of Family & Medical Leave Law" (Washington, DC: US Department of Labor, 1995). Photocopy.
7. Katherine A. McGonagle et al., "Commission on Leave Survey of Employees on the Impact of the Family and Medical Leave Act." (Ann Arbor, MI: Institute for Social Research, 1995): Photocopy, 23. See also, David Cantor et al., "The Impact of the Family and Medical Leave Act: A Survey of Employers" (Rockville, MD: Westat, 1995), Photocopy.
8. Yoon, Hartmann, and Braunstein, 4.
9. Ibid., Table 2.

QUESTIONS

1. What advantages does FMLA offer, particularly for women? Why is this Act under-utilized by employees?
2. Why would a plan modeled after Temporary Disability Insurance (TDI) be advantageous? What resistance might meet such a plan?
3. Are we interested in a more family-friendly workforce? Whose responsibility is it to provide a more family-friendly climate for workers? What economic and emotional benefits would be reaped from a more secure workforce? Would you be willing to pay the amount estimated to ensure a benefit like TDI to working parents? Why/Why not?

Historical Background of Child Care and Family Leave Issues (1995)

Margaret M. Conway, David W. Ahern and Gertrude Steuernagel

This excerpt from Women and Public Policy gives historical background on two neglected areas of public policy of significance for women-child care and family leave. Cultural change in attitudes toward parenting and care for the elderly, as well as controversy over the upper-class practice of employing working-class women as "nannies," has brought awareness to these issues. Still, public policymakers have not assumed responsibility for children's issues. Because women bear the cost of caring by relying upon private resources—especially after divorce—this lack of responsibility on policymakers' part contributes to the "feminization of poverty."

Although child care and family leave are often thought of as "new" issues, they have their roots in policies and societal dynamics that can be traced back to the beginning of industrial society. Changes in the nature of such care have often reflected changing societal ideas about the proper role of women in the family and in society, as well as economic necessity (women were needed in the work force during World War II).

Child Care

Child care in the United States has been influenced by the interplay of economic, social, and educational forces. According to John P. Fernandez, industrialization, urbanization, and mandatory public schooling all had a tremendous impact on the development of child care.[1] The industrial revolution changed familial relationships because it eliminated the necessity that all family members contribute to the provision of basic family needs. Previously, all family members had to work to earn a subsistence living. The industrial revolution enabled one person (normally the father) to become the "provider" for the entire family unit. Fernandez argues that this freedom from obligation to work allowed children (particularly boys) "to prepare themselves for the new industrial jobs which would allow them, in turn, to support their own families."[2] As people moved closer to their places of employment, urban centers were created, and there was a need for service industries near the manufacturing industries; women increasingly filled the demand for labor in the new service industries.

These economic and social changes were accompanied by a development in the field of education that would have an effect on child care—the establishment of nurseries and kindergartens. Nurseries were originally philanthropic institutions designed to provide care and protection for the needy children of Civil War widows and working women (particularly immigrants). Kindergartens, often located in the settlement houses that served the needy, stressed children's education and development.[3] The nursery school and the kindergarten represented the two competing perspectives concerning child care—custodial and developmental. Those who emphasized the developmental perspective (which

---

was influenced by Enlightenment philosophy) claimed that nurseries should contribute to the development of happy, educated, well-adjusted children. According to Lawrence Lynn, the earliest day nurseries in the United States reflected the optimism of European social reformers.[4] By the middle of the nineteenth century, however, influenced by developments in the field of medicine and the increase in the number of working women, supporters of the nursery movement began to favor the custodial perspective: nurseries should attend to the physical needs of the children of women who had to work because of the changes wrought by industrialization. By the end of the nineteenth century, the number of child care centers had greatly increased. But critics argued that such facilities "encouraged mothers to work, loosened family ties, and minimized the parents' sense of responsibility toward their children."[5] They also charged that there were few standards governing the type of child care provided. Scandals that emerged during World War I solidified in peoples' minds the idea, expressed at the first White House Conference on the Care of Dependent Children (1909) and at the White House Conference on Standards of Child Welfare (1919), that nurseries were nothing more than a temporary expedient and that the best care was home care.[6] Contributing to this idea was the unsympathetic approach to day care on the part of social workers. Lynn explains that the philanthropic view of working women as victims of industrialization was replaced by an emphasis on therapeutic intervention by social workers to help families whom they viewed as maladjusted or cared for by incompetent mothers.[7] Thus, the day care movement foundered. Facilities (such as Montessori schools) that emphasized the enlightenment perspective of providing the child with enriching experiences were still available to more affluent families, but for the vast majority, the child care provided was custodial and available only to "problem" families.

It was during the Depression that federal funds were first used to finance nursery schools as part of a program under the Works Progress Administration. Fernandez points out that although the primary aim of the program was not child care but the provision of jobs for the unemployed, the result was both the creation of an excellent child care program and the setting of a precedent for the public funding of child care.[8] In 1941 Congress passed the Lanham Act, which provided federal grants to states to establish child care facilities for women working in defense plants during World War II. Fernandez argues that the commitment of the federal government was less than total because it feared that such a program might communicate the wrong message about working women.[9] The demands of the war effort were paramount, however, and by 1945 more than $50 million had been spent of the construction and operation of day care facilities, and more than 1.6 million children were enrolled in federally assisted child care centers and nurseries.[10]

After the war, funding for child care centers was withdrawn and 95 percent of them had to close for lack of funds.[11] Servicemen returned to their jobs and women were expected to return to the home. Although the 1950s and early 1960s are generally viewed as a period of rapid economic expansion and population increase (the baby boom that resulted when veterans started families), in fact the percentage of working mothers increased steadily from 1940 (when one in eight mothers worked) to the end of the 1960s (when two in five mothers worked).[12] From the end of the war to the 1950s, the only government policy related to child care was a tax allowance for the deduction of some employment-related child care expenses. In the 1960s, the federal government again launched some programs, primarily of a remedial nature, for economically disadvantaged children. The most notable of these was Project Head Start, created under the Economic Opportunity Act of 1965 and intended as a preschool program to help prepare such children for school. As in the past, these programs were designed to assist economically disadvantaged families, not working mothers.

During the late 1960s, child care advocates began to lobby for a more general federal policy toward child care. The result was the proposed Comprehensive Development Act of 1971, which would have provided services for welfare recipients (with an increase in expenditures for new programs under Head Start), increased tax deductions for child care expenses for working families, and allocated funds for the construction of new facilities and for planning and technical assistance.[13] The monetary commitment would have been substantial, and although the proposed legislation appeared to have strong support and passed both houses of Congress, it was vetoed by President Nixon largely as a result of pressure by conservative groups such as the moral majority, which argued that such legislation was antifamily and would encourage women to leave the home for the workplace.[14]

Since the veto of the Comprehensive Development Act, the effort to establish a child care policy has succeeded only in the area of tax policy. In 1978, Congress replaced the proposed tax deduction with a tax credit for child care costs irrespective of income or marital status. Maximum deduction ceilings have been increased since then. Congress has also encouraged employers to provide child care assistance by allowing tax benefits for employers who do so. During the 1980s, there was a general recognition of the problem of child care, as evidenced by the proposal of hundreds of bills intended to resolve it.[15] The Act for Better Child Care, proposed in 1988, included provisions for federal grants to the states and the establishment of federal standards for child care. Conservative forces, led by President Bush, suggested that tax incentives rather than federal subsidies should be the key ingredients of child care policy. Some feminists also supported this approach, arguing that because tax credits could be utilized by both homemakers and working mothers, child care would be seen as an issue for all women, not just working women. Some groups argued the reverse position, that providing tax incentives for nonworking women would reinforce the notion that women should stay at home and raise the children by giving them an inducement to do so. As a result of the conflict between these opposing views, there have been no federal initiatives, and although some states have sought solutions to the child care problem, the attempt to reduce the budget deficit by cutting federal funds for state block grant programs has seriously hindered the states' efforts to increase their involvement in child care. As in the past, it is economic conditions that determine the policies and the debate with regard to child care.

Family Leave

The origins of current federal policies concerning family leave can be traced to state protective legislation of the nineteenth century that restricted the number of hours that women could work. Such restrictions were justified by medical testimony suggesting that certain types of work, as well as long periods of work, would have detrimental effects on the childbearing capabilities of women.[16] In its decision in *Muller* v. *Oregon* (1908), the Supreme Court prohibited regulations setting maximum hours of work for men but argued that such regulations for woman were necessary to protect offspring.[17] This legislation reflected prevailing attitudes concerning the health of women and the "proper" role of women as childbearers and nurturers.

In the 1920s and 1930s, women were still treated as "temporary workers," assumed to be present in the workplace only until they got married and began to raise children. Many employers refused to hire married women and dismissed single women after they became married. In businesses where married women were allowed to work, they were often forced to resign or were fired after they became pregnant.

World War II brought about some fundamental changes for women in the work force. The labor shortage created by the military draft necessitated the increased employment of women in key industries that supported the war effort. With women now playing an essential role, federal agencies had to establish standards for their protection, which included the recommendation of a six-week prenatal leave and a two-month postnatal leave. Many employers, however, cited "aesthetic and moral" reasons for not wanting women in the workplace, such as the "bad effect" that the sight of a pregnant woman had on male workers.[18]

Public policy with regard to pregnant women changed after passage of the Civil Rights Act of 1964. Although Title VII of the act prohibits discrimination in private and public employment on the basis of gender, initial rulings by the Equal Employment Opportunity commission held that "the denial of benefits to pregnant employees comparable to those provided to male and non-pregnant employees did not constitute sex discrimination."[19] In 1972, however, the guidelines were changed to define disabilities resulting from pregnancy (such as miscarriage, abortion, or childbirth) as "temporary disabilities" and to award those having such temporary disabilities all of the usual benefits associated with a temporary disability.[20] This ruling was the policy governing the treatment of pregnant women in the workplace until 1976–1977, when the guidelines were challenged in two cases decided by the Supreme Court.

In *General Electric Company* v. *Gilbert* (1976), the Court ruled that a company plan that failed to cover pregnancy-related disabilities did not discriminate on the basis of gender since the plan did not discriminate between men and women but between pregnant and nonpregnant persons.[21] In a related case, *Nashville Gas* v. *Satty* (1977), the Court ruled that sick pay could be refused to women who were unable to work because of pregnancy or childbirth.[22] Both cases suggested that the Court did not find that discrimination against pregnant women necessarily violated Title VII's prohibitions against gender discrimination. The task of establishing prohibitions against discrimination toward pregnant women was left to Congress.

In 1978 Congress responded by passing the Pregnancy Discrimination Act, which amended Title VII and prohibited discrimination against pregnant women. The act generally required employers who offer health insurance or disability plans (or both) to provide coverage to pregnant women for all conditions related to pregnancy and childbirth. In the area of abortion the act is less clear, since it does not require coverage for abortion unless the health of the mother is at stake. Abortions are not precluded from coverage, however. The Pregnancy Discrimination Act established the following: (1) discrimination on the basis of pregnancy or conditions related to childbirth is a form of gender discrimination; (2) such conditions must be treated the same as other forms of temporary disability; (3) abortions, except when the life of the mother is at stake, need not be covered by an employer plan although they may be, at the discretion of the employer; (4) an employer may not discriminate in the hiring, firing, or promotion of a pregnant woman; (5) an employer may not establish a mandatory leave policy for a pregnant woman that is not based on her inability to work; and (6) all reinstatement privileges and benefits provided to those who are temporarily disabled must be available to pregnant women.[23] Unfortunately, most women do not have jobs that provide them with disability benefits; thus, many women are not covered by the act.

Title VII and its amendment were federal actions that expanded the rights of pregnant women in the workplace; policies concerning maternity and family leave were generally left up to the private sector, with the assumption that they would be included in the fringe benefits packages negotiated between employers and unions. Unions historically have concentrated on increasing the basic wage rates for workers; however, fringe benefits packages have increasingly been a subject of collective bargaining between unions and employers. The most generally available maternity-related benefit is job-protected leave; the benefits provided tend to be proportional to the size of the firm, that is, the larger the firm, the more benefits are normally available to each woman.[24]

Business interests resisted inclusion of such benefits in their bargaining agreements. Dramatic increases in the cost of fringe benefit packages were often cited as a reason for opposition to family leave legislation. Opponents of leave policies frequently pointed to their destructive effects on the ability of U.S. business to compete abroad, but they were often confronted by the fact that virtually all the western industrialized nations have already adopted such policies, and most of them include some form of guaranteed leave and protection of wages; some (most notably those of Germany) include similar benefits for the male parent.

If the primary responsibility for providing family leave is assumed to be that of the business community, the evidence does not suggest that the burden would be too heavy. Judith Lichtman argues that statistics for 1987 presented by the United States Chamber of Commerce refute the argument that the costs of providing family leave are too high: (1) Chamber of Commerce estimates of the costs dropped from $16 billion per year to less than $3 billion per year; and (2) half of the firms surveyed by the Chamber of Commerce cited the benefits such programs provided them in the hiring and retaining of good employees.[25]

The Problems of Child Care and Family Leave: A Need for Public Awareness

Public policy with regard to child care and family leave, perhaps more than in any other area, reflects the attitudinal changes that have taken place in recent decades concerning the roles of women in the family and the workplace. The family as glorified in "Leave It to Beaver" and "Ozzie and Harriet" in the 1950s and 1960s does not exist. For reasons of personal career objectives or economic necessity, tens of millions of women go to work every day. Because of the virtually nonexistent or at best haphazard system of child care, many of them worry constantly about the type of care their children are receiving and whether that care will be there tomorrow.

Unfortunately for these working women, government and society have not been particularly sympathetic to their cause—in part because of the traditional notion that upper- and middle-class women should stay home while their husbands work or that they can work while their children are being cared for by working-class young women for wages low enough to make child care affordable. Thus the issue still has its class aspects. Working-class women who need to work must generally make other, more complex arrangements because they cannot afford professional child care; the alternative is to move out of the job market periodically and care for their children themselves. The fact that women's groups have found the child care and family leave issues so difficult to deal with demonstrates their complexity. Can some women enjoy the opportunities or gains resulting from the new role of women as members of the work force only at the expense of other women?

Government, for its part, has shown an unwillingness to become involved. Conservative forces will no doubt continue to fight government-supported day care options. By using adjectives such as profamily and antifamily to describe various proposals for reform, they endorse the traditional view of the family—the idealized version of Americans' recent past. Conservative forces will also continue to argue that government policies that regulate are an unnecessary governmental intrusion in people's lives. Many will also argue that at a time of scarce financial resources and a huge budget deficit, it is impossible to expand government programs.

Several developments have recently brought to the public's attention various issues related to the needs of children. The discussion of children's issues during the 1992 presidential campaign, the perceived debt that the Clinton administration owes to women, and the Nannygate controversy involving Zoë Baird and Kimba Wood have definitely raised the consciousness of Americans regarding the problems associated with work and family. The successful resolution of the problems of child care and family leave is of primary importance for women, for children, and for the future of society.

NOTES

1. John P. Fernandez, *Child Care and Corporate Productivity* (Lexington, Mass.: Lexington Books, 1986), 17.
2. Ibid.
3. Ibid., 18.
4. Lawrence E. Lynn, *Designing Public Policy* (Santa Monica, Calif.: Goodyear, 1980), 258.
5. Ibid., 259.
6. Ibid.
7. Ibid., 260.
8. Fernandez, *Child Care and Corporate Productivity*, 18.
9. Ibid., 19.
10. Lynn, *Designing Public Policy*, 26.
11. Fernandez, *Child Care and Corporate Productivity*, 19.
12. Lynn, *Designing Public Policy*, 261.
13. Fernandez, *Child Care and Corporate Productivity*, 19.
14. Ibid.
15. For a good description of some of these proposals, see Leslie W. Gladstone, "Parental Leave Legislation in the 100th Congress," Report no. IB 86–132, Congressional Reference Service, January 26, 1988.
16. Ibid., 8–9.
17. *Muller* v. *Oregon*, 208 U.S. 412 (1908).
18. Gladstone, 9.
19. Ibid., 11.
20. Ibid.
21. *General Electric Company* v. *Gilbert*, 429 U.S. 125 (1976).
22. *Nashville Gas* v. *Satty*, 434 U.S. 137 (1977).
23. Gladstone, 13–14.

24. Ibid., 20.

25. Judith L. Lichtman, "Leave Policies Establish Pro-Family Work Place," *Dayton Daily News and Journal Herald,* September 7, 1987, 7A.

Chronology

1908 In *Muller* v. *Oregon,* the Supreme Court prohibits regulations setting maximum number of work hours for men but rules that such regulations are necessary for women because of their maternal role.

1909 Meeting of the first White House Conference on the Care of Dependent Children.

1919 Meeting of the White House Conference on Standards of Child Welfare.

1941 Congress passes the Lanham Act, allocating federal funds to states to establish child care facilities for women working in defense plants during World War II.

1976 In *General Electric* v. *Gilbert,* the Supreme Court rules that a company plan that fails to cover pregnancy-related disabilities does not discriminate on the basis of gender because the plan does not discriminate between men and women but between pregnant and nonpregnant persons.

1977 In *Nashville Gas* v. *Satty,* the Supreme court rules that sick pay can be refused to women who are unable to work because of pregnancy or childbirth.

1978 Congress approves the allowance of tax credits for child care costs.

1978 Congress passes the Pregnancy Discrimination Act, amending Title VII of the Civil Rights Act of 1964.

1987 In *California Federal Savings and Loan Association et al.* v. *Guerra,* the Supreme Court upholds a California law that requires employers of fifteen or more workers to offer pregnant women four months of unpaid leave and the promise of a comparable job when they return to work.

1988 The Act for Better Child Care is proposed in Congress, but is not passed.

1993 Congress passes the Family and Medical Leave Act, which allows employees to take up to twelve weeks of unpaid leave because of their own illness, the illness of a family member, or the birth or adoption of a child.

QUESTIONS

1. Why does our society consider child care a "women's issue"? What is the effect of thinking about child care in this way? How else might we think about responsibility for child care?
2. What changes have taken place in child care and family leave policies over the years? Why is pregnancy considered a "temporary disability" for the purposes of public policy?
3. Why does the United States lag behind similar Western democracies in the area of family policy?

The "Nanny" Question in Feminism (2002)

Joan C. Tronto

Joan Tronto is a professor at Hunter College in the Department of Political Science. She has published several articles on the ethic of care and feminist political theory.

Danielle Slap [age 3] was looking out the window into the backyard when she spotted a group of four deer of varying sizes. "Look," she said. "There is a family: there's a daddy, mommy, baby and the baby sitter."

—Enid Nemy, Metropolitan Diary

I. The Question: Who is Responsible for Unjust Unintended Consequences?

Are social movements responsible for their unfinished agendas? One of the great accomplishments of second-wave feminism was to end the gender caste barrier that had kept women out of professions. Since most women professionals are heterosexual and marry, and because people generally marry within their socioeconomic status groups, one consequence of this greater freedom for women to become professionals has been to increase social and economic inequality between households (Milkman, Reese, and Roth 1998). Another consequence has been to make the problem of finding child care arrangements a concern for working mothers from all social classes. There are many options for child care in the United States: mothers can decide not to work or to arrange a work schedule with their partners so that they need no external support for child care. Where it is available, they can use professional day care at work or in the community. There are informal child care centers. Mothers can leave their children with a family member (Uttal 1999) or a neighbor. Mothers can also hire a nanny, *au pair*, or domestic worker who lives with them or who works in their own home full time. Such practices have become sufficiently widespread to be naturalized into the small joke quoted above published 6 September 1999 in the *New York Times*.

This essay mainly concerns the morality of practices of upper-class and upper middle-class men and women who are raising children in (usually) two-career (usually heterosexual) households.[1] Some suggest that two professional adults raising children constitute a new family type, the two-career household (Gregson and Lowe 1994). The two-career household is different even from dual-earner households in that both professionals in such a household hold down professional jobs where the time demands are excessive or unpredictable. The two-career households, and others similarly situated, are more likely to use a paid full-time domestic caretaker who either lives in the household or does not. This focus is narrow demographically, but these particular families are important. First, these are the families who have most benefited from the end of caste barriers to the professions, and part of my goal in this essay is to invoke long-standing feminist commitments of "sisterhood" and support for all women as a guide to moral action. Second, despite their small number in society, the broader ideology of "intensive motherhood" (Hays 1996) closely parallels what this group of men and women are doing, and their mothering ideals permeate and reflect prevailing ideology.

Of course, all child care work in the United States pays relatively poorly and has low prestige. Nevertheless, the women hired to do in-home, full-time child care endure the most difficult circumstances. In this essay, I shall primarily focus on two of the three groups described by Pirette Hondagneu-Sotelo in her recent study of domestic workers in Los Angeles. These are women who are hired as live-in help and those who are employed full time in a particular household.[2] Almost all of the workers employed in these ways in Los Angeles are immigrant women from Mexico, Central America, and Latin America. I shall use the terms domestic servants, domestic workers, and nannies to refer to these individuals.

In this essay I want to consider how the confluence of these two unintended consequences, greater social and economic inequality and greater demands for child care, have rearranged responsibilities in a way that undercuts basic feminist notions of justice. I shall first demonstrate that when the wealthiest members of society use domestic servants to meet their child care needs, the result is unjust for individuals and for society as a whole. I shall then consider whether there are ameliorating circumstances that make this solution, even if unjust, necessary. I shall consider some alternative ways in which women might think about child care to make it less unjust. Then I shall return to this question, under what circumstances should social movements be responsible for the unjust unintended consequences of their actions? I shall conclude that, in this case, the "nanny question" is a serious problem for feminists interested in justice.

II. Domestic Tyranny

> "[A] family with live-in servants is—inevitably I think—a little tyranny."
>
> —Michael Walzer, *Spheres of Justice: A Defense of Pluralism and Equality*

> "Isn't 'feminist domestic employer' a contradiction?"
>
> —Cynthia Enloe as quoted in Bakan and Stasiulis

Although the extent of domestic service in the United States is hard to measure (Hondagneu-Sotelo 1994, 50), there is no doubt that it is on the rise in the last twenty years. (This is also the case elsewhere; on Britain, see Gregson and Lowe 1994; on Canada see Giles and Arat-Koç 1994; Bakan and Stasiulis 1997.) In the United States, the use of domestic servants for child care and other "core" household care activities has increased, especially in those urban areas where economic inequality is greatest (Milkman, Reese, and Ross 1998). Thus, inequality is associated with increased use of domestic servants. Activists in industrial societies have been concerned to regulate the global trade in domestic servants (Glenn, Chang, et al. 1994; Bakan and Stasiulis 1997; Chang 2000).

In this section of the paper, I want to argue that the use of domestic servants is unjust in all but the most unusual cases, constituting a tyranny in Walzer's term (1983, 52) and contrary to feminist principles in Enloe's judgment (in Bakan and Stasiulis 1997, 13)

A. Moral Uniqueness of Domestic Service

[Quoting an employer who was hurt and angry that her live-in nanny had asked for a bonus:] So I made some points. I said, "You know, you say that I didn't give you a bonus, well, why don't you take back all those Christmas presents I gave you and cash them in? There's your bonus!". . . . I said, you know, "Is money just really all that's important to you?" (Hondagneu-Sotelo 2001, 120)

Let me first consider the objection that there is no reason to expend any special moral energy on this question because using domestic service is no different from purchasing services and goods on the market. One might argue that to make the choice to use domestic servants is only to participate in another market relation, no different from sending a child to a day care center, or purchasing prepared food, or eating in a restaurant that employs and underpays dishwashers. There are several morally relevant differences between hiring domestic servants and purchasing commodities and services on the market. First, the institutional setting of the household is a different setting than the market. Because domestic service takes place in a private home, it is often not regarded as employment at all. Michael Walzer writes: "The principles that rule in the household are those of kinship and love. They establish the underlying pattern of mutuality and obligation, or authority and obedience. The servants have no proper place in that pattern, but they have to be assimilated to it" (1983, 52). Feminist scholars have been more dubious than Walzer about the household as the realm of kinship and love; nonetheless, the household's personalism makes it distinctive. Insofar as domestic servants are conceived as a substitute for the wife in a traditional household, they are expected to conform to an account of their work that is only partly real "work." As Hondagneu-Sotelo observes, employers were often shocked to think that their child care workers were only working for the money (2001, 120). The household is a different kind of institution than a market.

Second, the relationships within a household are considerably more immediate and more intimate than in a market. The status of quasi-family member means that the domestic servant is enmeshed in the complete details of the lives of the people served. Domestic workers' work is expected to reflect the values (for example, in raising children or performing household duties), tastes (for example, in purchasing food, cleaning products, and other commodities for the household), and other aspects of the lives of their employers. The space in which they do their work is not a public work space, but someone else's most private space. Thus, the level of control that employers expect to be able to exert over domestic workers is very great, and noncompliance is often emotionally and psychologically charged.[3]

A third factor that distinguishes domestic service from other market relations. Insofar as the work of domestic service is care, one of the "products" of care is that it creates ongoing relationships among the care givers and care receivers. The quality of these relationships is thus one of the measures of the quality of the work that is done. Thus, part of the work of domestic service itself is to nurture and maintain care relationships. While these concerns also exist in market relations of care (for example, among nursing home aides and their charges), they are presumed to be paradigmatic of domestic relations, and thus, form a central part of domestic service.

B. Domestic Employment from within the Relationship: Three Perspectives

Within the relationship of domestic employment, there are different moral perspectives that we can consider. If, for the sake of simplicity, we consider the simplest pattern of relationship, then we need to consider three perspectives. We can consider the perspective of the worker, of the employing parent, usually a mother, and of the cared-for charge (to borrow a term from Kittay 1999). In this essay I shall assume that the charge is a child, but the argument is also true in part when the charge is an older person in need of sustained assistance.

Workers. The average domestic is paid woefully low wages. Hondagneu-Sotelo reports that job offers of $150 per week for a live-in worker are not unusual in Los Angeles. She estimates that live-in domestic workers earn less than minimum wage and work an average of sixty-four hours each week. Live-out nannies she surveyed averaged $5.90 an hour for approximately forty to forty-five hours each week (2001, 35, 38).

Nevertheless, according to the workers themselves, the most degrading aspect of their work is that they are not accorded sufficient respect and dignity. From the standpoint of workers, the moral stress of being a domestic worker is great. Not really "one of the family," domestics occupy a netherworld without support or moral acknowledgment for their roles (Rollins 1985; Romero 1992). The work that one is expected to do involves reflecting the values of an employer, which makes it alienating in many ways from one's own sense of value and worth. Domestic servants must work hard to establish and keep their dignity (Colen 1986) and to cope with the sense of anger and powerlessness that they often feel (Rollins 1985). Further, many domestic servants have families of their own, often left far away or far behind (Hondagneu-Sotelo 2001). While all working mothers have to cope somehow with the fact that they must leave their children in someone else's care, there is a poignant irony in the way in which domestic workers must leave their children so that they can ensure that "other people's children" receive the proper care (Romero 1992; Romero 1997). Live-in workers have still less control over the space that they occupy, the food that they can eat, and whether and how they can spend their leisure time. They might be vulnerable to sexual harassment or abuse by their employer or others in the household, and there is little recourse to anyone outside of the household for assistance. Although some employment laws do pertain to domestic workers, they are rarely enforced. Although there are a few organizations such as Domestic Workers of America, most domestics have little or no recourse to address complaints, no union protections, and so forth. While many low-paid workers in the United States lack such opportunities for collective action, the situation is obviously worse when each worker is in a separate workplace.

There are also moral rewards that can flow from this relationship. Caring for children and elderly people, though devalued in our culture, is very powerful and important. Domestic workers surely have an appreciation of the work that they do, and many find "respect and feelings" (Colen 1986) in their work. Domestic servants often find that a close personal relationship that might develop with an employer will be rewarding as well (Hondagneu-Sotelo 2001).

On balance, though, as Diemut Bubeck has observed, care workers are always especially vulnerable to a particular form of exploitation. "The exploitative mechanism," she writes, "is the social institution of the sexual division of labor which constructs women as carers and thus systematically 'extracts surplus labor' in the form of unpaid care from them (to hearken back to Marx's definition of exploitation)" (1995, 181). This is especially true for domestic workers. Among other aspects of the way in which the "circle of care" is exploitative, according to Bubeck, is the way in which workers can express their discontent. In most work, workers who wish to resist some aspect of their employment can respond by shirking their work responsibilities. In caring work, workers who shirk their duties impose the greatest harm on their charges. Because care work creates a relational bond between the worker and the charge, it is thus harder for any care worker to fight back, and this is especially so in a household where one is working intensively with others with whom one has established an ongoing caring relationship. We should conclude that the nature of domestic work makes likely the abuse of the workers and threats to their moral dignity. Given the low levels of pay, the working conditions, and the high level of arbitrariness that employers can exercise, domestic servants are highly vulnerable to abuse.

Employing Parents. Usually, the burden of hiring, firing, and supervising the domestic help, like all domestic duties, falls to women. A mother might think of the domestic worker as either her ally or her competition. In so doing, and in the assumptions about she makes about the competence of her worker, she has considerable control over the quality of the worker's work life. Nonetheless, given the intimacy and high stakes of this relationship, chances are high that some part of the work will be unsatisfactory on some terms. The power of the employer to change the conditions of employment, to act erratically, and to insult and degrade workers, is very high. It is likely, given such great power, to become tyrannical. The mother might think of the worker as competition for the affection of the children, for example. She might then fire workers after some time, regardless of the quality of their work (Hrdy 1999).

On the other hand, an employing mother might be aware of all of these potential abuses, of the low wages that she is paying, and so forth, and feel guilty about it. The guilt of mothers around using domestic workers is, thus, often great. But what positive role does such guilt have? It may in fact result in forms of behavior, such as gift-giving or enforced intimacy, that actually also may act as burdens on the lives of domestic workers (Rollins 1985; Bakan and Stasiulis 1997).

More recently, Hondagneu-Sotelo (2001) has noticed a different disparity. Very busy two-career mothers are less eager to spend time establishing a personal relationship with their workers. While the workers value such relationships, the interviewed employers resented the time that they spent learning about the workers' lives, concerns, and problems. Thus, there is a lack of reciprocity between the involvement of the worker in the life of the employer and a corresponding involvement of the employers in the lives of their workers.

Children. Finally, what is the consequence for children of growing up with another adult charged with their care? As feminists have asked about male domination in the household, what kind of moral education does one learn from being in a household in which one adult is so clearly subordinate to others? No doubt children do well when they are surrounded by adults who take care of them, and many testimonials suggest how vital the caregiver has been to the children (Romero 1997). On the other hand, there are a number of undesirable consequences of such care. Children may well come to expect that other people, regardless of their connection to them, will always be available to meet their needs. They may come to treat people as merely means, and not as ends in themselves. While it may be desirable for children to have another ally in a household, if that ally is not an independent person, what good will it do? Susan Okin has suggested (following J. S. Mill and Mary Wollstonecraft) that the family is the learning and proving ground for democracy and a sense of justice (Okin 1989). It does not bode well for the creation of democratic citizens if children witness the arbitrary and capricious interaction of parents and servants or if they are permitted to treat domestic servants in a similar manner.

Indeed, when we recall that race/ethnicity usually mark and distinguish the employers and the workers, children cared for by domestic servants are being more completely immersed into a racist culture. Sau-ling Wong goes further, and in writing about the role of people of color in recent Hollywood films, suggests that "in a society undergoing radical demographic and economic changes, the figure of the person of color patiently mothering white folks seems to allay racial anxieties" (1994, 69).

Mary Romero observes that the other side of this issue is also important. Working-class children are forced to learn early on that they have to endure the difficulties of life. What equality of opportunity can exist for a child who grieves as her mother goes off each day or week to serve, essentially, as a substitute mother for some other children and leaves her without her mother? Or, when the child is taken along to be a human toy for the children of the well-to-do (Romero 1997)? For the children as well as the mothers and the workers, then, there are likely to be unjust consequences from domestic service.

For a variety of reasons, then, hiring domestic servants seems an intrinsically unjust practice. In saying so, I do not deny that there are some employing mothers and fathers who are aware of these moral hazards and do their best to preserve the dignity of the workers that they employ. Nonetheless, study after study finds these similar patterns of abuse (Colen 1986; Romero 1992; Gregson and Lowe 1994; Bakan and Stasiulis 1997; Giles and Arat-Koç 1994; Chang 2000; Hondagneu-Sotelo 2001).

If it is unjust, though, why is this practice increasing? It is possible that, though unjust, there is no alternative to hiring domestic servants. People do not act in ways that they consider immoral. What might the parents who hire domestic servants be telling themselves as they hire domestic workers, and what moral status do such arguments have?

III. The Necessity Defense: Are There Alternatives to Hiring Domestic Servants?

> "You want someone who puts the children before herself," said Judy Meyers, 37, a mother of two in Briarcliff Manor, N.Y., who works for a health insurance company. "But to find someone for the right amount of money is not so easy."
>
> —Caren Rubenstein, Consumer's World: Finding a Nanny Legally

In an article entitled "Consumer's World: Finding a Nanny Legally," published in the *New York Times*, 28 January 1993, Caren Rubenstein says that working mothers who hire nannies do so because they believe it is in the best interests of their children, even if it means that they will try to take advantage of their nanny. Such a belief only outweighs the injustice of the practice, though, if it is the only way to provide adequate care for their children. Furthermore, simply because there is a rationalization for a belief does not make it just. In this section I shall first inquire about the values of upper middle-class mothers that might justify their belief. I will show that a set of beliefs that primarily benefit only well-off families make hiring nannies look necessary.

A. Upper Middle-Class Values and the Need for Competitive, "Intensive" Mothering

The well-off women who hire domestic servants believe that they are acting in the best interests of their children. For the upper middle-class, "good mothering" is inevitably tied to children's success in the context of a highly competitive capitalist environment.

Feminist philosophers in recent years have emphasized and taken some comfort in the ways that mothering stands against the hegemonic culture of capitalistic competition. Sara Ruddick (1989) and, more recently, Eva Kittay (1999) argue that mothering or caring for a charge follows a different, noncapitalist, logic. Virginia Held argues that, in a post-patriarchal world, we would be able to view the noncontractual relationship between mother and child as an alternative paradigm that could serve to inform a broad array of social relationships and institutions (Held 1993). Sharon Hays has argued that by stepping out of the labor market, young mothers defy capitalist logic (Hays 1996).

In fact, though, mothering practices can only ever partly defy their existing culture, and hiring domestic servants seems to be a part of capitalist logic. As Ruddick noted, one of the central tasks for mothers (that is, anyone who engages in mothering practices) is to help their children fit into existing societies. Thus, mothers are also in part enforcers of existing culture. It seems almost a truism to acknowledge that "the approach to child rearing—and the language used to articulate it—has always paralleled the ideology of the era" (Schwartz 1993, 262). Since World War II, as Ellen Seiter and others have argued, the model for child rearing that has predominated emphasizes the child's intellectual development. "The new child psychology was a child-centered model. Implicit in its proscriptions was a disavowal of maternal authority and an upgrading of the child's own desires as rational and goal directed. Because early life events for the child were of supreme importance, caretaking responsibilities expanded" (Seiter 1998, 308).

Ironically, then, as demands on mothers increased, their authority decreased. Their authority passed to experts. The standards for mothers' success become their capacities to produce children who meet or exceed expert predictions. Because these standards are often based on comparisons with other children, the dream of every good mother or parent is to produce, as Garrison Keillor has humorously noted, children who are all above average, reported Joe Pollack in his article, "Keillor Dazzling Down River," in the 19 July 1990 edition of the *St. Louis Post-Dispatch.* Mothers are asked to find a way to squeeze more out of limited resources, and have little authority to act to control this world. The perception that opportunities will not always expand means that children require an ever greater competitive advantage over other children (Schwartz 1993; Edwards 2001). Mothers are urged to provide their children with the right music, to have them participate in the best activities, attend the right schools, and so forth, to improve their chances later on in life. Mothers are caught in a cycle of competition to try to improve their children's lives. While mothers may unselfishly love their children and try to do the best for them, in a competitive society they must also try to gain and keep competitive advantage over other people's children.

This view is, of course, an ideal type and somewhat overdrawn. Research also suggests that though parents are constrained by the demands of raising their children, their children also connect them to a broader social network where they engage in care giving towards others (Gallagher and Gerstel 2001). Nonetheless, the justified anxiety about their children's futures makes parents, and especially middle-class parents (Lareau 2000), engage in practices designed to improve the competitiveness of their own children. That some other person's children (for example, the nanny's children) might be disadvantaged by this action may be regrettable, but it is a part of the "system" that individual mothers can well argue they are powerless to affect.

Short of hiring someone to come into their homes full time to take care of their children, upper middle-class parents could choose to take their children to day care centers, to use the services of women who provide day care in their homes, to leave their children with relatives, or to arrange for their children to spend their time in after-school programs. Any worthy form of day care provides workers who are deeply committed to the interests and needs of each child. But the fear for upper middle-class parents is that their children may not receive enough attention in such settings.

Relatively little high-quality, accessible day care is available in the United States. There is no guarantee that relatives and informal at-home day care providers will provide a sufficiently enriching environment for children (Uttal 1999). After-school programs may not be available, convenient, or of sufficient quality. In a book review published 16 April 1995 in the *New York Times*, Susan Chira points out that parents who are "obsessed with providing their children with sufficient intellectual stimulation" hire household work because they believe that the children are better off in their own homes where the parents can control the enriching environment to some extent by providing material benefits to their children.

Insofar as parents who hire household work are "obsessed with providing their children with sufficient intellectual stimulation" (Chira 1995), they believe that the children are better off in their own homes, where the parents can control the enriching environment to some extent by providing material benefits to their children. They then need to decide whether to hire a worker who is like them or different, either to reinforce their world views or to provide children with additional enriching experiences; for example, learning French or Spanish from a native speaking nanny (Wrigley 1995). For example, Los Angeles public relations consultant Kathleen Rogers, in an article entitled "A Real Nanny Dilemma: Many Caretakers Have Limited English Skills; Will Kids They Watch Fall Behind?" published 6 March 1995 in the *Los Angeles Times*, worries that if children spend all day with a Spanish-speaking maid they will be at a competitive disadvantage to children whose nannies speak grammatically correct English. Thus, the decisions made about who and how to provide care flow from the parental concern with the children's competitive advantage. The result is to further create a sense that, as long as an action is taken on behalf of one's children, then it cannot be morally questionable.

If there were opportunities for public discussions of needs, questions might open about the material needs of households, whether parents have to work so many hours, and about other ways to cope with competition among children. At present there is no discussion of the ways in which working more hours to earn enough money for all the "stuff" might distort other values, such as spending time with one's children. Barbara Omolade made a similar point when she reflected upon her own children's relatively poor economic background but their rich emotional and familial life and compared it to the material abundance but emotional impoverishment experienced by many suburban children (Omolade 1994). Yet there is no public arena for the discussion of such conceptions of needs. Fueled by a fear of the increasing competition for scarce future seats in competitive colleges, jobs, and so forth, the needs of children become greater and more expansive, without limit or public discussion.

Thus, the injustice of hiring domestic servants is obscured by the ideological construction of intensive and competitive mothering.

B. Obscuring Injustice

This problem is more intractable still. For exactly what makes domestic work potentially abusive is what makes it most adequate as the form of care for intensive and competitive mothering. This situation highlights two dimensions of caring not often stressed but crucially important.

The first complication is that caring work cannot be compressed into a manageable block of time (Stone 2000). As a result, given the ideology of "intensive motherhood," no working mother's care can be fully adequate. Anita Garey analyzed how mothers minimize their absence through distinctions between the routine work of care and the tasks that really require that they, and not a substitute worker or service, be present. She described three essential roles as "being there": the mother's relationship to the child, "family time"; the integration of children into the family's life (usually having to do with mediating the relationship of child and father); and "doing things," linking children to the larger public world (usually of school or activities) (1999, 31). Other activities, such as cooking, cleaning, driving children around, and so forth, could be delegated. While the mothers that Garey interviewed did not hire domestic workers, they either had to figure out a way to be present during the crucial times and to make certain that there was some way to provide the care during the other times, or think of themselves as less than perfect mothers. Nevertheless, what is difficult about these essential caring tasks is that they resist any logic of temporal control. Separating the wheat from the chaff in "being there" for one's child is not a simple matter. "Being there" is obviously important for a school play, but if a child injures herself during routine play that has been delegated to a sitter, then someone needs to fill in the "being there" role for the mother. In truth, no mother can ever be present for all of the "essential care" moments even though the ideology of intensive motherhood sets this standard. Domestic workers, because they are present in a full-time way and devoted only to these children, are more likely to seem an adequate substitute for the mother. (In fact, they realize that they need to finesse these anxieties; they will deliberately not mention, for example, a child's first steps but wait until the parent sees them (Hodagneu-Sotelo 2000).

Second, insofar as all caring involves "the politics of needs interpretation" (Fraser 1989), hiring a domestic worker greatly enhances the authority of parents to define their children's needs. Human needs are only set in the most basic form: what particular children "need" will depend upon their parents' views of what they need. But parents are not able to assert their view of needs unilaterally. Day care center staff, informal providers of home care, and school staff are all likely to provide competing definitions of children's needs. Domestic workers might disagree with parents, but they are not likely to remain employed for long if their views of the children's needs do not conform with the parents'. Hiring a nanny is a way for parents to try to keep control of their children's senses of their needs. This becomes increasingly difficult in our culture where increasingly the market defines the needs of people (Luttwak 1999; Schor 2000). Nonetheless, denied authority elsewhere, parents can view their imposition of their view of needs as a necessity for the children's well-being.

Thus, qualities intrinsic in the nature of care, the complexity of time, and of defining needs are made easier through the hiring of domestic workers. Ironically, the more the domestic servant's work approaches the ideal of meeting all of the desires of the parents to "be there" constantly and to adopt their account of what children need, the more the individual domestic worker loses her capacity to shape her work through control of her own time and to apply her own judgment.

By the same token, insofar as hiring domestic workers serves the economic self-interests of well-to-do mothers and fathers, it only does so insofar as it remains economically worthwhile for women to work in a second career. At the point where it is no longer to their economic advantage, mothers might make other decisions about their work. The idea of dramatically increasing the pay of domestic workers is not feasible because mothers' professions only "pay" if they make substantially more than they pay their domestic workers.

But such an advantage is very much at the cost of other people's children. The problem with this division of responsibility is that it makes men and women who are vulnerable economically more blameworthy for their lack of resources. Consider, as a simple matter, a parent's capacity to schedule time so that he or she can "be there" when his or her kids need him or her. As Jody Heymann has demonstrated, working and lower middle-class families are less likely to contain workers who have such job benefits as flex time, sick leave, personal days, and so forth. To be able to exercise some control over one's working time is very important to take care of children when they are sick, or have an important school event, and so forth. But if this allocation follows class structure, then the students most likely to be disadvantaged are those who are already disadvantaged (Heymann 2000). This image of mothering is thus not easy for anyone, but it is especially hard for less well off parents.

We have considered the possibility that hiring domestic servants is justified because it is necessary to provide adequate child care for children. We have seen that there are reasons why upper middle-class parents might think this way, but these reasons rest upon an account of good parenting that is, in its own way, also unjust.

IV. Feminist Responsibilities

According to Margaret Urban Walker, "An 'ethics of responsibility' as a normative moral view would try to put people and responsibilities in the right places with respect to each other" (Walker 1998, 78).

The question that remains for us, then, is whether feminists bear any responsibility for the increasing practice of hiring nannies. Assigning responsibility is a complex problem. Nevertheless, we can draw upon some familiar notions of justice to work our way to a conclusion.

Theorists of justice have long agreed that it is unjust if people directly benefit from harming others. There is no doubt that upper middle-class working men and women benefit greatly from hiring women to work as underpaid, exploited, domestic servants. As Audrey Macklin blunted states, "The grim truth is that some women's access to the high-paying, high-status professions is being facilitated through the revival of semi-indentured servitude. Put another way, one woman is exercising class and citizenship privilege to buy her way out of sex oppression" (1994, 34). But even if upper middle-class *women* who employ domestic servants are acting unjustly, do *feminists* share any responsibility for this injustice?

Obviously, feminists, who as a group made a political argument that had this consequence, cannot be held as responsible as the women who engage in the unjust practice. Indeed, we might say that a completely unexpected consequence should relieve actors from the consequences of their actions. Nonetheless, I suggest that if this consequence was foreseeable, even if unintended, then feminists have to bear some responsibility for it.

Should feminists have foreseen this danger lurking in their calls for more open professions? Several points suggest so. First, in retrospect, feminists should have recognized the class bias in their own professional desires. African American critics frequently worried that white, upper middle-class women were not thinking of all women when they drew up their agendas for action (hooks 1984). Consider, as another example, this reading of Betty Friedan's position: "For Friedan, housework can be done by 'anyone with a strong enough back' (and a 'small enough brain') and it is 'particularly suited to the capacities of feeble-minded girls.' When Friedan defined housework in these terms, she defined 'women's liberation' for the white, middle-class housewives she wrote for as getting out of the home" (Friedan quoted in Giles and Arat-Koç 1994, 4). Second, since feminists long argued that "the personal is political," they should have foreseen that changing the professions would affect private institutions, such as the family, as well.

While increasing economic inequality and the subsequent increase in domestic service are thus unintended consequences of feminist activity, they are not unforeseeable consequences of feminist positions. While feminists are clearly not as responsible for these developments as are the upper middle-class women who are hiring domestic servants, feminists need to recognize that they bear at least some responsibility for this situation.

The incomplete feminist revolution left unresolved the fundamental questions of how to allocate responsibility for child care in our society. For upper middle-class families, resorting to domestic service seems to be a way through the Scylla of mandated stay-at-home moms and the Charybdis of inadequate child care. To put it another way, the use of nannies allows upper middle-class women and men to benefit from feminist changes without having to surrender the privilege of the traditional patriarchal family. The hired household worker is an employee, but she is mainly treated as if she were a wife. Nannies can be imposed upon as if they were members of the family, and that imposition often proves to be abusive. By the same token, if we look at the question from the standpoint of the nanny's children, or from the standpoint of children whose parents have to jury-rig some form of care for them, what benefits the best off may not be the best solution.

V. Toward a Resolution of the Nanny Question

At a minimum, if the analysis of this paper is accurate, then it becomes incumbent upon feminists and other women of means to continue the struggle to realize the feminist revolutionary goals of reallocating household responsibilities within and among households. Short of revolutionary change, however, there is still a great deal that can be done:

Ameliorative Steps. Hondagneu-Sotelo wryly observes that Los Angeles could not function without the care labor of immigrant workers. She does not suggest the abolition of domestic service but urges that steps be taken to make working conditions more humane. These include enforcing the labor laws that exist, including laws for minimum wages and social security benefits. They require that workers and employers be informed of their legal obligations. Beyond these minimal steps, wages can be raised and working conditions made more standard. The Domestic Workers Association, for example, lists among its fundamental demands "an end to sexual harassment, adequate breaks and work schedules, no leftover food, sick days, paid vacations, medical benefits" (Hondagneu-Sotelo 2000, 217).

Radical Reforms. The United States needs to join other industrialized societies in providing child care facilities that are publicly supported, locally based and organized, and that provide for the needs of diverse children and families (compare Michel 1999). The shape and provision of such child care is a complex question, but the first step is to generate a sense that child care is a central public responsibility and that it is wrong to force families to try to solve the problem of child care on their own. Nor, obviously, is it adequate as an argument for justice to insist that women not work and return to their homes; among other reasons, such an answer ignores its own class bias by failing to notice that working-class women have often worked.

Revolutionary Changes. The most profound change that is necessary, however, is to recognize and rethink the ways in which the assignment of responsibility for children's success to their parents (and still, primarily, to their mothers) reinforces the "winner take all" attitudes in our culture. Children are not seen as a collective good in our society but as a good assigned to individual parents (Folbre 1993). Once parents see themselves in competition with all other parents, the prospect for collective action diminishes. Rethinking the balance between work and life, determining how everyone can be properly cared for in a way that exploits no caregivers in particular, is the most profound challenge that remains.

My goal, however, is not to condemn mothers, but to point to the way in which our individualized accounts of mothering make us inured to the social structures that contribute to the growing gaps among advantaged and less advantaged children. Injustice justified by care may not be worse than other forms of injustice, but it is often more difficult to see. Feminists cannot allow their approbation for care to obscure the ways in which current family practices further social and economic inequality and delay into a still more distant future, a time in which all people will be able to do their caring work well, and where all people will be well cared for. Recognizing the argument made in this paper requires feminists to recommit themselves to some very hard political work.

Notes

I thank the editors of this issue and anonymous reviewers for their assistance in writing this essay. An earlier version of this work was presented at Temple University and the comments received there were extremely helpful. I wrote this paper while a Laurance S. Rockefeller Fellow at Princeton University's Center for Human Values, and I am grateful for their support.

1. In this paper, I will switch between referring to mothers and to parents. Despite a generation of feminist activism, relatively little has changed in terms of the willingness of men to assume greater roles for child care duties. See (Bianchi, Milkie, Sayer and Robinson 2000; Hochschild 1989 and 1997). On one level this paper is more directly addressed to women. As the primary beneficiaries of feminist success, they should be most concerned about the unintended consequences of their benefits. Nonetheless, husbands and other family members also benefit from being part of two-career households. Thus, at some points in the paper, especially those that refer to the ways in which we think about children in society, I shall refer to parents and not just mothers.
2. I exclude Hondagneu-Sotelo's third category, women who clean homes one day a week or less, to simplify the argument about "need" and to focus this essay on child care; one can easily extend the argument to the need for a "clean house."
3. In one sense, since two working parents are likely to spend less time in the home than a non-working upper-class woman in the past, it may seem that domestic workers are less subject to such supervision than before. Nonetheless, parents will often resort to extraordinary means to control their nannies. See Rollins 1985; Romero 1992; and Hondagneu-Sotelo, especially where she shows an advertisement for a so-called "nanny-cam" (2001, 140).

References

Bakan, Abigail B., and Daiva Stasiulis, eds. 1997. *Not one of the family: Foreign domestic workers in Canada*. Toronto: University of Toronto Press.

Bianchi, Suzanne, Melissa A. Milkie, Liana C. Sayer, and John P. Robinson. 2000. Is anyone doing the housework? Trends in the gender division of household labor. *Social Forces* 79 (1): 191–228.

Bubeck, Diemut E. 1995. *Care, gender, and justice.* New York: Oxford.

Chang, Grace. 2000. *Disposable domestics: Immigrant women workers in the global economy.* Cambridge: South End Press.

Colen, Shellee. 1986. With respect and feelings: Voices of West Indian domestic workers in New York City. *All American women: Lines that divide and ties that bind,* ed. Johnetta Cole. New York: Free Press.

Edwards, Mark Evan. 2001. Uncertainty and the rise of the work-family dilemma. *Journal of Marriage and the Family* 63 (1): 183–96.

Folbre, Nancy. 1993. *Who pays for the kids?* New York: Routledge.

Fraser, Nancy. 1989. *Unruly practices: Power, discourse, and gender in contemporary social theory.* Minneapolis: University of Minnesota Press.

Friedan, Betty. 1963. *The feminine mystique.* New York: Norton.

Gallagher, Sally K., and Naomi Gerstel. 2001. Connections and constraints: The effects of children on caregiving. *Journal of Marriage and the Family* 63 (1): 265–75.

Garey, Anita I. 1999. *Weaving work and motherhood.* Philadelphia: Temple University Press.

Giles, Wenona, and Sedef Arat-Koç. 1994. Introduction. In *Maid in the market: Women's paid domestic labor,* ed. Wenona Giles and Sedef Arat-Koç. Halifax: Fernwood Publishing.

Glenn, Ellen Nakano, Grace Chang, and Linda Rennie Forcey, eds. 1994. *Mothering: Ideology, experience and agency.* New York: Routledge.

Gregson, Nicky, and Michelle Lowe. 1994. *Servicing the middle classes: Class, gender and waged domestic labor in contemporary Britain.* London, New York: Routledge.

Hays, Sharon. 1996. *The cultural contradictions of motherhood.* New Haven: Yale.

Held, Virginia. 1993. *Feminist morality: Transforming culture, society, and politics.* Chicago: University of Chicago Press.

Heymann, Jody. 2000. *The widening gap: Why America's working families are in jeopardy and what can be done about it.* New York: Basic.

Hochschild, Arlie R. 1989. *The second shift.* New York: Avon.

———. 1997. *The time bind: When work becomes home and home becomes work.* New York: Metropolitan Books.

Hondagneu-Sotelo, Pierrette. 1994 . Regulating the unregulated: Domestic workers' social networks. *Social Problems* 41 (February): 50–64.

———. 2001. *Doméstica: Immigrant workers cleaning and caring in the shadows of affluence*. Berkeley: University of California Press.

Hooks, Bell. 1984. *Feminist theory from margin to center*. Boston, Mass.: South End Press.

Hrdy, Sarah B. 1999. *Mother nature: A history of mothers, infants, and natural selection*. New York: Pantheon Books.

Kittay, Eva Feder. 1999. *Love's labor: Essays on women, equality and dependency*. New York: Routledge.

Lareau, Annette. 2000. Contours of childhood: Social class differences in children's everyday lives. Berkeley: Center for Working Families, University of California. Working Paper #19.

Luttwak, Edward N. 1999. Consuming for love. In *Consuming desires: Consumption, culture and the pursuit of happiness*, ed. Roger Rosenblatt. Washington, D.C.: Island Press.

Macklin, Audrey. 1994. On the outside looking in: Foreign domestic workers in Canada. In *Maid in the market: Women's paid domestic labor*, ed. Wenona Giles and Sedef Arat-Koç. Halifax: Fernwood Publishing.

Michel, Sonya. 1999. *Children's interests/mothers' rights: The shaping of America's child care policy*. New Haven: Yale University Press.

Milkman, Ruth, Ellen Reese, and Benita Roth. 1998. The macrosociology of paid domestic labor. *Work and Occupations* 25 (4): 483–507.

Okin, Susan Moller. 1989. *Justice, gender and the family*. New York: Basic.

Omolade, Barbara. 1994. *The rising song of African American women*. New York: Routledge.

Rollins, Judith. 1985. *Between women: Domestics and their employers*. Philadelphia: Temple University Press.

Romero, Mary. 1992. *Maid in the U.S.A.* New York: Routledge.

———. 1997. Who Takes Care of the Maid's Children? In *Feminism and families*, ed. Hilde Lindemann Nelson. New York: Routledge.

Ruddick, Sara. 1989. *Maternal thinking: toward a politics of peace*. Boston: Beacon Press.

Schor, Juliet, Ed. 2000. *Do Americans shop too much?* Boston: Beacon.

Schwartz, Judith D. 1993. *The mother puzzle: A new generation reckons with motherhood*. New York: Simon and Schuster.

Seiter, Ellen. 1998. Children's desires/mothers' dilemmas: The social contexts of consumption. In *The children's culture reader*, ed. Henry Jenkins. New York: New York University Press.

Stone, Deborah. 2000. Why we need a care movement. *The Nation* (March 12): 13–15.

Uttal, Lynet. 1999. Using kin for child care: Embedment in the socioeconomic networks of extended families. *Journal of Marriage and the Family*. 61 (4): 845–57.

Walker, Margaret Urban. 1998. *Moral understandings: A feminist study of ethics*. New York: Routledge.

Walzer, Michael. 1983. *Spheres of justice: A defense of pluralism and equality*. New York: Basic Books.

Wong, Sau-ling C. 1994. Diverted mothering: Representations of caregivers of color in the age of "multiculturalism." In *Mothering: Ideology, experience and agency*, ed. Evelyn Nakano Glenn, Grace Chang, and Linda Rennie Forcey. New York: Routledge.

Wrigley, Julia. 1995. *Other people's children*. New York: Basic.

QUESTIONS

1. How does Tronto differentiate between care work in the home and other kinds of work? Why does she think this distinction is important?
2. What are the different issues at stake for the worker, the employer, and the "cared for charge"? How are these issues related to feminist concerns of equality, choice, and women's domestic roles?
3. According to Tronto, how is "the nanny question" impacted or influenced by identities of race and class? Why might recognizing other social identities aside from gender be important for feminists who are researching domestic labor?
4. What does Tronto ultimately argue is a feminist's role or responsibility in relation to the issues of domestic labor and childcare? What are some changes that she advocates?

Excerpt from "Zero Balance: Watch out! Your retirement funds are in more trouble than you think" (2001)

By Meg Cox

Retirement may be the last thing college-aged women want to think about at a time when dreams of a career, financial stability, or a family seem more relevant to their immediate future. Yet, gender inequities built into the United States Social Security system and lifelong income disparities between men and women mean that without adequate preparation, American women—particularly women of color—are likely to face a retirement of poverty. Despite higher education levels and greater numbers working full time, women primarily work in low wage positions that offer little in the way of pensions *and less wage-earning power to contribute to Social Security. Currently, 42 percent of all women in the U.S. over the age of 75 live on less than $13,000 a year. Cox explains these economic conditions and emphasizes why women need to take steps now to bolster their financial status for the years to come.*

So you would think that when it comes to retirement, which is fast approaching for the older members of this group, they'd be better off than their mothers—the majority of whom were low-wage workers or homemakers dependent on a man's income. But think again.

"People have this notion that boomer women are just doing so well; many are earning a lot more than their mothers ever dreamed of," says Diana Zuckerman, former director of research at the Institute for Women's Policy Research, in Washington, D.C. "But when it comes to retirement, except for a select group of successful professionals, this generation of women isn't going to be nearly as well off as you might think." In fact, sociologist Nancy Dailey, author of *When Baby Boom Women Retire*, estimates that only 20 percent of boomer women will be financially secure in retirement. Adding insult to injury is this irony: despite all the gains of the women's movement, experts say the best indicator that this group of women will retire well is having a husband.

How Did This Happen?

First, when is impeding most women's ability to save for retirement is money, plain and simple: the leveler, across race and class differences, is that women earn 76 cents for every dollar men earn. Nearly 75 percent of women earn less than $30,000 a year. And while an estimated 8 million businesses in the U.S. are now owned by women, for every female executive in a corner office, there are hundreds of cashiers, secretaries, and cleaning women. And here's the second problem: these women are not just low wage; almost all of them work in jobs that don't even offer pensions, or they don't make enough to receive a pension that will keep them out of poverty. In fact, since benefits are computed based on earnings, many women will have lived in poverty while they worked and sink even deeper upon retirement.

And then there are the homemakers. Nearly all of them are or have been married and are dependent upon outmoded Social Security and pension rules that limit the amount of money they will receive from their husbands' retirement funds if they are divorced or widowed. Add in gender differences in life span and work patterns, and you wind up with a system that shortchanges women every step of the way.

All women suffer from these inequities. Older women are already paying the price; younger women still have to change things. But the group of women now approaching retirement is the least prepared for what is about to hit them. They thought things would be different.

Perhaps the most amazing aspect of this crisis-to-come is how little attention it has received. There is no "Million Matron March" being planned, no twenty-first century Gray Panther, like Maggie Kuhn rousing women to demand a better deal. More frequently, women look up one day and discover that they have too little to fall back on when they retire. It happened to Gail Krogstad when she opened a letter from the Social Security Administration—which now sends an annual letter predicting a person's retirement benefits. Krogstad, 47, an administrator for a senior center in Chicago, is college-educated and worked steadily both before giving birth to her son, who is now 13, and since he started kindergarten. She thought she and her husband were reasonably secure financially, but they are in the process of a divorce, and her husband has declared bankruptcy, so she won't be getting a settlement from him. Suddenly, the size of her future Social Security check is critical, and she was shocked to learn that her estimated take when she retires in 18 years will only be about $700 a month. "I'll be working till I'm 85," she says, only half-facetiously.

And it's even worse if you work at low-paying, traditionally female jobs without pensions, which half of all women do. Marva Diggins, 61, is a divorced mother of three who lives in New York City, one of the most expensive metropolitan areas in the country. She is a home health care aide, earning $7.25 an hour, barely enough to cover her living expenses, let alone save for retirement. She has no pension. Social Security will pay her less than $500 a month if she keeps working until she's 65. Retirement, says Diggins, is simply "too scary to think about."

In a recent survey, 41 percent of working women between 25 and 55 said they're afraid they'll spend their final years in poverty. Those numbers match almost perfectly with the actual numbers of elderly women now living in poverty: 42 percent of all women over 75 are living on less than $13,000 a year. And women of color are even worse off: "Older Women's League (OWL), which also found that only 25 percent of African American women and 33 percent of Latinas have any retirement income from savings or other assets. According to another study, 48 percent of African American women 65 and older who live alone are at or below the average federal poverty level of $9,000 a year for a single person. True, there are plenty of poor old men, but the risk of being poor in old age is 70 percent higher for a woman than for a man.

The fact that Krogstad and Diggins are both divorced is no coincidence. The high divorce rate is one of the factors contributing to baby boomers' bleak retirement prospects. Incredible as it may seem in this day and age, when fewer women are marrying than ever before, what most affects a woman's retirement is her marital status. The rate of divorce has increased dramatically since 1960, and poverty rates are higher for elderly divorced women than for widows. One reason is that the system doesn't recognize the reality of life today. Currently, the average marriage in the U.S. lasts somewhere between seven and nine years, but an ex-wife can't get Social Security spousal benefits unless she's been married for ten years. Many divorced women spend years at home caring for their families; often they had no input into how retirement funds were invested. And after divorce, women often end up with less money than their spouses and, therefore, less money to save. Some women don't even realize they are entitled to a share of their ex's pension benefits.

"I was so naïve when I got divorced," says Maggie Laughlin, 52, of Pittsburgh. Twelve years ago, Laughlin and her husband divorced after 18 years of marriage and two children. Even though she had mediators as well as lawyers handling the divorce, "no one told me that I should have insisted on getting a share of his pension. Instead, they told me to take the house, which I did, not realizing I couldn't afford to keep it," says Laughlin, who learned she had breast cancer a few years ago. Medical bills ate into her savings, and with no pension benefits, she's really worried. "My biggest fear is that I don't have so many years left to work," she says. "How can I ever catch up?"

Even though staying married helps financially, widows in the U.S. are hardly well-off, especially compared with women in countries where widows continue to receive the full amount of a spouse's benefit after his death. In the U.S., according to Karen Holden, a professor of public affairs and consumer science at the University of Wisconsin, married women face an average immediate decline in income of about 30 percent when their husbands die. That's because spousal benefits from both Social Security and pensions fall after a husband's death, and on top of that, a couple's combined savings are often depleted by a husband's final illness. And widowhood comes earlier than many expect, leaving some women to cope with reduced resources for years. "In the 1990s, one fourth of the women who became widows were younger than 65 when they lost their husbands," says Holden, and could expect to live another 15 to 20 years.

But at least heterosexual women are entitled to some benefits by law. Wanda Tritten-Robin, an artist living in Sebastopol, California, was drained, both emotionally and financially, when her long-term female partner died of cancer five years ago. "I've got a master's degree and had a business as a commercial photographer, with clients like the University of California," says Tritten-Robin. But because she was the primary caregiver, Tritten-Robin was "totally burned out" by the time her partner died. She'd spent so much time on caregiving that she wasn't able to pay attention to her business and, eventually, had to close it. Much of her savings had gone to caring for her partner, and because the government does not recognize their 15-year commitment, Tritten-Robin had no chance of receiving survivor's benefits from either a private pension or Social Security. Now 60 years old, she scrapes together a living by selling her artwork and doing odd jobs. "I feel sad that this is where I stand," she says. "I have no savings. I just try not to think about what will happen to me when I get old."

Never-married women—who now make up 20 percent of the boomer generation—generally do badly in retirement. According to OWL, the poverty rate of never-married women will rise from 23 percent now to 35 percent in 2020 as many start to retire. "It's a total myth that if you've never married and worked hard all your life, you'll be fine in retirement," says Nancy Dailey. That's because, except for a small percentage of professional women, the majority of never-married women are in low-paying jobs, have little or no pension, and one quarter of them are single mothers. And they all suffer from the inadequacies of Social Security.

Financial Insecurity

This past year, one question that drove election debates seemed to be, will Social Security be there when GenXers retire? But hardly anybody has addressed the gender inequities built into the system. While Social Security has literally kept millions of women alive—a fourth of elderly women today have no other source of income—it is biased toward men. Benefits are computed based on earnings for the highest paying 35 years of work. Men work an average of 39 years, while women work for pay an average of 27 years. All the years below 35 in which women neither work nor pay into Social Security are counted as zeros, thus pulling down their averages—and their benefits—drastically. It's not surprising then that married women who work outside the home find that half their husband's retirement benefit is usually larger than their own full one.

It's the same with pension benefits provided by individual companies (but regulated by the government). Because women are concentrated in lower-paying jobs, they are usually eligible for only small pensions. Or else these jobs—waitress, health care aide—provide no pensions at all. In addition, women at all points on the pay scale drop in and out of the workforce more often than men, and are three times more likely to work part-time, but the law does not require employers to pay part-time workers any pension benefits.

The system works against women in numerous ways: an employee generally needs five to seven years to become vested in a pension plan, for example, yet the average woman spends 4.4 years in a job. Only two out of five women working in the private sector have any pensions, according to former Secretary of Labor Robert Reich, and on average, their benefits are half those for men. Yet women need more retirement funds than men, because they live, on average, seven years longer. It's no wonder that OWL reiterates in many of its publications that the path to poverty in old age begins the first day women enter the workforce.

"All the young women we talk to about the inequities of retirement say, 'Didn't the women's movement fix all that?'" says Deborah Briceland-Betts, executive director of OWL. "But it isn't about being represented in the work-force in greater numbers. It's about the life patterns of women. The patterns that benefit from current retirement policies are those of men."

Another demographic land mine for boomer women will be the need to take care of their aging parents. For the first time in history, the majority of middle-aged people still have living parents: the fastest growing segment of the population is women 85 and older. "Boomer women will be facing issues of their own health while caring for the very old, and both generations will be operating on a fixed income," says Carroll Estes, founding director of the Institute for Health and Aging at the University of California, San Francisco.

And once again, there has been no planning to account for these women. Roberta Jackson, 52, of New York City, finds it ironic that the only reason her own aging mother is doing so well is because she has eight daughters. Jackson's mother has a small pension supplemented by Social Security, but what really keeps her going is that "every month, we have a sister meeting, and each one of us puts in $25 for Mother," says Jackson, who can't expect the same kind of help when she retires. In fact, she is raising two of her grandchildren and has nothing left at the end of the month for savings.

Not all the problems facing boomer retirees are gender-based. Both sexes have been harmed by changes in retirement benefits. Employers today rarely offer fully funded life-long pensions, common a generation ago. Instead, in so-called defined contribution pensions, employers leave it up to us to invest the money wisely, and we're responsible for making it last until we die. Even though men and women are both affected by these changes, evidence indicates that women play it too safe when it comes to investing and so end up with less than men. Worse still, says Teri Cavanagh, who runs a program for women entrepreneurs at Fleet Bank in Boston, there are countless women who don't even pay attention to the need to invest. Cavanagh says she is always surprised to hear women say, "I can't think about this right now."

. . .

Questions

1. What are the central reasons that women are most likely to end their lives in poverty? How can race and sexual identity intensify these circumstances?
2. How are Social Security benefits determined and allocated? How is the system inequitable for women?
3. According to Cox, why is having a husband the best indicator that women will retire well? How is this related to gender?
4. What significant social realities make the correlation between women's marital status and their retirement stability problematic? Can the same correlation be made for men? Why, or why not?
5. What steps can individual women take to protect themselves and their financial status as they age? What larger social changes seem necessary as well?

A Feminist Perspective on Hurricane Katrina (2005)

Loretta J. Ross

Loretta J. Ross is a founder and the national coordinator of SisterSong Women of Color Reproductive Health Collective, composed of 70 women of color organizations across the country (online at www.sistersong.net*). She was also the co-director of the National March for Women's Lives in Washington D.C. in 2004 and the former executive director of the National Center for Human Rights, a training and resource center for grassroots activists on using human rights education to address social injustices in the United States. Her areas of activism include reproductive rights, human rights, women's issues, diversity issues, and hate crimes. She is the co-author of* Undivided Right: Women of Color Organizing for Reproductive Justice *(South End Press, 2004).*

A tragedy of this magnitude forces all of us to examine the impact of this storm and the response to it on women and children. The Deep South has some of the highest poverty in America, affecting all races of people, and the world witnessed that great dirty secret that is America's shame. Black and brown people drowning in filthy floodwaters alerted the world that this country does not protect the human rights of its own citizens.

From a feminist perspective, there are certain predictions we can make concerning what will happen to some women and children based on our collective experiences in helping women and children survive trauma. Poverty in America is not only racialized but it is also gendered. The aftermath of Katrina must be examined through a gender lens that identifies the myriad of violations experienced by women. A disaster like Katrina is a violation against the entire community, but when threats to women's lives are not recognized, and steps are not taken to ensure that they are, women become doubly victimized—by the disaster and by the response to it.

Vulnerability of Women and Children

Many people could not escape not only because of poverty, but because they were not physically able to punch through rooftops, perch on top of buildings, or climb trees to survive. Horror stories of people abandoned to drown in nursing homes and hospitals emphasize that any disaster preparedness planning must take into account those unable to evacuate themselves. Instead, the mainstream media and government sources chose to blame the victims as if these vulnerable people simply made bad choices, ignoring the context in which these "choices" are made. Right-wing pundits are already saying that the tragedy was the fault of single mothers who were not married so that their husbands could lift them out of poverty! Those in power do not speak about the intentional chaos in people's lives created by constantly scrambling for survival while living in poverty or with disabilities that leave many women feeling simply overwhelmed by life itself.

We also know that women's issues will not be seen as "important" during the crisis, as we are advised that larger issues, such as maintaining law and order and securing the affected areas, are of higher priority. There is a risk of too much focus on the current crisis, shifting dollars from previous unmet needs, and forgetting older crises around the world and in our country. For example, Mississippi already had only one abortion provider before the storm. Women traveled to Louisiana or Alabama for services. What will an already under-served region do to help women receive reproductive health care?

Redefining Military Occupation

We witnessed a very authoritarian militarization of New Orleans during the crisis as police and the military were given permission to forcibly evict survivors, arrest or shoot lawbreakers, and impose martial law on the city. No one in authority questioned whether it is ethical to give orders to shoot flood survivors, even if they are supposedly looting. Many of the alleged "looters" were actually trying to find food to feed their families. Notably, while the police and military were protecting the property rights of business owners, they somehow neglected to protect the lives of women and children jammed into the Superdome and the Convention Center. Women, children, the sick and the elderly died waiting for help.

There are reports of massive arrests, police brutality and even deaths at the hands of the police and military during this crisis. Undoubtedly there were countless heroic actions as many people in law enforcement and the military risked their lives in contaminated water to rescue survivors. But as feminists, we should not confuse individual compassion with structural injustice. Both can exist in the same place at the same time.

Ironically, the occupation of New Orleans and the occupation of Iraq share one major obvious commonality. Both are greased by oil—its production and shipping. It is no coincidence that a port through which much of America's oil flows is quickly militarized while hundreds of people die in flooded houses. The same company that is profiting in Iraq—Halliburton—will receive major contracts to help in the rebuilding of New Orleans.

What was particularly telling about the Gulf Coast crisis was that the owners of casinos and Wal-Marts were apparently able to return to their businesses much more quickly to repair storm damages long before federal assistance arrived to reduce the needless loss of lives. They may be the first businesses to offer jobs to the massive numbers of people forced into unemployment because of the storm. Will we be in any position to challenge their labor practices and impact on communities if they are the only employers available? Wal-Mart already discriminates against the women it presently employs. With President Bush relaxing the minimum wage laws for companies hired to rebuild the Gulf Coast, will more women make even less money? You bet they will because more than 400,000 jobs were lost in the disaster.

The concept of peace and security is dreadfully misused during this crisis to impose a police state. The reality is that women live in a borderland of insecurity all the time, yet the needs of women are invisible during discussions on security preoccupied with criminals and terrorists. Poverty, hunger and deprivation of human rights are the real threats to security because security is determined by the extent to which people have their basic needs met and can live in freedom and safety, not by the number of armed occupiers in their communities. A militarized community does not feel safer, just more policed, so that what is allowed and what is accepted is constantly determined by those outside of the community.

Gender-Based Violence

Often poor women and children are the first ones forced into prostitution to survive. There will be an increase in the demand for prostitution created by the massive military and police presence in the affected states, similar to the rise in prostitution that surrounds our military bases around the world already. Women are not "opportunities to relieve stress" as many soldiers are encouraged to believe. Because of the limited real choices women face, we expect that there will be a rise in the prostitution and trafficking of women and children. We also expect that there will be a rise in the exploitation and sexual abuse of displaced children. Increases in the abuse of women and children will mean increases in unwanted pregnancies and sexually transmitted diseases, including HIV/AIDS.

We have already received reports of the rapes and murders of women and children among the survivors herded together in the Superdome and New Orleans Convention Center under inhumane conditions. We already know that some men do not know how to cope with a lack of control over their lives and they often express their frustration by abusing and violating women and children. Domestic violence and sexual assault will increase because women are more vulnerable and more men will become violent as the occupation and displacement continues.

Development for Whom? Using a Gender Lens to Rebuild

There is a difference in how women see what ought to happen and how men see what should be done. It will be important during this crisis to listen to the women of the Gulf Coast and incorporate their perspectives on what should be done to help people recover from this disaster.

Women must ask critical questions during this crisis: Why were we so vulnerable? Who are the groups benefiting from the disaster and who are the groups hurting or excluded? This is a chance to connect issues of poverty, war, occupation, racism, homophobia, militarism and sexism, and make the distinction between natural disasters and man-made ones.

Some humanitarian agencies or groups will actually facilitate the occupation of our communities by turning over lists of undocumented people to the authorities, not recognizing the family rights of same sex couples, or participating in redevelopment strategies that ignore the needs and perspectives of women.

To counter this, women must make our concerns known in the media, to government agencies, and to the humanitarian organizations. There are human rights standards that humanitarian agencies should follow and most require that women's perspectives are respected and incorporated. We cannot allow them to ignore the voices of local people or ignore the voices of women demanding inclusion.

It may take as long as five years to rebuild the Gulf Coast, and right now we need to demand that the services to which we are entitled—that are our human rights—are delivered with respect, efficiency, and dignity. We can use this moment to force bureaucracies to become more flexible, like changing normal admissions procedures to get our kids back in schools or demanding that quality public housing be provided instead of permanent refugee camps. We need schools, voter registration, immigrant services, drivers' licenses, housing, medical care, and public assistance put on the fast track, not bottle-necked services mired down in the typical bureaucratic snarls.

We need to demand economic redevelopment strategies that center on our needs, not those of casino owners. It will be mighty tempting to use this as an opportunity to not rebuild our communities in New Orleans or the rest of the Gulf Coast. New Orleans is particularly at risk of becoming a tourist mecca, where the only jobs available to people of color will be low-paying ones supporting the tourist and oil industries. We have to claim our human right to sustainable development. We have the right to quality schools for our children, jobs that pay living wages, communities free of environmental toxins, and opportunities to develop our full human potential. We have the right to reclaim our land, rebuild our homes, and restore our communities.

It is also predictable that the people who name the repression by our government will be attacked and we must defend the women who will come under assault. Women already get attacked even before we're in the public sphere, in our personal lives through gender-based violence, but we can expect an escalation of these attacks if we loudly demand accountability from authorities. They will threaten to take away our children, deny us benefits, and accuse us of being unpatriotic and selfish.

Specifically, we must demand the full funding of services women will need to recover from this crisis. Of the billions of dollars that will be poured into the region, we must demand increased funding for domestic violence shelters, rape crisis centers, abused children's services, reproductive health programs, and services for the elderly, immigrants, and people who are disabled. We must demand that those doing assessments of what is needed not use gender-blind methods that fail to see the differences between the conditions of women and men and fail to meet our need to be free from all forms of violence, especially sexual violence.

We need to demand support for local women's organizations, which are arguably the best way to get information to women and obtain information about women's needs. Yet often women's organizations are ignored either because they are not known to the decision-makers or their work is not valued. We need the solidarity of feminists from around to world to help us claim our human rights. Ignoring women as a resource to help recover from this tragedy will affect the entire society for years to come.

Questions

1. What is perceived to be the cause of poverty in New Orleans by right-wing pundits? What do you think of this interpretation?
2. Why does the author compare the military occupation of New Orleans to that of Iraq? What issues does she try to bring attention to by drawing this analogy?
3. Why does the author predict that there will be an increase of prostitution and other forms of gender violence against women in the rebuilding process of New Orleans?
4. This article invokes a human rights language in its critique of the social oppressions exposed by the disaster of Hurricane Katrina. How would you define human rights? What human rights are often denied to women? What human rights are demanded in the article?
5. Do you agree or disagree with the arguments made by the author in her discussion of Katrina? Why?

For the Poor, Defining Who Deserves What (1995)

Kimberly J. McLarin

Proposals to make welfare recipients work often ignore the difficulty of finding affordable child care when mothers work low-wage, no benefits jobs. U.S. citizens seem more willing to grant welfare benefits to the "working poor"—who live at 125% of the poverty line or above—than to those who live below the poverty line and do not or cannot work. This selection from The New York Times *(1995) examines the enduring distinction between the "deserving" and the "undeserving" poor. The "welfare queen" stereotype represents African-American women as "undeserving"—despite the fact that most women on welfare are white.*

Distinguishing the deserving poor from the simply lazy, the scammers from the unfortunate, the truly needy from those who just don't want to work, used to be easy.

Lots of people had humble beginnings, but poverty often seemed to be a temporary aberration brought on by elemental forces beyond an individual's control: a parent died or became disabled, the economy shriveled or collapsed. During the Depression, when thousands of desperate breadwinners lined up outside food pantries, Americans believed that it was society, and not the poor, that had failed. Hence the beginning of an enduring welfare experiment.

Congress was still grappling with the legacy of that experiment last week. In the Senate, moderates won more money for child care for poor women and fended off efforts by conservatives to deny any benefits to teen-age mothers and any additional benefits to women who had more children while on welfare. Conservatives applauded time limits and work requirements. A vote is due this week.

Society's attitude toward the poor has cycled like the seasons since the 16th century, when the Elizabethan Poor Laws provided beneficent relief for the young, the old and the infirm, and work for the able-bodied. By the 1800's poverty among the able-bodied had come to be viewed as a moral failing, but that attitude was tempered by humanitarianism later in the 19th century. The New Deal further codified welfare as a public responsibility, though some analysts say attitudes toward the poor hardened as government picked up the burden of charity from churches and other private sources.

But Lawrence M. Mead, a professor at Princeton University's Woodrow Wilson School, said that in the public eye, the line that separates deserving from undeserving has always been crystal clear: the willingness—given the physical ability—to work.

"The public is very upset by the fact that many poor people appear not to help themselves," he said. "Employment is the great badge of whether you are deserving. If you're working, you're in a completely different category."

Is a single mother considered "able" to work? Traditionally the answer was no. In fact, the nation's main welfare program, Aid to Families with Dependent Children, was created in 1935 with the goal of keeping women at home with their children. But those women were mostly widows or abandoned wives, alone through no choice of their own. They had the nation's sympathy.

"Welfare Queens"

That sympathy withered as out-of-wedlock births skyrocketed. And now that most women work, a single mother who relies solely on welfare for her income is seen as the most undeserving of the poor, said Michael B. Katz, a professor at the University of Pennsylvania and author of "The Undeserving Poor: From the War on Poverty to the War on Welfare" (Pantheon, 1990).

That woman became the welfare queen of public resentment—black, illiterate and producing babies at an alarming clip. (Blacks do account for a disproportionate number of welfare recipients, but the fact that most people on welfare are white—and are either children or elderly—has done little to dispel the stereotype.)

If the poor should work, do jobs exist? In the 1930's the answer was clear. They didn't. In 1960's, the consensus was that although jobs existed, barriers like discrimination and poor education could keep even the most determined poor person from getting a job.

Some of those roadblocks remain. And others, such as the shortage of affordable day care and the lack of health care benefits with minimum-wage jobs, have arisen, too,

Giving Credit

"There are jobs available, but there are a lot of issues that prevent women from taking those jobs," said William Grinker, a New York City Human Resources Commissioner in the Koch administration.

Mr. Mead says there is no evidence that women who leave welfare and then reapply do so because they lacked day care or health benefits. The public seems to agree.

There is evidence that Americans are more willing to provide aid to the working poor, though. Consider the earned income tax credit, which aids almost 14 million families who are poor but who make too much to qualify for welfare. The tax credit costs the Federal treasury $22 billion, a figure that mimics Federal spending on Aid to Families with Dependent Children.

"Yet that went through Congress with nary a peep," Mr. Katz said (although Republicans have since discussed scaling back the credit). "To me that is a fantastic illustration that money is not the real issue here."

The real issue, then, may be behavior. The deserving poor do not have babies out of wedlock. They are not mired in poverty, waiting for a handout.

"When people speak of the underserving poor, they are frequently thinking of those whose behavior seems disreputable to us, those people who share desperate behaviors, who don't take the alleged opportunities that exist," said the author Jonathan Kozol, who has researched the religious lives of poor children in the South Bronx. "But I've found that even seemingly irrational behavior is ultimately attributable to the fact that people know they are economically superfluous. They did not create the joblessness that engulfs them, and in that respect, they are blameless."

He argues that the issue should cut deeper than behavior. "The ultimate question is a theological one: What does any human being deserve?" he said. "The Bible tells us that a person's humanity is enough for our compassion."

What welfare revision really seeks to do, Mr. Grinker said, is alter the message, created in the 1960's and 1970's, that welfare is an acceptable way of life, or even an entitlement.

"For 15 or 20 years that was the message, and it began to get reversed in the 1980's," he said. "Now it's getting reversed with a vengeance."

QUESTIONS

---

1. What characteristics are associated with the "undeserving" poor? What characteristics are associated with the "deserving" poor? Why are these judgments significant? How do they affect policy?

2. Should those who receive welfare benefits be required to work even while they have sole responsibility for young children? What are the arguments for and against "workfare"?

3. What reasons can you give for why the nation's attitudes toward poor single mothers have changed over the years? If, as this article claims, money is not the "real issue," what is?

'So How Did I Get Here?' (1992)

Rosemary L. Bray

Rosemary L. Bray is a graduate of Yale University and a nationally recognized journalist. In this article from the New York Times, *Bray recounts her own experiences growing up in a family that needed the services provided by the welfare system. Her survival and success challenge public stereotypes about welfare and about race.*

Growing up on welfare was a story I had planned to tell a long time from now, when I had children of my own. My childhood on Aid to Families with Dependent Children (A.F.D.C.) was going to be one of those stories I would tell my kids about the bad old days, an urban legend equivalent to Abe Lincoln studying by firelight. But I know now I cannot wait, because in spite of a wealth of evidence about the true nature of welfare and poverty in America, the debate has turned ugly, vicious and racist. The "welfare question" has become the race question and the woman question in disguise, and so far the answers bode well for no one.

In both blunt and coded terms, comfortable Americans more and more often bemoan the waste of their tax money on lazy black women with a love of copulation, a horror of birth control and a

"'So How Did I Get Here?'" by Rosemary Bray, reprinted *The New York Times Magazine*, Vol. 35, No. 2, November 8, 1992. Reprinted by permission of the Elaine Markson Agency.

lack of interest in marriage. Were it not for the experiences of half my life, were I not black and female and of a certain age, perhaps I would be like so many people who blindly accept the lies and distortions, half-truths and wrongheaded notions about welfare. But for better or worse, I do know better. I know more than I want to know about being poor. I know that the welfare system is designed to be inadequate, to leave its constituents on the edge of survival. I know because I've been there.

And finally, I know that perhaps even more dependent on welfare than its recipients are the large number of Americans who would rather accept this patchwork of economic horrors than fully address the real needs of real people.

My mother came to Chicago in 1947 with a fourth-grade education, cut short by working in the Mississippi fields. She pressed shirts in a laundry for a while and later waited tables in a restaurant where she met my father. Mercurial and independent, with a sixth-grade education, my Arkansas-born father worked at whatever came to hand. He owned a lunch wagon for a time and prepared food for hours in our kitchen on the nights before he took the wagon out. Sometimes he hauled junk and sold it in the open-air markets of Maxwell Street on Sunday mornings. Eight years after they met—seven years after they married—I was born. My father made her quit her job; her work, he told her, was taking care of me. By the time I was 4, I had a sister, a brother and another brother on the way. My parents, like most other American couples of the 1950s, had their own American dream—a husband who worked, a wife who stayed home, a family of smiling children. But as was true for so many African-American couples, their American dream was an illusion.

The house on the corner of Berkeley Avenue and 45th Street is long gone. The other houses still stand, but today the neighborhood is an emptier, bleaker place. When we moved there, it was a street of old limestones with beveled glass windows, all falling into vague disrepair. Home was a four-room apartment on the first floor, in what must have been the public rooms of a formerly grand house. The rent was $110 a month. All of us kids slept in the big front room. Because I was the oldest, I had a bed of my own, near a big plate-glass window.

My mother and father had been married for several years before she realized he was a gambler who would never stay away from the track. By the time we moved to Berkeley Avenue, Daddy was spending more time gambling, and bringing home less and less money and more and more anger. Mama's simplest requests were met with rage. They fought once for hours when she asked for money to buy a tube of lipstick. It didn't help that I always seemed to need a doctor. I had allergies and bronchitis so severe that I nearly died one Sunday after church when I was about 3.

It was around this time that my mother decided to sign up for A.F.D.C. She explained to the caseworker that Daddy wasn't home much, and when he was he didn't have any money. Daddy was furious; Mama was adamant. "There were times when we hardly had a loaf of bread in here," she told me years later. "It was close. I wasn't going to let you all go hungry."

Going on welfare closed a door between my parents that never reopened. She joined the ranks of unskilled women who were forced to turn to the state for the security their men could not provide. In the sterile relationship between herself and the State of Illinois, Mama found an autonomy denied her by my father. It was she who could decide, at last, some part of her own fate and ours. A.F.D.C. relegated marginally productive men like my father to the ranks of failed patriarchs who no longer controlled the destiny of their families. Like so many of his peers, he could no longer afford the luxury of a woman who did as she was told because her economic life depended on it. Daddy became one of the shadow men who walked out back doors as caseworkers came in through the front. Why did he acquiesce? For all his anger, for all his frightening brutality, he loved us, so much that he swallowed his pride and periodically ceased to exist so that we might survive.

In 1960, the year my mother went on public aid, the poverty threshold for a family of five in the United States was $3,560 and the monthly payment to a family of five from the State of Illinois was $182.56, a total of $2,190.72 a year. Once the $110 rent was paid, Mama was left with $72.56 a month to take care of all the other expenses. By any standard, we were poor. All our lives were proscribed by the narrow line between not quite and just enough.

What did it take to live?

It took the kindness of friends as well as strangers, the charity of churches, low expectations, deprivation and patience. I can't begin to count the hours spent in long lines, long waits, long walks in pursuit of basic things. A visit to a local clinic (one housing doctors, a dentist and pharmacy in an incredibly crowded series of rooms) invariably took the better part of a day; I never saw the same doctor twice.

It took, as well, a turning of our collective backs on the letter of a law that required reporting even a small and important miracle like a present of $5. All families have their secrets, but I remember the weight of an extra burden. In a world where caseworkers were empowered to probe into every nook and cranny of our lives, silence became defense. Even now, there are things I will not publicly discuss because I cannot shake the fear that we might be hounded by the state, eager to prosecute us for the crime of survival.

All my memories of our years on A.F.D.C. are seasoned with unease. It's painful to remember how much every penny counted, how even a gap of 25 cents could make a difference in any given week. Few people understand how precarious life is from welfare check to welfare check, how the word "extra" has no meaning. Late mail, a bureaucratic mix-up . . . and a carefully planned method of survival lies in tatters.

What made our lives work as well as they did was my mother's genius at making do—worn into her by a childhood of rural poverty—along with her vivid imagination. She worked at home endlessly, shopped ruthlessly, bargained, cajoled, charmed. Her food store of choice was the one that stocked pork and beans, creamed corn, sardines, Vienna sausages and potted meat all at 10 cents a can. Clothing was the stuff of rummage sales, trips to Goodwill and bargain basements, where thin cotton and polyester reigned supreme. Our shoes came from a discount store that sold two pairs for $5.

It was an uphill climb, but there was no time for reflection; we were too busy with our everyday lives. Yet I remember how much it pained me to know that Mama, who recruited a neighbor to help her teach me how to read when I was 3, found herself left behind by her eldest daughter, then by each of us in turn. Her biggest worry was that we would grow up uneducated, so Mama enrolled us in parochial school.

When one caseworker angrily questioned how she could afford to send four children to St. Ambrose School, my mother, who emphatically declared "My kids need an education," told her it was none of her business. (In fact, the school had a volume discount of sorts; the price of tuition dropped with each child you sent. I still don't know quite how she managed it.) She organized our lives around church and school, including Mass every morning at 7:45. My brother was an altar boy; I laid out the vestments each afternoon for the next day's Mass. She volunteered as a chaperone for every class trip, sat with us as we did homework she did not understand herself. She and my father reminded us again and again and again that every book, every test, every page of homework was in fact a ticket out and away from the life we lived.

My life on welfare ended on June 4, 1976—a month after my 21st birthday, two weeks after I graduated from Yale. My father, eaten up with cancer and rage, lived just long enough to know the oldest two of us had graduated from college and were on our own. Before the decade ended, all of us had left the welfare rolls. The eldest of my brothers worked at the post office, assumed support of my mother (who also went to work, as a companion to an elderly woman) and earned his master's degree at night. My sister married and got a job at a bank. My baby brother parked cars and found a wife. Mama's biggest job was done at last; the investment made in our lives by the State of Illinois had come to fruition. Five people on welfare for 18 years had become five working, taxpaying adults. Three of us went to college, two of us finished; one of us has an advanced degree; all of us can take care of ourselves.

Ours was a best-case phenomenon, based on the synergy of church and state, the government and the private sector and the thousand points of light that we called friends and neighbors. But there was something more: What fueled our dreams and fired our belief that our lives could change for the better was the promise of the civil rights movement and the war on poverty—for millions of African-Americans the defining events of the 1960s. Caught up in the heady atmosphere of imminent change, our world was filled not only with issues and ideas but with amazing images of black people engaged in the struggle for long-denied rights and freedoms. We knew other people lived differently than we did, we knew we didn't have much, but we didn't mind, because we knew it wouldn't be long. My mother borrowed a phrase I had read to her once from Dick Gregory's autobiography: Not poor, just broke. She would repeat it often, as often as she sang hymns in the kitchen. She loved to sing a spiritual Mahalia Jackson had made famous: "Move On Up a Little Higher." Like so many others, Mama was singing about earth as well as heaven.

These are the things I remember every time I read another article outlining American's welfare crisis. The rage I feel about the welfare debate comes from listening to a host of lies, distortions and exaggerations—and taking them personally.

I am no fool. I know of few women—on welfare or off—with my mother's grace and courage and stamina. I know not all women on welfare are cut from the same cloth. Some are lazy; some are ground down. Some are too young; many are without husbands. A few have made welfare fraud a lucrative career; a great many more have pushed the rules on outside income to their very limits.

I also know that none of these things justifies our making welfare a test of character and worthiness, rather than an acknowledgment of need. Near-sainthood should not be a requirement for financial and medical assistance.

But all manner of sociologists and policy gurus continue to equate issues that simply aren't equivalent—welfare, race, rates of poverty, crime, marriage and childbirth—and to reach conclusions that serve to demonize the poor. More than one social arbiter would have us believe that we have all been mistaken for the last 30 years—that the efforts to relieve the most severe effects of poverty have not only failed but have served instead to increase and expand the ranks of the poor. In keeping women, children and men from starvation, we are told, we have also kept them from self-sufficiency. In our zeal to do good, we have undermined the work ethic, the family and thus, by association, the country itself.

So how did I get here?

Despite attempts to misconstrue and discredit the social programs and policies that changed—even saved—my life, certain facts remain. Poverty was reduced by 39 percent between 1960 and 1990, according to the Census Bureau, from 22.2 percent to 13.5 percent of the nation's population. That is far too many poor people, but the rate is considerably lower than it might have been if we had thrown up our hands and reminded ourselves that the poor will always be with us. Of black women considered "highly dependent," that is, on welfare for more than seven years, 81 percent of their daughters grow up to live productive lives off the welfare rolls, a 1992 Congressional report stated; the 19 percent who become second-generation welfare recipients can hardly be said to constitute an epidemic of welfare dependency. The vast majority of African-Americans are now working or middle class, an achievement that occurred in the past 30 years, most specifically between 1960 and 1973, the years of expansion in the very same social programs that it is so popular now to savage. Those were the same years in which I changed from girl to woman, learned to read and think, graduated from high school and college, came to be a working woman, a taxpayer, a citizen.

In spite of all the successes we know of, in spite of the reality that the typical welfare recipient is a white woman with young children, ideologues have continued to fashion from whole cloth the specter of the mythical black welfare mother, complete with a prodigious reproductive capacity and a galling laziness, accompanied by the uncaring and equally lazy black man in her life who will not work, will not marry her and will not support his family.

Why has this myth been promoted by some of the best (and the worst) people in government, academia, journalism and industry? One explanation may be that the constant presence of poverty frustrates even the best-intentioned among us. It may also be because the myth allows for denial about who the poor in America really are and for denial about the depth and intransigence of racism regardless of economic status. And because getting tough on welfare is for some a first-class career move; what better way to win a position in the next administration than to trash those people least able to respond? And, finally, because it serves to assure white Americans that lazy black people aren't getting away with anything.

Many of these prescriptions for saving America from the welfare plague not only reflect an insistent, if sometimes unconscious, racism but rest on the bedrock of patriarchy. They are rooted in the fantasy of a male presence as a path to social and economic salvation and in its corollary—the image of woman as passive chattel, constitutionally so afflicted by her condition that the only recourse is to transfer her care from the hands of the state to the hands of a man with a job. The largely ineffectual plans to create jobs for men in communities ravaged by disinvestment, the state-sponsored dragnets for men who cannot or will not support their children, the exhortations for women on welfare to find themselves a man and get married, all are the institutional expressions of the same worn cultural illusion—that women and children without a man are fundamentally damaged goods. Men are such a boon, the reasoning goes, because they make more money than women do.

Were we truly serious about an end to poverty among women and children, we would take the logical next step. We would figure out how to make sure women who did a dollar's worth of work got a dollar's worth of pay. We would make sure that women could go to work with their minds at ease, knowing their children were well cared for. What women on welfare need, in large measure, are the things key to the life of every adult woman: economic security and autonomy. Women need the skills and the legitimate opportunity to earn a living for ourselves as well as for people who may rely on us; we need the freedom to make choices to improve our own lives and the lives of those dear to us.

"The real problem is not welfare," says Kathryn Edin, a professor of sociology at Rutgers University and a scholar in residence at the Russell Sage Foundation. "The real problem is the nature of low-wage work and lack of support for these workers—most of whom happen to be women raising their children alone."

Completing a five-year study of single mothers—some low-wage workers, some welfare recipients—Edin is quantifying what common sense and bitter experience have told millions of women who rotate off and on the welfare rolls: Women, particularly unskilled women with children, get the worst jobs available, with the least amount of health care, and are the most frequently laid off. "The workplace is not oriented toward people who have family responsibilities," she says. "Most jobs are set up assuming that someone else is minding the kids and doesn't need assistance."

But the writers and scholars and politicians who wax most rhapsodic about the need to replace welfare with work make their harsh judgments from the comfortable and supportive environs of offices and libraries and think tanks. If they need to go to the bathroom midsentence, there is no one timing their absence. If they take longer than a half-hour for lunch, there is no one waiting to dock their pay. If their baby sitter gets sick, there is no risk of someone having taken their place at work by the next morning. Yet these are conditions that low-wage women routinely face, which inevitably lead to the cyclical nature of their welfare histories. These are the realities that many of the most vocal and widely quoted critics of welfare routinely ignore. In his book *The End of Equality*, for example, Mickey Kaus discusses social and economic inequity, referring to David Ellwood's study on long-term welfare dependency without ever mentioning that it counts anyone who uses the services for at least one month as having been on welfare for the entire year.

In the heated atmosphere of the welfare debate, the larger society is encouraged to believe that women on welfare have so violated the social contract that they have forfeited all rights common to those of us lucky enough not to be poor. In no area is this attitude more clearly demonstrated than in issues of sexuality and childbearing. Consider the following: A *Philadelphia Inquirer* editorial of Dec. 12, 1990, urges the use of Norplant contraceptive inserts for welfare recipients—in spite of repeated warnings from women's health groups of its dangerous side effects—in the belief that the drug "could be invaluable in breaking the cycle of inner-city poverty." (The newspaper apologized for the editorial after it met widespread criticism, both within and outside the paper.) A California judge orders a woman on welfare, convicted of abusing two of her four children, to use Norplant; the judge's decision was appealed. The Washington state legislature considers approving cash payments of up to $10,000 for women on welfare who agree to be sterilized. These and other proposals, all centering on women's reproductive capacities, were advanced in spite of evidence that welfare recipients have fewer children than those not on welfare.

The punitive energy behind these and so many other Draconian actions and proposals goes beyond the desire to decrease welfare costs; it cuts to the heart of the nation's racial and sexual hysteria. Generated neither by law nor by fully informed public debate, these actions amount to social control over "those people on welfare"—a control many Americans feel they have bought and paid for every April 15. The question is obvious: If citizens were really aware of who receives welfare in America, however inadequate it is, if they acknowledged that white women and children were welfare's primary beneficiaries, would most of these things be happening?

Welfare has become a code word now. One that enables white Americans to mask their sometimes malignant, sometimes benign racism behind false concerns about the suffering ghetto poor and their negative impact on the rest of us. It has become the vehicle many so-called tough thinkers use to undermine compassionate policy and engineer the reduction of social programs.

So how *did* I get here?

I kept my drawers up and my dress down, to quote my mother. I didn't end up pregnant because I had better things to do. I knew I did because my uneducated, Southern-born parents told me so. Their faith, their focus on our futures are a far cry from the thesis of Nicholas Lemann, whose widely acclaimed book *The Promised Land* perpetuates the myth of black Southern sharecropping society as a primary source of black urban malaise. Most important, my family and I had every reason to believe that I had better things to do and that when I got older I would be able to do them. I had a mission, a calling, work to do that only I could do. And that is knowledge transmitted not just by parents, or school, or churches. It is a palpable thing, available by osmosis from the culture of the neighborhood and the world at large.

Add to this formula a whopping dose of dumb luck. It was my sixth-grade teacher, Sister Maria Sarto, who identified in me the first signs of a stifling boredom and told my mother that I needed a tougher, more challenging curriculum than her school could provide. It was she who then tracked down the private Francis W. Parker School, which agreed to give me a scholarship if I passed the admissions test.

Had I been born a few years earlier, or a decade later, I might now be living on welfare in the Robert Taylor Homes or working as a hospital nurse's aide for $6.67 an hour. People who think such things could never have happened to me haven't met enough poor people to know better. The avenue of escape can be very narrow indeed. The hope and energy of the 1960s—fueled not only by a growing economy but by all the passions of a great national quest—is long gone. The sense of possibility I knew has been replaced with the popular cultural currency that money and those who have it are everything and those without are nothing.

Much has been made of the culture of the underclass, the culture of poverty, as though they were the free-floating illnesses of the African-American poor, rendering them immune to other influences: the widespread American culture of greed, for example, or of cynicism. It is a thinly veiled continuation of the endless projection of "disease" onto black life, a convenient way to sidestep a more painful debate about the loss of meaning in American life that has made our entire nation depressed and dispirited. The malaise that has overtaken our country is hardly confined to African-Americans or the poor, and if both groups should disappear tomorrow, our nation would still find itself in crisis. To talk of the black "underclass threat" to the public sphere, as Mickey Kaus does, to demonize the poor among us and thus by association all of us—ultimately this does more damage to the body politic than a dozen welfare queens.

When I walk down the streets of my Harlem neighborhood, I see women like my mother, hustling, struggling, walking their children to school and walking them back home. And I also see women who have lost both energy and faith, talking loud, hanging out. I see the shadow men of a new generation, floating by with a few dollars and a toy, then drifting away to the shelters they call home. And I see, a dozen times a day, the little girls my sister and I used to be, the little boys my brothers once were.

Even the grudging, inadequate public help I once had is fading fast for them. The time and patience they will need to re-create themselves is vanishing under pressure for the big, quick fix and the crushing load of blame being heaped upon them. In the big cities and the small towns of America, we have let theory, ideology and mythology about welfare and poverty overtake these children and their parents.

Questions

1. Why was Rosemary Bray motivated to write about her experiences growing up on welfare? What challenges did her family face when she was a child? What are some of the emotions Bray communicates as she reflects on her experiences? How does she feel about her mother?

2. What are some of the popular beliefs about poverty and welfare? How are these beliefs tied to stereotypes about people based on race and gender? How are these beliefs reflected in the solutions we develop to assist the poor?

3. What stereotypes about welfare does this personal narrative contradict? What hope does Bray offer?

From Norplant to the Contraceptive Vaccine: The New Frontier of Population Control (1997)

Dorothy Roberts

Dorothy Roberts is a law professor at Rutgers University. In this excerpt from her book Killing the Black Body, *Roberts details how race is deeply embedded in the politics of welfare and new efforts to control reproduction among poor women. Efforts to pass public policy that require women who receive welfare payments to use contraception like Norplant, Roberts argues, is tied to a long history of eugenics and racism in our country. Although the majority of people in the United States who receive welfare payments are white, the stereotype of the black woman as "Welfare Queen" is a powerful one that contributes to coercive efforts to control reproduction among black and poor women. Roberts startling article reminds us that the develop-*

ment of sophisticated forms of contraception do not necessarily translate to greater reproductive freedom and control for American women.

"They told us this and they told us that about the Norplant and I'm going through all these changes and I'm trying to have it removed." Yvonne Thomas, a thirty-year-old Baltimore mother, was describing her experience with Norplant, a new, long-acting contraceptive implanted in her arm at a family-planning clinic. When she began suffering from side effects, Thomas returned to have the device removed. But the clinic staff balked at her request. "Then they tell me that it's not putting me in bed, as if they know how I feel on the inside of *my* body. . . . I feel like because I'm a social service mother that's what's keeping me from getting this Norplant out of me. Because I've known other people that has the Norplant that spent money to have it put in and spent money to have it put out with no problems. . . . That's how they make me feel, like *'you got this Norplant you keep it.'*"[1]

Yvonne Thomas is one of thousands of Black women in the United States who have been pressured to try this controversial form of birth control. Like the others, she is a target of a campaign to push the drug on poor Black women in hopes of decreasing their birthrate. Population control policies designed to reduce births of an entire group of people for social ends are usually associated with Third World countries. In the 1990s, legislators and policymakers in the United States seized upon Norplant as a means of domestic population control.

Norplant appears destined to be replaced by injectable contraceptives such as the newly approved Depo-Provera or the experimental "contraceptive vaccine" as the method of choice for reducing Black women's fertility. Unlike that of Norplant, which can be removed (albeit by surgical incision), the contraceptive effect of an injection or vaccine cannot be reversed once the agents are shot into a woman's bloodstream. Injections and vaccines are also easier to administer without a woman's full awareness or consent. Negative publicity generated by women's adverse experiences with Norplant as well as class action lawsuits filed against its distributor may make it impossible to convince enough women to use it. Still, the speedy embrace of Norplant as a means of reproductive regulation and the injuries it has already inflicted are sobering omens of the future of birth control in America. In this article, I describe how racial politics created this latest threat to reproductive rights and explain why increasing access to new, highly effective contraceptives does not necessarily enhance reproductive freedom.

THE IDEAL CONTRACEPTIVE?

Norplant consists of six silicone capsules, each about the size of a matchstick, filled with a synthetic hormone called levonorgestral (the same type of progestin used in some birth control pills). The tubes are implanted in a fan-shaped design just under the skin of a woman's upper arm through a small incision. The minor surgical procedure, which takes ten to fifteen minutes, can usually be performed in a clinic or doctor's office under local anesthesia. Norplant prevents pregnancy for up to five years by gradually releasing a low dose of the hormone into the bloodstream. It works mainly by suppressing ovulation, but also keeps sperm from reaching the egg by thickening the cervical mucus. Originally developed by the Population Council, a nonprofit organization that promotes family planning in the Third World, Norplant is now distributed in the United States by the giant pharmaceutical company Wyeth-Ayerst Laboratories, a division of American Home Products.

When the FDA approved Norplant for marketing in December 1990, it was hailed as the first major birth control breakthrough since the pill. The press release from Wyeth-Ayerst proclaimed the "eagerly awaited medical advance" as "the most innovative contraceptive in thirty years."[2] From this perspective, Norplant is the ideal contraceptive—long-acting, effective, convenient. Once the tubes are inserted, a woman is protected against pregnancy for five years without any further hassle. There is no need to remember to take it daily, as with the pill. Women do not have to interrupt sex to use it, as with a diaphragm or contraceptive foam. Nor do women need their partner's cooperation, as with condoms. Norplant's failure rate is only 1 percent over the five-year period; in other words, it is 99 percent effective.[3] Only sterilization has a better record. In fact, Norplant is so foolproof that it is really a form of temporary sterilization. Yet it has the advantage over sterilization of being reversible once the tubes are removed. At first glance, Norplant seems like the answer to women's prayers. It has already been used by more than 1 million women in the United States and 3 million women worldwide.[4]

TESTING THE WATERS—THE *INQUIRER* EDITORIAL

Norplant's potential to enhance women's reproductive freedom was quickly overshadowed by its potential for reproductive abuse. The new contraceptive was instantly embraced by policymakers, legislators, and social pundits as a way of curbing the birthrate of poor Black women. On December 12, 1990, only two days after the FDA's approval, the *Philadelphia Inquirer* published a controversial editorial entitled "Poverty and Norplant: Can Contraception Reduce the Underclass?"[5] Deputy editorial-page editor Donald Kimelman began the piece by linking two recent news items: one announced the approval of Norplant, and the other reported the research finding that half of Black children live in poverty. Kimelman went on to propose Norplant as a solution to inner-city poverty, arguing that "the main reason more black children are living in poverty is that people having the most children are the ones least capable of supporting them."[6] No one should be compelled to have Norplant implanted, Kimelman conceded. But he endorsed giving women on welfare financial incentives to encourage them to use the contraceptive.

The Norplant editorial sent off shock waves across the country. Black leaders were quick to express their outrage at the editorial's racist and eugenic overtones. Norplant's creator, Dr. Sheldon J. Segal, shot off a letter to *The New York Times* unequivocally opposing the use of Norplant for any coercive purpose: "It was developed to improve reproductive freedom, not to restrict it."[7] Black reporters and editors at the *Inquirer* protested the editorial. An emotional meeting brought Black staff members to tears—was their boss implying that those who grew up in large, poor families should never have been born?[8] The *Inquirer*'s Metro columnist, Steve Lopez, issued a stinging rebuttal the following Sunday. "What we have, basically, is the *Inquirer* brain trust looking down from its ivory tower and wondering if black people should be paid to stop having so many damn kids," Lopez fumed. "By combining contraception and race, the voice of the *Inquirer* calls to mind another David. David Duke."[9] (Lopez was referring to the editorial-page editor, David Boldt, who okayed the editorial.)

The public outcry moved the *Inquirer* to print an apology eleven days later. Admitting that the piece was "misguided and wrongheaded," the paper said it now agreed with critics that the incentives it proposed were tantamount to coercion and that other strategies for eliminating poverty should be explored. As further evidence of America's racial cleavage, David Boldt later wrote that he was astonished by the adverse reaction.[10] He was unaware of Blacks' fear of genocide and had no idea that readers might be angered by the Norplant proposal. A telephone call from Jesse Jackson, he says, cleared things up.

The *Inquirer*'s apology did not put the idea of Norplant incentives to rest. Far from it. Journalists immediately came to the *Inquirer*'s defense. Within days of the apology, *Newsweek* offered careful praise of Kimelman's proposal: "However offensive the editorial, Kimelman was clearly on to something. . . . The old answers have mostly failed. After the shouting stops, the problem will remain. It's too important to become taboo."[11] The *Richmond Times-Dispatch* gave an even stronger endorsement, arguing that Norplant "offers society yet another way to curb the expansion of an underclass most of whose members face futures of disorder and deprivation."[12] A year later Matthew Rees, writing for the *New Republic,* similarly defended Norplant incentives on the ground that "the current threat to children in our inner cities makes it an option that the morally serious can no longer simply dismiss."[13] ("Our inner cities" and "the underclass," of course, are another way of referring to the *Black* urban poor.) Although Rees acknowledged the need to treat poverty's "deeper roots," as well as constitutional objections to interfering with a woman's reproductive decisions, he concluded that "right now, Norplant may be the only practical option we've got."

More ominously, people in positions to steer public policy followed the media's lead. David Frankel, director of population sciences at the Rockefeller Foundation, made light of tensions at the *Inquirer*, writing to the *Washington Post,* "Despite the infantile reaction of some black staffers, . . . birth control incentives would not be genocide. Such incentives would be a humane inducement to social responsibility."[14] Backers of the Norplant scheme were not uniformly white, as reflected by Washington, D.C., mayor

Marion Barry's support of mandatory Norplant for women on welfare. "You can have as many babies as you want," Barry stated. "But when you start asking the government to take care of them, the government now ought to have some control over you."[15]

MARKETING NORPLANT TO POOR WOMEN

The *Inquirer* episode inaugurated a new wave of birth control politics, with Norplant at the center. What appeared to be an expensive contraceptive marketed to affluent women through private physicians soon became the focus of government programs for poor women. Lawmakers across the country have proposed and implemented schemes not only to make Norplant available to women on welfare but to pressure them to use the device as well.

At a time when legislatures nationwide are slashing social programs for the poor, public aid for Norplant became a popular budget item. Without financial assistance, the cost of Norplant would be prohibitive. The capsules cost $365 and the implantation procedure can run from $150 to $500. Removal costs another $150 to $500, or more if there are complications. The government sprang into action. Every state and the District of Columbia almost immediately made Norplant available to poor women through Medicaid. Tennessee passed a law in 1993 requiring that anyone who receives AFDC or other forms of public assistance be notified in writing about the state's offer of free Norplant. Women in Washington State who receive maternity care assistance also get information about Norplant.

By 1994, states had already spent $34 million on Norplant-related benefits.[16] As a result, at least half of the women in the United States who have used Norplant are Medicaid recipients. When Planned Parenthood surveyed its affiliates it discovered that, although only 12 percent of its clients are Medicaid recipients, 95 to 100 percent of women implanted with Norplant at some of its clinics were on Medicaid.[17]

There were also efforts to provide Norplant to low-income women ineligible for Medicaid. California governor Pete Wilson allocated an extra $5 million to reimburse state-funded clinics for

Norplant going to women without Medicaid or Medi-Cal coverage. North Carolina's budget similarly set aside a "Women's Health Service Fund" to pay for Norplant for the uninsured. The Norplant Foundation, a nonprofit organization established by Norplant's distributor, Wyeth-Ayerst, devotes $2.8 million a year to donate Norplant kits to low-income women.[18]

Simply making Norplant more accessible to indigent women was not enough for some lawmakers. Within two years thirteen state legislatures had proposed some twenty measures to implant poor women with Norplant.[19] A number of these bills would pressure women on welfare to use the device either by offering them a financial bonus or by requiring implantation as a condition of receiving benefits. In February 1991, only a couple of months after Norplant was approved, Kansas Republican state representative Kerry Patrick introduced legislation that would grant welfare recipients a one-time payment of $500 to use Norplant, followed by a $50 bonus each year the implants remained in place. Patrick touted his plan as having "the potential to save the taxpayers millions of their hard-earned dollars" by reducing the number of children on the welfare rolls.[20] He suggested that women needed an extra incentive to get them to take advantage of the state's free supply of Norplant, pointing to a study indicating that only one out of eight women currently used birth control. Republican representative Robert Farr echoed these sentiments when he proposed a similar bill in Connecticut: "It's far cheaper to give you money not to have kids than to give you money if you have kids."[21]

In short order, Louisiana state representative and former Ku Klux Klan Grand Wizard David Duke proposed paying women on welfare $100 a year to use the device. Duke's bill was an attempt to fulfill his campaign promise to enact "concrete proposals to reduce the illegitimate birthrate and break the cycle of poverty that truly enslaves and harms the black race."[22] The scheme also reflected his earlier support for what he called "Nazism," when he claimed in 1985 that "the real answer to the world's problems" was "promoting the best strains, the best individuals."[23] Arizona, Colorado, Ohio, Florida, Tennessee, and Washington have considered similar Norplant bonuses. In addition to these financial incentives, a North Carolina bill would have required that all women who get a state-funded abortion be implanted with Norplant unless it is medically unsafe.

Several states have considered even more coercive means to ensure the infertility of women receiving welfare. In his 1993 State of the State address, Maryland governor William Schaefer suggested that the state should consider making Norplant *mandatory* for women on welfare. Similarly, bills introduced in Mississippi and South Carolina would require women who already have children to get Norplant inserted as a condition for receiving future benefits. Legislation proposed in other states would deny increases in AFDC payments to women who declined the device.

The notion of requiring women on welfare to use birth control had circulated decades earlier. In his 1973 book *Who Should Have Children?* University of Chicago physiologist Dwight J. Ingle advocated selective population control as an alternative to the growing welfare state.[24] Ingle proposed that individuals who could not provide their children with a healthy environment or biological inheritance—including people with genetic defects or low intelligence, welfare recipients, criminals, drug addicts, and alcoholics—should be encouraged, or forced if necessary, to refrain from childbearing. "By this I mean that millions of people are unqualified for parenthood and should remain childless," Ingle explained in the book's foreword. One of Ingle's proposals was the mandatory insertion of pellets containing an "antifertility agent" under the skin of every woman of childbearing age. Women would be required to apply for a license to have the pellet removed; only those who qualified for parenthood would be allowed to become pregnant. William Shockley made a similar proposal in a 1967 letter to the editor of the *Palo Alto Times*.[25] Norplant has the potential to fulfill these eugenicists' fantasies.

WHAT'S RACE GOT TO DO WITH IT?

If these proposals apply to all welfare recipients, what is the relevance of race? Clearly, welfare policy, which concerns how America deals with its poor, is governed by capitalist economics and class politics. Class divisions within the Black community also create differences in Blacks' attitudes toward welfare. Although we should not underestimate this class dimension of programs that regulate welfare mothers, it is crucial to see that race equally determines the programs' features and popularity. Because class distinctions are racialized, race and class are inextricably linked in the development of welfare policy. When Americans debate welfare reform, most have single Black mothers in mind.

Some Norplant proponents—Kimelman and Duke, for example—have explicitly suggested distributing the contraceptive to *Black* women. After the commotion over the *Inquirer* editorial, however, few politicians are likely to link birth control specifically to Black poverty, even if that is their intention. But race lurks behind proposals to induce poor women in general to use Norplant. Not only will these incentives disproportionately affect Black women, but they may be covertly targeted at these women as well.

Part of the reason has to do with numbers. Although most families on welfare are not Black, Blacks disproportionately rely on welfare to support their children. Black women are only 6 percent of the population, but they represent a third of AFDC recipients.[26] The concentration of Black welfare recipients is even greater in the nation's inner cities, where Norplant has primarily been dispensed. For example, in Baltimore, the site of a government campaign to distribute Norplant, 86 percent of women receiving welfare are Black.

It is also true that a larger percentage of Blacks than whites are poor. One-third of all Blacks and half of all Black children live in poverty. Black women are five times more likely to live in poverty, five times more likely to be on welfare, and three times more likely to be unemployed than are white women.[27] Welfare programs, then, have a greater direct impact on the status of Black people as a whole. Any policy directed at women on welfare will disproportionately affect Black women because such a large proportion of Black women rely on public assistance. These policies, in turn, affect all Blacks as a group because such a large proportion of Blacks are poor.

The second reason has to do with perceptions. Although most people on welfare are not Black, many Americans think they are. The American public associates welfare payments to single mothers with the mythical Black "welfare queen," who deliberately becomes pregnant in order to increase the amount of her monthly check. The welfare queen represents laziness, chicanery, and economic burden all wrapped up in one powerful image. For decades, the media and politicians have shown pictures of Black mothers when they discuss public assistance. Now the link between race and welfare is firmly implanted in Americans' minds.

When conservative activist Clint Bolick called Lani Guinier, President Clinton's repudiated Justice Department nominee, a "quota queen," he counted on the public's immediate association of the label with the pejorative "welfare queen."[28] The title automatically linked the Black Guinier to negative stereotypes of Black women on welfare, helping to shut off reasoned debate about her views. Similarly, it is commonplace to observe that "welfare" has become a code word for "race." People can avoid the charge of racism by directing their vitriol at the welfare system instead of explicitly assailing Black people.

In addition, poor Blacks pose a far greater threat to white Americans than do poor whites. The word "underclass" refers not only to its members' poverty but also to a host of social pathologies such as crime, drug addiction, violence, welfare dependency, and illegitimacy. Although poverty may be relatively race-neutral in people's minds, these other depravities are associated with Black culture. Contemporary welfare rhetoric blames Black single mothers for transmitting a deviant lifestyle to their children, a lifestyle marked not only by persistent welfare dependency but also by moral degeneracy and criminality.

White Americans resent the welfare queen who rips off their tax dollars, but even more they fear the Willie Horton she gives birth to. These images are distinctly Black; they have no white counterparts. . . . Many whites hold deeply embedded beliefs about the dangers of Black reproduction that infect any scheme to solve social problems through birth control. This panic is exacerbated by the predicted end of white numerical supremacy in the United States within decades.[29] Proposals designed to reduce the number of children born to poor parents are an attempt to fend off this threat to white people's welfare, a threat that is specifically Black.

Thus, race and class politics work together to propel coercive birth control policies. The impact of these policies, moreover, crosses the boundaries of race and class. Laws aimed at curbing Black women's fertility restrict poor white women's liberties as well. Programs that apply only to Black women who are poor help to devalue Black people as a whole.

To date, no state legislature has passed a bill offering bonuses for or mandating the use of Norplant. But the numerous proposals for Norplant incentives and the defense of the *Inquirer* editorial show that the idea is alive and well. Commentators and politicians have tested the waters and found growing support for the use of birth control as a solution to the Black underclass. As the social climate becomes increasingly hostile toward welfare mothers and supportive of drastic cuts in welfare spending, there is a good chance that these proposals could become a reality—unless people committed to racial equality, economic justice, and reproductive liberty fight back. . . .

NOTES

1. *Skin Deep* (September 1994), a documentary produced by Deb Ellis and Alexandra Halkin.
2. Lynn Smith and Nina J. Easton, "The Dilemma of Desire," *Los Angeles Times Magazine*, Sept. 25, 1993, p. 24.
3. American Medical Association Board of Trustees Report, "Requirements or Incentives by Government for the Use of Long-Acting Contraceptives," *Journal of the American Medical Association* 267 (April 1, 1992), p. 1818.
4. Albert G. Thomas, Jr., and Stephanie M. LeMelle, "The Norplant System: Where Are We in 1995?" *Journal of Family Practice* 40 (1995), p. 125.
5. Donald Kimelman, "Poverty and Norplant: Can Contraception Reduce the Underclass?" *Phildadelphia Inquirer*, Dec. 12, 1990. p. A18.
6. Ibid.
7. Sheldon J. Segal, "Norplant Developed for All Women, Not Just the Well-to-Do," *New York Times*, Dec. 29, 1990, p. A18.
8. David R. Boldt, "A 'Racist Pig' Offers Some Final Thoughts on Norplant" *Philadelphia Inquirer*, Dec. 30, 1990, p. F7.
9. Steve Lopez, "A Difference of Opinion," *Phildadelphia Inquirer*, Nov. 16, 1990, p. B1.

10. Boldt, "A 'Racist Pig' Offers Some Final Thoughts on Norplant," p. F7.

11. Jonathan Alter, "One Well-Read Editorial," *Newsweek*, Dec. 31, 1990, pp. 85, 86.

12. "Journalistic Thought Police," *Richmond Times-Dispatch*, Dec. 27, 1990, p. A12.

13. Matthew Rees, "Shot in the Arm: The Use and Abuse of Norplant; Involuntary Contraception and Public Policy," *New Republic*, Dec. 9, 1991, p. 16.

14. David Frankel, Letter to the Editor, *Washington Post*, Dec. 29, 1990, p. A18.

15. Quoted in Sally Quinn, "Childhood's End," *Washington Post*, nov. 27, 1994, p. C1.

16. Deborah L. Shelton, "Complications of Birth; Norplant Contraceptive," *American Medical News*_38 (Feb. 20, 1995), p. 15.

17. Planned Parenthood Federation of America, *Survey of Planned Parenthood Affiliates on Provision of Norplant*_(December 1992).

18. Smith and Easton, "Dilemma of Desire."

19. Ibid.

20. Rees, "Shot in the Arm," p. 16.

21. Quoted in Alan Harper, "Racism Suggested in Payments to Poor for Norplant Implants," *New York Beacon*, March 4, 1994 (available on Ethnic News Watch, Softline Information, Inc.).

22. Quoted in William H. Tucker, *The Science and Politics of Racial Research* (Urbana: University of Ilinois Press, 1994), p. 294.

23. Quoted in Craig Flourney, "Duke Says He's Proud of Years as Klan Chief," *Dallas Morning News*, June 17, 1992, pp. A1, A16.

24. Dwight J. Ingle, *Who Should Have Children? An Environmental and Genetic Approach* (Indianapolis and New York: Bobbs-Merrill, 1973).

25. Tucker, *Science and Politics of Social Research*, p. 193.

26. Staff of House Committee on Ways and Means, House of Representatives, *Overview of Entitlement Programs, 1994 Green Book*, 103d Cong., 2d sess., 1994, pp. 401, 444; Teresa L. Amott, "Black Women and AFDC: Making Entitlements Out of Necessity," in Linda Gordon, ed., *Women, the State, and Welfare* (Madison: University of Wisconsin Press: 1990), p. 280.

27. Nadja Zolokar, *The Economic Status of Black Women* (Washington, D.C.: U.S. Commission on Civil Rights, 1990), p. 1.

28. Clint Bolick, "Clinton's Quota Queens," *Wall Street Journal*, April 30, 1993, p. A12.

29. William Henry, "Beyond the Melting Pot," *Time*, April 9, 1990, pp. 28-31.

QUESTIONS

1. Why does the author believe that it is problematic to use Norplant as a solution to inner-city poverty? How do public policies to encourage use of Norplant by poor women disproportionately impact black women?

2. How would Roberts respond to Marion Barry's comment that women can have as many babies as they want "but when you start asking the government to take care of them, the government now ought to have some control over you"?

3. How are race and class linked in the development of welfare policy? How is race an underlying issue in inducing poor women to use Norplant? Should public policies of any kind be created to address reproductive issues

among *any* women? Why or why not? Why is reproduction believed by some to be a governmental issue?

4. What does it mean that certain forms of contraception like Norplant are paid for by Medicaid and others, like birth control pills, are not? What might Roberts say about the proposal to offer financial incentives to women to use Norplant? Why?

5. What perceptions exist about women and welfare? How would Roberts respond to those perceptions?

6. Why does Roberts suggest that black reproduction is threatening to white Americans? Why are poor blacks a greater threat than poor whites?

THE MOMMY WARS: HOW THE MEDIA TURNED MOTHERHOOD INTO A CATFIGHT (2000)

Susan Douglas and Meredith Michaels

Professors Susan Douglas and Meredith Michaels analyze representations of "celebrity" mothers in the popular press. Sexy, glamorous, contented, images of wealthy, white mothers such as Christie Brinkley and Kirstie Alley pervade popular magazines and assault readers with a vision of motherhood attainable only by lavish consumerism and extraordinary wealth. In contrast, images of "welfare mothers" demonize women who receive state support, portraying them as complaining and undeserving drains on the economy. The authors argue that these contrasting images construct motherhood as a competition between women—a catfight—in which some women triumph and some women fail because of what appear to be personal inadequacies rather than social and economic barriers. These divisive images also feed our rampant consumer culture in which energetic buying seems the only route to ideal motherhood.

Douglas is a Professor of Communication Studies at the University of Michigan and the author of Where the Girls Are, *an in depth analysis of the impact of the mass media on gender identity and development. Meredith Michaels is a Professor of Philosophy at Smith College and the co-author of* Fetal Subjects, Feminist Positions.

It's 5:22 p.m. You're in the grocery check-out line. Your three-year-old is writhing on the floor, screaming, because you have refused to buy her a Teletubby pinwheel. Your six-year-old is whining, repeatedly, in a voice that could saw through cement, "But mommy, puleeze, puleeze," because you have not bought him the latest Lunchables, which features as the four food groups: chips, a candy bar, fake cheese, and artificial coloring.

To distract yourself, and to avoid the glares of other shoppers who have already deemed you the worst mother in America, you leaf through *People* magazine. Inside, Uma Thurman gushes, "Motherhood is sexy." Moving on to *Good Housekeeping*, Vanna White says of her child, "When I hear his cry at 6:30 in the morning, I have a smile on my face, and I'm not an early riser." Brought back to reality by stereophonic wailing, you feel about as sexy and euphoric as Rush Limbaugh in a thong.

Meanwhile, *Newsweek*, also at the check-out line, offers a different view of motherhood. In one of the many stories about welfare mothers that proliferated until "welfare reform" was passed in 1996, you meet Valerie, 27, and "the three children she has by different absentee fathers." She used to live with her mother, "who, at 42, has six grandchildren." But now Valerie resides with other families, all of whom "live side-by-side in open trash-filled apartments." Hey, maybe you're not such a failure after all.

Motherhood has been one of the biggest media fixations of the past two decades. And this is what so many of us have been pulled between when we see accounts of motherhood in the me-

---

"The Mommy Wars: How the Media Turned Motherhood into a Catfight," by Susan Douglas and Meredith Michaels. Reprinted from *Ms.* Magazine, February/March 2000. pp. 62–67.

dia: celebrity moms who are perfect, most of them white, always rich, happy, and in control, the role models we should emulate, versus welfare mothers who are irresponsible, unmarried, usually black or Latina—as if there were no white single mothers on the dole—poor, miserable, and out of control, the bad examples we should scorn.

Beginning in the late 1970s, with the founding of *People* and *Us*, and exploding with a vengeance in the '90s with *InStyle*, the celebrity-mom profile has spread like head lice through popular magazines, especially women's. "For me, happiness is having a baby," gushed Marie Osmond on a 1983 cover of *Good Housekeeping*, and Linda Evans added in *Ladies' Home Journal*, "All I want is a husband and baby." These celeb biographies, increasingly presented as instruction manuals for how the rest of us should live our lives, began to proliferate just as there was a dramatic rise in the number of women who worked outside the home while raising small children. Pulled between established wisdom—if you worked outside the home before your child entered kindergarten you were bound to raise an ax murderer—and the economic and psychic need to work, many of these mothers were searching for guidance. And celebrity mom magazine articles seemed to provide it.

Celebrity moms were perfect for the times. They epitomized two ideals that sat in uneasy but fruitful alliance. On the one hand, they exemplified the unbridled materialism and elitism the Reagan era had spawned. On the other, they represented the feminist dream of women being able to have a family and a job outside the home without being branded traitors to true womanhood. Magazine editors apparently figured they could use stars to sell magazines and to serve as role models.

But now, in the year 2000, things have gotten out of control. Celebrity moms are everywhere, beaming from the comfy serenity and perfection of their lives as they give multiple interviews about their "miracle babies," what an unadulterated joy motherhood is, and all the things they do with their kids to ensure they will be perfectly normal Nobel laureates by the age of 12. These stories are hardly reassuring. They make the rest of us feel that our own lives are, as the great seventeenth century philosopher Thomas Hobbes put it, nasty, brutish, and short. So why should we care about something so banal as the celebrity mom juggernaut? One answer is that it bulldozed through so much of American popular culture just when working mothers, single mothers, and welfare mothers were identified, especially by conservative male pundits, as the cause of everything bad, from the epidemic of drug use to the national debt to rising crime rates. Remember all the hand-wringing by George Will, William Bennett, and Allan Bloom about America's "moral decay"? The biggest culprit, of course, was the single welfare mother. These guys attacked celebrity single mothers now and then, but the mud never stuck—not even, heaven help us, on that fictional celebrity single mother Murphy Brown.

As the push "to end welfare as we know it" gained momentum and reached its climax in the welfare reform of 1996, the canonized celebrity mom and the demonized welfare mother became ever more potent symbols, working in powerful opposition to each other. We rarely saw these very different mothers in the same publication, or even considered them in the same breath. Celebrity moms graced the covers of magazines designed for self-realization and escape; welfare mothers were the object of endless stories in newspapers and newsmagazines and on the nightly news that focused on public policy and its relation to the tenuous state of morality in America.

But what if we put these portrayals side by side and compare what these different mothers were made to stand for? Could it be that the tsunami of celebrity-mom profiles helped, however inadvertently, to justify punitive policies toward welfare mothers and their children? While the "you can have it all" ethos of these pieces made the rest of us feel like failures as mothers, and upped the ante in the eyes of employers and coworkers about how much working mothers can handle, a little side-by-side reading also exposes some rather daunting hypocrisy. Often, one group is glamorized and the other castigated for precisely the same behavior.

Let's take a look at a celebrity mom first. Kirstie Alley, for example. It's 1994. The star of *Cheers* and the *Look Who's Talking* movies graces the cover of *InStyle*, a magazine that pays fawning tribute to the charming indiosyncrasies and lifestyle choices of our nation's most glamourous. Among Kirstie's recent choices is the purchase of her third house. *InStyle* advises us respectfully that "as with all of her houses, Kirstie paid cash." On a tour of her new Bangor, Maine, retreat (the renovation of which was paid for by a quick voice-over job she did for Subaru), we discover that both Kirstie and her house are "at once down-to-earth and whimsical."

Kirstie must be down-to-earth, of course, because now, at long last, she is a mother. Her "playful sense of style" is made evident by the decoupage grapes that grace her son True's high chair. "It was painted and cracked to make it look old," *InStyle* informs us. (Why not simply rely on natural toddler effluvia to give the chair that petroglyph look?) True has just turned one; his whimsical high chair faces an equally whimsical ceramic pig holding a blackboard on which a new word appears each day to encourage his reading.

In our tour through Kirstie's hideaway, we encounter an entourage—decorators, a nanny, a cook, and various personal assistants. Kirstie spends True's two-hour nap time working out with her personal trainer and then being served a healthful, fat-free lunch by the cook. Lounging in her living room (painted to "echo" the surrounding firs and elms), reflecting on the challenges of motherhood, Kirstie gushes, "Being a mother has given me a whole new purpose. Every day when I wake up it's like Christmas morning to me, and seeing life through True's eyes gives me a whole new way of looking at the world." Perfect house. Perfect husband. Perfect child. Perfect career. Perfect life. Kirstie is a perfect mother. *InStyle* invites you to curl up on the sofa with Kirstie, but then implies that you'd probably just spill your tea on it.

Forward to 1997. There's Kirstie again, now the star of the television series *Veronica's Closet*, beaming at us once more from *InStyle*. "A new man, a new show, a brand-new life," proclaims the cover. Since 1994, her island mansion has "become a place to play." Each of the 15 bedrooms is decorated with Kirstie's "eclectic and playful eye." According to *InStyle*, most people would have found decorating this 16,000-square-foot house daunting, but not Kirstie. "I'm very fast," she explains. "I don't shop. I just point: boom, boom, boom." Having outgrown his high chair, True now has his own miniature lobster boat. In addition, he and his new sister, Lillie, can frolic in their personal nursery-rhyme garden, complete with Mother Goose figures especially commissioned by "fun-loving" Kirstie because, as she puts it, "I hope I give my children a spirit of play."

Kirstie swears by the facial treatment she receives every morning on her terrace as the fog burns off Penobscot Bay. It involves "blasting her face with oxygen and enzymes . . . through a plastic hose hooked up to two pressurized tanks." Though her life was perfect in 1994, she has since set aside her husband, Parker Stevenson, in favor of her "soul mate," James Wilder, who "is a cross between Houdini, Errol Flynn, and Marlon Brando." Apparently Kirstie uses the same technique for choosing her lovers as she does for choosing sofa fabrics. With James, "it was like comet to comet. Boom . . ."

Not that we ought to single out Kirstie (although such self-serving bilge makes it irresistible). Celebrity-mom profiles are almost all alike and haven't changed much over the years, except that the houses and toys are more lavish. Celebrity moms are shown embracing motherhood after years of sweating under klieg lights, which apparently brings them in touch with their true, essential, feminine natures. Most important, motherhood is a powerfully transforming experience, akin to seeing God. It always changes these women, and always for the better. "I feel more enriched and compassionate toward others since having my son," says Elle McPherson.

Ladies' Home Journal tells us that Christie Brinkley's third child, daughter Sailor (her father, Brinkley's fourth husband, is a descendant of Captain Cook), "barely tipping the scale at eight pounds . . . has become Brinkley's anchor, a midlife miracle well worth waiting for." Of her second child, Jack (from her third marriage, which lasted only a few months), Christie was equally lyrical: "It's like I went to hell and came back with this angel."

We assume that most (but not all) of these celebrity moms are not trying to gloat, or to rub our noses in our own poor lifestyle choices (which invariably include the failure to choose being thin, white, gorgeous, and rich). And we've all said mushy things about how much our kids mean to us, especially in the immediate aftermath of birth, before the months of sleep deprivation and projectile vomiting produce a slightly more jaundiced view of the joys of motherhood.

But there's little deviation in the celebrity mom profile: it is a sturdily ossified genre, and those who choose to contribute to it must embody and emphasize certain traits. She is everything that you—poor, stupid, imcompetent slob—are not: serene, resourceful, contented, transformed, perky, fun-loving, talented, nurturing, selfless, organized, spontaneous, thin, fit, pore-free, well-rested, well-manicured, on-the-go, sexy and rich. She has absolutely no ambivalence about motherhood, would prefer to spend all her time with her kids if only she could, and finds that when she comes home from a draining day, her children recharge her as if they were Energizers. She is never furious, hysterical, or uncertain. She is never a bitch. She is June Cleaver with cleavage and a successful career. In a 1997 cover story titled "The New Sexy Moms," *People* told us that "postpartum depression isn't an option for such celebrity moms as Whitney Houston, Madonna, and supermodel Miki Taylor." Being subjected to sleep deprivation and raging hormones was a choice for these women, and they just said no.

The celebrity-mom profile is predicated on the interview, in which we hear extensively from the mother herself. This is a media form designed to showcase the mother's subjective processes and inner life and, thus, to celebrate her distinctive individuality. We're meant to hang on her every word, no matter how banal. She hasn't fallen through the cracks, ended up part of some vast, nameless, harried horde like the rest of us. What makes her such a great mother and enviable person is her ability to take action, make smart choices, and impose discipline on herself while being loving and spontaneous with her kids. The myth of the determined individual, fully capable of vaulting over all sorts of economic, political, and social barriers, is beautifully burnished in these profiles. It's all up to you, if only you'll try, try, and try again. There are no such things in this gauzy world as economic inequalities, institutional sexism, racism, or class privilege. Nor are there tired, pissed-off partners or kids who've just yelled, "I hate you! I wish you were dead!"

Celebrity children don't wreak havoc with work, they enhance it and even fortify their mothers' bargaining position with the boss. Says actress Gigi Rice, "Now, if they want you to do a job, you say, 'well, my baby comes with me.' What are they going to say—no?" In addition, *People* tells us, "Contractually mandated star perks typically include first-class airfare for the entire entourage, a separate trailer for the kiddies and a 24-hour limousine on standby to ferry them wherever they want to go, paid hotel accommodations for the nanny, even a nanny allowance." Sounds just like your workplace, *n'est-ce pas?*

Celebrity moms exemplify what motherhood has become in our intensified consumer culture: a competition. They rekindle habits of mind, pitting women against women, that the women's movement sought to end, leaving the notion of sisterhood in the dust. More perniciously, these portraits resurrect so many of the stereotypes about women we hoped to deep-six 30 years ago: that women are, by genetic composition, nurturing and maternal, that they love all children and prefer motherhood to anything, especially work—so they should be the main ones responsible for raising the kids. In the pages of the glossies, motherhood becomes a contest in which the reader is always the loser. Why do Kirstie and Cindy and Whitney love being mothers in some unequivocal way that you do not? Because they're good and you're bad.

Ah, but you could be worse. What about media motherhood on the other side of the tracks? Celebrity mom profiles place us on the outside looking in; stories about welfare mothers invite us to look down from on high. Welfare mothers have not been the subject of honey-hued profiles in glossy magazines. They are not the subjects of their own lives, but objects of journalistic scrutiny. We don't hear about these women's maternal practices—what they do with their kids to nurture them, educate them, soothe them, or keep them happy. It is simply assumed that these women don't have inner lives. Emotions are not ascribed to them; we don't hear them laugh or see their eyes well up with tears. One of the most frequent verbs used to describe them is "complain," as when they complain about losing health care for their kids when they go off welfare. When they are quoted, it is not their feelings about the transformative powers of motherhood to which we are made privy. Rather, we hear their relentless complaints about "the system." In many articles about welfare, we don't hear from the mothers at all, but instead from academic experts who study them, or from politicians whose careers are devoted to bashing them. The iconography of the welfare mother is completely different, too—she's not photographed holding her child up in the air, whizzing her about. In fact, she's rarely, if ever, shown smiling at all. It's as if the photographer yelled "scowl" just before clicking the shutter.

These mothers are shown as sphinx-like, monolithic, part of a pathetic historical pattern known, familiarly, as "the cycle of dependency." In a major article in *Newsweek* in August 1993 titled "The Endangered Family," we learned that "For many African Americans, marriage and childbearing do not go together." Not to mention the 25 percent of white women for whom they don't go together either, or the celebrity single mothers like Jodie Foster, Madonna, and Farah Fawcett.

It isn't just that the conservative right has succeeded in stereotyping welfare mothers as lazy, promiscuous parasites; the media in which these mothers appear provide no point of identification with them. At best, these mothers are pitiable. At worst, they are reprehensible opposites of the other mothers we see so much of, the new standard-bearers of ideal motherhood—the doting, conscientious celebrities for whom motherhood is a gateway to heaven.

During the height of welfare bashing in the Reagan, Bush, and Clinton administrations, the stereotype of the "welfare queen" gained mythological status. But there were other, less obvious, journalistic devices that served equally well to dehumanize poor mothers and their children. Unsavory designations proliferated with a vengeance: "chronic dependents," "the chronically jobless," "welfare mothers in training," "hardcore welfare recipients," "never-married mothers," "welfare careerists," and "welfare recidivists" became characters in a distinctly American political melodrama. Poor women weren't individuals; instead their life stories became case-studies of moral decay, giving substance to the inevitable barrage of statistics peppering the media's presentation of "Life on the Dole." In publications everywhere, we met the poster mother for welfare reform. She only had a first name, she lived in the urban decay of New York, Chicago, or Detroit, she was not married, she had a pile of kids each with a different absent father, and she spent her day painting her nails, smoking cigarettes, and feeding Pepsi to her baby.

As sociologists have pointed out, even though there consistently have been more white people than black on welfare, the news media began, in the mid-1960s, to rely almost exclusively on pictures of African Americans to illustrate stories about welfare, reinforcing the stereotype that most welfare recipients are black. Occasionally readers are introduced to the runner-up in the poster competition: the white welfare mother, whose story varies only in that she lives in a trailer in some godforsaken place we have never heard of and is really, really fat.

For example, in a 1995 edition of CBS's *48 Hours*, titled "The Rage Over Welfare," we met two overweight white women who live on welfare in New Hampshire. The very first shots—just to let us know the kind of lazy, selfish mothers we are in for—are close-ups of hands shuffling a deck of playing cards and, next, a mom lighting a cigarette. The white male journalist badgers one of the women, who says she can't work because she has epilepsy and arthritis in both knees. "People with epilepsy work. People with bad knees work. People do," he scolds. As she answers, "I don't know what kind of a job I could find," the camera again cuts to her hands shuffling the cards, suggesting, perhaps, a bright future in the casino industry if she'd only apply herself.

Or there's Denise B., one of the "True Faces of Welfare," age 29, with five daughters, from ages one to 13. "All, after the first, were conceived on welfare—conceived perhaps deliberately," *Reader's Digest* sniffs, conjuring up the image of Denise doing some quick math calculations, saying to herself, Oh boy, an extra 60 bucks a month, and then running out to find someone to get her pregnant. The other thing we learn about Denise is that she's a leech. Why not get a job, even though she has toddlers? Because she's lazy. "To get a good job, she would first have to go to school, then earn her way up to a high salary," *Reader's Digest* reminds us, and then lets the ingrate, Denise, speak. "'That's going to take time,' she says, 'It's a lot of work and I ain't guaranteed to get nothing.'" What we learn of Denise's inner life is that she's a calculating cynic. Her kids don't make her feel like every day is Christmas; no, we're supposed to think she uses her kids to get something for nothing.

Even the *New York Times'* Jason De Parle, one of the more sympathetic white male journalists to cover welfare, gets blinded by class privilege. Roslyn Hale, he wrote in 1994, who had been trying to get off welfare, had a succession of jobs that "alternatively invite and discourage public sympathy." She had worked as a maid and as a clerk in a convenience store during the overnight shift when drunks came in and threatened her with a knife. Hale "blames economics for her problems," De Parle reports, since these were crappy jobs that paid only minimum wage. "And sometimes she blames herself. 'I have an attitude,' she admitted." Hello? What middle-class woman would not have "an attitude" after having been threatened at knifepoint or being expected to be grateful for such jobs? In the *Boston Globe*'s "Welfare Reform Through a Child's Eyes" we see little Alicia, who now has a room of her own, Barbies, four kittens, and a ferret because her mother got a job. But although this story appears to be through the child's eyes (never the mother's), it's actually through the judgmental eyes of the press. Sure, the mom has quit drinking, quit crack, and is now working at a nursing center. But the apartment is "suffused with the aroma of animal droppings and her mother's cigarette smoke." Presumably everyone but welfare mothers and former welfare mothers knows how to make their litter boxes smell like gardenias.

One of the sentences most commonly used to characterize the welfare mother is "Tanya, who has ____ children by ____ different men . . ." (you fill in the blanks). Their lives are reduced to the number of successful impregnations by multiple partners—like zoo animals, but unlike Christie Brinkley, although she has exactly the same reproductive M.O. And while the celebrity magazines gush that Christie, Kirstie, and Cindy are sexier than ever, a welfare mother's sexuality is depicted as her downfall.

In the last three years, we've seen the dismantling of the nation's welfare system. Meanwhile, the resentment over the ridiculous standards we're supposed to meet is rising. Sure, many of us ridicule these preposterous portraits of celebrity mom-dom, and we gloated when the monumentally self-righteous "I read the Bible to Cody" Kathie Lee Gifford got her various comeuppances. But the problem is bigger than that: the standards set by celebrity motherhood as touted by the media, with their powerful emphasis on individual will, choice, and responsibility, severely undercut sympathy for poor mothers and their children. Both media characterizations have made it easier for middle-class and upper-middle-class women—especially working women facing speed-ups at work and a decline in leisure time—to resent welfare mothers instead of identifying with them and their struggles.

Why does the media offer us this vision? Not surprising, many reporters bought into the myths that began in the Reagan era, with its dogma of trickle-down economics, its attacks on the poor and people of color, and its antifeminist backlash, through which patriarchy got a new name—family values. Becoming rich and famous came to be the ultimate personal achievement. Reagan's message was simple—the outlandish accumulation of wealth by the few is the basis of a strong economy.

In that context, celebrity-mom profiles haven't been just harmless dreck that help sell magazines. They have encouraged self-loathing, rather than reassurance, in those of us financially comfortable enough not to have to worry about where our kids' next meals are coming from. And they play a subtle but important role in encouraging so many of us to think about motherhood as an individual achievement and a test of individual will and self-discipline. That mind-set—the one that promotes individual responsibility over community and societal obligations—justifies letting poor women and their children fend for themselves until mom makes the right lifestyle choices.

These stories suggest that we, too, can make it to the summit if we just get up earlier, laugh more, and buy the right products. These stories are about leaving others behind, down below. Phony images of joyful, ever-nurturing celebrity moms sitting side-by-side in the newsstands next to humorless, scowling welfare mothers naturalize a pecking order in which some kids deserve to eat well, have access to a doctor, or go to Disney World, and others do not. Under the glossy veneer of maternal joy, generosity, and love lurks the worst sort of narcissism that insists it's every woman for herself. Paying lip service to a collagen-injected feminism, celebrity momism trivializes the struggles and hopes of real women, and kisses off sisterhood as hopelessly out of style.

QUESTIONS

1. How are "celebrity moms" portrayed in the popular press? How are "welfare moms" portrayed? Give specific examples. Why do Douglas and Michaels think these contrasting images are damaging? What specifically do they damage?

2. List every social support and resource you can think of that women need to fulfill the duties associated with mothering. Be as specific as possible, drawing from your own experience if relevant. What financial and social resources do celebrity moms have access to that women who receive state support do not? How do these resources shape celebrity women's attainment of the idealized perfect mother?

3. Why might it be dangerous to glorify celebrity women as ideal mothers? Why do different standards of mothering exist for different groups of women? For example, why are women on welfare with children forced to work under new

welfare laws while other women are encouraged to stay at home with their children?

4. Brainstorm about what kind of information about the daily lives of "welfare" moms and "celebrity" moms might be left out of popular accounts. For example, what might be an obstacle to working full time for a single mother who receives state support? Also, who is taking care of the children of "celebrity" moms?

5. Why do you think that the popular press focuses so frequently on celebrity moms? Why does the public find these stories appealing? Why, in contrast, might the stories about mothers on welfare be unappealing or cause discomfort?

Health and Medicine

Linda A. Bernhard

Health is more than the absence of disease. The World Health Organization (WHO) defines health as a state of complete physical, mental, and social well being. Feminist scholars and activists focus on the ways gender influences standards of health, access to health care, quality of treatment, status in the health care professions, and research. Moreover, health, health care and medical research are affected not only by gender, but also by race, class, sexual orientation, age, (dis)ability status, and nationality and by the intersections of these categories.

For example, poverty is the number one cause of poor health, and women are disproportionately represented among the poor, mostly as young, single mothers or as older women. Most people obtain health insurance as a benefit of employment; however, low-paying, temporary, or contingent jobs usually do not provide that benefit. Women are most likely to have those jobs. Black women have a lower survival rate from breast cancer than white women. This lower survival rate may be associated with the lack of early detection due to limited access to preventive health care. Research shows that many lesbians avoid seeking health care for fear of discrimination or prejudice by health care providers.

As both formal and informal providers of health care, women are largely responsible for the world's health. Women comprise the majority of all health care providers, both in the allopathic (regular) and the alternative/complementary health care systems. But most women are employed in health care occupations, such as nursing, with limited authority, prestige, and income. Physicians, who have the highest authority, prestige, and income, among health care providers, are primarily men.

As informal non-paid health providers, women are directly responsible for the health and health care of their families. As mothers and wives, women are socialized to provide good nutrition and sanitary living conditions for children and men to maintain their health. Women also provide non-paid health services to their families, most often children and dependent elderly family members. Today these types of services are called *caregiving*. In many parts of the world, women often receive the health care information that they use for informal care from their mothers and grandmothers, and pass on these health care traditions to their daughters.

Gender bias occurs in research when women are excluded from or underrepresented in clinical trials of new drugs or when gender effects are not fully analyzed. For example when drugs are only tested on men we cannot assume that the effect will be the same in women. Research must include women. Most early AIDS research included only men. Not until 1993 did the diagnostic criteria for AIDS include problems unique to women.

As the second wave of feminism developed, women realized that the medical system was an institution that required critique and change. The Women's Health Movement grew from, and parallel to, the second wave women's movement. The Movement began in 1969 when a group of women in Boston came together to compile a list of obstetrician/gynecologists who were respectful of women and responsive to questions. But the task was so difficult that they decided to collect their own health information. They formed the Boston Women's Health Book Collective and published the first *Our Bodies Ourselves*, as an underground newspaper, because what they wrote was so radical at the time.

Simultaneously in Los Angeles, another group of women began discussing the link between reproduction and women's oppression and the role of government and physicians in controlling women by controlling reproduction. Believing that women could take responsibility for reproduction, they formed the first Feminist Women's Health Center in 1971. Reproductive rights—specifically abortion—were among the first issues addressed by the movement. Educating women about their bodies and how to care for them to maintain health was also part of the movement.

The goal of today's Women's Health Movement is to improve health care for women, realizing that when health care for women is improved, health care for everyone will be better.

The Women's Health Movement was initially very anti-professional, specifically anti-physician, because women believed that doctors had ignored women's needs and that women could take care of their own health needs. Women's health activists began to discuss *medicalization*, the process through which physicians turn many women's developmental processes, such as menstruation and pregnancy, into illnesses or health problems to be diagnosed, treated, and cured.

The movement changed from grassroots activism when nurses and other health care providers became involved, beginning in the early 1980s. Then women's health became economically attractive and by the late 1980s physicians were joining, many simply to make money, but others who were seriously concerned about women's issues and wanted to change the way medicine was practiced.

The early Women's Health Movement was comprised of white and middle class women almost exclusively. Since the 1980s many women's health groups and organizations devoted to health of specific groups of women (e.g., National Black Women's Health Project) or to single health issues (e.g., National Breast Cancer Coalition) have been established. Increasing numbers of people and organizations raise awareness of women's health and help to strengthen the overall movement for enhanced women's health. Some would argue that today there are numerous women's health movements.

In 1988, at the request of the Congressional Caucus for Women's Issues, the Government Accounting Office conducted a study which revealed that only 13% of the budget of the National Institutes of Health (NIH), the nation's largest sponsor of health research, was used for research on women's health. Such negative publicity helped to bring women's health to the nation's attention as it had never been before. Subsequently, in 1990, NIH created an Office of Research on Women's Health and developed policies to mandate study of women's health problems, inclusion of women as participants in research, and recruitment of women into biomedical research careers.

Nearly every kind of health situation or disease is subject to feminist research and critique. For example, heart disease is the number one killer of women in the United States, but most women do not know that it is as great a problem for women as it is for men. Men receive health screenings more frequently than women do. Violence against women has numerous physical and mental health consequences. Both physical and mental health of women in prison deteriorate during incarceration. These situations, and many others, suggest a need for feminist analysis and research. Women's health activists and other feminist scholars approach these issues from multiple perspectives and continue to work for better health for all of us.

FURTHER READINGS

Boston Women's Health Book Collective (1992). *The New Our Bodies, Ourselves*. New York: Touchstone.

Delgado, Jane L. and The National Hispanic Women's Health Initiative (Eds.) (1997). *Salud!: A Latina's Guide to Total Health-Body, Mind, and Spirit*. New York: Harperperennial Library.

Geary, Mary Ann S. (1995). An Analysis of the women's health movement and its impact on the delivery of health care within the United States. *Nurse Practitioner*, 20(10), November 1995, 24–35.

Moss, Kary L. (Ed.) (1996) *Man-Made Medicine: Women's Health, Public Policy, and Reform*. Durham, NC: Duke University Press.

Rosser, Sue V. (1994). *Women's Health—Missing from U.S. Medicine*. Bloomington, IN: Indiana University Press.

Ruzek, Sheryl Burt, Olesen, Virginia L., & Clark, Adele E. (Eds.) (1997). *Women's Health: Complexities and Differences*. Columbus, OH: Ohio State University Press.

Schaps, Margie J., Linn, Edward S., Wilbanks, George D., & Wilbanks, Evelyn Rivers. (1993). Women-centered Care: Implementing A Philosophy. *Women's Health Issues*, 3(2), pp. 52–54.

White Evelyn C. (Ed.). (1994). *The Black Women's Health Book: Speaking for Ourselves* (2nd ed.). Seattle: Seal Press.

White, Jocelyn and Marissa C. Martinez (Eds.) (1997). *The Lesbian Health Book: Caring for Ourselves*. Seattle: Seal Press.

Roe v. Wade, 1973; Planned Parenthood of Southeastern Pennsylvania v. Casey (1992)

Linda K. Kerber
and Jane Sherron De Hart, eds.

Historians Linda K. Kerber and Jane Sherron De Hart provide a twenty-year legal history of reproductive rights and a social context for understanding that history. Their commentary and the excerpted remarks of various US Supreme Court justices over the past twenty years help us to understand the evolution of reproductive rights law and various challenges to that law. Paying close attention to the rhetoric of the legal arguments, and the reasoning of the justices, helps us to understand the constitutional, moral, and social dimensions of this issue.

The Comstock Law had been echoed by a series of anticontraception and antiabortion laws throughout the country. James Mohr observes, "Every state in the Union had [by 1900] an antiabortion law of some kind on its books . . . except Kentucky, where the state courts outlawed the practice anyway."* In 1962 the ethics of abortion became a pressing problem when it was revealed that thalidomide, a drug extensively used in Europe and occasionally in the United States, resulted in the birth of thousands of babies with phocomelia (deformed or missing arms and legs). Sherry Finkbine, an Arizona woman who had taken the drug, demanded a legal abortion. Although her doctors supported her, the county medical society refused to approve the procedure, and, lacking confidence that she and her doctors would be spared immunity from prosecution, she fled to Sweden, where abortion was legal.

Her plight, and her challenge to hospital practice, helped to shift public opinion, both within the medical profession, which would subsequently be instrumental in advocating liberalization of abortion legislation, and among women's groups, who began to articulate dismay that women were generally denied access to safe abortion services. Estimates of the number of illegal abortions performed each year before 1973 range from 200,000 to 1,200,000; it is estimated that 200 women died each year as a result. Abortion was virtually the only medical procedure to which middle-class women did not have access. The issue was less intense for black women's groups; working-class minority women lacked a wide range of medical services, and abortion was only one among many which they needed. Thus at the beginning of the reinvigorated women's movement of the late 1960s, black and white women were divided about the place that access to legal abortion should hold in their list of priorities for legal change.

In 1970, Alaska, Hawaii, New York, and Washington legalized abortion. Texas law, like the law of most states, continued to prohibit abortion except for the purpose of saving the mother's life. In 1970, Norma McCorvey, a single pregnant woman, known as Jane Roe to protect her privacy, brought a class action suit challenging the constitutionality of that law as a violation of her right to liberty as guaranteed by the due process clause of the Fourteenth Amendment.

The Supreme Court's decision in *Roe v. Wade* marked a sharp change from long-established practice. As the opening lines of the majority decision make clear, the justices were aware they were making a sensitive and important decision.

Mr. Justice Blackmun delivered the opinion of the Court.

> We forthwith acknowledge our awareness of the sensitive and emotional nature of the abortion controversy, of the vigorous opposing views, even among physicians, and of the deep and seemingly absolute convictions that the subject inspires. One's philosophy, one's experiences, one's exposure to the raw edges of human existence, one's religious training, one's attitudes toward life and family and their values, and the moral standards one establishes and seeks to observe, are all likely to influence and to color one's thinking and conclusions about abortion.
>
> In addition, population growth, pollution, poverty, and racial overtones tend to complicate and not to simplify the problem.
>
> Our task, of course, is to resolve the issue by constitutional measurement free of emotion and of predilection. We seek earnestly to do this. . . .
>
> The principal thrust of the appellant's attack on the Texas statutes is that they improperly invade a right, said to be possessed by the pregnant woman, to choose to terminate her pregnancy. Appellant would discover this right in the concept of personal "liberty" embodied in the Fourteenth Amendment's Due Process Clause; or in personal, marital, familial, and sexual privacy said to be protected by the Bill of Rights . . . or among those rights reserved to the people by the Ninth Amendment. . . .
>
> It perhaps is not generally appreciated that the restrictive criminal abortion laws in effect in a majority of States today are of relatively recent vintage. Those laws, generally proscribing abortion or its attempt at any time during pregnancy except when necessary to preserve the pregnant woman's life, are not of ancient or even of common-law origin. Instead, they derive from statutory changes effected, for the most part, in the latter half of the 19th century. . . . At common law, at the time of the adoption of our Constitution, and throughout the major portion of the nineteenth century . . . a woman enjoyed a substantially broader right to terminate a pregnancy than she does in most states today. . . .
>
> When most criminal abortion laws were first enacted, the procedure was a hazardous one for the woman. This was particularly true prior to the development of antisepsis. . . . Abortion

mortality was high. . . . Modern medical techniques have altered this situation. Appellants . . . refer to medical data indicating that abortion in early pregnancy, that is, prior to the end of the first trimester, although not without its risk, is now relatively safe. Mortality rates for women undergoing early abortions, where the procedure is legal, appear to be as low or lower than the rates for normal childbirth. Consequently, any interest of the State in protecting the woman from an inherently hazardous procedure . . . has largely disappeared. . . . The State has a legitimate interest in seeing to it that abortion, like any other medical procedure, is performed under circumstances that insure maximum safety for the patient. . . .

The Constitution does not explicitly mention any right of privacy. In a line of decisions, however . . . the Court has recognized that a right of personal privacy, or a guarantee of certain areas or zones of privacy, does exist under the Constitution. . . . This right . . . whether it be founded in the Fourteenth Amendment's concept of personal liberty . . . or . . . in the Ninth Amendment's reservation of rights to the people, is broad enough to encompass a woman's decision whether or not to terminate her pregnancy. . . . We . . . conclude that the right of personal privacy includes the abortion decision, but that this right is not unqualified and must be considered against important state interests in regulation. . . .

. . . the State does have an important and legitimate interest in preserving and protecting the health of the pregnant woman . . . and . . . it has still *another* important and legitimate interest in protecting the potentiality of human life. These interests are separate and distinct. Each grows in substantiality as the woman approaches term, and, at a point during pregnancy, each becomes "compelling."

With respect to the State's important and legitimate interest in the health of the mother, the "compelling" point, in the light of present medical knowledge, is at approximately the end of the first trimester. This is so because of the now-established medical fact . . . that until the end of the first trimester mortality in abortion may be less than mortality in normal childbirth. It follows that . . . for the period of pregnancy prior to this "compelling" point, the attending physician, in consultation with his patient, is free to determine, without regulation by the State, that in his medical judgment, the patient's pregnancy should be terminated.

. . . For the state subsequent to approximately the end of the first trimester, the State, in promoting its interest in the health of the mother, may, if it chooses, regulate the abortion procedure in ways that are reasonably related to maternal health.

For the state subsequent to viability, the State in promoting its interest in the potentiality of human life may, if it chooses,

> regulate, and even proscribe, abortion except where it is necessary, in appropriate medical judgment, for the preservation of the life or health of the mother.
>
> Our conclusion . . . is . . . that the Texas abortion statutes, as a unit, must fall. . . .

In the years before 1973, when abortion was generally illegal, commonly performed in the private offices of doctors and unlicensed practitioners without emergency medical support, and generally without anesthesia, death from abortion was substantial. It is estimated that at least 200 deaths a year occurred when abortion was illegal. In 1985, it was estimated that only two deaths occurred from illegal abortion and only six deaths resulted from legal abortion.

The issues that were raised by *Roe v. Wade* have not been fully settled and are not likely to be easily resolved, touching as they do on basic religious and ethical beliefs. Because only women become pregnant, and because there is no obvious parallel to pregnancy in male experience, arguments about abortion are less easily made on the equal treatment grounds that served women's rights activists well in *Frontiero* (see *Frontiero v. Richardson)* and other similar cases. Advocates must ask what equal treatment would mean for men and women, who are differently situated in relation to abortion.

In the 1980s, a number of states tested what boundaries would be considered reasonable limits on the abortion rights sustained in Roe. In 1980, the Supreme Court upheld the "Hyde Amendment" by which Congress refused to fund even medically necessary abortions for indigent women *(Harris v. McRae,* 448 U.S. 297). This decision was not the focus of massive public protest, and it was replicated in the laws of many states. An effort to defeat the Hyde Amendment failed in Congress in 1993, but some states did revise their practice, covering some abortions for indigent women, usually in the case of rape or incest.

Missouri legislators developed further the position that the state could deny any form of public support or facilities for the performance of abortions. A 1986 law prohibited the use of public employees and facilities to perform or assist abortions not necessary to save the life of the mother and also prohibited the use of public funds for counseling a woman in abortion decisions not necessary to save her life. It included a preamble that claimed that the life of each human being begins at conception and a provision that required that medical tests of fetal viability—tests whose efficacy was disputed—be performed before any abortion on a fetus estimated to be twenty weeks or more in gestation. Since 97 percent of all late abortions (done at an estimated sixteen-week gestational age) were performed at a single hospital in Kansas City that, although private, received public aid and was located on public property, the practical impact of the law was great.

In deciding *Webster v. Reproductive Health Services* in July 1989, by a 5–3 vote, the Supreme Court majority claimed that the conclusions of *Roe* had not been changed.** Missouri law left a pregnant woman free to terminate her pregnancy so long as neither public funds nor facilities were used for it; this was, the Court majority said, a "value judgment" favoring childbirth over abortion. But the majority raised a general question about *Roe.* [T]he rigid Roe framework," wrote Chief Justice Rehnquist in the majority opinion, "is hardly consistent with the notion of a Constitution cast in general terms, as ours is, and usually speaking in general principles, as ours does. The key elements of the *Roe* framework—trimesters and viability—are not found in the text of the Constitution or in any place else one would expect to find a constitutional principle . . . the result has been a web of legal rules that . . . [resemble] a code of regulations rather than a body of constitutional doctrine." Justice Anthony Scalia concurred, adding that in his view, *Roe* should have been overturned; abortion is, he thought, a field in which the Court "has little proper business since the answers to most of the cruel questions posed are political and not juridical." He was appalled at efforts to bring the pressure of public opinion to bear on the decisions of the Court, notably the March on Washington of some 200,000 people that had been sponsored by pro-choice groups shortly before the *Webster* case was argued in April 1989.

Justice Harry A. Blackmun, who had written the Court's opinion in *Roe,* now wrote a bitter dissent for the minority. He denied that Rehnquist's opinion left *Roe* "undisturbed." Rather it challenged a large body of legal precedent that had established a "private sphere of individual liberty," which although not explicitly specified in the Constitution had long been taken to have been implied by the Fourth Amendment guarantee against unreasonable searches. The right to privacy had been invoked in the 1960s when the Court protected the sale and use of birth control devices; the *Webster* decision, Blackmun feared, bypassed "the true jurisprudential debate underlying this case: . . . whether and to what extent . . . a right to privacy extends to matters of childbearing and family life, including abortion." Justice John Paul Stevens argued that the preamble's claim that life begins at conception was a religious view, and to write it into law was to ignore First Amendment requirements for the separation of church and state. Finally, Blackmun argued that the state had a distinct interest in maintaining public health, and that as safe and legal abortions became more difficult to get, an increase in deaths from illegal abortions could be predicted. "For today," he concluded, "the women of this Nation still retain the liberty to control their destinies. But the signs are evident and very ominous, and a chill wind blows."

The Court's decision in *Webster* left many questions open. If states could deny public funds for abortions, what other limitations was it reasonable for state legislatures to impose? Was it reasonable to require a waiting period? Was it reasonable to require minors to get the consent of one parent? of both parents? The Court had ruled in 1976 that a state could not require a married woman to get her husband's consent before having an abortion (*Planned Parenthood* v. *Danforth*, 428 U.S. 52 [1976]); could a state require a married woman to *notify* her husband?

In 1988 and 1989 Pennsylvania amended its Abortion Control Act of 1982 extensively, requiring a twenty-four-hour waiting period and the provision of "certain information" twenty-four hours before the abortion is performed. Minors were required to have the consent of one parent, and married women to have notified their husbands, although it was possible for a court to waive that requirement and all requirements could be waived in the event of a "medical emergency." Because most of the Justices had made public substantial reservations about the decision in *Roe*, it seemed to many observers not unreasonable to predict that the Court would uphold the entire Pennsylvania statute and, possibly, overturn *Roe* v. *Wade*. Instead, a majority organized by Justices Sandra Day O'Connor, Anthony Kennedy, and David Souter, joined by Harry Blackmun and John Paul Stevens, wrote a complex opinion, which began with a ringing affirmation of *Roe*. But O'Connor, Kennedy, and Souter also made it clear that they shared Rehnquist's skepticism of the trimester framework of *Roe*. How does the majority think the principle of equal protection of the laws should be applied in abortion decisions?

Note the comments on coverture at the end of the majority opinion; this statement marks the first explicit recognition by the court of the end of coverture.

Why do the dissenting Justices think *Roe* should be overturned?

Planned Parenthood of Southeastern Pennsylvania v. Casey.

Justices O'Connor, Kennedy, Souter:

> Liberty finds no refuge in a jurisprudence of doubt. Yet 19 years after our holding that the Constitution protects a woman's right to terminate her pregnancy in its early stages . . . that definition of liberty is still questioned. . . . After considering the fundamental constitutional questions resolved by *Roe,* principles of institutional integrity, and the rule of *stare decisis* [the principle that decisions of previous courts should be let stand unless there is overwhelming reason to change them], we are led to conclude this: the essential holding of *Roe* v. *Wade* should be retained and once again reaffirmed. . . . Constitutional protection of the woman's decision to terminate her pregnancy derives from the Due Process Clause of the Fourteenth Amendment. It declares that no State shall "deprive any person of life, liberty, or property, without due process of law." . . . It is a premise of the Constitution that there is a realm of personal liberty which the government may not enter. We have vindicated this principle before. Marriage is mentioned nowhere in the Bill of Rights and interracial marriage was illegal in most States in the 19th century, but the Court was no doubt correct in finding it to be an aspect of liberty protected against state interference by the substantive component of the Due Process Clause in *Loving* v. *Virginia* 388 U.S. 1 (1967). . . .
>
> Men and women of good conscience can disagree, and we suppose some always shall disagree, about the profound moral and spiritual implications of terminating a pregnancy, even in its earliest stage. Some of us as individuals find abortion offensive to our most basic principles of morality, but that cannot control our decision. Our obligation is to define the liberty of all, not to mandate our own moral code. . . .
>
> Our law affords constitutional protection to personal decisions relating to marriage, procreation, contraception, family

relationships, child rearing, and education. . . . These matters, involving the most intimate and personal choices a person may make in a lifetime, choices central to personal dignity and autonomy, are central to the liberty protected by the Fourteenth Amendment. At the heart of liberty is the right to define one's own concept of existence, of meaning, of the universe, and of the mystery of human life. Beliefs about these matters could not define the attributes of personhood were they formed under compulsion of the State. The woman's right to terminate her pregnancy before viability is the most central principle of *Roe v. Wade.* It is a rule of law and a component of liberty we cannot renounce.

On the other side of the equation is the interest of the State in the protection of potential life. The *Roe* Court recognized the State's "important and legitimate interest in protecting the potentiality of human life." . . . That portion of the decision in *Roe* has been given too little acknowledgment and implementation by the Court in its subsequent cases. . . . Though the woman has a right to choose to terminate or continue her pregnancy before viability, it does not at all follow that the State is prohibited from taking steps to ensure that this choice is thoughtful and informed. Even in the earliest stages of pregnancy, the State may enact rules and regulations designed to encourage her to know that there are philosophic and social arguments of great weight that can be brought to bear in favor of continuing the pregnancy to full term. . . . We reject the trimester framework, which we do not consider to be part of the essential holding of *Roe*. . . . Measures aimed at ensuring that a woman's choice contemplates the consequences for the fetus do not necessarily interfere with the right recognized in *Roe* . . . not every law which makes a right more difficult to exercise is, ipso facto, an infringement of that right. . . .

. . . We . . . see no reason why the State may not require doctors to inform a woman seeking an abortion of the availability of materials relating to the consequences to the fetus. . . . Whether the mandatory 24-hour waiting period is . . . invalid because in practice it is a substantial obstacle to a woman's choice to terminate her pregnancy is a closer question. [We do not agree with the District Court] that the waiting period constitutes an undue burden. . . . [From Part D: We have already established the precedent, and] we reaffirm today, that a State may require a minor seeking an abortion to obtain the consent of a parent or guardian, provided that there is an adequate judicial bypass procedure. . . .

. . . Pennsylvania's abortion law provides, except in cases of medical emergency, that no physician shall perform an abortion on a married woman without receiving a signed statement from the woman that she has notified her spouse that she is about to undergo an abortion.

The woman has the option of providing an alternative signed statement certifying that her husband is not the man who impregnated her; that her husband could not be located; that the pregnancy is the result of spousal sexual assault which she had reported [or that she fears bodily harm from him.] A physician who performs an abortion on a married woman without receiving the appropriate signed statement will have his or her license revoked, and is liable to the husband for damages.

. . . In well-functioning marriages, spouses discuss important intimate decisions such as whether to bear a child. But there are millions of women in this country who are the victims of regular physical and psychological abuse at the hands of their husbands. . . . Many may have a reasonable fear that notifying their husbands will provoke further instances of child abuse [or psychological abuse]. . . .

. . . [A]s a general matter . . . the father's interest in the welfare of the child and the mother's interest are equal. Before birth, however, the issue takes on a very different cast. It is an inescapable biological fact that state regulation with respect to the child a woman is carrying will have a far greater impact on the mother's liberty than on the father's. [That is why the Court has already ruled that when the wife and husband disagree on the abortion decision, the decision of the wife should prevail.]

. . . There was a time, not so long ago, when a different understanding of the family and of the Constitution prevailed. In *Bradwell v. Illinois,* three Members of this Court reaffirmed the common–law principle that "a woman had no legal existence separate from her husband." . . . Only one generation has passed since this Court observed that "woman is still regarded as the center of home and family life," with attendant "special responsibilities" that precluded full and independent legal status under the Constitution *(Hoyt v. Florida).* These views, of course, are no longer consistent with our understanding of the family, the individual, or the Constitution. . . . [The Pennsylvania abortion law] embodies a view of marriage consonant with the common–law status of married women but repugnant to our present understanding of marriage and of the nature of the rights secured by the Constitution. Women do not lose their constitutionally protected liberty when they marry.

CHIEF JUSTICE REHNQUIST, WITH WHOM JUSTICE WHITE, JUSTICE SCALIA, AND JUSTICE CLARENCE THOMAS JOIN:

> The joint opinion . . . retains the outer shell of *Roe v. Wade* . . . but beats a wholesale retreat from the substance of that case. We believe that *Roe* was wrongly decided, and that it can and should be overruled consistently with our traditional approach to *stare decisis* in constitutional cases. We would . . . uphold the challenged provisions of the Pennsylvania statute in their entirety.... [B]y foreclosing all democratic outlet for the deep passions this issue arouses, by banishing the issue from the political forum that gives all participants, even the losers, the satisfaction of a fair hearing and an honest fight, by continuing the imposition of a rigid national rule instead of allowing for regional differences, the Court merely prolongs and intensifies the anguish.
>
> We should get out of this area, where we have no right to be, and where we do neither ourselves nor the country any good by remaining.

Abortion is an issue of concern to men as well as to women. It is an issue on which women and men hold a wide variety of views. Among the questions raised are:

1. What are the limits of a woman's right to make her own reproductive decisions?
2. Should the unborn be afforded legal rights?
3. What rights does the father have? In 1976 the Supreme Court held that a state could not require a married woman to get her husband's consent before having an abortion (*Planned Parenthood v. Danforth,* 428 U.S. 52 [1976]). Is the husband's claim of a role in an abortion decision a reinstatement of the old law of coverture?
4. What rights does the community have to set general policy? What are the appropriate limits of government intervention? The state may not require a woman to conceive a child; can the state require a woman to bear a child?
5. Will any of these rights change as improvements are made in the technology for the discovery of birth defects and genetic abnormalities, for the implantation of embryos, and for caring for premature infants at earlier ages?

Notes

* James C. Mohr, *Abortion in America: The Origins and Evolution of National Policy, 1800–1900* (New York, 1978), pp. 229–30.

** *William L. Webster, Attorney General of Missouri* v. *Reproductive Health Services*, 109 Sup. Ct. 3040 (1989).

QUESTIONS

1. What medical controversy in the early 1960s brought the abortion issue before the public? What type of suit did Norma McCorvey (Jane Roe) bring before the Supreme Court and what legal rationale was used on her behalf?
2. What did the Supreme Court rule in *Roe v. Wade*? What two constitutional amendments were used in this case and why? What type of limits on abortion were left standing in the original *Roe. v. Wade* decision?
3. How was *Roe v. Wade* challenged by various states and by congress? What limits did they seek to impose on a woman's right to an abortion? What arguments were used? Which state laws has the Supreme Court upheld and which ones have been denied? What is significant about the Casey decision?
4. Why is this body of law so controversial? What are some of the ethical arguments involved in this issue? Do you believe it is a matter for the courts to decide?

Jane Doe's Choice

Lynda Zielinski

Lynda Zielinski is an Ohio-based freelance writer who recently retired from her job as a licensed social worker in the juvenile court system. The Jane Doe and judges depicted are composites based on her experience.

"Your Jane Doe is here," the secretary tells me.

In juvenile court, a Jane Doe is not a dead person: She is a pregnant teenager, under 18, who wants an abortion but doesn't want to tell her parents about it. Ohio law allows her to have a court hearing before a judge, who can grant permission for the procedure—a "judicial bypass"—without the parental consent required in this and other states.

The young woman's identity has to be kept confidential; that's why we call her Jane Doe. I am a social worker in the court's diagnostic clinic. I interview juveniles before their court appearances—Jane Does, Delinquents and Unrulies, as they are called.

The interview takes place in my closet-sized basement office. The only real bright spot here is a photo of my twin granddaughters in oversized, flowery hats. When I first started working here, I was concerned that the image might upset the Jane Does, so I considered taking it down. But I learned that it didn't matter. These girls are desperate to get on with the abortion, get on with their lives. They are undeterred by pictures of young children.

Before she meets with me, the Jane Doe has already cleared several other hurdles. First, she visited our intake department, located in one of the city's toughest neighborhoods. There she was given the phone number of an attorney, who will also serve as her guardian ad litum—someone to look out for her best interests. She was also randomly assigned to one of our courtrooms. This assignment will pretty much seal her fate.

The intake department and the court itself are open only on weekdays, 8:30 a.m. to 4:00 p.m. School hours. Except in summertime, Jane Doe will have to cut class to get here. Truancy—one of the court's major concerns for all other juveniles—becomes a moot point for these young women.

Jane Doe had to arrange a meeting with her lawyer, who's located somewhere within our large county. A few of the kinder-hearted attorneys will arrange to meet Jane Does at a place more convenient than their offices, or at least accessible to bus lines. The lawyers realize that time is important for pregnant young women: Any delay could put them into the second trimester, making the bypass more difficult to obtain.

At the meeting with her lawyer, Jane Doe would have brought proof from a doctor confirming her pregnancy—another expense for her. (The result of a home test is not permissible.) She also had to show that she has received pregnancy counseling and knows her three options: having a baby and keeping it, having a baby and giving it up for adoption, or having an abortion.

When she finally gets to me, I start with the usual question, "How did you find out about the judicial bypass?"

"I did some research on the Internet and then I talked to a school counselor," she tells me.

Good. She has sought out an adult for guidance. I will be asked to give my opinion to the judge on whether Jane Doe is sufficiently mature to deserve a bypass, and well-enough informed to seek an abortion without parental consent. The informed part is relatively easy: In front of the judge, she must simply be able to go over her three options, explain why she has decided on abortion and describe the abortion procedure and its health risks.

But the "mature" part is insane. Mature compared to an adult woman? To an older teenager? More mature than a teenager who has decided to give birth? Maturity is ultimately in the eye of the judge; there are no specified psychological or legal criteria.

In our juvenile court I have observed a number of judges, who fall into several categories. Each is guided by personal beliefs—not about maturity, but about abortion.

One type of judge believes that the agencies we rely on for pregnancy counseling don't give proper emphasis to the "pro-life" viewpoint, and so provides a separate list to the Jane Does. Judges in that category require them to visit one of these places and bring back some literature as proof, then quiz the young women on their errant sexual behavior. Nonetheless, those judges usually grant the bypass.

Another kind of judge never grants a bypass, under any circumstance. This is because of the judges' religious beliefs—which are then justified by finding the Jane Doe to be "immature."

Other judges grant the bypass only after delivering a stern and lengthy lecture. They are well-intentioned, believing in promoting family unity. "Don't you trust your parents, who love you and provide for you?" they might ask the Jane Does. I have heard this lecture many times. It is given regardless of the girl's actual family circumstances—an alcoholic mother, say, or a father in prison for rape. I caution my Jane Doe not to show anger toward this type of judge, even if what he or she says isn't true of her family. "You have to show that you are mature," I remind her.

Finally, we have judges who grant bypasses without my testimony. Their reasoning is that any minor who can navigate through all the appointments ahead of the hearing *has* to be mature.

My latest Jane Doe enjoys her life. She looks forward to skating lessons, the prom, a trip with Mom to visit a college campus. She's worried about her reputation: She is a role model to her younger siblings and has never been in trouble. She doesn't want to upset her mother, who trusts her.

Most Jane Does say they are seeking the bypass because they don't want to disappoint their parents. Some, from dysfunctional homes, fear that their pregnancy may exacerbate problems between their parents. Some worry that it will add stress to a parent with emotional or substance-abuse issues. A few worry that they will be kicked out of their homes. Still others are certain that their parents would support their abortion decision, but prefer to handle it themselves.

This Jane Doe looks at me with pleading eyes. "I've been a basket case about this," she says. "I just can't have a baby now; I'm not ready. My boyfriend's been accepted to college on a football scholarship. He said he would support me, no matter what I decide. He's a good kid. I don't want to ruin his life too." She starts crying, searching for tissues in her tiny handbag. "I'm not a slut," she continues softly. "I haven't slept around. I know we should have waited to have sex."

"How do you think you'll feel after your abortion?" I ask her. "Relieved," she says. I always ask this of Jane Does, and this is their stock answer. It is the response given most often by women of all ages who have chosen to have an abortion. Relief. Earlier, we had talked about the risks. I asked her, "Which carries a greater risk, having an abortion or giving birth?" and she got it wrong. The impression many girls have is that abortion is risky but having a baby is, well, *normal*. In fact, while the fatality risk is 0.1 per 100,000 surgical abortions at eight weeks or less in the U.S., pregnancy carries a fatality risk of 11.8 per 100,000. And what about psychological harm? Teens suffer much more stress as a result of carrying an unwanted pregnancy than they do from having an abortion.

Yet mandatory parental-involvement laws—designed to make abortions that much harder for teens—are now in effect in 35 states. In comparison, 34 states and the District of Columbia allow most pregnant minors to obtain prenatal care and delivery services without parental notification or consent. Furthermore, all 50 states and D.C. give all or most minors the right to obtain treatment for sexually transmitted diseases without telling their folks.

On the day of the court hearing, I tell the judge that Jane Doe is 16, a good student, involved in various sports and responsible enough to drive. I testify that Jane Doe is appropriate in conduct and demeanor. She appears forthright and credible. Her thought processes are clear and goal-directed. These are some of the pat phrases I use in the courtroom to make her appear reasoned and stable. It's a good thing she doesn't seem crazy or un-grounded—then she might have to have a baby.

Jane Doe is asked to describe the abortion procedure and the risks. All goes well. As predicted, this judge grants the bypass.

Jane Doe is all smiles. She thanks me and her attorney. She goes on her way looking confident; she has jumped through the last hoop. But she doesn't know how lucky she is: She got a judge who is kind and follows the law. I'm thinking, this Jane Doe believes she is the exception here—a good girl. But I see a lot of exceptions just like her.

Meanwhile, courts whittle away at abortion rights under the guise of protecting young women from harm. If they would say, "We love the innocent fetus much more than the pregnant teen," then at least they would be honest. In Ohio this September, another obstacle was added to the bypass steeplechase: a face-to-face talk with the doctor to learn about the procedure a day before the abortion. Another expense. Are the other professionals, who were quite capable before of explaining abortion, no longer qualified? To make matters worse, the law also now eliminates a young woman's ability to obtain a bypass solely because she faces abuse from a parent or guardian.

The determined, middle-class young woman will still manage to do what is required to get the bypass. She will then finish school, and at some time in her future may have a baby shower and go shopping for adorable wallpaper and an educational mobile.

Meanwhile, those who can't ace the bypass procedure, or lack financial resources, may find their options severely limited—and their burdens greatly increased. If they don't opt for an illegal—and often unsafe—abortion, they'll be expected to stay in school, work part-time, get to doctors' appointments and prepare to give birth and support a child.

If only they could have shown they were mature.

QUESTIONS

1. The author points out that for a pregnant teenager to obtain a judicial bypass for abortion without parental consent, she has to prove her "maturity" in front of a judge. What are the girls required to do in the court to show their "maturity"? How do the judges measure the girl's "maturity"? What social and cultural beliefs are actually guiding these judgments?
2. What procedures and rhetoric associated with the current abortion policy for pregnant teenagers are discussed and critiqued by the author? How do they curtail young girls' reproductive rights?
3. Which social groups of teenagers might be especially disadvantaged by this process?

STUDY SAYS BABIES IN CHILD CARE KEEP SECURE BONDS TO MOTHERS (1996)

Susan Chira

The question of who should bear the responsibility for child care has become a pressing socio-economic issue, and a concern for many working parents. Journalist Susan Chira reports on recent research which contradicts previous findings that child care hinders child development. The research Chira reports on here offers important new information to the debate about the need for a federal child care policy.

The most far-reaching and comprehensive study to date has found that using child care does not affect infants' trust in their mothers.

The results, announced yesterday at a conference in Providence, R.I., run counter to several previous studies that seemed to show that infants in child care were slightly more likely to have an insecure relationship with their mothers than those whose mothers stayed at home with them .

"Study Says Babies in Child Care Keep Secure Bonds to Mothers" by Susan Chira, reprinted by permission form *The New York Times,* April 21, 1996.

The earlier research had alarmed some experts and parents because other studies indicate that troubled bonds between infants and mothers could signal emotional and behavioral problems later.

The new study was designed to try to address one of the most emotionally charged issues in society today: Does a mother put her child at risk by working outside the home? It reported that the sense of trust felt by 15-month-old children in their mothers was not affected by whether or not the children were in day care, by how many hours they spent there, by the age they entered day care, by the quality or type of care or by how many times care arrangements were changed. Instead, what affected that trust was a mother's sensitivity and responsiveness to her child.

"Part of what elicited this study was real worries that child care in and of itself was unhealthy," said Dr. Deborah Lowe Vandell, one of the 25 researchers on the project, which was sponsored by the National Institute of Child Health and Human Development, part of the National Institutes of Health. "I think that is the wrong analysis. One message from the study is that if the quality of the interaction with the mother is sensitive, then the child is likely to develop a secure relationship with her. I'm sure that will be reassuring to many mothers and families.

But the researchers cautioned that the study found some aspect s of child care appeared to pose risks for certain vulnerable children. When a mother does not handle her child sensitively, the likelihood of a troubled mother-child bond can be increased by child care that is of poor quality, changes several times or extends more than 10 hours a week.

The ongoing study, which brought together researchers who have often clashed about the risks of child care, has been following more than 1,300 families nationwide since 1991. Compared with previous studies, this one includes more diverse families and more types of child care. It has observed children at home as well as in child care and laboratories, following children from birth through 7 years of age.

Researchers emphasize that many questions remain unanswered, and they must await later stages of the project to see if the links described yesterday last. Children who look secure now could be insecure later. What seem to be risks of child care now could prove unimportant as children grow, or new risks could surface.

Later stages of the study will examine children's bonds to their mothers at 3 years old, and their cognitive and language development physical development, health, behavior and relationships with peers.

In a result that intrigued several researchers who said they were still not entirely sure how to interpret it, the study also found that more time in child care was linked to some risks for boys but that less time was potentially risky for girls. Boys who were in child care for more than 30 hours a week were slightly more likely to have an insecure relationship to their mothers, while girls were more likely to have an insecure bond if they were in child care less than 10 hours a week.

While this finding was statistically significant, it was weaker than the other results and researchers cautioned against overreacting to it.

Previous studies of older children have found that child care can have some ill effects for boys, particularly middle-class boys and that girls of working mothers tended to be more independent and focused on achievement.

Dr. Jay Belsky, one of the researchers, said it was possible that "separation might prove stressful for boys, but girls who are home with mothers extensively may become almost too close and enmeshed."

The study offered researchers in the often-acrimonious world of social science a chance to test competing ideas. Psychologists have long disagreed over how important and lasting are the effects of the mother-child bond this study measures, which is known as "attachment."

The scientists measured attachment by watching children's reactions when their mothers returned after brief separations. Children who sought comfort from their mothers were judged to be secure. Researchers evaluated mothers by videotaping them with their children and grading the mothers' sensitivity according to accepted criteria.

While many researchers say the quality of a child's first relationship sets the tone for all future ones, others say that impact has been exaggerated. Usually, the first relationship is with the mother, which is why this study and others measure that bond.

This study confirms researchers' belief that a mother's sensitive care is crucial in forging a secure attachment, said Dr. Cathryn L. Booth, one of the researchers. But some researchers, as well as some popular baby experts and pediatricians, have argued that working during the first year of a child's life would be harmful, either because long hours spent away from a child would interfere with the mother's ability to be sensitive or because a baby would experience a mother's absence as a devastating abandonment and feel unable to count on her. Although the earlier studies seemed to offer some support for that argument, this more comprehensive study questions that assumption, Dr. Booth said.

The study offered further evidence of what experts have been telling parents for years: smaller groups of children, more adults per child and more sensitive caregivers spell higher-quality child care, defined as environments in which children are stimulated and get adequate attention. Child-care centers were ranked lowest in quality; care by fathers or relatives or in the home by a caregiver were ranked the highest.

Because researchers were able to follow children from birth, they were also able to figure out what influenced parents' choices for child care. Children who were in better-quality care had more stimulating home environments and mothers who were more likely to believe that working put children at risk. At the same time, children who were most securely attached had mothers who were better off economically and who appeared to be more sensitive and were more likely to believe that day care could be harmful.

Dr. Belsky, who ignited a firestorm in 1986 when he became one of the first researchers to raise questions about the potential risks of day care, suggested that while the study offered reassurance to working parents, it also indicated that some guilt might be productive.

"It may be that some guilt and anxiety keeps you alert, vigilant and able to monitor the quality of care," Dr. Belsky said. "Being cavalier about the effects of work turns out to be risky."

The study also departed in several other ways from previous ones. By the time the children studied were a year old, 80 percent of them had been in child care for at least a few hours a week, a higher percentage than previous surveys have found. And the overall quality of child care, the researchers observed, was better than the usually dismal picture revealed by several recent studies.

Dr. Sarah Friedman, the study's coordinator at [the] institute, said that researchers were not sure why, but one explanation might be that previous studies had focused on child care centers, which were found to provide the lowest-quality care in this study.

Questions

1. How can gender and class differences affect a child's response to child care? What evidence does Chira offer?
2. How does Chira report her information? Why do research efforts sometimes produce contradictory results? What reasons does Chira offer to explain the contradictions in research on child care? What is the significance of these reasons for the use of research findings in the development of national child care policy?
3. What effects might child care research have on women's ability to negotiate work and family responsibilities? Would working men be similarly affected? Why/why not?

THE VIOLENCE AGAINST WOMEN ACT (1994)

The following selection has been adapted from the Violence Against Women Act, passed by the House and Senate in 1994. The first act to specifically address violence against women as a national concern, the VAWA calls for more funding and training to prevent violence before it begins, as well as legal and economic provisions for women who have already suffered from battering, rape or sexual assault. Recognizing that violence is both a health concern and a civil rights issue, activists now have more comprehensive resources to help victims of gender-motivated crime.

Violence against women is a serious health problem for women in the United States. Until recently women have had little protection from domestic violence, sexual assault, or stalking. Although physical assault is a crime, when women are hurt by people they know, the police have been reluctant to enforce orders of protection or even respond to calls to domestic violence situation. Out of fear, women do not ask to press charges against their attacker in these situations. As a result, often women have not been pro-

"The Violence Against Women Act," adapted from Title IV of The Violent Crime Control and Law Enforcement Act of 1994, Public Law 103–322 [H.R. 3355], September 13, 1994.

tected, and the perpetrator has not been prosecuted. In order to protect women's lives, health and safety both in public and in their homes, the Violence Against Women Act (VAWA) was enacted in 1994. The rationale for enacting the Violence Against Women Act (VAWA) was founded on the inability of the criminal and civil justice systems to protect victims of gender-motivated crime. For example, in certain states, interspousal immunity laws prevented a battered spouse from suing her husband for monetary damages for medical expenses and pain and suffering. Orders of protection were not usually considered enforceable outside the state where it was obtained.

Purpose of the Act

- train police, prosecutors, and judges to deal more effectively with sexual assault and domestic violence and provide funds for increased law enforcement efforts;
- authorize funds for rape prevention and education;
- provide for training of probation and parole officers who deal with released offenders to prevent repeat offenses;
- eliminate loopholes in state domestic violence laws by requiring interstate enforcement of protection orders and encouraging arrests of abusive spouses;
- provide federal penalties for abusers who stalk their spouses or partners across state lines; and
- protect immigrant women trapped in abusive marriages and create a civil remedy for victims of gender-based crimes.

Provisions of the Act

- Stricter sentencing for sexual offenders;
- Mandatory restitution for sex crimes for the full amount of victim's financial losses and costs incurred for:

- medical services relating to physical, psychiatric, or psychological care
- physical and occupational therapy or rehabilitation,
- necessary transportation, temporary housing, and child care expenses
- lost income
- attorney's fees, plus any cost in obtaining a civil protection order
- any other losses suffered by the victim as a proximate result of the offense,

- Law enforcement and prosecution grants to reduce violent crimes against women, including education programs, data collection, training, additional personnel, victim services programs, programs addressing stalking, and programs specifically for American Indian women;
- Safety for women in public transit and public parks—improved lighting, increasing camera surveillance, providing emergency phone lines to contact law enforcement or security personnel, etc;
- New evidentiary rules to protect a victim from having her sexual history disclosed as evidence in sex crime cases; and a
- National domestic violence hotline

Remedies

The VAWA provides a civil remedy to women who have suffered criminal acts. To utilize the protection of the VAWA, the crime must be a crime of violence motivated by gender. There is no requirement that the act or acts actually result in a criminal charge, prosecution or conviction. Additionally, although the violent act must constitute a felony crime, the burden of proving that the perpetrator committed the act is by a preponderance of the evidence and not the beyond-a-reasonable-doubt standard. The act also provides a four-year statute of limitations for such claims.

Insofar as homeowners policies routinely exclude intentional acts of the insured, a claim under the VAWA for damages might be limited unless the perpetrator has substantial assets. Regarding damages, the VAWA permits recovery for all compensatory damages suffered by the victim. The victim is also entitled to injuctive relief, declatory relief, punitive damages and such other remedies as the court may deem appropriate. In addition, attorney fees are recoverable.

Overall, the VAWA recognizes that women in our society have been forced to alter their lifestyles substantially in order to protect themselves from violent crimes (Hunn, 1995. Adapted by Sarah Liros).

QUESTIONS

1. What is the rationale behind the Violence Against Women Act? What provisions of the act are designed to further protect women from violence? What provisions are designed to aid women who have already been victims of crime? Why might violence be considered a gender-motivated crime?

2. Why have the criminal and civil justice systems been unable to adequately address this issue? What factors complicate orders of protection, police response to calls, and the judicial process? Why does the government have a responsibility to address violence against women?

3. How well does the VAWA include provisions that will accommodate the many differences among women, such as race, age, class and geography? Look closely at the Act to imagine how the elements will apply to the different realities of women's lives. What doesn't this Act address?

"The Rape" of Mr. Smith

Unknown

In this piece of unknown origin, the author uses parody to illustrate the damaging cultural assumptions about rape that infiltrate our legal system and threaten a rape victim's ability to receive a fair trial. In this selection, a man robbed at gunpoint is subjected to a line of questioning similar to that often directed at rape victims—one that puts the victim, and not the attacker, on trial.

The law discriminates against rape victims in a manner which would not be tolerated by victims of any other crime. In the following example, a holdup victim is asked questions similar in form to those usually asked a victim of rape.

"Mr. Smith, you were held up at gunpoint on the corner of 16th & Locust?"

"Yes."

"Did you struggle with the robber?"

"No."

"Why not?"

"He was armed."

"'The Rape' of Mr. Smith," by Unknown, reprinted from *Issues in Feminism: An Introduction to Women's Studies*, 1980, Mayfield Publishing Company.

"Then you made a conscious decision to comply with his demands rather than to resist?"

"Yes."

"Did you scream? Cry out?"

"No. I was afraid."

"I see. Have you ever been held up before?"

"No."

"Have you ever given money away?"

"Yes, of course—"

"And did you do so willingly?"

"What are you getting at?"

"Well, let's put it like this, Mr. Smith. You've given away money in the past—in fact, you have quite a reputation for philanthropy. How can we be sure that you weren't *contriving* to have your money taken from you by force?"

"Listen, if I wanted—"

"Never mind. What time did this holdup take place, Mr. Smith?"

"About 11 p.m."

"You were out on the streets at 11 p.m.? Doing what?"

"Just walking."

"Just walking? You know that it's dangerous being out on the street that late at night. Weren't you aware that you could have been held up?"

"I hadn't thought about it."

"What were you wearing at the time, Mr. Smith?"

"Let's see. A suit. Yes, a suit."

"An *expensive* suit?"

"Well—yes."

"In other words, Mr. Smith, you were walking around the streets late at night in a suit that practically *advertised* the fact that you might be a good target for some easy money, isn't that so? I mean, if we didn't know better, Mr. Smith, we might even think you were *asking* for this to happen, mightn't we?"

"Look, can't we talk about the past history of the guy who *did* this to me?"

"I'm afraid not, Mr. Smith. I don't think you would want to violate his rights, now, would you?"

Naturally, the line of questioning, the innuendo, is ludicrous—as well as inadmissible as any sort of cross-examination—

unless we are talking about parallel questions in a rape case. The time of night, the victim's previous history of "giving away" that which was taken by force, the clothing—all of these are held against the victim. Society's posture on rape, and the manifestation of that posture in the courts, help account for the fact that so few rapes are reported.

QUESTIONS

1. What questions are victims of rape frequently asked in court cases that are similar to the questions in this selection? How do such questions further victimize rape victims?
2. What cultural stereotypes and assumptions are used to justify these types of questions? Why are such questions tolerated in rape trials that would never be tolerated in other types of trials, like Mr. Smith's?

Raped: A Male Survivor Breaks His Silence (1992)

Fred Pelka

Fred Pelka combats the myth that rape only happens to women by describing his experience as an adult male rape victim. Although women are the primary victims of sexual assault, Pelka clarifies that rape is not a crime of sex but an act of power and control in which women, children and men can all be targets. Rapists use their bodies as weapons to degrade and humiliate others and to assert a sense of their own strength and power. The crime of male rape offers insight into cultural gender norms because it upsets the typical construction of masculinity as "in control" and femininity as "weak" and "vulnerable." Pelka felt—and was treated by other males—as if his rape had made him less than a man and "'reduced' him to the status of women."

The man who raped me had a remarkable self-assurance which could only have come from practice. He picked me up just outside

"Raped: A Male Survivor Breaks His Silence" by Fred Pelka. Reprinted from *On the Issues*, Spring 1992.

Cleveland, heading east in a van filled with construction equipment. That early morning in May I'd already spent a sleepless 24 hours trying to hitchhike from Oxford, Mississippi to Buffalo, New York, so it felt good when I was offered a ride through the western fringe of Pennsylvania. First, though, the driver told me he needed to stop along the way, to pick up some building supplies. We drove to a country club undergoing renovation, where I hung out with his co-workers while he signed for several boxes of equipment which we carried back to his van. Getting back onto the turnpike he told me about one more stop he had to make.

As a man, I've been socialized never to admit to being vulnerable, to discuss those moments when I wasn't in control. I know also how women and children are routinely punished when they speak out about abuse, how they are blamed for their own victimization. The examples are endless: Witness the contempt with which Anita Hill was treated. For these reasons and more I'm still reticent, years after it happened, to recount what happened to me that day in Ohio. This article marks the first time in 15 years I have publicly discussed it under my own name.

The second building seemed deserted. We went up a flight of stairs, down a corridor into a side room. I looked around for the equipment he'd mentioned, and noticed him locking the door behind us. He slugged me before I could react, forced me down with his hands around my throat. As I began to lose consciousness I heard him say, "If you scream, if you make one wrong move, I'll kill you."

The police told me later that the man who raped me was a suspect in the rapes of at least six other young men. During the assault his mood swung from vicious, when he promised to strangle me or break my neck, to self-pity, when he wept because we were both among "the wounded ones." In that enormous calm that comes after the acceptance of death, I wondered who would find my body.

Most rapes don't happen like this. Most victims know their attacker(s)—he is a neighbor, friend, husband, or father, a teacher, minister or doctor. The vast majority of rapes are committed by men against women and children, and the FBI estimates that anywhere from 80 to 90 percent go unreported. Rape is an integral part of our culture, and fully one third of all women in this country will be raped at some point in their lives. But this sexist violence does occasionally spill over onto boys and men. The

National Crime Survey for 1989 estimated that one in 12 rape survivors is male.

For all this, nobody really knows how many men are raped each year, or how many boys are sexually abused. One study at the University of New Hampshire found that one in 11 young men surveyed had been sexually abused before their 18th birthday. I've seen articles which speculate that anywhere from one in nine to one in seven men will be raped or sexually abused in their lifetime, most often by other males, but these are little more than guesses.

"Since rape is generally misconstrued to be a sexually motivated crime," writes Dr. A. Nicholas Groth and Anne Wolbert Burgess, "it is generally assumed that males are unlikely targets of such victimization, and then when it does occur, it reflects a homosexual orientation on the part of the offender. However, the causes of male rape that we have had an opportunity to study do not lend much support to either assumption." Groth and Burgess interviewed men in the community who had been raped, and men who admitted to raping other men, and published their findings in the *American Journal of Psychiatry*. In half the cases they studied, the gender of the victim "did not appear to be of specific significance" to the rapist. "Their victims included males and females, adults and children," and "may symbolize . . . something they want to conquer or defeat. The assault is an act of retaliation, an expression of power, and an assertion of their strength or manhood."

In their article, Burgess and Groth dispute some of the prevalent myths about male rape. The first is that men simply don't get raped, at least not outside prison. Of course, if men don't get raped then what happened to me either wasn't male rape (the police asking, "Did you come?"), or I'm not a man (my male friends wanting to know how I could "let something like this" happened to me). The second myth—that all men who are raped or rape other men are gay—is a product of our culture's homophobia, and our ignorance of the realities of sexual violence. Most people find it difficult to understand why a straight man would rape another straight man. But if you see rape as a way of exerting control, of confirming your own power by disempowering others, then it makes perfect sense. If it makes you feel powerful and macho to force sex on a woman or child, think of how much more powerful you feel raping another man.

* * *

**

"I have a special place," the man who raped me said after a long while. "It's out in the country where we can make all the noise we want." It seemed obvious what would happen to me once we arrived at "His special place," but I knew there was no hope for my survival as long as we stayed in that room. So I agreed to go with him to "the country." I promised not to try to escape. It is perhaps an indication of his fragile hold on reality that he believed me.

We walked back to his van and drove away. I waited until I saw some people, then jumped as we slowed to make a turn, rolling as I hit the pavement. I ran into the nearest building—a restaurant—just as patrons were finishing their lunch. Conversation stopped, and I was confronted by a roomful of people, forks raised in mid-bite, staring.

"I think you'd better call the police," I told the waitress. This was all I could say, placing my hands flat on the counter between us to control their trembling. She poured me a cup of black coffee. And then the police arrived.

The two detectives assigned to my case conformed to the standard good cop/bad cop archetype. The good cop told me how upset he'd seen "girls" become after being raped. "But you're a man, this shouldn't bother you." Later on he told me that the best thing to do would be to pull up my pants "and forget it ever happened." The bad cop asked me why my hair was so long, what was I doing hitchhiking at seven o'clock in the morning? Why were my clothes so dirty? Did I do drugs? Was I a troublemaker?

I used to be puzzled at how the bad cop obviously didn't believe me, in spite of the fact that, by his own account, in the months before my assault six other men had come to him with similar stories. Then I heard of the Dahmer case in Milwaukee, how in May 1991 Dahmer's neighbors saw him chasing a naked 14-year-old boy, bleeding from the anus, through the alley behind their building. The responding officers returned the boy to Dahmer's apartment, where Dahmer explained that this was just a lover's spat, which the police believed in spite of the youth's apparent age, and the photos scattered on Dahmer's floor of murdered and mutilated boys and men. The police reassured a neighbor who called again, saying that everything was all right—this at the very moment Dahmer was murdering Konerak Sintha-somphone. Afterwards Dahmer dismembered Sinthasomphone's body.

Sinthasomphone was one of at least 17 boys and men raped and murdered by Dahmer, their body parts stored in vats and freezers in his apartment. It was reported that his first assaults were committed in Ohio, so I had to brace myself before I could look at Jeffrey Dahmer's photo in the paper. At first I was relieved to find that he was not the man who raped me. Then I thought how this meant my assailant is likely still out there, looking for more "wounded ones."

Because I gave them such detailed information—the country club, the name painted on the side of his van—the detectives were able to locate my assailant not too many hours after I was brought into their precinct. The good cop asked, after I identified the rapist, whether I wanted to press charges. He explained how I'd have to return to Ohio to appear before a grand jury, and then return again for the trial, how the newspapers would publish my name, how little chance there was of a conviction.

"He says you seduced him," the good cop said. "So it's your word against his."

The bad cop glared at me when I told them there was no way I wanted any of this to be made public. "You mean," he fumed, "I wasted my whole afternoon on this shit?" Standing in front of me with an expression of disgust, he asked, "How do you think this makes me feel?"

By then it was getting dark. I hitchhiked the remaining 200 miles home, studying every movement of every man who offered me a ride. I arrived at my apartment after midnight, walking the last 10 miles.

In the weeks that followed the assault, every stupid, insensitive thing I'd ever said about rape came back to haunt me. A friend of mine had been attacked several months earlier, also while hitchhiking. She told me just a few hours after it happened how she'd missed her bus, and didn't want to be late to work. She said the man offering her a lift seemed normal enough, even "nice."

"You should have waited for the next bus," I lectured. Today I cringe at my arrogance. Hitchhiking, like walking alone after dark, or feeling safe on a date, at work, at home, is another prerequisite to which only men are entitled. How dare she not understand the limits of her freedom?

While women tell me that the possibility of rape is never far from their minds, most men never give it a first, let alone a second, thought. This may explain why they react so negatively to accounts by male survivors. To see rape as "a women's issue" is a form of male privilege most men would prefer not to surrender. They would rather believe that they can move with immunity through the toxic atmosphere of violence and fear they and their compatriots create. Being a male survivor meant I'd lost some of that immunity. No wonder I felt as if I'd been poisoned, as if I were drowning.

For years I pretended, as per the good cop's recommendation, that nothing had happened, secretly feeling that I was somehow responsible, somehow less masculine. The turning point came with the media storm that swirled up around the Big Dan rape in New Bedford, Massachusetts. The movie "The Accused" is based on that incident—a woman assaulted in a bar while other men looked on and cheered. Naive as I was, I figured this was a pretty clear-cut case. Where the police might have doubted my will to resist (no broken bones, no massive lacerations), here was a victim overpowered by half a dozen men. How could anyone doubt that she had been brutalized? Yet, during the trial, *The Boston Herald* ran the front page headline "SHE LED US ON!" I realized then that, even had I been murdered, someone would have inevitably questioned my complicity: "He probably likes rough sex."

It's just this sort of victim-blaming that discourages survivors from reporting their trauma, or seeking treatment, but there are other factors which may discourage males in particular. Homophobia for one: The sort of gender McCarthyism that labels any man a faggot who cannot or will not conform to accepted norms of masculine feeling or behavior. Men who rape other men capitalize on this, knowing that straight victims don't want to appear gay, and gay victims might fear coming out of the closet. Groth and Burgess report, for instance, that "a major strategy used by some offenders . . . is to get the victim to ejaculate." This "strategy" was attempted in roughly half the cases they studied, and in half of those the rapist succeeded in ejaculating his victim. This confuses the victim, who often misidentifies ejaculation with orgasm. It confirms for the rapist the old canard about how victims "really want it." And, as Groth and Burgess say, it leaves the survivor "discouraged from reporting the assault for fear his sexuality may be suspect."

For male survivors of child sexual abuse there is also the unfortunate theory that boys who are abused inevitably grow up to be men who rape. One survivor told me it was for this reason he had decided never to be a father. Not that he'd ever wanted to abuse children, nor was there any evidence he ever would. He eventually came to realize that because some rapists are themselves survivors doesn't mean that all male survivors of child sexual abuse turn out to be rapists.

Finally, rape-crisis centers, the only institutions in our society founded expressly to help rape survivors, are identified by some men as hotbeds of feminism, and many men take "feminist" to mean "Man-hating." It's true that the vast majority of rape crisis counselors are women, that the entire stop-rape movement is an extension of the women's movement. For the record, though, I have never felt any hostility in response when calling a rape-crisis center, this in spite of the fact that RCCs are often plagued by "hotline abusers"—men who call to masturbate to the sound of a female voice.

On the other hand, I've run across a good deal of hostility toward women from male survivors with whom I've talked. One man told me how certain he was that the counselors at his local RCC hated men, even though, by his own admission, he'd never called, and knew no one who had. A while back I attended a survivors' conference organized by a Boston women's group, attended by several hundred women and maybe a dozen men. One of these men stood up during a plenary session to shout at the women on the podium. As an incest survivor, he said, he felt "marginalized" and "oppressed" by the way the conference was run, despite the fact that a number of the workshops were specifically geared toward males, and that a keynote speaker received a standing ovation when he described his work with boys and men. Some male survivors even blame women for the denial and homophobia they encounter after their assault. They openly resent the (pitifully few) resources available to female survivors, as if any help women receive is at the expense of men. Even Geraldo has picked up this theme: His show on male survivors ended with an attack on rape crisis centers for their alleged refusal to acknowledge male victimization.

This hostility has been exacerbated by the so-called men's movement, the Robert Bly/mythopoetic crowd, with their "Wild Man" and "Inner Warrior" archetypes. These men say a lot of absurd things about sexual violence, not the least of which is that "just as many men get raped as women." This last statement is often repeated by Chris Harding, editor of *Wingspan*, which *The Boston Globe* calls "the bible of the new men's movement." Harding is generally quick to add that most of these rapes "occur in prison"—a statement which is as inaccurate as it is pernicious, assuming as it does that a disproportionate number of male rapes are committed by working-class and minority men. The men's movement claims that rape is a "gender-neutral issue." and thus has nothing to do with sexism.

What is ironic about all this is that what little acknowledgment there is of male victimization generally comes from the *women's* stop-rape movement. To the extent that male survivors *can* tell their stories, it is because of the foundation laid by feminists. So this woman-bashing is as ungrateful as it is gratuitous.

One source of confusion appears to be the distinction between victimization and oppression. Male survivors charge that feminists see rape as a "man vs. woman" issue, emphasizing the central role male violence plays in stunting and destroying women's lives, and they're right. The distinction is that while many women, and some men, are victimized by rape, all women are oppressed by it, and any victimization of women occurs in a context of oppression most men simply do not understand. Rape for men is usually a bizarre, outrageous tear in the fabric of reality. For women, rape is often a confirmation of relative powerlessness, of men's contempt for women, and its trauma is reinforced every day in a thousand obvious and subtle ways.

For myself, I don't need for rape to be gender neutral to feel validated as a male survivor. And I certainly don't need to denigrate women, or to attack feminists, to explain why I was abused by the male police, ridiculed by my (male) friends and marginalized by the male dominated society around me. It is precisely because we have been "reduced" to the status of *women* that other men find us so difficult to deal with. It was obvious to me at the police station that I was held in contempt because I was a *victim*—feminine, hence perceived as less masculine. Had I been an accused criminal, even a rapist, chances are I would have been treated with more respect, because I would have been seen as more of a man. To cross that line, to become victims of the violence which works to circumscribe the lives of women, marks us somehow as traitors to our gender. Being a male rape survivor means I no longer fit our culture's neat but specious definition of masculinity, as one empowered, one always in control. Rather than continue to deny our experience, male survivors need to challenge that definition.

As Diana E.H. Russell says in *The Politics of Rape*, "Women must start talking about rape: Their experiences, their fears, their thoughts. The silence about rape must be broken."

The same must be true for men. And so I offer this article as my first contribution to that effort.

I've been back to northern Ohio exactly once in the 15 years following that day. Seven years ago I was traveling from Boston to Chicago with a car full of friends. It was early morning, and I was sleeping in the back seat when we pulled off the highway, and steered onto a street that looked oddly, disturbingly familiar. Rubbing my eyes, I felt a strange sense of deja vu. And then I remembered.

"Time for some coffee," the driver said, and I wondered then if we would eat breakfast at that same restaurant, if I would meet that same waitress. We didn't and I chose not to tell my companions what had happened to me all those years ago.

Today I think I might be less disconcerted. Today I think I just might have told them what happened.

QUESTIONS

1. How is "masculinity" defined in our culture? How is femininity defined? Why did Pelka's rape "reduce him to the status of women"? What does this statement mean?

2. How did other men treat Pelka after the assault? How did the police treat him? Give specific examples. Why did other men react to him differently than if he had been the victim of another type of violent crime?

3. What are some of the widespread myths about male rape? What is homophobia and how is it a factor? What in actuality motivates a rapist to assault his victims?

4. What distinction does Pelka draw between victimization by rape and oppression by it? What relationship does the sex of the victim have to the likelihood of becoming a victim of rape?

5. Why did Pelka choose not to press charges against his rapist? What is the cultural climate for survivors who choose to prosecute? How did he feel in the days, months, and years after the assault? What avenues did Pelka have to report and work through the trauma of his rape?

Introduction: Myths and Realities Regarding Battered Women (1996)

Albert R. Roberts

Albert Roberts' introduction to Helping Battered Women: New Perspectives and Remedies *(1996) challenges persisting myths about female battering, offering personal narratives, scholarship and statistical information to construct a more realistic portrait of domestic violence. Roberts also provides a brief overview of historical efforts to seek change on women's behalf.*

Rachel, age thirty-four, described her abusive partner's self-destructive patterns and his death threats against her:

> He had been doing drugs, and he started getting paranoid and accused me of making signals out to someone in the hall—and there was no one out there. He asked me to go downstairs to get something and he locked himself in the room, and I knew that he

> was upset and I heard the click of a gun being dry fired, and I could hear him spinning the barrel and I started getting scared. Finally I convinced him to open the door. He acted like he was gonna shoot himself. I begged him not to. The kids were down the hall [sleeping]. I got angry with him and said, "Go ahead, do it"; then I said, "Give it to me—I'll do it." He gave me the gun. I put it down and went downstairs. He came after me and held the gun to my head and said, "If I can't have you, no one can!" He cocked it [the gun]. We were there for a long time. I was crying and told him I never cheated on him, and finally through talking, I convinced him not to do it. For a long time I thought I was gonna die that night.

Mindy, age twenty-two, a visiting nurse with a five-year-old son, briefly described her self-destructive coping attempts. In order to cope with the violent abuse—being hit with a lead pipe and empty beer bottles by her boyfriend—she took drugs and attempted suicide. In her words,

> I O-Ded on cocaine intravenously. Purposely! I couldn't take it anymore. I was real depressed and upset and afraid that he was going to beat our son. I went to the hospital; they pumped my stomach, then told me that I was a drug addict. Then they put me in a ninety-day inpatient drug program which I didn't complete. The psychiatrist put me on Fisterol, an antidepressant, and then Haldane.

In Chapter 3, Albert R. Roberts describes in vivid and graphic detail typical illustrations of critical incidents during childhood and adolescence, incidents triggering the worst battering episodes, terroristic and death threats, the nature and extent of injuries, and suicide attempts among a representative sample of 210 battered women.

During the late 1970s and the 1980s, the pendulum shifted from an emphasis on providing emergency shelter and counting the high rates of spouse abuse to an emphasis in the mid-1990s on implementing legal remedies, proarrest policies, case management services, and treatment programs for battered women.

Common Myths

A number of myths and stereotypes hinder both an accurate knowledge of the nature, extent, and intensity of woman battering and effective intervention. Enormous progress has been made in the past few years in regard to major policy reforms and program developments. Recent legislation, more sensitive police and court responses, and communitywide case management approaches offer much promise to lessening the battering of women in the United States. But in order for agency policies and clinical practices to be implemented effectively, our attention needs to be directed toward the realities of domestic violence against women, rather than the myths. This book was written to debunk the traditional myths and replace them with new knowledge, research, social action, public policy, and intervention strategies.

Although considerable progress has been made in funding domestic violence programs in the past ten years, much still remains to be done. There is disproportionately less funding for victim assistance programs when compared with programs and institutions for convicted felons. For example, the Violent Crime Control and Law Enforcement Act of 1994 authorizes nearly $9.9 billion for prisons and an additional $1.7 billion for alternative detention programs, whereas the Violence Against Women Act of the 1994 crime bill authorizes a total of only $1.2 billion over five years for criminal justice programs and social services to aid battered women and victims of sexual assault.

Myth 1. Woman battering is a problem in only the lower socioeconomic class.

Reality: Woman battering takes place in all social classes, religions, races, and ethnic groups. Although violence against women seems to be more visible in the lower class because it is more frequently reported to the police and hospital emergency rooms in inner-city poor neighborhoods, it is increasingly being recognized as a pervasive problem in middle- and upper-class homes as well. For example, the murder of Nicole Brown Simpson in 1994 received intensive media scrutiny because of reports that she had been beaten by her ex-husband, former football legend O.J. Simpson. In her new book, Georgette Mosbacher, former wife of the CEO of Fabergé, describes the battering she endured while married.

Although woman battering occurs in all socioeconomic classes, it is reported to be more prevalent in the lowest economic groups. The U.S. Department of Justice's 1994 National Crime

Victimization Survey Report states that women with a family income under $9,999 were more than five times as likely to be a victim of a violent incident perpetrated by an "intimate" than were women with a family income over $30,000 (BJS, 1994).

Myth 2. Woman battering is not a significant problem because most incidents are in the form of a slap or a punch that do not cause serious injury.

Reality: Woman battering is a very serious problem. National Crime Survey data estimate the number of visits each year for medical care resulting from domestic violence: 28,700 visits to a hospital emergency room, 39,900 visits to a physician's office, 21,000 in-patient hospitalizations, and 99,800 days of hospitalization. The total health-care costs per year is approximately $44,393,700 (McLeer & Anwar, 1989; National Crime Surveys, 1981).

For example, Delores, age forty-two, described her injuries from years of battering: "Two broken ribs, scars on my elbows and thighs, bruises on my back and neck. Broke my bridge in five places. All of my top teeth are loose. My glasses were broken." In addition, "he threatened to kill me. If he was drunk enough, I thought he would. He always said, 'If I ever catch you with another man, I'll kill you' and 'If you leave me, I'll blow your brains out'."

Myth 3. Elder abuse (abuse of one's elderly parent) is not much of a problem.

Reality: According to the 1990 report of the House of Representatives Select Committee on Aging, *Elder Abuse: A Decade of Shame and Inaction,* more than 1.5 million older persons may be victims of abuse by their adult children. This figure is only an estimate because there is no accurate reporting system for elder-abuse incidents. Researchers have discussed battered elderly women, police complaint reports as a source of early case findings, the need for statutory or mandatory reporting of elder abuse and financial exploitation (as is done in child-abuse cases), and a model case-management strategy.

Myth 4. The police do not want to arrest the batterer because they view domestic violence calls as a private matter.

Reality: I had black eyes from his hitting and punching me. I called 911 and the police came, and I said to arrest him. He told them I was nuts because I was on pills from the doctor. The house was a mess, and I had the baby. The police officer believed me, and they arrested him. One officer asked me if I had anywhere to go, so I said I was from New Jersey and my mother was there. He advised me to go back to New Jersey with the money I had. The police said otherwise it would happen again. So I called my mother; bought a ticket and left the next morning. He [the batterer] called and told me to drop the charges while I was packing to leave. I told him no.

Reality: Before 1985, the police often did not want to arrest the batterer when they were called to the scene in a domestic violence case. However, the court decision in the case of *Thurman v. The City of Torrington* (1985) served notice to police departments across the country to treat domestic violence reports as they would any other crime in which the perpetrator and victim do not know each other.

In this Torrington, Connecticut, case, Tracey Thurman had repeatedly begged the police for protection from her former husband, Charles "Buck" Thurman. In one instance, the police were called to Ms. Tracey Thurman's residence because her former husband was beating and stabbing her just outside her home. When the police officer finally arrived (his arrival was delayed for approximately twenty minutes while he went to the station to "relieve himself"), he asked Buck for the knife but did not handcuff or attempt to arrest him. Buck then continued to brutalize Tracey, kicking and stomping on her. Tracey suffered very serious injuries, including partial paralysis. She won her lawsuit against the Torrington police department for its negligence in not arresting Buck and for violating her constitutional rights to equal protection. Ms. Tracey Thurman was awarded $2.3 million in compensatory damages, which was later reduced to $1.9 million. Because of the large settlement in the Thurman case, this case is credited as being the catalyst for the development of mandatory arrest laws in a growing number of states.

. . . By 1989, thirteen states had enacted mandatory arrest policies for the perpetrators of domestic violence, although in several of the states, arrest is mandatory only when the batterer violates a restraining order. In addition, there have been far-reaching changes in New York State's Family Court Act, Domestic Relations Law, and Criminal Procedural Law. New York's Family Protection and Domestic Violence Intervention Act of 1994 requires police to make arrests in cases in which there is reasonable cause to believe that a felony or misdemeanor was committed by one family or household member against another or if an order of protection was violated. As of 1991, in New Jersey, arrest is mandatory if a woman suffers an injury or complains of injury. New Jersey law states that arrest is mandatory for violating a restraining order if it involves a new act of domestic violence.

Myth 5. All batterers are psychotic, and no treatment can change their violent habits.

Reality: The majority of men who assault women can be helped. There are two main types of intervention for men who assault women: arrest and counseling. Studies have shown that mandatory arrest has worked for some types of batterers, but not others. In their 1992 study of 1,200 cases in Milwaukee, Sherman and associates found that arrest seemed to result in an escalation of battering among unemployed minorities, whereas arrest had a deterrent effect among abusers who were employed, white, and married at the time of the study. . . .

The Duluth, Minnesota, Domestic Abuse Intervention Project (DAIP) conducted a twelve-month follow-up study in which battered women were asked their opinion of the intervention that the project had used in an effort to make the batterer change his violent habits. Of the women studied, 60 percent said they felt there was improvement when the batterer took part in education and group counseling, whereas 80 percent of the women stated that the improvement had resulted from a combination of involvement by the police and the courts, group counseling, and the shelter (Pence & Paymar, 1993).

Myth 6. Although many battered women suffer severe beatings for years, only a small percentage experience symptoms of posttraumatic stress disorder (PTSD).

Reality: Tina, age twenty-five, recounted her suicide attempt and intrusive thoughts about the traumatic abusive incidents:

> I tried to kill myself because of depression over life in general. I was fed up—sick and tired of being beaten and miserable and taken advantage of. I kept having recurring nightmares about the battering and death threats. Thoughts of the beatings kept popping into my mind almost every morning. . . . My body took the drugs. I couldn't O-D [overdose]. I tried to hang myself in my backyard, but someone pulled into my driveway and rescued me. I found recently I have a lot to live for.

Three clinical studies of battered women living in shelters or women attending community-based self-help groups found PTSD rates ranging from 45 to 84 percent (Astin et al., 1990; Houskamp & Foy, 1991; Kemp, Rawlings, & Green, 1991). These studies revealed a significant association between the extent and intensity of battering experiences by abused women and the severity of their PTSD symptoms. . . .

There has been discussion of the admissibility of expert testimony on battered women syndrome and PTSD to support self-defense claims made by battered women charged with homicide of their abusers. In some cases the expert testimony and the distortions of it by the press leads to a more severe sentence (e.g., fifteen to twenty years or a life sentence).

Myth 7. Battered women who remain in a violent relationship do so because they are masochistic.

Reality: Most battered women who remain in an abusive relationship do so for the following reasons:

1. Economic need (e.g., financial dependency);
2. Intermittent reinforcement and traumatic bonding (e.g., the development of strong emotional attachments between intimate partners when the abusive partner is intermittently kind, loving, and apologetic for past violent epi-

sodes and promises that it will never happen again, interspersed with beatings and degrading insults);

3. Learned helplessness (e.g., when someone learns from repeated, unpleasant, and painful experiences that he or she is unable to control the aversive environment or escape, that person will gradually lose the motivation to change the situation);

4. The far that the abuser will hunt down the victim and kill her if she leaves; and

5. Concern that leaving the relationship and moving to a new location will be a major disruption for the children.

Myth 8. Children who have witnessed repeated acts of violence by their father against their mother do not need to participate in a specialized counseling program.

Reality: We had been arguing; I can't remember what about. He became violent and ripped the phone wire off because I tried to call the police. He tied me up with the wire and burned me with an iron. He ran outside and ripped some kind of plug from my car so that it wouldn't work. Both my children were there. My daughter was six, and she was screaming. My son was five, and he just stayed away and hid under his bed.

A report from the American Bar Association (1994) entitled *The Impact of Domestic Violence on Children* urges lawyers and judges to try more actively to protect children from the devastating impact (both physical and psychological) of domestic violence. The report provides the following revealing statistics about children and youth who have witnessed domestic violence: Seventy-five percent of the boys who were present when their mothers were beaten were later identified as having demonstrable behavior problems. Between 20 and 40 percent of chronically violent teens lived in homes in which their mother was beaten. Sixty-three percent of males in the eleven-to-twenty age group who are incarcerated on homicide charges had killed the man who battered their mother.

Jaffe, Wolfe, and Wilson (1990) found that although group counseling was helpful for children with mild to moderate behavior problems, more extensive individual counseling was required for children who had witnessed ongoing and severe violent episodes. Jaffe and associates reported on a four-year study of 371 children who had lived in violent homes. They found that group counseling had helped the children "improve their self-concept, understand that violence in the home was not their fault, become more aware of protection planning, and learn new ways of resolving conflict without resorting to violence" (p. 90). . . .

Myth 9. Alcohol abuse and/or alcoholism causes men to batter their partners.

Reality: Although research indicates that among heavy drinkers there seems to be a higher rate of domestic violence than among nondrinkers, the majority of batterers are not alcoholics and the overwhelming majority of men classified as high level or binge drinkers do not abuse their partners (Straus & Gelles, 1990).

In many cases, alcohol is used as an excuse for battering, not a cause. Disinhibition theory suggests that the physiological effects of heavy drinking include a state of lowered inhibitions or control over the drinker's behavior. Marlatt and Rohsenow (1980) found that the most significant determinant of behavior right after drinking is not the physiological effect of the alcohol itself, but the expectations the individuals place on the drinking experience. Removing the alcohol does not cure the abusive personality. . . .

Historical Background

Women have been battered by their partners for centuries. Indeed, in most societies, brutal whippings and beatings have to have been the most salient way of keeping spouses from leaving their husbands. In 1885, the Chicago Protective Agency for Women and Children was established, and according to feminist historian Elizabeth Pleck (1987), this organization was the most important agency effort of the nineteenth century to help women who were victims of physical abuse. This agency provided legal aid, court advocacy, and personal assistance to women victims of assault. An abused woman could receive up to four weeks of shelter at a refuge run by the Women's Club of Chicago, and in addition, battered women were able to receive an equitable amount of property in divorce settlements. The agency also helped abused women secure legal separations and divorces after proving extreme cruelty and/or drunkenness on the part of their husband.

Between 1915 and 1920, twenty-five cities followed Chicago's lead in establishing protective agencies for women.

Of these cities that followed the lead of Chicago's wealthy women advocates, only a few lasted beyond the 1940s. The new Women's Bureaus were a separate unit of the police department and were responsible for helping runaway girls, prostitutes, abused women and abused children. Although these police social workers did not provide legal aid, they did provide counseling, court advocacy, and job placement and arranged for temporary housing for abused women and transient youths. The largest number of police social workers in Women's Bureaus was in Chicago, Cleveland, Baltimore, Detroit, Pittsburgh, Los Angeles, Minneapolis, New York City, Portland, Seattle, St. Louis, St. Paul, and Washington, D.C. (Roberts, 1990). However, by the 1940s all the police Women's Bureaus had been eliminated by a new police chief, city manager, or mayor. In a few police departments the Bureaus were changed to crime prevention bureaus, and a male police administrator replaced the woman director. As a result of the downfall of the police social work movement, it was rare for any help to be offered to battered women until the women's rights movement, which began in the 1970s.

By the late 1970s, emergency shelters, twenty-four-hour hotlines, and a network of volunteer host homes were developed to aid battered women throughout the United States, Canada, and Great Britain. The first shelter, Chiswick Women's Aid, was opened in London in 1972 by Erin Pizzey. Pizzey's efforts to provide emergency shelter for abused women and their children inspired others throughout the Western world to do the same. By 1977, eighty-nine shelters for battered women had been opened throughout the United States, and during that year, the shelter's twenty-four-hour hotlines received over 110,000 calls from battered women.

The major self-reported strengths of emergency services were shelter, twenty-four-hour hotlines, peer counseling, court advocacy, legal aid, and the commitment of staff and volunteers (many of whom work fifty to sixty hours a week, evenings, and weekends). The major problems were overcrowding in the shelters, lack of stable funding, rapid turnover of full-time staff and attrition of volunteers, lack of cooperation by local police and the courts, and poor interagency relations and linkages (Roberts, 1981).

By 1990, there were more than 1,250 battered women's shelters throughout the Untied States and Canada (Roberts, 1990). In addition, crisis-oriented services for battered women are provided at thousands of local hospital emergency rooms, hospital-based trauma centers, emergency psychiatric services, suicide prevention centers, community mental health center crisis units, and pastoral counseling services (Roberts, 1995).

A number of states have enacted special legislation that provides funding for hotlines and shelters for victims of domestic violence. Every state and major metropolitan area in the country now has crisis-intervention services for battered women and their children. Although the primary focus of these services is to ensure the women's safety, many shelters have evolved into much more than just a place for safe lodging. Crisis intervention for battered women generally includes a twenty-four-hour telephone hotline, a safe and secure emergency shelter (the average length of stay is three to four weeks), an underground network of volunteer homes and shelters, and welfare and court advocacy by student interns and other volunteers (Roberts, 1984). Many shelters also offer peer counseling, support groups, information on women's legal rights, and referral to social service agencies.

In some communities, emergency services for battered women have expanded to include parenting education workshops, assistance in finding housing, employment counseling and job placement for the women, and group counseling for the batterers. In the all-too-often neglected area of assessment and treatment for the children of battered women, a small but growing number of shelters provide either group counseling or referral to mental health centers.

Planned social change and a sharp reduction in a major social problem usually takes place after (1) legislators, human service administrators, prosecutors, and judges become aware that the problem (e.g., women battering) affects a large number of people (more than 1 million) and is life threatening; and (2) collective action is taken by large organizations, interest groups, and statewide coalitions to remedy or lessen the problem.

In this book, the contributors document the extensive efforts, demonstration projects, research, and recent legislation on behalf of battered women. We know that the passage of legislation aimed at resolving a social problem has the most potential for encouraging a resolution of the problem if a major appropriation is attached to compliance with the legislation. For example, each state had to develop and implement a plan to deinstitutionlize all status offenders and neglected and abused youths from juvenile institutions and adult jails in order to receive federal funds from the Juvenile Justice and Delinquency Prevention Act of 1974. A number of states complied with the mandate and monitored adult jails for many years afterward to make sure that juvenile status offenders were not confined with adult offenders.

The incremental approach to building support year after year to ultimate passage of the Violence Against Women Act of 1994 has been documented. This recent legislation includes a $1.2 billion appropriation (1) to improve the criminal justice response to violent crimes against women; (2) to expand services and community support for domestic violence victims; (3) to improve safety for women in public transit and public parks and assistance to victims of sexual assault; and (4) to provide support for a variety of educational, health, and database services (e.g., educating youth about domestic violence, developing national projections of domestic violence—caused injuries and recommended healthcare strategies, and improving the incorporation of data regarding stalking and domestic violence into local, state, and national crime information systems). National and statewide coalitions and how these advocacy groups were instrumental in encouraging legislators to pass far-reaching federal and state legislation, including the Violence Against Women Act of 1994 and stalking legislation in a growing number of states have been discussed.

Starting in 1984 with the passage of the Victims of Crime Act (VOCA), millions of dollars have been allocated by the federal government through state and local agencies to support battered women's shelters and court-based victim assistance. The Violence Against Women Act (VAWA) was signed into law by President Clinton on September 13, 1994. This act provides an appropriation of $1.2 billion to improve and expand crisis services, criminal justice agency responses, housing, and community support programs for victims of domestic violence and sexual assault.

References

American Bar Association. 1994. *The Impact of Domestic Violence on Children.* Chicago: American Bar Association.

Astin, M. C., K. Lawrence, G. Pincus, and D. Foy. 1990, October. "Moderator Variables for PTSD Among Battered Women." Paper presented at the convention of the International Society for Traumatic Stress Studies, New Orleans.

Bachman, R. 1994. *Violence Against Women: A National Crime Victimization Survey Report.* Washington, D.C.: U.S. Department of Justice, Bureau of Justice Statistics.

Bureau of Justice Statistics (BJS). 1994. *Criminal Victimization in the United States, 1992.* Washington, D.C.: U.S. Department of Justice, Bureau of Justice Statistics.

Houskamp, B.M., and D. W. Foy. 1991. "The Assessment of Postraumatic Stress Disorder in Battered Women." *Journal of Interpersonal Violence* 6: 367–75.

Jeffe, P.G., D.A. Wolfe, and S. K. Wilson. 1990. *Children of Battered Women.* Newbury Park, Calif.: Sage.

Kempt, A., E. I. Rawlings, and B. L. Green. 1991. "Post-Traumatic Stress Disorder (PTSD) in Battered Women: A Shelter Sample." *Journal of Traumatic Stress* 4:137-48.

Klingbeil, K., and V. Boyd. 1984. "Detection and Assessment of Battered Women in the Emergency Room." In *Battered Women and Their Families: Intervention Strategies and Treatment Programs,* ed. A. R. Roberts, pp. 7–32. New York: Springer.

Marlatt, G.A., and D. J. Rohsenow. 1980. "Cognitive Processes in Alcohol Use: Expectancy and the Balanced Placebo Design." In *Advances in Substance Abuse Behavioral and Biological Research.* ed. Nancy K. Mello, pp. 159-99. Greenwich, Conn.: JAI.

McLeer, S. V., and R. Anwar. 1989. "A Study of Battered Women Presenting in an Emergency Department." *American Journal of Public Health* 79: 65-66.

National Crime Surveys. 1981. "National Sample, 1973-1979." Ann Arbor, Mich.: Inter-University Consortium on Political and Social Research, University of Michigan.

Pence, E., and M. Paymar. 1993. *Education Groups for Men Who Batter: The Duluth Model,* New York: Springer.

Pleck, E. 1987. *Domestic Tyranny.* New York: Oxford University Press.

Roberts, A.R. 1981. *Sheltering Battered Women.* New York: Springer.

Roberts, A.R. 1984. *Battered Women and Their Families: Intervention Strategies and Treatment Programs,* New York: Springer.

Roberts, A.R. 1995. *Crisis Intervention and Time-Limited Cognitive Treatment.* Thousand Oaks, Calif.: Sage.

Roberts, A.R., ed. 1990. *Crisis Intervention Handbook: Assessment, Treatment and Research.* Belmont, Calif.: Wadsworth.

Sherman, L.W. 1992. *Policing Domestic Violence: Experiments and Dilemmas.* New York: Free Press.

Straus, M., and R. Gelles. 1990. *Physical Violence in American Families.* New Brunswick, N.J.: Transaction Books.

QUESTIONS

1. Why do myths and stereotypes about violence hinder effective intervention? Why is the disproportionate level of funding for victim assistance programs and programs for convicted felons significant? What philosophy about violence does this policy difference reveal? What possible consequences might this philosophy or attitude have for women?

2. What myths does Roberts challenge in this selection? What might be the consequences for women of viewing violence as a "private" matter rather than a "major social problem"? How did the case of Thurman v. The City of Torrington alter the way police dealt with domestic violence calls?

3. What physical, emotional and economic effects can violence have on women? On their children? Why do women sometimes remain in violent relationships?

4. Is there evidence in the article that the conceptualization of "violence"—what "violence" has meant—has changed through time? How have the responses to domestic battery and protections available to women changed?

The Reality of Acquaintance Rape (1988)

Robin Warshaw

In this selection from her 1988 text, I Never Called It Rape, *journalist Robin Warshaw explores acquaintance rape and its prevalence on college campuses. Discussing research that examines assumptions about dating and sexual expectations, Warshaw challenges the myth that a woman is more likely to be raped by a stranger than by a man that she knows. Warshaw's work has appeared in* The New York Times, The Nation, *the* Philadelphia Inquirer Magazine, Woman's Day, *and* Ms. Magazine.

Women raped by men they know—acquaintance rape—is not an aberrant quirk of male-female relations. If you are a woman, your risk of being raped by someone you know is *four times greater* than your risk of being raped by a stranger.

A recent scientific study of acquaintance rape on 32 college campuses conducted by *Ms.* magazine and psychologist Mary P.

Koss showed that significant numbers of women are raped on dates or by acquaintances, although most victims never report their attacks.

Ms. SURVEY STATS

- 1 in 4 women surveyed were victims of rape or attempted rape.
- 84 percent of those raped knew their attacker.
- 57 percent of the rapes happened on dates.

Those figures make acquaintance rape and date rape more common than left-handedness or heart attacks or alcoholism. These rapes are no recent campus fad or the fantasy of a few jilted females. They are real. And they are happening all around us.

The Extent of "Hidden" Rape

Most states define rape as sexual assault in which a man uses his penis to commit vaginal penetration of a victim against her will, by force or threats of force or when she is physically or mentally unable to give her consent. Many states now also include unwanted anal and oral intercourse in that definition and some have removed gender-specific language to broaden the applicability of rape laws.

In acquaintance rape, the rapist and victim may know each other casually—having met through a common activity, mutual friend, at a party, as neighbors, as students in the same class, at work, on a blind date, or while traveling. Or they may have a closer relationship—as steady dates or former sexual partners. Although largely a hidden phenomenon because it's the least reported type of rape (and rape, in general, is the most underreported crime against a person), many organizations, counselors, and social researchers agree that acquaintance rape is the most prevalent rape crime today.

Only 90,434 rapes were reported to U.S. law enforcement agencies in 1986, a number that is conservatively believed to represent a minority of the actual rapes of all types taking place. Government estimates find that anywhere from three to ten rapes are committed for every one rape reported. And while rapes by strangers are still underreported, rapes by acquaintances are virtually nonreported. Yet, based on intake observations made by staff at various rape-counseling centers (where victims come for treatment, but do not have to file police reports), 70 to 80 percent of all rape crimes are acquaintance rapes.

Those rapes are happening in a social environment in which sexual aggression occurs regularly. Indeed, less than half the college women questioned in the *Ms.* survey reported that they had experienced *no* sexual victimization in their lives thus far (the average age of respondents was 21). Many had experienced more than one episode of unwanted sexual touching, coercion, attempted rape, or rape. Using the data collected in the study . . . , a profile can be drawn of what happens in just one year of "social life" on America's college campuses.

Over the years, other researchers have documented the phenomenon of acquaintance rape. In 1957, a study conducted by Eugene J. Kanin of Purdue University in West Lafayette, Indiana, showed that 30 percent of women surveyed had suffered attempted or completed forced sexual intercourse while on a high school date. Ten years later, in 1967, while young people donned flowers and beads and talked of love and peace, Kanin found that more than 25 percent of the male college students surveyed had attempted to force sexual intercourse on a woman to the point that she cried or fought back. In 1977, after the blossoming of the women's movement and countless pop-culture attempts to extol the virtues of becoming a "sensitive man," Kanin found that 26 percent of the men he surveyed had tried to force intercourse on a woman and that 25 percent of the women questioned had suffered attempted or completed rape. In other words, two decades had passed since Kanin's first study, yet women were being raped by men they knew as frequently as before.

In 1982, a doctoral student at Auburn University in Auburn, Alabama, found that 25 percent of the undergraduate women surveyed had at least one experience of forced intercourse and that 93 percent of those episodes involved acquaintances. That same year, Auburn psychology professor and acquaintance-rape expert Barry R. Burkhart conducted a study in which 61 percent of the men said they had sexually touched a woman against her will.

Further north, at St. Cloud State University in St. Cloud, Minnesota, research in 1982 showed 29 percent of women surveyed reported being physically or psychologically forced to have sexual intercourse.

In 1984, 20 percent of the female students questioned in a study at the University of South Dakota in Vermillion, South Dakota, said they had been physically forced to have intercourse while on a date. At Brown University in Providence, Rhode Island, 16 percent of the women surveyed reported they were raped by an acquaintance and 11 percent of the men said they had forced sexual intercourse on a woman. And another study coauthored by Auburn's Burkhart showed 15 percent of the male respondents reporting having raped a date.

That same year, the study of acquaintance rape moved beyond the serenity of leafy college quadrangles into the hard reality of the "dangerous" outside world. A random sample survey of 930 women living in San Francisco, conducted by researcher Diana Russell, showed that 44 percent of the women questioned had been victims of rape or attempted rape—and that 88 percent of the rape victims knew their attackers. A Massachusetts Department of Public Health study, released in 1986, showed that two-thirds of the rapes reported at crisis centers were committed by acquaintances.

These numbers stand in stark contrast to what most people think of as rape: that is, a stranger (usually a black, Hispanic, or other minority) jumping out of the bushes at an unsuspecting female, brandishing a weapon, and assaulting her. The truth about rape—that it usually happens between people who know each other and is often committed by "regular" guys—is difficult to accept.

Most people never learn the truth until rape affects them or someone they care about. And many women are so confused by the dichotomy between their acquaintance-rape experience and what they thought rape really was that they are left with an awful new reality: Where once they feared strange men as they were taught to, they now fear strange men *and* all the men they know.

Lori's Story

How can a date be a rape?

The pairing of the word "date," which conjures up an image of fun shared by two companions, with the word "rape," which evokes the total loss of control by one person to the will of another, results in the creation of a new phrase that is nearly impossible for most people to comprehend. To understand how date rape happens, let's look at a classic case.

The Setup

It was natural. Normal. Lori's friend Amy wanted to go out with Paul, but felt awkward and shy about going out with him alone. So when Paul's roommate, Eric, suggested that he and Lori join Amy and Paul for a double date, it made sense. "I didn't feel anything for Eric except as a friend," Lori says of her reaction to the plan. "I said, 'Okay, maybe it will make Amy feel better.'"

Agreeing to go out with Eric was no great act of charity on Lori's part. He *was* attractive—tall, good-looking, in his mid-20s and from a wealthy family. Lori, who was 19 at the time, knew Eric and Paul as frequent customers at the popular Tampa Bay restaurant where she worked as a waitress when she was between college semesters.

On the day of the date, Eric called several times to change their plans. Finally, he phoned to say that they would be having a barbecue with several of his friends at the house he and Paul shared. Lori agreed.

> We went to his house and I mentioned something about Paul and Amy and he kind of threw it off, like, "Yeah, yeah." I didn't think anything of it. There we are, fixing steaks, and he was saying, "Well, this is obviously something to help Amy."
>
> He kept making drinks all night long. He kept saying, "Here, have a drink," "Here, drink this." I didn't because I didn't want it. He was just downing them right and left.

The Attack

Unknown to Lori, Amy had canceled her plans to see Paul the day before. Paul told Eric, but Eric never told Lori. As the barbecue party progressed and her friend failed to show up, Lori questioned Eric again. He then lied, telling her that Paul had just called to say he and Amy weren't coming.

> I was thinking to myself, "Well, okay." Not in my wildest dreams would I have thought he was plotting something.

> Then all of his friends started leaving. I began to think, "Something is wrong, something is going on," but I've been known to overreact to things, so I ignored it.
>
> After his friends left, we're sitting on the couch and he leans over and he kisses me and I'm thinking, "It's a date, it's no big deal." So then we started kissing a little bit more and I'm thinking, "I'm starting to enjoy this, maybe this isn't so bad." Then the phone rang and when he came back I was standing up. He grabbed me from behind and picked me up. He had his hands over my eyes and we were walking through his house. It was really dark and I didn't know where on earth he was taking me. I had never actually walked through his house.
>
> He laid me down [on a bed] and kissed me.... He starts taking off my clothes and I said, "Wait—time out! This is not what I want, you know," and he said to me something like this is what I owed him because he made me dinner.
>
> I said, "This is wrong, don't do this. I didn't go out with you with this intent."
>
> He said, "What do you call that on the couch?"
>
> I said, "I call it a kiss, period."
>
> And he said, "Well, I don't."

The two struggled until Eric rolled off her momentarily. Lori jumped up and went into the bathroom. Her plan was to come out in a few minutes and tell him it was time to take her home.

> The whole time I'm thinking, "I don't believe this is happening to me." I didn't even have time to walk fully out of the bathroom door when he grabbed me and threw me on the bed and started taking my clothes off. I'm yelling and hitting and pushing on him and he just liked that. He says, "I know you must like this because a lot of women like this kind of thing." Then he says, "This is the adult world. Maybe you ought to grow up some."
>
> I finally got to the point where there was nothing I could do.

Eric pushed his penis into her and, after a few minutes, ejaculated. Lori had had only one other experience with sexual intercourse, about a year before with a longtime boyfriend.

> Then Eric just rolled over and I started to get my clothes together. He said, "Don't tell me you didn't like that." I looked at him and said, "No," and by this time I'm crying because I don't know what else to do. I never heard of anybody having that happen to them.

The Aftermath

Finally, Eric took her home.

> In the car he said, "Can I call you tomorrow? Can I see you next weekend?" I just looked at him and he just looked at me and started laughing.
>
> My mom had gone out and I just laid on my bed with the covers up. Everything I could possibly put on I think I put on that night—leg warmers, thermal underwear—everything imaginable in the middle of summer I put on my body. That night I dreamed it was all happening again. I dreamed I was standing there watching him do it.
>
> For two weeks I couldn't talk. People would talk to me and I felt nothing. I felt like a zombie. I couldn't cry, I couldn't smile, I couldn't eat. My mom said, "What's wrong with you? Is something going on?" I said, "Nothing's wrong."
>
> I thought it was my fault. What did I do to make him think he could do something like that? Was I wrong in kissing him? Was I wrong to go out with him, to go over to his house?

After two weeks, she told her mother what happened and they talked about what to do. Lori decided not to report it to the police for fear Eric would blame her. Eric continued to frequent the restaurant where she worked. Several weeks after their date, he cornered her in a hallway near the kitchen.

> He touched me and I said, "Get your hands off me." At first, he thought it was funny. He said, "What's wrong?" then he started pulling me, trying to hug me. I pushed him and said, "Leave me alone," and I was starting to get a little loud. As I was walking away, he said, "Oh, I guess you didn't get enough."
>
> I walked in the kitchen and picked up this tray full of food. I don't know how it happened, I just dropped the

> whole tray and it went everywhere. My friend, another waitress, went to the manager and said, "She's not going to be much good to you tonight," so they sent me home.

Lori decided to move to a town about 150 miles away to avoid continued encounters with Eric. There she found work as an office assistant and cashier and enrolled for a few classes at a new college. . . .

The Myths About Acquaintance Rape

Like most women with date-rape or acquaintance-rape experiences, Lori did not report the incident to police and did not, at first, even understand it to be rape. Instead, she felt almost totally isolated and blamed herself for what happened. She changed her life in order to feel physically safe from her attacker. She is now filled with doubts about her own judgment, fears socializing with men, and despairs about her ability to have a "normal" relationship.

But ask a group of college students what they think of a story like Lori's and they might tell you:

- "She deserved it."
- "What did she expect? After all, she went to his house."
- "That's not rape. Rape is when a guy you don't know grabs you and holds a gun to your head."
- "She wasn't a virgin, so no harm was done."
- "He bought her dinner. She owed him."
- "She liked kissing him. What's the big deal if he went farther?"
- "She just 'cried rape' later because she felt guilty about having sex."

Those are the kinds of comments heard recently on all kinds of campuses—Ivy League, state universities, small schools—when date rape was discussed by both male and female undergraduates. But let's not blame college students alone for their views: Their parents, indeed most of our society, would agree with one or more of those statements.

These are the myths that have formed what we believe to be the truth about women who are raped by men they know. But the actual truth is different indeed. Here are several of the most common myths about acquaintance rape juxtaposed with the reality:

Myth	**Reality**
Rape is committed by crazed strangers.	Most women are raped by "normal" acquaintances.
A woman who gets raped deserves it, especially if she agreed to go to the man's house or ride in his car.	No one, male or female, deserves to be raped. Being in a man's house or car does not mean a woman has agreed to have sex with him.
Women who don't fight back haven't been raped.	You have been raped when you are forced to have sex against your will, whether you fight back or not.
If there's no gun or knife, you haven't been raped.	It's rape whether the rapist uses a weapon or his fists, verbal threats, drugs or alcohol, physical isolation, your own diminished physical or mental state, or simply the weight of his body to overcome you.
It's not really rape if the victim isn't a virgin.	Rape is rape, even if the woman isn't a virgin, even if she willingly had sex with the man before.
If a woman lets a man buy her dinner or pay for a movie or drinks, she owes him sex.	No one owes sex as a payment to anyone else, no matter how expensive the date.
Agreeing to kiss or neck or pet with a man means that a woman has agreed to have intercourse with him.	Everyone has the right to say "no" to sexual activity, regardless of what has preceded it, and to have that "no" respected.
When men are sexually aroused, they need to have	Men don't physically need to have sex after becoming

sex or they will get "blue balls." Also, once they get turned on, men can't help themselves from forcing sex on a woman.	aroused any more than women do. Moreover, men are still able to control themselves even after becoming sexually excited.
Women lie about being raped, especially when they accuse men they date or other acquaintances.	Rape really happens—to people you know, by people you know.

Like most of our beliefs, we absorb these myths as we grow up: from the people around us, from the books we read, from the movies and television programs we watch, even from the way products are sold to us in advertisements.

Because of the myths, the reality of acquaintance rape is largely ignored. On college campuses, when a woman is raped in a dormitory or fraternity house by another student, university officials announce new plans for better lighting in the parking lots and expanded hours for escort services—positive safety precautions that have nothing to do with stopping acquaintance rape. The few women who report their date rapes (and whose cases are accepted for prosecution) are usually met with skepticism and disbelief from jurors and judges when they testify about being raped by a man they knew or chose to be with in a social setting.

No wonder that while many rape-prevention activists would like to see more prosecutions for acquaintance-rape cases, many admit privately that they counsel women not to press charges because of the difficulty of convincing jurors—whose views are shaped by the myths—that a rape has really taken place.

Rape Is Rape

Rape that occurs on dates or between people who know each other should not be seen as some sort of misguided sexual adventure. Rape is violence, not seduction. In stranger rape *and* acquaintance rape, the aggressor makes a decision to force his victim to submit to what he wants. The rapist believes he is entitled to force sexual intercourse from a woman and he sees interpersonal violence (be it simply holding the woman down with his body or brandishing a gun) as an acceptable way to achieve his goal.

"All rape is an exercise in power," writes Susan Brownmiller in her landmark book *Against Our Will: Men, Women and Rape.* Specifically, Brownmiller and others argue, rape is an exercise in the imbalance of power that exists between most men and women, a relationship that has forged the social order from ancient times on.

Today, that relationship continues. Many men are socialized to be sexually aggressive—to score, as it were, regardless of how. Many women are socialized to submit to men's wills, especially those men deemed desirable by society at large. Maintaining such roles helps set the stage for acquaintance rape.

But despite their socialization, most men are not rapists. That is the good news.

The bad news, of course, is that so many are.

MS. SURVEY STAT

- 1 in 12 of the male students surveyed had committed acts that met the legal definitions of rape or attempted rape.

Blaming the Acquaintance-Rape Victim

Without question, many date rapes and acquaintance rapes could have been prevented by the woman—if she hadn't trusted a seemingly nice guy, if she hadn't gotten drunk, if she had acted earlier on the "bad feeling" that many victims later report they felt but ignored because they didn't want to seem rude, unfriendly, or immature. But acknowledging that in some cases the woman might have prevented the rape by making a different decision does not make her responsible for the crime. Says a counselor for an Oregon rape-crisis agency: "We have a saying here: 'Bad judgment is not a rapeable offense.'"

As a society, we don't blame the victims of most crimes as we do acquaintance-rape survivors. A mugging victim is not believed to "deserve it" for wearing a watch or carrying a pocketbook on the street. Likewise, a company is not "asking for it" when its profits are embezzled; a store owner is not to blame for handing over the cash drawer when threatened. These crimes occur because the perpetrator decides to commit them.

Acquaintance rape is no different. There are ways to reduce the odds, but, like all crimes, there is no way to be certain that it will not happen to you.

Yet acquaintance-rape victims are seen as responsible for the attacks, often more responsible than their assailants. "Date rape threatens the assumption that if you're good, good things happen to you. Most of us believe that bad things don't happen out of the blue," says psychologist Koss, chief investigator of the *Ms.* study, now affiliated with the department of psychiatry at the University of Arizona Medical School in Tucson, Arizona. Society, in general, is so disturbed by the idea that a "regular guy" could do such a thing—and, to be sure, many "regular guys" are made uncomfortable by a concept that views their actions as a crime—that they would rather believe that something is wrong with the woman making such an outlandish claim: She is lying, she has emotional problems, she hates men, she is covering up her own promiscuous behavior. In fact, the research in the *Ms.* survey shows that women who have been raped by men they know are not appreciably different in any personal traits or behaviors than women who are not raped.

Should we ask women not to trust men who seem perfectly nice? Should we tell them not to go to parties or on dates? Should we tell them not to drink? Should we tell them not to feel sexual? Certainly not. *It is not the victim who causes the rape. . . .*

Date Rape and Acquaintance Rape on College Campuses

Despite philosophical and political changes brought about by the women's movement, dating relationships between men and women are still often marked by passivity on the woman's part and aggression on the man's. Nowhere are these two seen in stronger contrast than among teenagers and young adults who often, out of their own fears, insecurity, and ignorance, adopt the worst sex-role stereotypes. Such an environment fosters a continuum of sexual victimization—from unwanted sexual touching to psychologically coerced sex to rape—that is tolerated as normal. "Because sexually coercive behavior is so common in our male-female interactions, rape by an acquaintance may not be perceived as rape," says Py Bateman, director of Alternatives to Fear, a Seattle rape-education organization.

Indeed, we speak of "the battle of the sexes" and, for many, it is just that. In their teens, many boys are counseled by their friends and older males to practice the "4Fs" when dealing with women: "Find 'em, feel 'em, fuck 'em, forget 'em." On the other hand, many girls, who have been admonished to "save it" for Mr. Right, want sexual intercourse to take place in the context of a relationship with some continuity attached to it. Kurt Weis and Sandra S. Borges, researchers at the University of California at Berkeley, pointed out in a 1973 paper that dating places individuals with these highly socialized but differing expectations into an ambiguous situation in which there is maximum privacy.

That is, dating can easily lead to rape.

Not surprising, then, that the risk of rape is four times higher for women aged 16 to 24, the prime dating age, than for any other population group. Approximately half of all men arrested for rape are also 24 years old or younger. Since 26 percent of all 18- to 24-year-olds in the United States attend college, those institutions have become focal points for studying date rape and acquaintance rape, such as the *Ms.* research.

Ms. SURVEY STAT

- For both men and women, the average age when a rape incident occurred (either as perpetrator or victim) was 18½ years old.

Going to college often means going away from home, out from under parental control and protection and into a world of seemingly unlimited freedoms. The imperative to party and date, although strong in high school, burgeons in this environment. Alcohol is readily available and often used in stultifying amounts, encouraged by a college world that practically demands heavy drinking as proof of having fun. Marijuana, cocaine, LSD, methamphetamines, and other drugs are also often easy to obtain.

Up until the 1970s, colleges adopted a "substitute parent" attitude toward their students, complete with curfews (often more strict for females than males), liquor bans, and stringent disciplinary punishments. In that era, students were punished for violating the three-feet-on-the-floor rules during coed visiting hours in dormitories or for being caught with alcohol on college property.

Although those regulations did not prevent acquaintance rape, they undoubtedly kept down the number of incidents by making women's dorms havens of no-men-allowed safety.

Such regulations were swept out of most schools during the Vietnam War era. Today, many campuses have coed dorms, with men and women often housed in alternating rooms on the same floor, with socializing unchecked by curfews or meaningful controls on alcohol and drugs. Yet, say campus crisis counselors, many parents still believe that they have properly prepared their children for college by helping them open local bank accounts and making sure they have enough underwear to last until the first trip home. By ignoring the realities of social pressures at college on male and female students—and the often catastrophic effects of those pressures—parents help perpetuate the awareness vacuum in which date rape and acquaintance rape continue to happen with regularity.

"What's changed for females is the illusion that they have control and they don't," says Claire P. Walsh, program director of the Sexual Assault Recovery Service at the University of Florida in Gainesville. "They know that they can go into chemical engineering or medical school and they've got their whole life planned, they're on a roll. They transfer that feeling of control into social situations and that's the illusion."

When looking at the statistical results of the *Ms.* survey, it's important to remember that many of these young people still have years of socializing and dating ahead of them, years in which they may encounter still more acquaintance rape. Students, parents of college students, and college administrators should be concerned. But many are not, lulled by the same myths that pervade our society at large: Rape is not committed by people you know against "good" girls, in "safe" places like university campuses. . . .

QUESTIONS

1. Explain how myths and stereotypes affect the awareness and understanding of rape. How do they affect the responses to acquaintance rape on both an individual and social level?

2. How do expectations about dating contribute to acquaintance rape on college campuses? How do these expectations affect men's an women's different experiences of the same event?

3. What is the typical social response to rape? Why is this significant? What effect does this response have on efforts to reduce violence against women?

Men Changing Men (1994)

Robert L. Allen and Paul Kivel

Crimes like battery, sexual assault and rape are often thought to be "women's issues." Media coverage of these topics frequently focuses on increasing women's awareness and encouraging the development of self-defense techniques. The following 1994 essay taken from Ms. Magazine *shifts our attention to the ways men are organizing to prevent violence against women and analyzing the cultural definition of masculinity. Robert Allan and Paul Kivel describe their efforts to help men better understand how their own gender socialization promotes aggressive behavior.*

Batterers need to be penalized for their actions, but the future safety of women and children depends on stopping the violence before it starts. With prevention in mind, "Ms." asked Robert Allan and Paul Kivel to discuss the work they do with boys and men in the Oakland Men's Project (OMP). Formed in 1979, this California-based group is a nonprofit, multiracial organization of men and women, devoted to community education and eradicating male

"Men Changing Men," by Robert L. Allen and Paul Kivel, reprinted from *Ms.*, September/October 1994.

> violence, racism, and homophobia. The group has worked with thousands of boys and men. Its workshops are designed to encourage participants to examine gender roles, violence and discrimination, and alternatives to violence.

Why do men batter women? We have to discard the easy answers. Portraying batterers as ogres only serves to separate "them" from "us." But men who batter and men who don't are not all that different. Male violence is normal in our society and vast numbers of men participate. Men batter because we have been trained to; because there are few social sanctions against it; because we live in a society where the exploitation of people with less social and personal power is acceptable. In a patriarchal society, boys are taught to accept violence as a manly response to real or imagined threats, but they get little training in negotiating intimate relationships. And all too many men believe that they have the right to control or expect certain behavior from "their" women and children; many view difficulties in family relationships as a threat to their manhood, and they respond with violence.

Young people's definitions of femininity and masculinity often reflect rigid expectations of what they must live up to in order to be a "real" woman or a "real" man. Time and again we hear boys say that they are supposed to be tough, aggressive, in control, that they are not to express any feelings except anger, not to cry, and never to ask for help. And many boys expect girls to acquiesce to men and be dependent on them.

How do boys get these ideas about male identity and manhood? Often from parents, but our whole society contributes to the process. As many as one of every six boys are sexually assaulted, and many, many more are hit, yelled at, teased, and goaded into fighting to prove they're tough. At the project, we believe that many boys become convinced that they will be violated until they learn to use force to protect themselves. Then they move to take their pain and anger out on others the way older males have done to them.

In our work we often use role play as a way of getting at some of these issues. One particularly effective exercise involves a ten-year-old and his father; the father arrives home from work and demands that the boy turn off the TV, then berates him for the messiness of his room. The boy tries to explain; the father tells him to shut up, to stop making excuses. Fueling the father's anger is the fact that he's disappointed by the boy's school report card. The father shoves the report card in his son's face and demands to know why he has gotten a "D" in math. The boy says he did his best. The father tells him that he is stupid. The boy protests and begins to stand up. The father shoves him down, saying, "Don't you dare get up in my face!" The boy is visibly upset, and begins to cry. The father explodes: "Now what? You little mama's boy! You sissy! You make me sick. When are you going to grow up and start acting like a man?"

When we do this exercise in schools, it gets the boys' undivided attention because most have experienced being humiliated by an older male. Indeed, the power of this exercise is that it is so familiar. When asked what they learned from such encounters, the boys often say things like: A man is tough. A man is in control. A man doesn't cry. A man doesn't take crap.

We write the boys' comments on a blackboard, draw a box around them, and label it the "Act Like a Man" box. We talk about how males in this culture are socialized to stay in the box. Eventually we ask: What happens if you step out of it, if you stop acting tough enough or man enough? Invariably we hear that you get called names like "fag," "queer," "mama's boy," "punk," "girl." Asked why, the boys say it's a challenge, that they're expected to fight to prove themselves. Homophobia and fear of being identified with women are powerful messages boys get from an early age, and they are expected to fight to prove that they're tough and not gay—that they're in the box.

Using exercises, like the father/son interchange, helps us examine how the male sex role often sets men up to be dominating, controlling, and abusive. We ask: How safe is it to stay in the "Act Like a Man" box? Usually, most admit that it isn't safe, because boys and men continually challenge each other to prove that they're in the box. When a boy or man is challenged, he can prove he's a man either by fighting the challenger or by finding someone "weaker"—a female or a more vulnerable male—to dominate. Hurting girls relieves any anxiety that we may not be tough enough and establishes our heterosexual credentials. It's both a sign of our interest (we're paying attention to them) and a symbol of our difference (we're in control).

Because we are taught that women are primarily sexual objects, this behavior seems perfectly natural. And many men come to believe that a woman is just another material possession. We initiate dates, pay for our time together, protect them on the streets, and often marry them. We are trained to think that in return, girls should show their appreciation by taking care of us emotionally, putting their own concerns and interests aside, and putting out sexually.

This unspoken contract is one that many heterosexual men operate by, and it often leads to the assumption that women are our dumping grounds. If we've had a hard day at work, were embarrassed or humiliated by a boss—challenged in the box—the contract leads us to believe that we can take those feelings out on "our" women, and thus regain our power. If we end up hitting her, then we have to blame her in order to deny our aggression and keep our self-esteem intact. So we say things like: She asked for it. She pushed my buttons. She deserved it.

Invariable it comes as a surprise to us that women don't meekly accept our violence. So we respond by minimizing and justifying our actions: I didn't mean it. You're too sensitive. That's the way guys are. It was just the heat of the moment.

In order to get men to take responsibility for their own actions, we have to get them to talk about what they did, and what they said, and what they felt. Making the connection between how they have been trained and hurt and how they have learned to pass that pain on by hurting women or young people is essential.

To get men to reflect on their experiences and behaviors, we use exercises we call "stand ups." We ask everyone to be silent, and then slowly pose a series of questions or statements, and ask men to stand every time one applies to them. For example, we may ask, Have you ever:

- worried you were not tough enough?
- been called a wimp, queer, or fag?
- been told to "act like a man"?
- been hit by an older man?
- been forced to fight?
- been physically injured and hid the pain?
- been sexually abused, or touched in a way you didn't like?
- used alcohol or drugs to hide your pain?
- felt like blowing yourself away?

Later in the workshop we ask, Have you ever:

- interrupted a woman by talking louder?
- made a comment in public about a woman's body?

- discussed a woman's body with another man?
- been told by a woman that she wanted more affection and less sex from you?
- used your voice or body to intimidate a woman?
- hit, slapped, shoved, or pushed a woman?
- had sex with a woman when you knew she didn't want to?

Each participant is asked to look around and see other men standing, which helps break down their sense of isolation and feelings of shame. Since we are not a therapy group, no one is questioned or confronted about his own experiences. All of our work involves challenging the notion that males are naturally abusive and that females are natural targets of male abuse. We give boys and men a way of analyzing social roles by drawing insights from their own experiences, and help them to recognize that social interactions involve making choices, that we can break free of old roles by supporting each other in choosing alternatives to violence.

An important part of our work is getting men and boys to look at how power, inequality, and the ability to do violence to others are structured into social relationships in this country. We discuss how these inequalities are maintained and how violence against one targeted group encourages violence against others. This is not to excuse men's behavior; it is done in the belief that in order to make better choices, men must understand the framework of power and violence that constantly pressures us to be in control and on top.

There are growing numbers of men who are critical of sexism. All too often they are isolated and fearful of raising their concerns with other men because they worry about being targeted for violence. We try to help them break through the fear and reach out to other men. But we also work to get men to understand how they are damaged by sexism and how male violence against women keeps us from the collective action needed to confront racial, gender-based, and economic injustice.

For us personally this is powerful, life-changing work. We were each drawn to it because of troubling issues in our own lives: issues around our relationships with our fathers (one emotionally abusive, the other emotionally distant); relationships with women partners where we found ourselves repeating controlling, sexist behaviors that made us feel guilty, ashamed, defensive; and the fear that we might do to our children what had been done to us as children. Through the work we have discovered that many men share these concerns, but they are hesitant to talk about this with other men. Sadly, we have all learned that "real" men don't admit vulnerability. But despite their initial hesitation, many men are eager to talk about their lives, and to change the controlling and abusive behavior they've been trained to pass on. Doing this work is healing for us and for those we work with.

Men are responsible for battery and for stopping male violence. If we are to counter the myth that men's abuse of women is natural, men must challenge each other to stop the violence. We must defy notions of manhood that lead us to injure or kill those we say we love. We must confront male friends when we see them heading down the destructive path of domestic violence and urge them to get help. While it is critical that domestic violence cases be taken more seriously by the police and criminal justice system, it is equally important to examine and to change underlying social attitudes and practices that promote and excuse domestic violence. This is truly men's work.

QUESTIONS

1. What are the effects of shifting our attention from violence as a "women's issue" to men's responsibility for preventing crimes against women? How is violence against women also a crime against men?

2. In our culture, how do men have to behave to stay in the "Act Like a Man" box? How are little boys and men hurt by these messages that they receive from childhood? According to Allen and Kivel, how is violence promoted by these social constructions of masculinity? How do they perpetuate homophobia?

3. How can individual men make a difference even though they may not have the opportunity to participate in such a group?

407
363
printout

Gendered War Crimes: Reconceptualizing Rape in Time of War (1995)

Rhonda Copelon

Among all the atrocities that occur in war, rape is a crime that is distinctly gendered, and as such, can be particularly devastating to the subjectivity and humanity of women. However, as Rhonda Copelon explores in this 1995 essay, the types of rape that occur in war are not all considered equally grave, and some do not receive sufficient attention from a legal standpoint—few military tribunals recognize rape explicitly as a crime against humanity, few measures are established to punish offenders. Copelon describes some of the legal ambiguity involved in this issue, the implications for women, and possible avenues for change.

"Gendered War Crimes: Reconceptualizing Rape in Time of War," by Rhonda Copelon, reprinted from *Mass Rape: The War Against Women in Bosnia-Herzegovina,* edited by Andrea Stiglmayer by permission of the University of Nebraska Press.

Introduction

Historically, the rape of women in war has drawn occasional and short-lived international attention. It comes to light as part of the competing diplomacies of war, illustrating the viciousness of the conqueror or the short-lived innocence of the conquered. When war is done, rape is comfortable filed away as a mere and inevitable "by-product," a matter of poor discipline, the inevitable bad behavior of soldiers revved up, needy, and briefly "out of control."

Military histories rarely refer to rape, and military tribunals rarely either indict or sanction it.[1] This is the case even where rape and forced prostitution are mass or systematic, as in both theatres of World War II, which included the rape of German women by the conquering Russian army and the enslavement on the battlefields of 200,000–400,000 "comfort women" by the Japanese army.[2] It is even the case where open, mass, and systematic rape has ostensibly shocked the conscious of the world, as in the "rape of Nanking"[3] or the rape of an estimated 200,000 Bengali women during the war of independence from Pakistan.[4] Rape was ignored by the International Tribunals at Nurenberg and, although it was discussed in the Judgment of the Military Tribunal in Tokyo, it was not treated as a crime for which the Japanese Commander would be separately charged. In Bangladesh, amnesty was quietly traded for independence.

More recently, the rape of women in the wars in the former Yugoslavia—most often committed by Serbs against Bosnian-Muslim women as part of the campaign of "ethnic cleansing"—broke through media barriers and briefly captured international attention.[5] The rape of women in Bosnia-Herzegovina, however, appeared unique because the rape of women in history (as well as in the present) has been rendered invisible. Moreover, geopolitical factors—that the locale is Europe, that the conflict threatens to set off a new world war and that the agents are White men and the victims White (albeit largely Muslim) women—cannot be ignored when explaining the visibility of these rapes. By contrast, the routine rape of women in the civil wars and military dictatorships in Haiti, Peru, Liberia, and Burma (to name a few) goes largely unreported until women's voices are heard.[6] Nor does the international press report that mercenaries hired by an international agribusiness company rape 50 percent of the women of the indigenous Yuracruz people in Ecuador in order to "cleanse" the land of the Yuracruz people.

When the rapes in Bosnia-Herzegovina were revealed, feminists had already been working for decades on rape and gender violence.[8] It was also a moment in which women were organizing, regionally and globally, to put recognition of women's human rights on the agenda at the 1993 World Conference on Human Rights in Vienna. In this effort, violence against women—both official and personal—was a central issue. Thus the issue of the rape of women in Bosnia became part of the broader global feminist effort, less influenced by nationalist diplomacies,[9] at the same time that it advanced the feminist campaign by underscoring the gravity of ongoing gender violence just two hundred miles from the conference site. The Vienna *Declaration and Programme of Action* condemned gender violence generally and made special mention of "systemic rape, sexual slavery and forced pregnancy" in armed conflict.[10] The statute of the International Tribunal, created by the United Nations to prosecute war crimes in the former Yugoslavia, included widespread or systematic rape as an indictable offense.[11]

Nonetheless, the question today is whether the terrible wartime rape of women in former Yugoslavia will disappear into history or survive but be viewed as an exceptional case. Just as, historically, the condemnation of rape in war has rarely become an outcry against crimes of gender, so the mass rape in Bosnia captured world attention largely because of its association with "ethnic cleansing" or genocide. In a single week, a midday television talk show opened with, "In Bosnia, they are raping the enemy's women,"[12] and a leading Croatian-American scholar distinguished genocidal rape from "normal" rape, with very little reaction from the audience.[13] When women argued that rape is a weapon of war, rather than a by-product, they were referring to all its various purposes (e.g., to dilute ethnic identity, destabilize civilian populations, or reward soldiers). This assessment, however was accepted by the public only as regards rape as a vehicle of genocide.

The elision of genocide and rape in the focus on "genocidal rape" as a means of emphasizing the heinousness of the rape of Muslim women in Bosnia is thus dangerous. Rape and genocide are each atrocities. Genocide is an effort to debilitate or destroy a people based on its identity as a people, while rape seeks to degrade and destroy a woman based on her identity as a woman. Both are grounded in total contempt for and dehumanization of the victim, an both give rise to unspeakable brutalities. Their intersection in the Serbian (and, to a lesser extent, the Croatian) aggressions in Bosnia creates an ineffable living hell for women there. From the standpoint of these women, they are inseparable.

But to emphasize as unparalleled the horror of genocidal rape is factually dubious and risks rendering rape invisible once again. When the ethnic war ceases or is forced back into the bottle, will the crimes against women matter? Will their suffering and struggles to survive be vindicated? Or will condemnation be limited to this seemingly exceptional case? Will the women who are brutally raped for purposes or domination, terror, booty, or revenge in Bosnia and elsewhere be heard?

The situation presents an historic opportunity (indeed an imperative) to insist on justice for the women of Bosnia as well as to press for a feminist reconceptualization of the role and legal understanding of rape in war.

To do this, we must surface gender in the midst of genocide at the same time that we avoid dualistic thinking. We must examine critically the claim that rape as a tool of "ethnic cleansing" is unique, worse than, or incomparable to other forms of rape in war or in peace—even while we recognize that rape coupled with genocide inflicts multiple, intersectional harms.[14] This is critical if the horrors experienced by women in Bosnia are to be fully acknowledged and understood and if that experience is to have meaning for women brutalized in less-known theatres of war or in the by-ways of daily life.

Although there are significant concerns about the viability of the new International War Crimes Tribunal generally,[15] the rules that have been adapted articulate a commitment to sensitively and effectively prosecute sex crimes.[16] If the Tribunal functions and takes rape and the abuse of women seriously, it will be the first time—even if its actions are largely symbolic. The Tribunal also will be called upon to apply international law to rape in ways that could provide significant precedents for other situations.[17]

This essay examines the evolving legal status of rape in war with attention both to the particular context in which rape is occurring and to the general gender dimension, as well as to the tension between them. It focuses on two central conceptual questions: first, whether these crimes are fully recognized as war crimes under the Geneva Conventions—the cornerstone of what is called "humanitarian" law (i.e., the prohibitions that, by regulating war also acknowledge it as permissible)—and, second, whether international law does, and should, distinguish between "genocidal rape" and mass rape for purposes other than genocide. In this regard, it examines the limitations of, and the potential inherent in, the concept of "crimes against humanity," as well as the relationship between gender and nationality/ethnicity in the crimes committed against women in Bosnia. The Conclusion suggests the relationship between everyday rape and rape in armed conflict or under military rule.

Rape, Forced Prostitution, and Forced Pregnancy as War Crimes

Although news of the mass rape of women in Bosnia was significant factor in the demand for the creation of the International Tribunal, international law experts debated whether rape and other forms of sexual abuse are "war crimes" of the gravest dimension, subject to universal jurisdiction and therefore prosecutable before an international tribunal as well as in the courts of every country. The answer is not yet clear.

Rape and other forms of sexual assault have long been prohibited under national and international rules of war, and to prevent rape, the Geneva Conventions require separate quarters for women prisoners, as well as supervision and searches by women only.[18] But these crimes have been categorized as crimes against honor, not as crimes of violence[19] comparable to murder, mutilation, cruel and inhuman treatment, and torture.

Traditionally, rape has been condemned as a violation of a man's honor and exclusive right to sexual possession of his woman/property, and not because it is an assault on a woman.[20] Today, the mass rape in Bosnia is often referred to as the rape of "the enemy's women"—the enemy in this formulation being the male combatant and the seemingly all-male nation or religious or ethnic group. The victim is male, humiliated and emasculated by having failed as both warrior and protector. While this describes a significant patriarchal dimension of rape, it ignores the fact that women, too, are the enemy, and are raped as such.

The Geneva Conventions characterize rape as a crime against the honor and dignity of women.[21] But this too is problematic. Women's "honor" has traditionally been equated with virginity or chastity.[22] Loss of honor implies the loss of station or respect, reinforcing the social view—often internalized by women—that the raped woman is dishonorable. While the concept of dignity potentially embraces more profound concerns, the emphasis on honor obfuscates the fact that rape is violence against women—against women's body, autonomy, integrity, selfhood, security, and self-esteem, as well as standing in the community.

This failure to recognize rape as violence is critical to the traditionally lesser or ambiguous status of rape in humanitarian law. Under the Geneva Conventions, international crimes are those identified as "grave breaches."[23] On the level of discourse, this calls attention to the egregiousness of the assault. As a legal matter, only grave breaches are subject to universal jurisdiction under the Geneva Conventions, triggering the obligation of every nation to bring the perpetrators to justice and justifying the trial of such crime before an international tribunal.

Under the Geneva Conventions, rape is not specified in the list of crimes considered grave breaches, which includes "killing, torture or inhumane treatment" and "willfully causing great suffering or serious injury to body or health."[24] Clearly these categories are broad and generic enough to encompass rape and sexual abuse. But if the egregiousness of rape is to be fully recognized, rape must be explicitly recognized as a form of torture.

When the Conventions were drafted, torture was largely understood as a method of extracting information. By contrast, today, as the historian Edward Peters writes, "It is not primarily the victim's information, but the victim, that torture needs to win—or reduce to powerlessness."[25] Recent treaties define torture as the willful infliction of severe physical or mental pain or suffering not only to elicit information but also to punish, intimidate, discriminate, obliterate the victim's personality, or diminish her personal capacities.[26] Thus, torture is now commensurate with willfully causing great suffering or injury. Increasingly its definition encompasses not only the inflicting of physical pain but also methods of humiliation and debilitation that work directly on the mind. In the contemporary understanding of torture, degradation is both vehicle and goal.[27]

Although largely ignored by human rights advocates,[28] the testimonies and studies of women tortured during dictatorial regimes and military occupations make clear that rape is one of the most common, terrible, and effective forms of torture used against women.[29] Rape attacks the integrity of the woman as a person as well as her identity as a woman. It renders her, in the words of Lepa Mladjenovic, a psychotherapist and Serbian feminist antiwar activist, "homeless in her own body."[30] It strikes at a woman's power; it seeks to degrade and destroy her; its goal is domination and dehumanization.[31]

The impact of rape is multiplied and becomes sexual enslavement when it is institutionalized as forced prostitution or linked with the threat, fear, and/or reality of pregnancy. The expressed intent to make women pregnant is an additional form of psychological torture; the goal of impregnation leads to imprisoning women and raping them until they are pregnant; the fact of pregnancy, whether aborted or not, continues the initial torture in a most intimate and invasive form; and the fact of bearing the child of rape, whether placed for adoption or not, has a potentially lifelong impact on the woman, on her liberty, and on her place in the community.

Because rape is a transportation of the intimate into violence, rape by acquaintances, by those who have been trusted, is particularly world-shattering and thus is a particularly effective method of torture and tool of ethnic cleansing.[32] In Bosnia, the fact that the rapists are, in many cases, former colleagues, neighbors, or even friends further exacerbates the trauma and degradation. There are reports that some Bosnian-Serbs are being recruited as rapists through methods commonly used in training torturers: exposure to and engagement in increasingly unthinkable violence and humiliation.[33]

Although rape and related crimes are widely accepted as grave breaches in the context of the former Yugoslavia, it is not clear that this acceptance applies to contexts in which rape is neither widespread nor linked to ethnic cleansing.[34] The statute establishing the jurisdiction of an International War Crimes Tribunal does not explicitly list rape, forced prostitution, and forced pregnancy in its definition of grave breaches, although it is implicit in the recognized categories.[35] But if, as a consequence of women's interventions, these are prosecuted as such by the International Tribunal, this will effectively amend or expand the meaning of grave breach. This emphasizes the importance, from a practical as well as moral perspective, of insisting that all rape in war, not only mass or genocidal rape, be understood as torture.

Genocide Rape vs. "Normal" Rape: When Is Mass Rape a Crime Against Humanity?

"Crimes against humanity" were first formally recognized in the Charter and Judgment of the Nuremberg Tribunal. They are viewed as violations of mandatory customary norms that brook no exceptions. This means they do not depend on adherence to a treaty and are subject to universal jurisdiction. The statute of the International Tribunal lists rape as a crime against humanity, and the commentary mentions forced prostitution as an example of a related offense.[36] Local Council Law No. 10, which provided the foundation for the trials of lesser Nazis by the Allied forces, also listed rape, although no one was prosecuted for it.[37] While it is critical to have rape identified, the meaning of this designation and its import for other contexts in which women are subjected to mass rape apart from ethnic cleansing is not clear. The danger, as always, is that extreme examples produce narrow principles.

The commentary on this aspect of the jurisdiction of the International Tribunal signals this danger. It explains crimes against humanity as "inhumane acts of a very serious nature, such as willful killing, torture or rape, committed as part of a widespread or systematic attack against any civilian population on national, political, ethnic, racial or religious grounds."[38] Several aspects of this definition deserve comment.

On the positive side, the statute correctly encompasses violations that are widespread but not necessarily systematic. The law wisely does not require massive numbers but, rather, patterns of abuse. (This is particularly important vis-a-vis rape, since only a small percentage of women will ultimately come forward, and statistics therefore, conceal, rather than reveal, the significance of the pattern.) Moreover, rape need not be ordered or centrally organized for commanders to be held accountable: they are responsible for failing to take steps to prevent patterns of violence of which they were aware or should have been aware.[39] While it is politically and ethically important for the Tribunal to investigate and prove the chain of command, it is likewise important that the leadership be held legally responsible without such proof.

The important gender question is whether widespread or systematic rape, apart from genocide or ethnic cleansing, would qualify as a crime against humanity. The original concept of crimes against humanity recognized two separate and independent criteria: gross acts of violence and persecution-based offenses. The statute of the Tribunal listed rape alongside torture and, thus, might be understood as recognizing rape as a gross act of violence. But by merging the criteria of gross violence with persecution-based offenses, the commentary might be seen to limit prosecution to those rapes undertaken as a method of persecution on the specified grounds.]

The latter narrow view, expressed in the popular distinction between so-called "normal" rape and genocidal rape, is unfortunately quite prevalent. This distinction contrasts the common and tolerable with the unique and heinous. It is proffered not as a typology but rather as a hierarchy. To thus exaggerate the distinctiveness of genocidal rape obviates the atrocity of common rape. Genocidal rape in Bosnia involves gang rapes, often in public or in front of children or partners. It involves imprisoning women in rape "camps" and raping them repeatedly. These characteristics are unfortunately not unique but rather common to most rape in war—rape for booty or to boost the morale of soldiers—just as they are to the use of rape as a form of torture and terror by dictatorial regimes.

The notion that genocidal rape is uniquely a weapon of war is also problematic. The rape of women is a weapon of war where it is used to spread political terror, as in the military repression in Haiti, and the civil war in Peru. It is a weapon of war where, as with the Russian rape of German women at the close of World War II, it is used against women to destabilize a society and break its resistance.[40] It is a weapon of war where, as in Bosnia and the indigenous Yuracruz homeland in Ecuador, it is part of a calculated effort to terrorize and shame women into fleeing their homes, and often their families and communities.

The rape of women as the "booty" of war, where permitted or systematized, is likewise a tactic or engine of war: it maintains the morale of soldiers, feeds their hatred and sense of superiority, and keeps them fighting. During World War II, the Japanese military industrialized and made invisible the enslavement of women as booty: women—mostly Korean, but also Filipino, Chinese, Indonesian and some Dutch—were deceived or disappeared into "comfort stations" where they were raped repeatedly, and moved from battlefield to battlefield to motivate and reward the Japanese soldiers. Genocide was not a goal, but it is believed that 90 percent of these women died in captivity. Among the known survivors, few if any were able subsequently to bear children.[41] For similar reasons, the United States military in Vietnam raped Vietnamese women and established brothels, relying on the women's desperate poverty and family pressures, rather than kidnapping, to fill them.[42]

While testimonies of women from Bosnia reveal, in fact, an admixture of all these tactics, genocidal or ethnic cleansing rape as practiced in Bosnia has some aspects particularly designed to drive women from their homes or destroy their possibility of reproducing within and "for" their community.[43] Since war and propaganda have made enemies of neighbors, women are raped by men familiar to them, thus exacerbating the trauma, shame, betrayal, and impulse to flee. The second and more generally distinctive feature of genocidal rape is the focus on women as reproductive vessels. The commonly articulated goal to make Muslim women bear "Serbian babies" (as if the child is the product of sperm only)justifies repeated rape and aggravates the terror of—as well as the future stigma on—the women. Similarly, Bengali women were raped by the Pakistani army to lighten their race and produce a class of outcast mothers and children. Enslaved African women in the southern United States were raped as property to produce babies who were then bartered, sold, and used as property.[44]

While intentional impregnation is properly treated as a separate offense,[45] this should not obscure the fact that pregnancy is a common consequence of rape. In situations where women are raped repeatedly, most fertile women will become pregnant at some point. When the U.S. Navy took over Saipan, for example, one observer reported that virtually all the women who had been enslaved as "comfort women" by the Japanese army were pregnant.[46]

These distinctive characteristics do not, however, place genocidal rape in a class by itself; nor do they reflect the full range of atrocities, losses, and suffering that the combination of rape and genocide inflict. Bosnian-Muslim women are being persecuted based on multiple elemental aspects of identity: gender and ethnicity or religion. But the effect on women of rape apart from genocide may be no less life-shattering, given the enormity of the assault on a woman's integrity and personality and the unacceptablity of a raped woman to the patriarchal community and, as a result, to herself. The crystallization of the concept of "crimes against humanity" in the wake of the Holocaust has meant that it is popularly associated with religious and ethnic genocide. The categories of persecution, however, are explicitly open-ended, capable of expanding to embrace new understandings of persecution and of embracing persecution based on gender as a category of crimes against humanity. The problem is, of course, that historically gender has not been recognized as a category of persecution. The frequency of mass rape and the absence of sanction is sufficient evidence. In the Holocaust, the gender persecutions—the rape and forced prostitution of women as well as the extermination of gays—were obscured.[47] A parallel problem exists in the context of political asylum, which requires a well-founded fear of persecution but has not yet explicitly recognized gender as a source of persecution.[48] Expansion of the concept of crimes against humanity to include gender is thus part of the broader movement to end the historic invisibility of gender violence as a humanitarian and human rights violation.

Moreover, the particular goals and defining aspects of genocidal rape do not detract from, but rather underscore, the nature of rape as a crime of gender. Women are targets not only because they "belong to" the enemy but also because they keep the civilian population functioning and are essential to its continuity. They are targets because they too *are* the enemy; because of their *power* as women; because of hatred of their power including their sexual and reproductive powers; because men delight in the objectification and degradation of women.

The crime of forced impregnation—central as it is to genocidal rape—also underscores the gender component. Since in a patriarchy women are viewed as little more than vessels for childbearing, involuntary pregnancy is commonly viewed as natural, divinely ordained perhaps, or simply an unquestioned fact of life. As a result, the risk of pregnancy in all rape is treated not as an offense but as a sequela. Forced pregnancy has drawn condemnation only when it reflects an intent to harm the victimized race.

Since, in Bosnia, ethnically mixed families are common in certain areas, the issue is not so much about racial impurity as it is about the perpetrator's purpose and the victim's choice. The taunt that Muslim women shall bear Serbian babies is not simply an ethnic harm. The intent to impregnate is equally an assault on the reproductive self-determination of women; it marks the rape and rapist upon a woman's body and spirit and upon her life.

Finally, the fact that the rape of women is also designed to humiliate men or destroy "the enemy" to whom the women "belong" itself reflects the fundamental objectification of women. Women are the targets of abuse at the same time that their existence and subjectivity are completely denied. The persistent failure to acknowledge the gender dimension of rape and sexual persecution is thus a most effective means of perpetuating it.

In sum, the international attention focused on Bosnia challenges the world to recognize squarely that sexual violence against women in war is a form of torture. Widespread or systematic rape, forced prostitution, and forced pregnancy must be viewed as crimes against humanity not only when they are the vehicles of some other form of persecution but also independently, because they are invariably forms of persecution based on gender. Nor is it enough for the Tribunal statute simply to recognize rape as a crime; those responsible for rape and related crimes must be charged and prosecuted in accordance with bias-free standards and recognized procedure. This is essential if the women of Bosnia are to be understood as full subjects, as well as objects, of this terrible victimization, and if the international attention focused on Bosnia is to have meaning for women subjected to rape in other parts of the world.

Given the formidable pressure being brought to bear by women survivors and the women's movement globally, it may well be that some few men will be indicted and even tried before the International Tribunal or national courts—*if* impunity is not once again the price of peace. This would be precedent setting in international law and provide symbolic vindication of the untold numbers of women rendered homeless in so many senses by this war. It would strengthen the claims women in other countries can make on their governments to prosecute such criminals when they come within their territory and would enable victims and survivors to sue perpetrators for damages based on the incorporation of international law into national law.[49] But unless the gender dimension of rape in war is recognized, it will mean little for women where rape is not also a tool of genocide.

Conclusion

When women charge rape in war, they are more likely to be believed because their status as enemy, or at least as belonging to the enemy, is recognized and because rape in war is seen as a product of exceptional circumstances. When women charge rape in everyday life, they are disbelieved largely because the ubiquitous war against women is denied. Emphasis on the gender dimension of rape in war is critical not only to surfacing women as full subjects of sexual violence in war but also to recognizing the atrocity of rape in so-called times of peace.

This is not to say that rape is identical in the two contexts. There are differences, just as there are differences between rape for the purposes of genocide and rape in which women are considered booty. War tends to intensify the brutality, repetition, public aspect, and likelihood of rape. War diminishes sensitivity to human suffering and intensifies men's sense of entitlement, superiority, avidity, and social license to rape. But the line between rape committed during wartime and at other times is not so sharp. Gang rape in civilian life shares the repetitive, gleeful, and public character of rape in war. Marital rape, the most private of all, also shares some of the particular characteristics of genocidal rape in Bosnia: it is repetitive, brutal, and exacerbated by a profound betrayal of trust; it assaults a woman's reproductive autonomy, may force her to flee her home and community, and is widely treated as legitimate by law and custom.[50]

From a feminist human rights perspective, gender violence has escaped sanction because it has not been viewed as violence and because the public/private dichotomy has insulated it most common, private forms.[51] The recognition of rape as a war crime is thus a critical step toward understanding rape as violence. The next step is to recognize that rape that acquires the imprimatur of the state is not necessarily more brutal, relentless, or dehumanizing than the private rapes of everyday life, nor is violation by a state official or enemy soldier necessarily more devastating than violation by an intimate.[52]

Every rape is grave violation of physical and mental integrity. Every rape has the potential to debilitate profoundly, to alienate a woman from her own body and destroy her sense of security in the world. Every rape is an expression of male domination and misogyny, a vehicle for terrorizing and subordinating women. Like torture, rape takes many forms, occurs in many contexts, and has different repercussions for different victims. Every rape is multidimensional, but not incomparable.

The rape of women in the former Yugoslavia challenges the world to refuse impunity to atrocity and to resist the powerful forces that would make the mass rape of Muslim women in Bosnia appear exceptional, thus neutralizing its meaning for women raped in different contexts. We must recognize situational differences without losing sight of the commonalities. To fail to make distinction flattens reality; to rank the egregious demeans it.

NOTES

Credit for extensive research into the historical and current understanding of war crime and crimes against humanity is due to Krishna Stark and Ethan Taubes. I also appreciate Celina Romany's and Marilyn Young's comments on the draft, as well as conversations with Jennifer Green, Vesna Kesic, Guadeloupe Leon, Sara Sharett, Ann Snitow, and Dorothy Thomas, among others.

1. See, e.g., Susan Brownmiller, *Against Our Will: Men, women, and Rape,* (New York: Simon and Schuster, 1975), pp. 31–113.
2. Attina Grossman, unpublished paper; and Lourdes Sajor, "Women in Armed Conflict Situations" MAV/1993/WP. 1 (September 21, 1993) (prepared for Expert Group meeting on Measures to Eradicate Violence Against Women, UN division for the Advancement of Women).
3. The "rape of Nanking" refers to the brutal taking of Nanking by Japanese forces, which involved several months of mass and open killing, looting, and rape. It is estimated that 20,000 women were raped in the first month. See Leon Friedan, *The Law of War, A Documentary History,* Vol. 2 (New York: Random House, 1972), p. 46.
4. Brownmiller, *supra* n. 1, pp. 78–86. Among the motives for these rapes was a genocidal one—to destroy the racial distinctiveness of the Bengali people.
5. Although the Serbian campaign against the Bosnian-Muslims is the

most extensive, the hatred inflamed and the atrocities committed in the wars in the former Yugoslavia are far too complicated to describe as a one-way street. Croatian women were also targets. Moreover, from before the outset of the war, the Croatian government has sought to "cleanse" Croatia of Serbs and has waged a bitter war against Muslims in Bosnia in the effort to claim territory as Croatian. There are reports as well of rape and other atrocities committed by Muslims. See Jeri Laber, "Bosnia: Questions of Rape," *New York Review of Books* (March 25, 1993), pp. 3–6; and Alexandra Stiglmayer, *Mass Rape: The War Against Women in Bosnia-Herzegovina* (Lincoln, NB: Univ. of Nebraska Press, 1994). There are some reports that men have been subjected to rape, which is also a crime of gender, but rape has been, as usual, overwhelmingly directed against women (telephone conversation with Patrick Cotter, January 1994.)

6. See, for example, America's Watch and Women's Rights Project, *Untold Terror: Violence Against Women in Peru's Armed Conflict* (New York: Human Rights Watch, 1992); Asia Watch and Women's Rights Project, *Burma: Rape, Forced Labor, and Religious Persecution in Northern Arakan* (Washington, DC: Human Rights Watch, 1992); Shana Swiss, *Liberia: Women and Children Gravely Mistreated* (Boston: Physicians for Human Rights, 1991). For other examples, see Shana Swiss and Joan E. Giller, "Rape as a Crime of War," *Journal of the American Medical Association* 270 (August 4, 1993): p. 612.

7. The routine rape of Haitian women identified as Aristide supporters was ignored in the periodic reports of the Inter-American Commission on Human Rights until the pressure of women forced the UN/OAS Observer Mission to conduct a special investigation. As a result of a brief investigation in Cite Soleil, a very poor and pro-Aristide section of Port-au-Prince, the Mission reported that "rape appear[s] to form an integral part of the political violence and terror" (UN/OAS Observer Mission, Communique, March 21, 1994). See also presentation of Guadalupe Leon, Panel on Military Violence and Sexual Slavery, 1993 UN Conference on Human Rights, NGO Parallel Activities, June 1993.

8. See Cynthia Enloe, "Afterword" in Stiglmayer, *supra, n. 5,* and Lourdes, Sajor, *supra,* n. 2.

9. National experience and divisions have, however, divided women and feminists. See Vesna Kesic, "A Response to Catherine MacKinnon's 'Turning Rape into Pornography: Postmodern Genocide,'" *Hasting's Women's Law Journal* 5(1) (Winter 1994) (written to refute Catherine MacKinnon, "Turning Rape into Pornography: Postmodern Genocide," in Stiglmayer, *supra* n. 5, pp. 73-81), and C. Carr, "Battle Scars: Feminism and Nationalism Clash in the Balkans" *Village Voice,* July 13 1993, p. 25.

10. *Report of the Drafting Committee, Addendum*, Final Outcome of the World Conference on Human Rights, A/conf. 157/PC/Add. 1 (June 24, 1993) (hereinafter, "Vienna Declaration").

11. The full title is "International Tribunal for the Prosecution of Persons Responsible for Serious Violations of International Humanitarian Law Committed in the Territory of the Former Yugoslavia Since 1991," *Report of the Secretary-General, pursuant to para. 2 of the Security Council Resolution 808* (1993), S/25704 (May 3, 1993), para. 48 at 13. Discussion infra pp. 8–9.

12. CNN, *Sonya Live*, January 26, 1993.

13. Bogdan Denitch, panel held at CUNY Law School, May 22, 1993, sponsored by the Queens Coalition for Political Alternatives. Some feminists have also made this distinction. See MacKinnon, *supra* n. 9; Carr, *supra* n. 9.

14. On the significance of the intersection of categories of oppression, see Kimberle Crenshaw, "Demarginalizing the Intersection of Race and Sex: A Black Feminist Critique of Anti-Discrimination Doctrine, Feminist Theory, and Antiracist Politics," *University of Chicago Legal Forum* (1989), pp.139–67. For examination of the particularities of ethnogender violence, see Stiglmayer, "The Rapes in Bosnia-Herzegovina," *supra* n. 5, pp. 82–169; Azra Zalihic-Kaurin, "The Muslim Women," in Stiglmayer, *supra* n. 5, pp. 170–73; MacKinnon, "Rape, Genocide, and Women's Human Rights," in Stiglmayer, *supra* n. 5, pp. 183–196; Adrien Katherine Wing and Sylke Merchan, "Rape, Ethnicity, and Culture: Spirit Injury from Bosnia to Black America," *Columbia Human Rights Law Review* 25(1) (Fall 1993), 1-46; International Human Rights Law Group, *No Justice, No Peace* (Washington, DC: 1993).

15. More than one year after its creation, the Tribunal still has no Chief Prosecutor, the Deputy Prosecutor has just begun hiring a skeletal staff, the project is substantially underfunded, and only two of the eleven judges are women. The Tribunal is politically compromised by its ad hoc status, and the risk remains that formal impunity will again be the price of peace. Further, the power of the Tribunal is sorely limited; it cannot compel the appearance of the accused without the cooperation of a willing state. Thus, in relation to major figures who remain in or close to power in their countries, the Tribunal can generate only an international "wanted" list that will, at least, restrict the ability of the accused to travel internationally.

16. See International Tribunal for the Prosecution of Persons Responsible for Serious Violations of International Humanitarian Law Committed in the Territory of the Former Yugoslavia since 1991, *Rules of Procedure and Evidence*, UN Docs. IT/32 (March 14, 1994) and IT/61/Rev. 1 (May

6, 1994). The rules clearly reflect the influence of feminist approaches to rape. See, e.g., rule 75 (protection of witnesses); rule 79 (closed sessions); and, particularly, revised rule 96 (evidence in cases of sexual assault), which precludes requiring corroboration of the victim's testimony, precludes the defense of consent where violence, duress, detention, or psychological oppression are shown, and prohibits evidence of the prior sexual conduct of the victim. An extensive proposal for the treatment of war crimes was submitted to the Tribunal by the International Women's Human Rights Law Clinic at CUNY Law School, an the Harvard Human Rights Program.

17. The international legal meaning of rape is also under consideration in petitions before the Inter-American Commission on Human Rights concerning Haiti and Peru.

18. See, e.g., Yougindra Khusalini, *Dignity and Honour of Women As Basic and Fundamental Human Rights* (Boston: Martinus Nijhoff, 1982). Also, *Geneva Convention Relative to the Protection of Civilian Persons in Time of War*, common art. 3, 1(a) and (c), arts. 27, 76, and 97 (hereinafter referred to as Geneva Convention IV); *Protocol Additional to the Geneva Conventions of 12 August 1949, and relating to the Protection of Victims of International Armed Conflicts (Protocol I)*, art. 76; *Protocol Additional to the Geneva Conventions of 12 August 1949, and relating to the Protection of Victims of Non-International Armed Conflicts (Protocol II)*, art. 4. All of the conventions above reprinted in Center for Human Rights, *Human Rights: A Compilation of International Instruments*, Vol. 1 (pt. 2) (New York: United Nations, 1993), pp. 799–939.

19. Khusalini, *supra* n. 18; *Geneva Convention IV*, art. 27, para. 2; *Protocol II*, art. 4.

20. In the United States, the death penalty for rape was prevalent in the Southern states as a result of a combination of sexism and racism. See *Coker v. Georgia*, 433 U.S. 584 (1977).

21. Khusalini, *supra*, n. 18, pp. 39-76.

22. See, e.g., America's Watch, *Untold Terror, supra* n. 6.

23. *Geneva Convention IV*, note 9, art. 147; *Protocol I*, note 9, arts. 11 and 85(3). The concept of "grave breach" applies only to international conflict and not to civil war. With respect to the question of whether the conflict in former Yugoslavia is international or internal, the UN has taken the position that the warring parties have agreed to abide by the rules governing international armed conflicts. United Nations, *Report of the Secretary-General, supra* n. 11, para. 25, p. 8.

24. *Geneva Convention IV*, note 9, art. 147; *Protocol I*, note 9, arts. 11 and 85(3).

25. Edward Peters, *Torture* (New York: Basil Blackwell, 1985), p. 164.

26. *UN Convention Against Torture,* art. 1; *Inter-American Convention Against Torture,* art. 2 reprinted in J. Herman Burgers and Hans Danelius, *The United Nations convention Against Torture and Other Cruel Inhuman and Degrading Treatment or Punishment* (Boston: Martinus Nijhoff, 1988), Appendix.

27. Amnesty International, *Report on Torture* New York: Farrar, Straus and Giroux, 1974). See Rhonda Copelon, "Recognizing the Egregious in the Everyday: Domestic Violence as Torture" *Columbia Human Rights Law Review,* 25(2) (Spring 1994): pp. 291–367.

28. It was not until 1991 that a mainstream human rights non-governmental organization recognized rape in detention or under military occupation as a form of torture. Amnesty International, *Women in the Front Line* (New York: Amnesty International, 1991). In 1992, the UN Commission on Human Rights' Special Rapporteur on Torture did likewise. *Report of the Special Rapporteur P. Kooijmans, Pursuant to Commission on Human Rights Resolution 1992/32,* UN Doc. E/CN.4/1993/26 (15 December 1992), e.g., paras. 355, 371. For a discussion of the recognition of rape as torture by the United Nations Commission on Human Rights' Special Rapporteur on Torture, see *Token Gestures: 1, the UN Special Rapporteur on Torture* (Washington, DC: International Human Rights Law Group, June 1993). See also, Deborah Blatt "Recognizing Rape as a Method of Torture." *NYU Review of Law and Social Change* 19:821 (1992); and Theodor Meron, "Rape As a Crime Under International Humanitarian Law," *American Journal of International Law* 87:424 (1993).

29. See, e.g., Ximena Bunster-Bunalto, "Surviving Beyond Fear: Women and Torture in Latin America," *Women and Change in Latin America,* edited by June Nash and Helen Safa (Westport, CT: Bergin and Garvey, 1986), pp. 297–325; F. Allodi and S. Stiasny, "Women As Torture Victims," *Canadian Journal of Psychiatry* 35 (March 1990): 144–48; Inge Lunde and Jorge Ortmann, "Prevalence and Sequelae of Sexual Torture," *The Lancet* 336 (August 1990): 289-91. While not the subject here, the rape of men is also a devastating crime of gender, designed as it is to humiliate through "feminization."

30. Testimony before the Global Tribunal on Violations of Women's Human Rights part of the NGO Parallel Activities, 1993 World Conference on Human Rights, Vienna, June 15, 1993.

31. See, e.g., Brownmiller, *supra* n. 1; Bunster-Bunalto, *supra* n. 29; Amnesty International, *Women in the Front Line, supra* n. 28.

32. See Amnesty International, *Report on Torture, supra* n. 27; Elaine Scarry, *The Body in Pain: The Making and Unmaking of the World* New

York: Oxford Univ. Press, 1985), p. 41; Judith Lewis Herman, *Trauma and Recovery* (New York: Basic Books, 1992); David Finkelhor and Kersti Yllo, *License to Rape: Sexual Abuse of Wives* (New York: Free Press, 1985); Diana E. H. Russell, *Rape in Marriage* (New York: Collier, 1982).

33. See Stiglmayer, *supra* n. 5. See also, e.g., Stanley Milgram, "Some Conditions of Obedience and Disobedience to Authority," *Human Relations* 18(1) (1965): 57–74. On the training of torturers, see Amnesty International, *Torture in Greece: The First Torturers' Trial 1975* (New York: Amnesty International, 1977); Mika Haritos-Fatouros, "The Official Torturer: A Learning Model for Obedience to the Authority of Violence," *Journal of Applied Social Psychology* 18(13) (October 1988): pp. 107–120.

34. UN Commission on Human Rights *Rape and Abuse of Women in the Territory of the Former Yugoslavia*, Report on the 49th Session, February 1-March 12, 1993 Economic and Social Council Suppl. No. 3, E/CN4/1993/122: e.g., "Rape and abuse of women and children in the former Yugoslavia which, *in the circumstances*, constitutes a war crime." (emphasis added). Likewise, the Vienna Conference limited its condemnation to "systematic rape" (Vienna Declaration, *supra* n. 10). See also Meron, *supra* n. 28.

35. Article 2 of the statute identifies as grave breaches "(a) willful killing; (b) torture or inhuman treatment, including biological experiments; (c) willfully causing great suffering or serious bodily injury to body or health." United Nations, *Report of the Secretary-General, supra* n. 11, art. 2, paras. 37-40, pp. 10-11.

36. *Report of the Secretary-General supra* n. 11, art. 5, paras. 47-49, p. 13.

37. Khusalini, *supra* n. 18, p. 23; see discussion therein, pp. 13-38.

38. *Report of the Secretary-General, supra* n. 11, para. 48, p. 13.

39. Idem, art. 7(3), p. 15.

40. America's Watch and Women's Rights Project, *Untold Terror, supra* n. 6; Swiss and Giller, *supra* n. 6.

41. Sajor, *supra* n. 2. Testimony of Bok Dong Kim before the Global Tribunal on Violations of Women's Human Rights, NGO Parallel Activities, 1993 World Conference on Human Rights, Vienna, June 15, 1993. See also *Hearings before the United Nations Secretary-General* (February 25, 1993) (testimonies of Hyochai Lee, MA; Soon-Kum Park, and Chung-Ok Yum, MFA Korean Council for the Women Drafted for Military Sexual Service in Japan).

42. Brownmiller, *supra* n. 1, pp. 86-113.

43. See e.g., Stiglmayer, *supra*, n. 5.

44. Angela Y. Davis, *Women, Race and Class* (New York: Vintage, 1983), p. 172.

45. See Anne Tierney Goldstein, "Recognizing Forced Impregnation as a War Crime Under International Law," Special Report of the Center for Reproductive Law and Policy (1993).

46. Conversation with D. B., New Haven, CT, April 1993.

47. See Brownmiller, *supra* n. 1, pp. 48-78, for the unrecognized sexual violence against women on the part of Allied as well as Axis forces. See also Erwin J. Haeberle, "Swastika, Pink Triangle, and Yellow Star: The Destruction of Sexology and the Persecution of Homosexuals in Nazi Germany," in *Hidden from History: Reclaiming the Gay and Lesbian Past*, edited by Martin Duberman, Martha Vicinus, and George Channcez, Jr., pp. 375-79 (New York: Meridian, 1990) (noting the gender aspect of the Nazi attacks on homosexuals reflected in the use of the pink triangle and charges of emasculation).

48. The *Convention Relating to the Status of Refugees* recognizes persecution based on race, religion, nationality, membership in a particular social group, or political opinion. The "social group" category is currently being expanded to encompass gender claims, but this is not enough. See Pamela Goldberg, "Anyplace But Home: Asylum in the United States for Women Fleeing Intimate Violence." *Cornell International Law Journal 26:565* (Symposium 1993).

49. Two lawsuits have been filed against the Bosnian-Serbian leader, Radovan Karadzic. *Jane Doe v. Radovan Karadzic* Civil Action No. 93 Civ. 0878 (PKL) (U.S. Southern District of New York, filed 1993); *S. Kadic v. Radovan Karadzic*, Civil Action No. 93 Civ. 1163 (PKL) (U.S. Southern District of New York, filed 1993). The Center for Constitutional Rights in New York City has a number of cases, including *Doe v. Karadzic*, and is the leading source of information on this strategy for domestic implementation of international law.

50. Amnesty International, *Report on Torture, supra* n. 27; Scarry, *supra* n. 32; Herman, *supra* n. 32; Finkelhor and Yllo, *supra* n. 32; Russell, *supra* n. 32.

51. See Charlotte Bunch, "Women's Rights as Human Rights: Towards a Re-Vision of Human Rights," *Human Rights Quarterly* 12 (1990); Celina Romany, "State Responsibility Goes 'Private': A Feminist Critique of the Public/Private Distinction in International Human Rights Law," in *The Human Rights of Women*, edited by Rebecca Cook (Philadelphia: Univ. of Pennsylvania Press, 1994); Copelon, *supra* n. 27.

52. Herman, *supra* n. 32.

QUESTIONS

1. What are the various ways rape in war is conceptualized? When is it considered a crime? How well do rapes in war fit the definition of a human rights violation?
2. Why do certain types of rape get the most attention internationally? Why does Copelon find it problematic to make distinctions between genocidal rape and other types of mass rape occurring in war? What solutions does she pose?
3. What connections does Copelon make between rape in war and rape occurring in non-war contexts?

INTRODUCTION: REIMAGING TRANSNATIONAL SISTERHOOD (2002)

Stanlie M. James and Claire C. Robertson

Stanlie M. James is professor of Afro-American studies and women's studies at the University of Wisconsin-Madison. She is the editor of Theorizing Black Feminisms: The Visionary Pragmatism of Black Women *(with Abena Busia). Her articles have appeared in Signs,* Women's Studies International Forum, Women in Politics, Africa Today, *and the* Journal of African Policy Studies. *Her areas of interest include black feminisms and women's international human rights.* (info quoted from the "contributors" section in the book) *Claire Robertson is a listed author in the RWL database.*

Popular Western Perceptions reduce Africa and African women in three distinct ways that could be called the "three Rs." First, they reduce Africa's fifty-four countries and hundreds of cultures to one uncivilized, "traditional" place outside of history to be compared with the "modern" "West." Second, they reduce Africans, and African women in particular, to the status of their genitals, to being malicious torturers or hapless victims. Finally, uniform depictions reduce all cutting of female genitals to the most severe practice—infibulation. The cumulative effect of these reductions is that all African women are represented as having been infibulated due to unreasoned adherence to tradition and/or malicious ignorance.

As feminist scholars from diverse backgrounds and activists committed to eliminating harmful genital cutting, we are distressed by these perceptions and by media misrepresentations of those practices often referred to as female genital mutilation (FGM) or sometimes female genital surgeries (FGS). Whether through exaggeration, overgeneralization, stereotyping, inaccuracy, voyeurism, or misplaced militance, the U.S. media has succeeded in portraying African women as victims of sensationalized FGM in a manner that has eclipsed any reasoned consideration of historical contexts, contemporary experiences, and the agency of African women themselves.

Positions on this issue range from cultural relativism to a militant stance that would forbid all U.S. aid to countries where these customs continue to be practiced by any of their citizens. Recognizing that neither of these approaches appeared to be effective in struggles to eradicate such practices, in 1983 the Women's Caucus of the African Studies Association (ASA) advocated a different approach in the "Position Paper of the Women's Caucus of the African Studies Association on Clitoridectomy and Infibulation," which is included as the prologue to this volume. The caucus concluded that "changes in the practice of clitoridectomy and infibulation in Africa must be initiated and carried out by members of those African cultures in which the custom exists." The paper also observed that "many African women need food for themselves and their children, greater control over the means of food production, access to clean water, a secure fuel supply, access to health care including family planning and ways to acquire cash income. *Concern about clitoridectomy and infibulation as the sole issue affecting the status of women may be a luxury that only the West can afford*" (emphasis added).

A decade later in 1993, Lynda Dey attended the New York City opening of the "documentary" *Warrior Marks* by Alice Walker and Pratibha Parmar. Dey reported to the Women's Caucus that she was appalled by the film's implications for those engaged in efforts to eradicate the practices. She urged caucus members to see it (it was available for viewing at the annual meeting of the African Studies Association that year) and argued that members should take a stand against such simplistic constructions. It was decided that the keynote speaker for the caucus's annual luncheon the following year would address this issue and that the caucus would sponsor at least one roundtable on the subject. Although invitations were issued to both Alice Walker and Pratibha Parmar to attend the annual meeting and participate in the roundtable, we received no response from Walker and an oblique refusal from Parmar. Seble Dawit, an attorney who specializes in international human rights and is an activist engaged in the struggle to eradicate the practices, did accept the invitation, however. Her moving address, "African Women in the Diaspora and the Problem of Female Mutilation," provided the inspiration for this volume, as did years of Women's Caucus discussions.

The editors of this volume eventually began to work independently on papers, excerpts of which were presented on panels at later ASA meetings and were subsequently published in *Signs*.[1] Despite those efforts, we still felt an obligation as Western women to respond in a more consistent manner to the admonition found in the Women's Caucus's Position Paper "that outsiders' contributions to this [eradication] effort can be most effective in the areas of collaborative research, discussion and dissemination of information about the progress of efforts elsewhere, and technical support." Although the caucus recognized the great need for work in this area, with "significant opportunities for genuine collaboration" the paper had also insisted that the practices must be contextualized rather than be addressed as isolated phenomena.

Genital Cutting and Transnational Sisterhood: Disputing U.S. Polemics represents our efforts to respond to the challenge of the position paper. It problematizes the often simplistic, sensationalized, and inaccurate portrayals of female genital cutting (FGC, the term we will use) in U.S. media and legal discourses. It plots a third course between the relativistic and the militant approaches that appear to have been ineffective in eradicating these harmful practices. We suggest that these approaches have sometimes demonized and/or victimized African women in a manner that has been detrimental to fragile endeavors to construct the bonds of transnational sisterhood. There may be elements, however, within these approaches that, when combined, could provide new ways to push beyond polarization and the immediate, visceral feelings of revulsion the topic provokes in the United States. If, as Parker Palmer suggests, "opposites do not negate each other [but] . . . cohere in mysterious unity at the heart of reality," then those of us committed to eradicating FGC must intentionally engage in the creative synthesis of paradox through scholarship that carefully examines the specificities of history and culture.[2]

* * *

Challenging Western perceptions and misrepresentations around the cutting of women's genitalia requires careful examination of overgeneralizations. One critical, and frequent, area of overgeneralization concerns terminology, where both the terms *female circumcision* and *female genital mutilation* have currency. Each contributor to this volume has her own critique of these terms, which are loaded with theoretical and political implications. Suffice it to say that "female circumcision" as a blanket term to cover FGC is misleading because it makes a false analogy to the much more minor operation performed on men and then places all FGC in this category, minimizing the impact of sometimes drastic and harmful cutting. Meanwhile, "female genital mutilation" as a term errs in the other direction, assuming that all FGC is mutilating. The contributors have therefore chosen to use several more precise terms to describe the cutting of women's and girls' genitalia. Stanlie James and Claire Robertson use "female genital cutting," while Isabelle Gunning uses "female genital surgeries" and Christine Walley uses "female genital operations." Cheryl Chase uses "clitoridectomy" to refer to the particular operation that is the chief subject of her essay and "pediatric genital surgeries" for the general category.

In Africa the widespread practices of FGC are as differentiated as the people themselves. In general, there are two different bundles of characteristics that have often been uncritically lumped together in the literature as "female circumcision" or "female genital mutilation." They differ according to what is done, the cultural significance of the practices, where they occur, and the pattern of spread or diminution. The following description and analysis is a summation of more extensive material available elsewhere.[3]

The first and most drastic type of female genital cutting is often called pharaonic circumcision or infibulation in the literature.

Here we will call it infibulation, which includes the excision of the clitoris. It is an ancient practice, recorded as far back as pharaonic Egypt, which Westerners have found to be most repulsive. The practice involves removing a woman's entire external genital area, the labia majora and minora and the clitoris, and sewing the wound together to leave a single opening the size of a pencil to allow for evacuation of urine and menses. Infibulation is often performed privately on young girls, or even infants, by older women relatives or hired operators of either gender in various locations and often without ritual. The drastic nature of the cutting and the usually unsanitary conditions in which it occurs often bring massive complications. Even if the initial wound heals properly without infection, the inelasticity of the resultant scar tissue and the smallness of the opening may require routine defibulation using a knife or other instrument at the time of marriage and childbirth.[4] In some cases, women are reinfibulated after childbirth.

The psychological effects of such mutilation may also be drastic, all the more so because it is often done to small children with no preparation or warning, with force used to restrain the unanesthetized girls. Because female relatives are usually those who forcibly restrain the girls it seems likely that the resultant feelings of mistrust might well militate against female solidarity, while sexual intercourse would be strongly associated with pain.[5]

What are the reasons behind what could easily be termed an unprovoked attack on young girls by their female or male relatives, who if they do not do it themselves will at least make the arrangements to have it done? Understanding the reasons for infibulation invites us to venture beyond simplistic statements of "it's a ritual" or a "tradition." According to the literature on infibulation, the goal is to make the girl into a desirable bride, meaning that she will be chaste and virginal until marriage and faithful after marriage. Many are convinced that a girl who has not been infibulated will not find a husband. Their duty to the child then requires that infibulation be done. Female genitalia in their unaltered state may be regarded as dirty and ugly. Thus some people believe that the aesthetics of beauty, fertility, and health are enhanced by removal of the external genitalia.[6]

Infibulation occurs chiefly in the Horn of Africa: Ethiopia, Sudan, Egypt (including among Egyptian Coptic Christian communities), Eritrea, and Somalia, and sporadically in West African

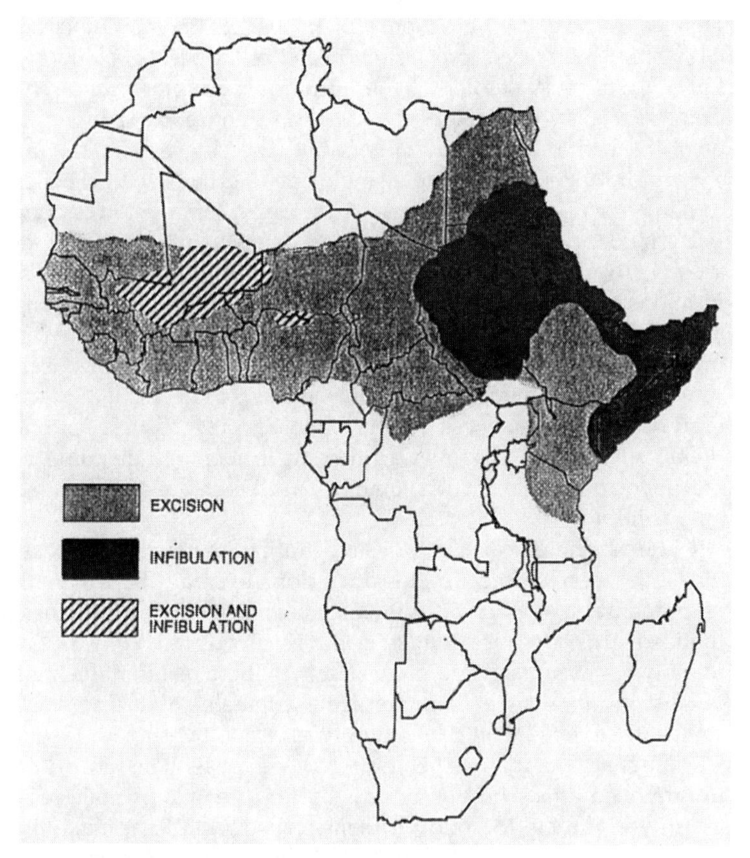

Fig. 1. Africa.
From Hanny Lightfoot-Klein, *Prisoners of Ritual: An Odyssey into Female Genital Circumcision in Africa* (New York: Haworth Press, 1989), 32. Map by Daniel V. Klein.
Reprinted by permission of The Haworth Press, Inc.

countries like Chad (fig. 1).[7] The practice is almost universal in some countries of the Horn (an exception is Eritrea, where it largely stopped during the long war of independence from Ethiopia) and has even spread into new areas along with Islam. Despite the lack of justification for it within the Koran itself, scholars acknowledge that Islam has incorporated and accommodated practices of genital cutting into its religious and worldviews.[8] Its persistence and spread are also associated with lesser economic opportunities for women that encourage economic dependency on a husband, with the misery caused by the longstanding civil war in Sudan, and with the neocolonial economies of these countries, in which well-paying jobs are scarce. The rise of fundamentalist Islam has also promoted the practice.

Clitoridectomy or excision of the clitoris, the other form of female genital cutting that is widely practiced, varies according to the portion of the clitoris removed and whether or not the labia majora or minora are also removed.[9] There is, as well, more minor cutting that may be mislabeled as clitoridectomy, but that involves only pricking or nicking the clitoris or removing the prepuce of the clitoris, as described by Emmanuel Babatunde with the Yoruba.[10] This practice, which is most analogous to male circumcision, will be referred to as female circumcision, or *sunna*, in this volume. Clitoridectomy also has a history of being practiced in Western countries as well as in parts of Africa.[11] In France, it began to be promoted as a cure for female homoeroticism as early as the late sixteenth and seventeenth centuries.[12] It is now practiced in the United States as one of the pediatric genital surgeries discussed by Cheryl Chase in this volume.

Less drastic procedures, ranging from merely pricking the clitoris to removing most but not all of the external genitalia, extend over a larger area of Africa than infibulation but are more discontinuous. The southernmost extent is usually accounted to be northern Tanzania, while people who most engage in clitoridectomy live in a belt that crosses Africa's mid-section from Senegal to Kenya and Tanzania, although there have been reports that certain women in southern Africa also practice clitoridectomy. The practices seem not to occur north of the Sahara. There are many people in countries where clitoridectomy exists who have never engaged in any of its variations, such as the Akan people in Ghana and Ivory Coast who compose the dominant portion of the population of both of those countries. Some Igbo in Nigeria continue to practice clitoridectomy, whereas some stopped doing it during the 1920s. In West Africa, clitoridectomy is more common upcountry, away from the coast in less urbanized areas; in Kenya it is not practiced on the predominantly Islamic coast. One of the chief areas where it was practiced extensively was around Nairobi, the largest city, where there has now been a substantial diminution in clitoridectomy among the largest ethnic group, the Kikuyu. The reasons for that decline are connected to the meanings people invest in clitoridectomy, which differ sharply from those accompanying infibulation.

In many societies, clitoridectomy was often performed as a part of puberty rites for girls, preceding or at the time of the first menses. The reason that clitoridectomy was frequently referred to as "female circumcision" in the anthropological literature was because it was viewed as being analogous to male circumcision and was often performed at the same time. Most people who practice clitoridectomy in the context of puberty rites also practice male circumcision. Excising the clitoris or its prepuce only was thought to remove the male principle from females, and many believed that male circumcision removed the female principle from males. Elders, who deemed these rites necessary to establish gender identity and induct the youth into adulthood, also believed the rites to be critical to the survival of the society. Senior males or senior females usually performed the procedures in sex-segregated settings, sometimes accompanied by isolation of the participants from the rest of the village for some period of time. Their elders prepared boys and girls for the ceremonies by instructing them in proper behavior and the significance of the rites. Those being excised were supposed to demonstrate bravery by keeping silent during their surgeries, which were usually performed without anesthetic. Other tests of courage and sometimes of athletic skills for both sexes also accompanied the rites. Groups of boys and girls experienced these procedures alongside rites that included education on how to be a successful adult.[13] Often initiates became an age-set pledged to each other for life; male and female solidarity was fostered, and healing together became one of the factors solidifying the group.[14]

In Sierra Leone, women initiated girls into Sande, a powerful women's secret society, and gave extensive instruction over several years in housewifery, beauty culture, arts and crafts, fishing, farming, childrearing, hygiene and sanitation, care of the sick, singing, drumming, dancing and drama, herbal lore, and respect for the elders.[15] The new initiates reentered society with great celebration, showered with gifts and acclaimed as newly fledged adults. Many women in societies where clitoridectomy was practiced recalled their experiences during and after initiation with pleasure as the most carefree time of their lives.[16]

The past tense here reflects changes that seem to be pervasive in many societies that still practice clitoridectomy. Although fostering sexual control among initiates was one motive for clitoridectomy, in some places that has assumed primary motivation for the practices, which are now done when girls are younger so they will not protest. Securing a husband has also become more important in a few areas. As more girls attend school, the seclusion and education period has diminished.[17] Many people have simply stopped doing initiation rites at all. Paradoxically, where women's groups that use puberty rites as induction rituals remain powerful, clitoridectomy may continue along with the substantial power of such groups. But where women's groups have been weakened or have transformed themselves, the practices may be disappearing. Their disappearance thus has ambivalent implications, for some women signaling an overall lessening of women's power. Yet the disappearance may also symbolize a transformation toward more democratic forms of women's power.[18] Thus, the chief declines in the cutting of women's and girls' genitals have occurred in areas where clitoridectomy or circumcision rather than infibulation have been prevalent.

It is this kind of specific context that is critical to our attempts to diminish the practices. The best knowledge about the practices is local. That knowledge must be respected and learned by those who work to eradicate female genital cutting, including Africans from other cultures. Thus, neither criminalization in the United States and Africa nor U.S. media condemnations that distort the complicated situations in Africa are very helpful. To avoid over-generalization and set these practices within the complex contexts from which they emerge, we have tried to use terminology as precisely as possible for the specific practice that is under discussion.

Exploding the Binaries: Rethinking Gender in the United States

Claude Lévi-Strauss suggested that the human brain tended to establish binaries as a way of knowing due to its binary structure, but it is not clear that this form of biological determinism must govern our practice.[19] The terminological issue is only one of several problems of binaries that this volume hopes to address. The range of terms for varied FGC practices in Africa reflect colonialist perspectives and polarize cultural relativist and militant feminist positions (see Christine J. Walley, "Searching for 'Voices': Feminism, Anthropology, and the Global Debate over Female Genital Operations" and Claire C. Robertson, "Getting beyond the Ew! Factor: Rethinking U.S. Approaches to African Female Genital Cutting," both in this volume). There are as well rigid concepts of gender established by sex in the United States that have had a detrimental impact on society's responses to intersexed individuals (those with ambiguous genitalia) and in far too many instances resulted in pediatric genital surgeries intended to established definitive gender/sex (see Cheryl Chase, "'Cultural Practice' or 'Reconstructive Surgery'? U.S. Genital Cutting, the Intersex Movement, and Medical Double Standards" in this volume). Although second-wave feminists have been at the forefront of critiquing binary gender definitions, neither second-nor third-wave feminists have often dealt well with the issues of FGC and pediatric genital surgeries.

Problematic feminist approaches to issues of FGC and pediatric genital surgeries are frequently connected to what one might call the colonial flaw. In the African case, these are heavily inflected by race, whereas the U.S. case may be affected by the analogue to the African case. That is, although many feminists by now are aware that clitoridectomy was practiced at different times and places in the United States, most confine it to the past. Routine pediatric genital surgeries continue in the United States, which suggests that the distance between some African cultures and U.S. society is not as great as many would like to imagine; these surgeries are regularly categorized as different from African practices and necessary, medically not culturally ordained. In some African societies, "ugly" female genitalia are made "beautiful" by infibulation; in the United States, nonconforming genitalia are regarded with aesthetic distaste, theoretical puzzlement, and possibly even fear. In both contexts, questions arise as to how conventional gender analysis can be applied to such individuals. Are we as feminists actually covertly, and perhaps even unconsciously, committed to the very categories of sex/gender that we deconstruct? What if a society developed in which all sex/gender categories were fluid, recognized, and accepted? Why are definitive categories necessary anyway? Why is it necessary to claim biological sex and/or sexual orientation as identity to achieve at least a modicum of acceptance and comfort within society? If we can move beyond our preoccupation with reconstructing binary gender by deconstructing it as the preeminent feminist project, and beyond colonial othering in terms of race and gender, perhaps we can begin to think through the paradox of a multicultural, multigendered world that may, in turn, be more hospitable to difference.

Notes

1. Clarie C. Robertson, "Grassroots in Kenya: Women, Genital Mutilation and Collective Action, 1920–1990," *Signs: Journal of Women in Culture and Society* 21, no. 2 (1996): 615–42; Stanlie M. James, "Shades of Othering: Reflections on Female Circumcision/Genital Mutilations," *Sings: Journal of Women in Culture and Society* 23, no. 4 (1998): 1031–48.

2. Parker Palmer, *Let Your Life Speak: Listening for the Voice of Vocation* (San Francisco: Jossey Bass, 2000), 99.

3. Short texts that give excellent overview of the female genital surgeries issue are those by Efua Dorkenoo, *Cutting the Rose: Female Genital Mutilation* (London: Minority Rights Group, 1994), and Lillian Passmore Sanderson, *Against the Mutilation of Women: The Struggle to End Unnecessary Suffering* (London: Ithaca Press, 1981).

4. Aamina Warsame, Sadiya Ahmed, and Aud Talle, *Social and Cultural Aspects of Female Circumcision and Infibulation* (Mogadishu/Stockholm: Somali Academy of Sciences and Arts and Swedish Agency for Research Cooperation, 1985), 10–11, have noted that women see the prospect of defibulation as the second trauma in their sexual lives; many try to postpone consummation of a marriage by running away. The prevalence of routine episiotomies in the United States is also worth noting in this regard; see Robbie E. Davis-Floyd, "Gender and Ritual: Giving Birth the American Way," in *Gender in Cross-Cultural Perspective*, ed. Caroline B. Brettell and Carolyn F. Sargent (Upper Saddle River, N.J.: Prentice-Hall, 1997).

5. The psychological impacts of FGC seem to be analyzed very sparsely in the literature, which looks only at infibulation and notes a decline in self-confidence. Ahmed Ibrahim Ballal's *Psychological Effects of Female Circumcision* (New York: Vantage Press, 1992) falls into this category in looking only at women in Khartoum. He goes further, however, to exculpate men entirely by noting that men, whatever they say, "are

puppets in the hands of mothers and grandmothers" (33), and women can enjoy sex (not defined) after infibulation. See also Mahdi Ali Dirie, *Female Circumcision in Somalia: Medical and Social Implications* (Collaborative Report between SOMAC and SAREC, 1985), 9.

6. As Dirie aptly stated, "[T]radition as a reason does not explain the underlying motives, which first made the practice necessary and later allowed it to continue, hereby becoming 'traditional'" (*Female Circumcision*, 91). The best summations of justifications for FGC can be found in Olayinka Koso-Thomas, *The Circumcision of Women: A Strategy for Eradication* (London: Zed Press, 1987), 2–12; Sanderson, *Against the Mutilation of Women*, 46–52; and Dorkenoo, *Cutting the Rose*, 46.

7. Esther Hicks, *Infibulation: Female Mutilation in Islamic Northeastern Africa* (New Brunswick: Transaction Publishers, 1996), 8.

8. Jonathan P. Berkey, "Circumcision Circumscribed: Female Excision and Cultural Accommodation in the Medieval Near East," *International Journal of Middle East Studies* 28 (1996): 19–38. See also Dorkenoo, *Cutting the Rose*, 37, for an excellent discussion of arguments by Muslim scholars for and against FGC.

9. Dorkenoo's discussion of the different procedures belies the singularity that her title implies (*Cutting the Rose*, 5–6).

10. Emmanuel D. Babatunde, *Women's Rights versus Women's Rites: A Study of Circumcision among the Ketu Yoruba of South Western Nigeria* (Trenton: Africa World Press, 1998).

11. In Great Britain and the United States, the reasons for the practices were also various, whether as a cure for epilepsy, frigidity, masturbation, or nymphomania. In Russia it was part of a sectarian religious rite. Sanderson, *Against the Mutilation of Women*, 28–29; Raqiya Abdalla, *Sisters in Affliction: Circumcision and Infibulation of Women in Africa* (London: Zed Press, 1982), 60.

12. Katharine Park, "The Rediscovery of the Clitoris: French Medicine and the *Tribades*, 1570–1620," in *The Body in Parts: Fantasies of Corporeality in Early Modern Europe*, ed. David Hillman and Carla Mazzio (New York: Routledge, 1997), 186–87.

13. There is a long history of human societies using pain as a social mechanism to manipulate or transform identity or to induce spiritual revelations.

14. One of the key misrepresentations of clitoridectomy in Alice Walker's novel *Possessing the Secret of Joy* (New York: Harcourt Brace, 1992) is the solitary confinement of the chief character undergoing the rite. When performed properly, initiation rites were and are

normatively collective in nature, which makes them easier to modify than to eradicate. It may be that clitoridectomy, in some areas where initiation is disappearing, is left without its original context and collective aspects but has new meaning as an individual procedure, but we have no evidence to that effect.

15. Koso-Thomas, *The Circumcision of Women*, 21.
16. Christine J. Walley, "Searching for `Voices': Feminism, Anthropology, and the Global Debate over Female Genital Operations," chapter 1 in this volume. Claire Robertson found that older women among traders in Nairobi in 1987–88 invariably cited this time as the happiest in their lives and the most free.
17. Koso-Thomas, *The Circumcision of Women*, 23; Dorkenoo, *Cutting the Rose*, 40.
18. Robertson, "Grassroots in Kenya."
19. Claude Lévi-Strauss, *The Raw and the Cooked* (New York: Harper Torchbooks, 1969).

QUESTIONS

1. What types of female genital cutting (FGC) practiced in Africa are discussed by the authors? How do they differ from each other in terms of the surgical content, cultural significance, regions of practice and patterns of spread?
2. Why do the authors object to the use of terms like "female circumcision" and "female genital mutilation" in descriptions of the cutting of women's genitalia? What binaries are invoked by these dominant terminologies and critiqued in this article?
3. According to the author, how are Africa and African woman usually portrayed in popular Western perceptions? How is FGC constructed in these perceptions? Why do the authors link FGC to pediatric genital surgeries in the U.S.?
4. How does this article suggest that feminists approach the issue of FGC? How does this article illustrate their recommended approach?

THE GLOBETROTTING SNEAKER (1995)

Cynthia Enloe

Cynthia Enloe, professor of government at Clark University and author of The Morning After: Sexual Politics at the End of the Cold War, *discusses the production and marketing of the American athletic shoe and what it means for women workers in Asia. Companies like Nike and Reebok borrow the empowerment rhetoric of the U.S. women's movement to sell their product to women at home. At the same time, they abandon corporate responsibility for fair wages and safe working conditions for women workers abroad.*

Four years after the fall of the Berlin Wall marked the end of the Cold War, Reebok, one of the fastest growing companies in United States history, decided that the time had come to make its mark in Russia. Thus it was with considerable fanfare that Reebok's executives opened their first store in downtown Moscow in July 1993. A week after the grand opening, store managers described sales as well above expectations.

"The Globetrotting Sneaker," by Cynthia Enloe, from *Ms.* magazine, Vol. 5, No. 5, March/April 1995. Reprinted by permission of *Ms.* magazine,

Reebok's opening in Moscow was the perfect post-Cold War scenario: commercial rivalry replacing military posturing; consumerist tastes homogenizing heretofore hostile peoples; capital and managerial expertise flowing freely across newly porous state borders. Russians suddenly had the "freedom" to spend money on U.S. cultural icons like athletic footwear, items priced above and beyond daily subsistence: at the end of 1993, the average Russian earned the equivalent of $40 a month. Shoes on display were in the $100 range. Almost 60 percent of single parents, most of whom were women, were living in poverty. Yet in Moscow and Kiev, shoe promoters had begun targeting children, persuading them to pressure their mothers to spend money on stylish, Western sneakers. And as far as strategy goes, athletic shoe giants have, you might say, a good track record. In the U.S. many inner-city boys who see basketball as a "ticket out of the ghetto" have become convinced that certain brand-name shoes will give them an edge.

But no matter where sneakers are bought or sold, the potency of their advertising imagery has made it easy to ignore this mundane fact: Shaquille O'Neal's Reeboks are stitched by someone; Michael Jordan's Nikes are stitched by someone; so are your roommate's, so are your grandmother's. Those someones are women, mostly Asian women who are supposed to believe that their "opportunity" to make sneakers for U.S. companies is a sign of their country's progress—just as a Russian woman's chance to spend two months' salary on a pair of shoes for her child allegedly symbolizes the new Russia.

As the global economy expands, sneaker executives are looking to pay women workers less and less, even though the shoes that they produce are capturing an ever-growing share of the footwear market. By the end of 1993, sales in the U.S. alone had reached $11.6 billion. Nike, the largest supplier of athletic footwear in the world, posted a record $298 million profit for 1993—earnings that had nearly tripled in five years. And sneaker companies continue to refine their strategies for "global competitiveness"—hiring supposedly docile women to make their shoes, changing designs as quickly as we fickle customers change our tastes, and shifting factories from country to country as trade barriers rise and fall.

The logic of it all is really quite simple; yet trade agreements such as the North American Free Trade Agreement (NAFTA) and the General Agreement on Tariffs and Trade (GATT) are, of

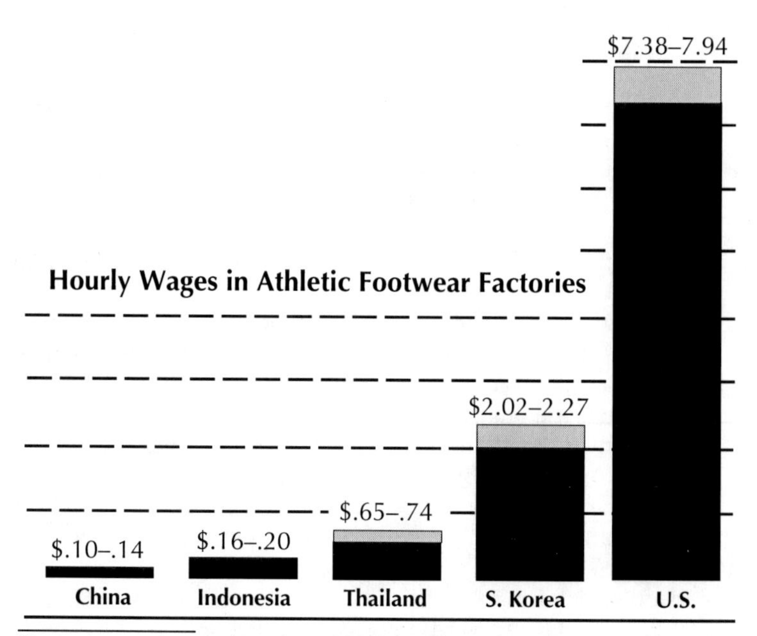

Figures are estimates based on 1993 data from the International Textile, Garment, and Leather Workers foundation; International Labor Organization; and the U.S. Bureau of Labor Statistics.

course, talked about in a jargon that alienates us, as if they were technical matters fit only for economists and diplomats. The bottom line is that all companies operating overseas depend on trade agreements made between their own governments and the regimes ruling the countries in which they want to make or sell their products. Korean, Indonesian, and other women workers around the world know this better than anyone. They are tackling trade politics because they have learned from hard experience that the trade deals their governments sign do little to improve the lives of workers. Guarantees of fair, healthy labor practices, of the rights to speak freely and to organize independently, will usually be left out of trade pacts—and women will suffer. The recent passage of both NAFTA and GATT ensures that a growing number of private companies will now be competing across borders without restriction. The result? Big business will step up efforts to pit working women in industrialized countries against much lower-paid working women in "developing" countries, perpetuating the misleading notion that they are inevitable rivals in the global job market.

All the "New World Order" really means to corporate giants like athletic shoemakers is that they now have the green light to accelerate long-standing industry practices. In the early 1980s, the field marshals commanding Reebok and Nike, which are both U.S.-based, decided to manufacture most of their sneakers in South Korea and Taiwan, hiring local women. L.A. Gear, Adidas, Fila, and Asics quickly followed their lead. In short time, the coastal city of Pusan, South Korea, became the "sneaker capital of the world." Between 1982 and 1989 the U.S. lost 58,500 footwear jobs to cities like Pusan, which attracted sneaker executives because its location facilitated international transport. More to the point, South Korea's military government had an interest in suppressing labor organizing, and it had a comfortable military alliance with the U.S. Korean women also seemed accepting of Confucian philosophy, which measured a woman's morality by her willingness to work hard for her family's well-being and to acquiesce to her father's and husband's dictates. With their sense of patriotic duty, Korean women seemed the ideal labor force for export-oriented factories.

U.S. and European sneaker company executives were also attracted by the ready supply of eager Korean male entrepreneurs with whom they could make profitable arrangements. This fact was central to Nike's strategy in particular. When they moved their production sites to Asia to lower labor costs, the executives of the Oregon-based company decided to reduce their corporate responsibilities further. Instead of owning factories outright, a more efficient strategy would be to subcontract the manufacturing to wholly foreign-owned—in this case, South Korean—companies. Let them be responsible for workers' health and safety. Let them negotiate with newly emergent unions. Nike would retain control over those parts of sneaker production that gave its officials the greatest professional satisfaction and the ultimate word on the product: design and marketing. Although Nike was following in the footsteps of garment and textile manufacturers, it set the trend for the rest of the athletic footwear industry.

But at the same time, women workers were developing their own strategies. As the South Korean pro-democracy movement grew throughout the 1980s, increasing numbers of women rejected traditional notions of feminine duty. Women began organizing in response to the dangerous working conditions, daily humiliations, and low pay built into their work. Such resistance was profoundly threatening to the government, given the fact that South Korea's emergence as an industrialized "tiger" had depended on women accepting their "role" in growing industries like sneaker manufacture. If women re-imagined their lives as daughters, as wives, as workers, as citizens, it wouldn't just rattle their employers; it would shake the very foundations of the whole political system.

At the first sign of trouble, factory managers called in government riot police to break up employees' meetings. Troops sexually assaulted women workers, stripping, fondling, and raping them "as a control mechanism for suppressing women's engagement in the labor movement," reported Jeong-Lim Nam of Hyosung Women's University in Taegu. It didn't work. It didn't work because the feminist activists in groups like the Korean Women Workers Association (KWWA) helped women understand and deal with the assaults. The KWWA held consciousness-raising sessions in which notions of feminine duty and respectability were tackled along with wages and benefits. They organized independently of the male-led labor unions to ensure that their issues would be taken seriously, in labor negotiations and in the pro-democracy movement as a whole.

The result was that women were at meetings with management, making sure that in addition to issues like long hours and low pay, sexual assault at the hands of managers and health care were on the table. Their activism paid off: in addition to winning the right to organize women's unions, their earnings grew. In 1980, South Korean women in manufacturing jobs earned 45 percent of the wages of their male counterparts; by 1990, they were earning more than 50 percent. Modest though it was, the pay increase was concrete progress, given that the gap between women's and men's manufacturing wages in Japan, Singapore, and Sri Lanka actually *widened* during the 1980s. Last but certainly not least, women's organizing was credited with playing a major role in toppling the country's military regime and forcing open elections in 1987.

Without that special kind of workplace control that only an authoritarian government could offer, sneaker executives knew that it was time to move. In Nike's case, its famous advertising slogan—"Just Do It"—proved truer to its corporate philosophy than its women's "empowerment" ad campaign, designed to rally women's athletic (and consumer) spirit. In response to South

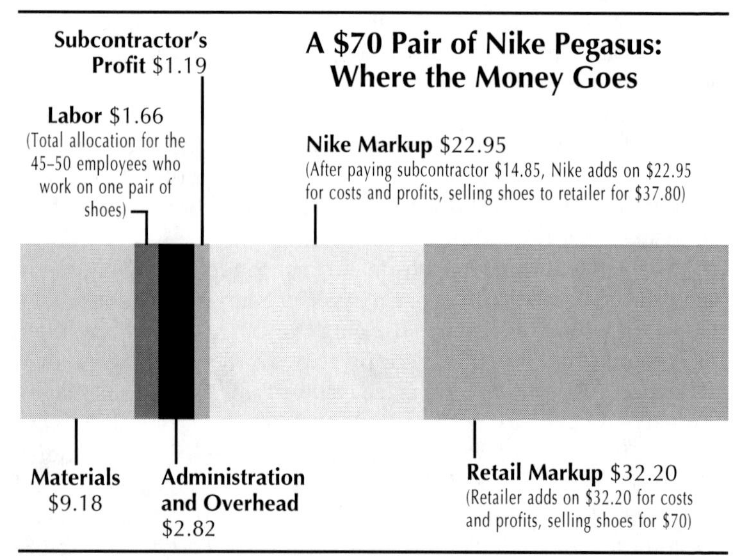

Source: Nike, Inc.

Korean women workers' newfound activist self-confidence, the sneaker company and its subcontractors began shutting down a number of their South Korean factories in the late 1980s and early 1990s. After bargaining with government officials in nearby China and Indonesia, many Nike subcontractors set up shop in those countries, while some went to Thailand. China's government remains nominally Communist; Indonesia's ruling generals are staunchly anti-Communist. But both are governed by authoritarian regimes who share the belief that if women can be kept hard at work, low paid, and unorganized, they can serve as a magnet for foreign investors.

Where does all this leave South Korean women—or any woman who is threatened with a factory closure if she demands decent working conditions and a fair wage? They face the dilemma confronted by thousands of women from dozens of countries. The risk of job loss is especially acute in relatively mobile industries; it's easier for a sneaker, garment, or electronics manufacturer to pick up and move than it is for an automaker or a steel producer. In the case of South Korea, poor women had moved from rural villages into the cities searching for jobs to support not only themselves, but parents and siblings. The exodus of manufacturing jobs has forced more women into the growing "entertainment" industry. The kinds of bars and massage parlors offering sexual services that had mushroomed around U.S. military bases during the Cold War have been opening up across the country.

But the reality is that women throughout Asia are organizing, knowing full well the risks involved. Theirs is a long-term view; they are taking direct aim at companies' nomadic advantage, by building links among workers in countries targeted for "development" by multinational corporations. Through sustained grassroots efforts, women are developing the skills and confidence that will make it increasingly difficult to keep their labor cheap. Many looked to the United Nations conference on women in Beijing, China as a rare opportunity to expand their cross-border strategizing.

The Beijing conference will also provide an important opportunity to call world attention to the hypocrisy of the governments and corporations doing business in China. Numerous athletic shoe companies followed Nike in setting up manufacturing sites throughout the country. This included Reebok—a company claiming its share of responsibility for ridding the world of "injustice, poverty, and other ills that gnaw away at the social fabric," according to a statement of corporate principles.

Since 1988, Reebok has been giving out annual human rights awards to dissidents from around the world. But it wasn't until 1992 that the company adopted its own "human rights production standards"—after labor advocates made it known that the quality of life in factories run by its subcontractors was just as dismal as that at most other athletic shoe suppliers in Asia. Reebok's code of conduct, for example, includes a pledge to "seek" those subcontractors who respect workers' rights to organize. The only problem is that independent trade unions are banned in China. Reebok has chosen to ignore that fact, even though Chinese dissidents have been the recipients of the company's own human rights award. As for working conditions, Reebok now says it sends its own inspectors to production sites a couple of times a year. But they have easily "missed" what subcontractors are trying to hide—like 400 young women workers locked at night into an overcrowded dormitory near a Reebok-contracted factory in the town of Zhuhai, as reported last August in the *Asian Wall Street Journal Weekly*.

Nike's co-founder and CEO Philip Knight has said that he would like the world to think of Nike as "a company with a soul that recognizes the value of human beings." Nike, like Reebok, says it sends in inspectors from time to time to check up on work conditions at its factories; in Indonesia, those factories are run largely by South Korean subcontractors. But according to Donald Katz in a recent book on the company, Nike spokesman Dave Taylor told an in-house newsletter that the factories are "[the subcontractors'] business to run." For the most part, the company relies on regular reports from subcontractors regarding its "Memorandum of Understanding," which managers must sign, promising to impose "local government standards" for wages, working conditions, treatment of workers, and benefits.

The minimum wage in the Indonesian capital of Jakarta is $1.89 *a day*—among the highest in a country where the minimum wage varies by region. And managers are required to pay only 75 percent of the wage directly; the remainder can be withheld for "benefits." By now, Nike has a well-honed response to growing criticism of its low-cost labor strategy. Such wages should not be seen as exploitative, says Nike, but rather as the first rung on the ladder of economic opportunity that Nike has extended to workers with few options. Otherwise, they'd be out "harvesting coconut meat in the tropical sun," wrote Nike spokesman Dusty Kidd, in a letter to the *Utne Reader*. The all-is-relative response craftily shifts attention away from reality: Nike didn't move to Indonesia to help Indonesians; it moved to ensure that its profit margin continues to grow. And that is pretty much guaranteed in a country where "local standards" for wages rarely take a worker over the poverty line. A 1991 survey by the International Labor Organization (ILO) found that 88 percent of women working at the Jakarta minimum wage at the time—slightly less than a dollar a day—were malnourished.

A woman named Riyanti might have been among the workers surveyed by the ILO. Interviewed by *The Boston Globe* in 1991, she told the reporter who had asked about her long hours and low pay: "I'm happy working here. . . . I can make money and I can make friends." But in fact, the reporter discovered that Riyanti had already joined her coworkers in two strikes, the first to force one of Nike's Korean subcontractors to accept a new women's union and the second to compel managers to pay at least the minimum wage. That Riyanti appeared less than forthcoming about her activities isn't surprising. Many Indonesian factories have military men posted in their front offices who find no fault with managers who tape women's mouths shut to keep them from talking among themselves. They and their superiors have a political reach that extends far beyond the barracks. Indonesia has all the makings for a political explosion, especially since the gap between rich and poor is widening into a chasm. It is in this setting that the government has tried to crack down on any independent labor organizing—a policy that Nike has helped to implement. Referring to a recent strike in a Nike-contracted factory, Tony Nava, Nike representative in Indonesia, told *The Chicago Tribune* in November 1994 that the "troublemakers" had been fired. When asked about Nike policy on the issue, spokesman Keith Peters struck a conciliatory note: "If the government were to allow and encourage independent labor organizing, we would be happy to support it."

Indonesian workers' efforts to create unions independent of governmental control were a surprise to shoe companies. Although their moves from South Korea have been immensely profitable [see chart, previous page], they do not have the sort of immunity from activism that they had expected. In May 1993, the murder of a female labor activist outside Surabaya set off a storm of local and international protest. Even the U.S. State Department was forced to take note in its 1993 worldwide human rights report, describing a system similar to that which generated South Korea's boom 20 years earlier: severely restricted union organizing, security forces used to break up strikes, low wages for men, lower wages for women—complete with government rhetoric celebrating women's contribution to national development.

Yet when President Clinton visited Indonesia, he made only a token effort to address the country's human rights problem. Instead, he touted the benefits of free trade, sounding indeed more enlightened, more in tune with the spirit of the post-Cold War era than do those defenders of protectionist trading policies who coat their rhetoric with "America first" chauvinism. But "free trade" as actually being practiced today is hardly *free* for any workers—in the U.S. or abroad—who have to accept the Indonesian, Chinese, or Korean workplace model as the price of keeping their jobs.

The not-so-new plot of the international trade story has been "divide and rule." If women workers and their government in one country can see that a sneaker company will pick up and leave if their labor demands prove more costly than those in a neighbor country, then women workers will tend to see their neighbors not as regional sisters, but as competitors who can steal their precarious livelihoods. Playing women off against each other is, of course, old hat. Yet it is as essential to international trade politics as is the fine print in GATT.

But women workers allied through networks like the Hong Kong-based Committee for Asian Women are developing their own post-Cold War foreign policy, which means addressing women's needs: how to convince fathers and husbands that a woman going out to organizing meetings at night is not sexually promiscuous; how to develop workplace agendas that respond to family needs; how to work with male unionists who push women's demands to the bottom of their lists; how to build a global movement.

These women refused to stand in awe of the corporate power of the Nike or Reebok or Adidas executive. Growing numbers of Asian women today have concluded that trade politics have to be understood by women on their own terms. They came to Beijing in September 1996, ready to engage with women from other regions to link the politics of consumerism with the politics of manufacturing. If women in Russia and eastern Europe can challenge Americanized consumerism, if Asian activists can solidify their alliances, and if U.S. women can join with them by taking on trade politics—the post-Cold War sneaker may be a less comfortable fit in the 1990s.

QUESTIONS

1. According to Enloe, why do trade deals between countries do little to improve the lives of workers? How are women pitted against each other in the global competition for expanding markets and cheap labor? What factors keep women's labor cheap?

2. Describe the working conditions for those who produce the shoes. How are women and human rights advocates organizing to end harmful labor practices? What are the risks and benefits for working women? How are the companies responding?

3. Why are consumers at home and abroad willing to pay so much for shoes? Where does the money go? What are some of the contradictions involved in Nike's support for women's athletics?

The Feminization of Immigration (1996)

National Council for Research on Women

Global economic shifts have thrown enormous numbers of women into migrant work in factories or as domestics. Immigrant women—often women of color—are scapegoated in ways similar to "welfare queens" because of the belief that immigrants drain more resources than they provide. In the following 1996 article, anthropologist Lorraine Kenny examines this belief, suggesting that the United States has always been deeply dependent on immigrant labor. Kenny, a guest faculty member at Sarah Lawrence College, is the author of the forthcoming Daughters of Suburbia: Growing Up White, Middle-Class and Female *(1998).*

Give us your tired, your hungry, your poor, no more.

Among their election strategies, proponents of California's "Save Our State" initiative deployed the image of a young, brown-skinned, pregnant, single mother from Mexico living ille-

"The Feminization of Immigration," by the National Council for Research on Women, from *Issues Quarterly,* Vol. 1, No. 3, 1996. Reprinted with permission of the National Council for Research on Women.

gally in the barrios of Los Angeles, sending her children to public schools, and making her way to the state-funded health clinic for free prenatal care.

The approach worked.

Californians passed the initiative, Proposition 187, by a three-to-two margin. Whites constituted 75 percent of the voting electorate, which cast its ballots in favor of cutting off social services like schooling and nonemergency medical care to undocumented immigrants and their children.[1]

Why was the *idea* of this immigrant woman and her children so effective in getting out the vote?

Pierrette Hondagneu-Sotelo, author of *Gendered Transitions: Mexican Experiences of Immigration,* contends that the recent anti-immigration campaign in California and in the nation at large scapegoats women because women are key players in settling and building communities. "The xenophobia of the early '80s focused on labor, while the more recent backlash against immigrants focuses on reproduction, or everything it takes to bring a new generation into the labor force," says Hondagneu-Sotelo.

Since the passage of the first immigration restrictions in the late nineteenth century, immigration opponents in the U.S. have blamed "unchecked" immigration for the country's so-called overpopulation and the depletion of its social and natural resources. One such group, the Federation for American Immigration Reform (FAIR), played a significant role in promoting California's Proposition 187 and in fostering similar anti-immigrant forces in other states, including Florida, Arizona, and Texas. Founded in 1979 by the former president of Zero Population Growth, John Tanton, FAIR is a national educational and lobbying network "concerned with the adverse effects of out-of-control immigration." The group believes that immigration causes overpopulation, which in turn encroaches on the country's fragile coastal wetlands and consumes its prime farmlands. Likewise, immigration fuels unemployment, depresses wages, and overburdens the U.S.'s "sophisticated social safety net."[2] With a membership of over 50,000, FAIR is living proof that "invasion rhetoric" sells.

Who overpopulates a nation more than an influx of young, nonwhite women? Or so the argument goes.

The Immigration Reform and Control Act (IRCA) of 1986 ostensibly sought to limit immigration in the name of safeguarding jobs for U.S.-born laborers by penalizing employers who hire undocumented workers. However, efforts by a strong agricultural lobby saw to it that their sector of the workforce, the mostly male Mexican and Central American seasonal employees, could now apply for permanent resident status under a Special Agricultural Workers provision. As a result of what amounted to IRCA's gender-biased amnesty program, more Mexican women and their children began to cross the border without legal authorization.[3] Some came to join their newly legalized husbands and fathers and some to fill the growing demand for female workers in the hidden service economy.

The Immigration and Naturalization Service (INS) calculates that between 1980 and 1990, the total population of unauthorized immigrants in the U.S. hovered at 2.6 million, and following the 1986 IRCA amnesty program, the total number of unauthorized immigrants in California decreased. As such, an INS report concludes, "Population size is not the primary reason for the greater concern about unauthorized immigrants . . . in California in 1994."[4]

Likewise, it is not true that immigrants drain more than they contribute to the economy. Recent Urban Institute studies show that immigrants pay significantly more in taxes than they cost in services: when all is said and done, they generate a $25 to $30 billion annual net surplus.[5] Similarly, immigrants create more jobs than they take. And as factory workers, housekeepers, and home-based child-care and health-care providers, immigrants fill low-wage, no-benefits jobs that the native population doesn't want, while providing needed services that substantially contribute to middle-class quality of life. Researchers also project that as baby boomers come of age and start to cash in on their entitlements, employed young-adult immigrants will ultimately keep the Social Security system solvent.[6]

So what's really going on? Why all the public outcry over immigration, and why are women bearing the brunt of the attacks?

"The easiest thing for a politician to do is blame immigrant women and children because they don't vote," says Wendy Walker-Moffat, author of the forthcoming *The Other Side of the Asian American Academic Success Story*. Walker-Moffat suggests that singling out women in the anti-immigration/social services debate masks the real problem: the graying of America. The Center on Budget and Policy Priorities in Washington, D.C., reports that in 1993, nearly two-thirds of the federal Medicaid budget underwrote the costs of providing health care to the elderly. In 1994, the Congressional Budget Office estimated that cutting off Medicaid to immigrants would only save the federal government 2 billion dollars in a budget that nears 100 billion. In light of these numbers and the fact that the elderly represent a solid and consistent voting bloc, targeting immigrant women and children is politically expedient.

Class Comforts

Ironically, immigrant women increasingly care for our aging population as well as our children through informal, private-sector employment. While recent U.S. Department of Labor statistics show a shrinking pool of domestic workers—942,000 in 1983 to 755,000 in 1991—they also show a rise in the number of women working. In 1991, nearly two-thirds of all women age 16 and over were in the labor force; in 1992, more than 16 million mothers with pre-school children worked full time.[7] Such figures beg the question: Who is home cleaning the house, making the meals, and taking care of the kids?

The "Nannygate" scandal of 1993—set off when a congressional committee discovered that Clinton's first nominee for attorney general, Zoë Baird, had hired two illegal Peruvian immigrants to work in her home—vividly answered the question. The International Labour Office estimates that more than 350,000 illegal immigrant women work as domestics in the current U.S. market.[8] Though these women are ultimately statistically invisible, the effects of their labor are more than apparent in the lives of professional families throughout the U.S.

Among legal immigrants, women significantly outnumbered their male compatriots in 1993 for the first time since the early 1980s. A study by the Rand Corporation attributes this recent demographic shift to the fact that women can now easily find jobs in the unregulated private sector.[9] Like their illegal sisters, documented women domestics remain hidden from government statisticians because many of their employers pay them under the table and do not pay Social Security taxes on their wages.

What is known about the last decade paints a polarized picture of the U.S. economy. The Women's Bureau of the U.S. Department of Labor documents that though women's overall earnings grew faster than men's, the number of women living in poverty skyrocketed and the disparity between white and black workers of either gender also grew. "What's true in today's economy is a greater inequality of income among women. Anytime you create a situation where rich women can buy poor women's labor, you create divisions among women," cautions economist Nancy Folbre.

The Center for Immigrants Rights (CIR) in New York City is one of several organizations around the country that advocates for immigrant household workers through its Workers' Rights Project. "This is a worldwide women's issue, for household workers are increasingly immigrant women from the Caribbean, from Eastern Europe, Central America, and the Philippines. For these women work, any kind of work in the developed world, still means a step up, from the limited opportunities at home," argues Ursula Levelt, director of education at CIR.[10] Through a joint project with NOW Legal Defense and Education Fund, "Nannies, Caretakers, Housekeepers: You Have Rights!," CIR distributes information to immigrant women and their employers about domestic-workers' rights under U.S. immigration and labor laws.

The Global Picture

As Levelt suggests, women's immigration experiences in the U.S. are part of a complex global story that has been in the making for some time. The international debt crisis; trade agreements; foreign assistance programs; the end of the cold war; civil, ethnic, and religious strife; government-sponsored human rights violations; famine; AIDS and other infectious diseases; floods, earthquakes, and massive fires; industrial disasters; overpopulation; and economic inflations, recessions, and embargoes have all set the stage for an unprecedented number of people to leave their homes in pursuit of safety, economic stability, and cultural freedoms. The Women's Commission for Refugee Women and Children reports that in 1993, 80 percent of the world's 44 million refugees were women and their dependent children either displaced within their own countries or compelled by dire living conditions to migrate across international borders.[11]

A statement issued by the 1994 American Assembly on World Migration and U.S. Policy, "Threatened Peoples, Threatened Borders," notes that during the cold war, U.S. migration policy intended to stabilize "friendly" governments like El Salvador and destabilize "unfriendly" ones, like Cuba.[12] Recent U.S. military interventions in Haiti, along with the Clinton administration's struggle to rescue Mexico's plummeting currency and its failed attempts to leverage peace treaties and work with UN forces in the former Yugoslavia, underscore the degree to which the U.S. still bears considerable responsibility for fostering or disrupting global stability in the post-cold war era.

U.S. domestic and foreign policies play an instrumental role in setting international populations in motion—a fact largely missing from current state and federal immigration debates. "We have chosen to not view ourselves as part of the international situation," says Wendy Walker-Moffat. Such blind spots make it easier to scapegoat certain groups of people rather than address the larger national and global policy issues.

Where Do We Go From Here?

Given that the world has undergone major political and social shifts since the U.S. last recast its immigration policies in 1986 and 1990, it is not surprising that the nation is currently embroiled in a battle over whom to welcome and how to welcome them. The legacy of U.S. immigration policy is deeply entrenched in racial, ethnic, class, and gender battles. Starting with the Chinese Exclusion Act of 1882, immigration legislation ebbed and flowed around national-origins quotas and prohibitions, until the 1965 Immigration and Nationality Act made it illegal to base INS policy on nationality, race, or ancestry. As current anti-immigrant forces increasingly hold pregnant immigrant women and their children responsible for the nation's woes, it becomes clear that race, ethnicity, class, and gender still motivate the discussion. Congressional leaders underscore this connection in their strident calls for cutting welfare benefits to immigrant *and* low-income women of color.

Organizations throughout the country are starting to forge links between immigrant populations and U.S.-born communities of color. For example, the Filipina Career Awareness Program in Union City, CA, partners immigrant with U.S.-born Filipina girls to strengthen the leadership, academic, and social skills of girls in both groups. The new Workers' Center Movement unifies immigrant and nonimmigrant workers around labor and community concerns. "The Workers' Center model functions across racial, ethnic, and regional differences. It allows for diversity," explains JoAnn Lum of the Chinese Workers' Association in New York City's Chinatown. Leni Marin of the Family Violence Prevention Fund in San Francisco reports that the battered immigrant women's provision made it into the 1994 Violence Against Women's Act because immigrant-rights and anti-domestic violence advocates worked together. And, in the wake of the passage of Proposition 187, immigrant advocacy organizations and progressive social service groups in California are shoring up their joint opposition to welfare reform proposals currently making their way through Congress. These and other programs underscore the fact that the immigration debate is as much about community issues and values as it is about the economy, legislation, and the INS. As Pierrette Hondagneu-Sotelo asserts, "Political and economic transformations may set the stage for migration, but they do not write the script."[13] How factory-owners and professional families treat the immigrant women they employ affects the day-to-day lives of individual women workers as well as public perceptions of immigrants and immigration. Likewise, understanding how the national discussion positions immigrant women as the literal and figurative bearers of culture makes it clear that the current anti-immigration fervor is not just about demographics and labor markets; it is about how we see ourselves as a nation at home and abroad.

NOTES

1. B. Drummond Ayres Jr., "Californians Pass Measure on Aliens; Courts Bar It," *New York Times*, Thursday, November 10, 1994: B7.

2. Federation for American Immigration Reform, "Are You Concerned About Immigration? You Should Be." Brochure.

3. Pierrette Hondagneu-Sotelo, *Gendered Transitions: Mexican Experi-*

ences of Immigration (Berkeley: University of California Press, 1994), 26.

4. Robert Warren, "Estimates of the Unauthorized Immigrant Population Residing in the United States, by Country of Origin and State of Residence: October 1992." Immigration and Naturalization Services, Statistics Division, April 29, 1994. Photocopy, 23, 21.

5. "A Sourcebook for the Immigration Debate," *Urban Institute Policy and Research Report*, volume 24, number 2 (Summer 1994): 21.

6. David E. Hayes-Bautista, Werner O. Schink, and Jorge Chapa, *The Burden of Support: Young Latinos in an Aging Society* (Stanford, CA: Stanford University Press, 1988).

7. U.S. Department of Labor, Women's Bureau, *1993 Handbook on Women Workers: Trends & Issues* (Washington, D.C.: U.S. Department of Labor, 1994), 19, 1.

8. Peter Stalker, *The Work of Strangers: A Survey of International Labour Migration* (Geneva, Switzerland: International Labour Office, 1994), 149.

9. Frank D. Bean, Barry Edmonston, Jeffrey S. Passel, *Undocumented Migration to the United States: IRCA and the Experience of the 1980s* (Santa Monica, CA: Rand Corporation, 1990).

10. Ursula Levelt, "Household Work: The Oldest Sweatshop," *Women & Philanthropy News*, volume 17, number 3 (Fall/Winter 1994): S4.

11. Women's Commission for Refugee Women and Children, *Annual Report 1993*, 2. According to the United Nations high commissioner for Refugees, in the 1970s there were approximately 2.7 million refugees worldwide, and in the 1980s, 8.2 million. Sima Wali, "Developing Gender-Based Program and Donor Policies as if Refugee and Displaced Women Mattered," (Washington, D.C.: Refugee Women in Development, 1994). Photocopy, 1.

12. *Threatened Peoples, Threatened Borders: World Migration and U.S. Policy.* Final report of the 86th American Assembly, (November 10–13, 1994), 8.

13. Hondagneu-Sotelo, 187.

QUESTIONS

1. Why are immigrant women and children targeted in the

debate over immigration restriction?

2. How does immigrant women's employment contribute to differences between women?

3. What does employers' treatment of immigrant factory workers and domestics say about U.S. cultural values? Could public policy be used to improve the situation of recent immigrants and, if so, how?

The Deportation of Barbie from Iran (1999)

Farzaneh Milani

Like fast food and Gap jeans, the Barbie doll has gone global—but you won't find her in Iran. Although this 11 inch American plastic doll adorns store shelves in more than 140 countries, she was recently "deported" from Iran because her Western wardrobe and makeup conflicts with traditional Islamic values, according to Iranian authorities. Since 1979, Iran has been governed according to a strict interpretation of Muslim law—that is, by Islamic fundamentalism. Like many parts of the world, it views it necessary to resist and counter the dominant influence of Western materialism and values. Thus, as Milani argues, even dolls are powerful bearers of symbolic meanings about culture and gender. We can see this cultural clash over meanings in different interpretations of the practice of veiling, which Westerners often view as a symbol of Islamic women's oppression, but Islamic authorities

"The Deportation of Barbie from Iran," by Farzaneh Milani, from *Iris,* 1999.

believe frees Islamic women from the obsession with physical looks, fashion and thinness that so plagues women in the West.

With much fanfare and publicity, the Islamic Republic of Iran recently deported Barbie. Considered a serious threat to Islamic values, Barbie was compared to a "Trojan Horse" by Majid Ghaderi, the Director of the Recreation Department at the government-sponsored Institute for the Intellectual Development of Children and Young Adults. "She carries her Western cultural influences such as makeup and indecent clothes," said Mr. Ghaderi. "Barbie is an American woman who never wants to get pregnant and have babies. She never wants to look old. These contradict our culture. . . . Once she infiltrates our society, she will affect our children."[1]

Mr. Fitzgerald, the Vice President of Mattel Corporation, Barbie's manufacturer, has a different version of the story. In answer to my personal query, he wrote, on May 21, 1997, that his company has "purposefully chosen not to enter" the Iranian market. "As Barbie represents freedom of expression, individuality and self-determination for girls and women," claimed Mr. Fitzgerald, "the brand is in direct conflict to the religious teachings of those countries. In deference to those teachings, Mattel has elected not to sell Barbie in fundamentalist Islamic countries. As with many other U.S.-based multi-national companies, there are a variety of reasons beyond Barbie's brand identity that comprise our decision not to conduct business of any kind in Iran."

Be that as it may, the Institute has promised to replace Barbie with its own indigenous doll by the end of the year. Sara, as she is called, is "properly" attired young woman who wears no makeup and has long, flowing clothes. A Chador—the all encompassing veil—covers her hair and her body. What Barbie displays, Sara encloses. If Barbie's companion is her boyfriend, Ken, Sara is accompanied—or rather, chaperoned—by a family member, her brother, Dara. If Barbie is obsessed with clothes, looks, and thinness, Sara, it is claimed by the Institute, can develop her mind and be accepted for who she is rather than how she looks. If Barbie wears makeup and indecent clothes, Sara is a symbol of modesty and morality.

What, we might ask ourselves, is so dangerous about an eleven-and-a-half-inch plastic doll? If Barbie is viewed as an agent of corruption, why replace her with another adult-bodied doll rather than the baby doll little girls traditionally play with? Had Sara been younger than nine—when traditionally Muslim girls have to start covering themselves—she would not have needed to veil herself. Or, if Barbie is criticized because of her obsession with youth, why not replace her with an old Sara? If Barbie promotes ageism and sexism, the belief that a woman's young body is her most valuable asset, why focus attention on the young body—albeit covered—of Sara? If Barbie does not invoke the maternal, how does Sara embody motherhood? Why, indeed, bother with a doll, even if it is the most popular toy ever created?

Part of the answer must surely lie in the fact that as bearers of symbolic meanings, dolls can and do play important and varied roles in cultural politics—as religious icons, as means to disseminate values, beliefs, and attitudes. They can serve ritualistic and ceremonial functions. Dolls are cultural symbols, and political battles have been "fought over and through the manipulation of cultural symbols. People use them to signal political identities, to effect political coalitions, to disrupt and challenge beliefs and connections that have come to seem natural."[2] Dolls have functioned as a screen upon which to project dreams and nightmares and I would like to use them as tools to meditate on power relations. Indeed, the sociopolitical circumstances of the attempted—even though still unrealized—replacement of Barbie with Sara not only yield insights about the cultural and political conflicts between Iran and America, they also provide an opportunity to study the centrality of gender relations in contemporary Iran.

Ever since she entered the international market in 1961 when she was exhibited in a showcase of American toy products in London, Barbie has attained quasi-mythic dimensions throughout the world. She has come to be a symbol of American culture and America's most popular female icon. She has become a global space-age goddess, inspiring numerous poems, short stories, vignettes, sculptures, portraits, and exhibitions. She has her own personal museum—the Barbie Hall of Fame in Palo Alto, California. She commands a devoted army of experts, dealers, restorers, auctioneers, appraisers, and groupies in various parts of the world. She also threatens a sizable battalion of adversaries who are as interested in her as her admirers. A growing publishing industry revolves around her. Her authorized and unauthorized biographies abound. Oral-history projects, documentary films, and scholarly books on her proliferate. Barbie enjoys an unprecedented popularity which cannot be explained in marketing terms. She must have touched a nerve not only locally but also globally. Modeled after Lilli, a voluptuous German sex doll for adult men which itself was based on a playgirl character in a cartoon series, Barbie, whose proportions if life-size would be 36–18–33, has invaded the international toy market.

Sold in more than 140 countries, Barbie has assumed more than forty nationalities and many more ethnicities. This commodification of ethnic diversity has not displaced the white, blonde, American Barbie who remains the norm, the standard of beauty, the ideal of femininity. The "Barbie Look" continues to be a rigidly defined Euro-American standard of beauty. Sara's veiling, one might argue then, democratizes beauty in the sense that it promotes diversity and views an ethnic look as attractive. After all, Barbie's multi-cultural and multi-ethnic wardrobe has never included the veil. Ann DuCille astutely has remarked that the "rainbow coalition of colors, races, ethnicities, and nationalities" of Barbie dolls are "remarkably like the stereotypical white Barbie, modified only by a dash of color and a change of clothes."[3] Has the veil, even as a garment, as a simple change of clothes and marketing strategy, as an effort to merchandise difference, proven to be inappropriate for Barbie?

Sara's differences from Barbie are mainly articulated through her different body semantics. Through the symbolism of her veiling, a distinct and modern Islamic/Iranian identity is reconstructed at the transnational level: an identity that rejects the universalism and homogenizing forces of Western modernity and asserts Islamic/Iranian difference. Sara's veiling represents a community striving to define itself as a cohesive religious entity. For the veil is one of the most politicized symbols of Islamic movements today. It has become a badge of Islamic identity, a flag, a line of demarcation separating "us" from "them," a no-trespassing sign delineating protected space and property. Woman's veiled body has become the emblem of an Islamic society built upon the ruins of a decayed, "westernized" one. As the protected core of the community, it has come to represent the symbolic attempts of the society to protect its culture, its history, its tradition, its independence.

Before contemporary Islamic movements adopted the veil as a badge of their identity, it was considered the most defining feature of the Islamic world in the West. Actually, Zoraida is the first and the prototype of the veiled Muslim woman who appeared on the Western literary scene in Cervantes' *Don Quixote.* Prior to her, none of the Muslim women protagonists of European Medieval and early Renaissance literature—and there are many of them—were either veiled or submissive.[4] For the last four centuries, however, the veil has sealed Muslim women in an image of essential difference. It has embodied otherness. This restrictive stereotype has fixed a perpetually shifting reality. For veiling is a context-bound institution. It is neither monolithic nor homogeneous. It cannot be understood without taking the issues of time, place, class, gender, and power into account. Although veiling has an amazingly rich range of meanings and implications, it has suffered a shrinking of definitions in the West. According to Webster's *Thesaurus* "masking, disguising, concealing, hiding, and camouflaging" are some of its synonyms. All of these words share one basic premise: the prevention of transparency. But there is no real nakedness, and transparency is an illusion that refuses to be called what it is. Self, like an onion, has many layers. We gradually peel off one layer to find yet another. The more skin we peel off, it seems, the more there is to peel off. We reject and cling to the veil simultaneously. We cast aside one veil as we weave another. There is always another veil—visible or invisible—to rend.

Although there is no conclusive evidence to indicate when and where veiling originated, we do know that it predates Islam and was a mark of distinction reserved for women of the court and high aristocracy. The Islamic veil, like the pre-Islamic practice, was also originally a mark of distinction and social rank. Verse 59 of Chapter 33 of the Qurían marks Muslim women as members of a new elite: "O Prophet! Say to thy wives and daughters and the believing women, that they draw their veils close to them; so it is likelier they will be known, and not hurt." Veiling was considered such a privileged prerogative of the elite that at times marginalized groups were officially discriminated against by being prevented from veiling.

The function of clothing in Islam, for men and women alike, is, generally speaking, not to display the body, but to conceal it. Even in the Islamic paradisaical order, Adam and Eve are covered.

The Qurianic story of the Fall from the Garden of Eden best exemplifies this point. Verse 115 of chapter 20 reads: "He brought your parents out of the Garden, stripping them of their garments to show them their shameful parts." Nakedness was a punishment for the fallen Adam and Eve. In the Christian version of this story, the original couple are naked in the garden and must cover themselves on expulsion. Although the conclusion is the same for both versions—covering is mandatory in a fallen world—the ideal state for the Christian seems to be uncovered, and for the Muslim, covered. Accordingly, the Persian word "Pushidan" means to cover up, to conceal from view, whereas its English equivalent, "to dress," means, among other things, to decorate, to adorn.

With the veil as her most defining feature, Sara is an adult-bodied doll, utilized as a valuable transmitter of religious/cultural norms and political messages. Islamic laws, however, do not encourage human representation and the use of the human figure for indoctrination by the Islamic Republic of Iran is surely fascinating. Customarily, the clergy has relied on words and the authority of received texts to promote Islamic values and to regulate the community of believers. A doll, an adult-bodied doll at that, as an agent of persuasion and symbol of national identity is indeed a novelty. Sara is not only a bearer but a maker of meanings in Iran's turbulent political scene. She is neither secluded nor erased from the field of visibility. She is not concealed from view by walls, closed doors, and codes of sex-segregation.

Sara has become a member of "the national family" and this gives her a place in the public eye. With this expansion of "domestic" boundaries, with this shifting meaning of the veil, Sara is neither eliminated from the public scene nor relegated to the domain of the private. She has a public presence and her veil does not impose anonymity. As a matter of fact, it has developed new connotations of its own, quite different from the traditional notions. The equation veiled=silent=absent no longer applies to Sara. Her symbolically charged veil does not exclude her from the public. It does not shield her from the public gaze. On the contrary, it marks her as a political agent of historical and cultural significance—nationally and internationally. Sara's veil affords her political and cultural options outside the traditional domain of women—the home. This redefinition of the veil from tool of segregation to vehicle of desegregation is surely revolutionary.

The banning of Barbie and her replacement by Sara, however, is not only an assertion of local values and ideals by the Islamic Republic of Iran. It is also closely connected to dramas currently unfolding within Iranian society. It is another manifestation of intense ideological anxieties pertaining to questions of national identity, the reclamation of an indigenous culture, and about the (real or imagined) eroding authority of Iranian men. In other words, Barbie is another site upon which Iran's internal conflicts could be played out. After all, it is easy to blame her, to expel her, to reject her. She is from a distant land, and can be more readily lambasted and disposed of.

Although the castigation of Barbie is a recent development in Iran, the vilification of the "Western doll" is nothing new. In the 1940s any Iranian woman who was condemned for imitating the West was labeled a "Western Doll." Originally a compliment for a woman endowed with much beauty, "Western Doll" became a term of insult. Not only the religious fanatics but also the revolutionaries, the royalists, the rightists, and the leftists vented their anger against this domestic enemy. Implicitly, and at times quite explicitly, the ills of the society were all blamed on her. She personified the pollution of native and authentic culture. She was viewed as the potential or actual fifth column, a tool of imperialist conspiracies, the primary accomplice of the superpowers that exploited Iran. Considered a fatal threat to Irano-Islamic culture, she was accused of national infidelity.

With gusto and passion, many writers, philosophers, and social critics wrote about this mutant character. Ali Shari'ati, a Western-educated intellectual and considered by many the ideologue of the Islamic Revolution, found her appalling. "These Western Dolls," he wrote, "empty-headed, made-up and masked, neither have the feelings of our own women of yesteryear nor the intelligence of Western women of today. They are mechanical dolls which are neither Adam nor Eve! . . . They are a hodgepodge kind of woman, assembled in local industries with a made in Europe sticker."[5] This bad imitation of the West, this unauthentic replica of traditional Iranian women—this hybrid, this made-up doll—personified the painful loss of cultural identity. Hard to control, define, and immobilize, she became the emblem of threatening changes in the social organization of gender relations in Iran. Blurred now was the boundary between masculine and feminine, and blurred with it, too, was any sense of stability.

Shari'ati's nostalgia for a past when authentic feminine identity and values were not compromised, when women were "women," exemplifies the sense of loss that permeates the works of many mid-twentieth-century Iranian writers—men and women alike. According to many critics the degeneracy of Iranian culture was brought about by this new "Westernized," "half-naked," that is, unveiled, woman. They attacked this "Western Doll" with openly sexual language. Time and again, they portrayed her as sexually promiscuous, an easy prey, open to alien "penetration." Her "uncovered," hence, "uncontained," body became synonymous and licentiousness. Soon this violated (and violating) woman became the paradigm of Iran, the country, the motherland, the pure mother, and Iranian men became the emasculated sons who could not protect the mother. This masculinization of the West became a real challenge to the manliness of Iranian men who were forced constantly to prove themselves, their bearing, their control.

Persian narratives of the last few decades are saturated with the theme of imperiled manhood. A sizable body of literature decried the "dishonored man," the soft male, the womanly man. It lamented the sharp decline in the old and cherished ideals of masculinity. From Muslim clergy to secularist writers to politicians and scholars, men and women warned against this unfortunate decay. In his pioneering book, *Possessed by Western Culture,* published in 1947, Seyed Fakhr-ed-din Shadman, a prolific writer and politician, portrayed a pathetic image of effeminate Iranian men. In *Persian Requiem,* the most popular Iranian novel by Iran's first woman novelist, published in 1964, the author, Simin Daneshvar, mourned the "castration" of Iranian men by Western forces. And in his highly acclaimed and controversial book, *Westomania,* Al-e-Ahmad equated the infiltration of Western culture in Iran with the loss of Iranian manliness.

Not only were fictive characters denounced as being unmanned, but so too were prominent political figures. Mohammad Reza Shah Pahlavi described his own prime minister, Mohammad Mossadeq, as a person who "cried like a woman and indulged in hysterical tirades." Prime Minister Amir Abbas Hoveida was denigrated as an effeminate homosexual. The Shah himself was not spared from such allegations. A book titled *Ernest Peron, the Husband of the Shah of Iran,* typifies the attempt to portray him as lacking "manliness."

A society characterized for centuries by its glorification of masculinity was witnessing a crisis. The implications and ramifications of this challenge remain to be fully analyzed and understood. But as gender categories eroded, the desire for a more familiar, reassuring lifestyle intensified. As notions of masculinity were further challenged, the need to accentuate the differences between the sexes increased and veiling became essential to the articulation of manhood. For, as a system of visual communication, the veil expresses gendered identity unambiguously. It evokes femininity and creates an essential woman who is presumed to be different from men. The veil is a distinct, almost theatrical optical emblem. It separates rather than unites the sexes. It dramatizes and polarizes the differences between men and women. It is a defining female garment. A veiled woman makes a man, any man, appear more masculine by contrast. No wonder, throughout its long history, not a single man has sought equality in the arena of veiling.

Sara's veil, in other words, is not only symbolic of the effort to free the country of alien ideologies, establishing women's independence from Western domination of styles, it is also meant to define gender boundaries between the sexes within Iran. It is to maintain the social, or rather the "natural" order, accentuating the differences between men and women. And in this political theater, it is not surprising if, once again, woman's body becomes a battleground and upon it are projected the society's doubts about itself, about modernity, about change, about its relations with the West, about its struggles with gender identity. Barbie's banishment from Iran is a symbolic bearer of these trials and tribulations just as Sara's veiling is an attempt to reconstitute and reestablish a lost order and a lost community.

Notes

1. Afshin Valinejad, "Iran Debuts Islamic Barbie," Associated Press, October 21, 1996.

2. Erica Rand, *Barbie's Queer Accessories* (Durham: Duke University Press, 1995), 5.

3. Ann DuCille, *Skin Trade* (Cambridge: Harvard University Press, 1996), 38.

4. See Mohja Kahf, *From Turmagon to Odalisque* (Austin: University of Texas Press, 1999).

5. Ali Shari'ati, *Zan* [Woman] (Tehran: n.p., 1983), 76.

QUESTIONS

1. What Western values and beauty norms does Barbie represent and why do these characteristics trouble Iranian officials? What characteristics do they believe make Sara a more appropriate role model for Islamic children?

2. What do you think of Mattel's spokesperson's assessment of what Barbie symbolizes for American girls and women? Based on the article, how might some Iranian authorities respond to these claims? How does this debate over dolls reflect larger political issues between America and Iran?

3. What does Milani mean when she says that Barbie's worldwide availability and varied ethnicities is a "commodification of difference"? Why might some cultural groups not want a Barbie doll representing them? How do we tell the difference between representing diversity and commodifying it?

4. Discuss ways that wearing a veil can have more than one meaning. What are some of the different meanings veiling has had? How do Americans and Iranian authorities interpret the veil differently?

5. What is ethnocentrism? How does it affect the way Westerners perceive Islamic attire? How does clothing serve as a marker of identity and "difference" in the US as well? Based on the article, how might some Iranian observers evaluate American women's status based on their clothing?

AIDS: Women Are Not Just Transmitters (1991)

Claudia Garcia-Moreno

Throughout the world, women continue to be infected with HIV at high rates as a result of heterosexual sex with infected men. The persistent misconception that AIDS was a "gay man's disease" coupled with the concentration on women as carriers, rather than sufferers, has slowed research into the varied ways HIV and AIDS impact women. Garcia-Moreno, a health advisor who is interested in AIDS and policy, describes some of the issues faced by women with the virus in Latin America and Africa. Initial observations are presented in a 1989 article and Garcia-Moreno's 1990 follow-up summarizes improvements and new obstacles.

Until recently, AIDS was perceived in the West as a problem affecting mainly homosexual men. The biggest impact of AIDS on women's lives there had been until recently as carers for people

"AIDS: Women Are Not Just Transmitters," by Claudia Garcia-Moreno, from *Changing Perceptions: Writing on Gender and Development*, reproduced with permission of Oxfam Publishing, 274 Banbury Road, Oxford, OX2 7DZ

with HIV disease or AIDS. However, more women are now becoming infected and the number is likely to increase in the next few years—in New York AIDS is already the leading cause of death in women between 25 to 34.[1] In Africa and some parts of Latin America, mainly the Caribbean, HIV has always been transmitted predominantly through heterosexual sex, and in these areas AIDS has affected women and men equally.[2] Yet women have received, until recently, little attention in the AIDS literature and when they are referred to it is usually only in their role as transmitters of the infection. There has been little focus on women as sufferers from AIDS.

Prostitutes

Prostitutes especially have been singled out as a high risk group, and have even been portrayed as being responsible for the spread of the HIV and AIDS epidemic in some places. The word "prostitute" means different things in different cultures. In some countries prostitutes are an easily identifiable group, whereas in others they are much less visible. Where prostitutes form a definable group they are accessible and easy to study and have become the focus of research in some cities of Africa.[3] They have been found to have a higher rate of HIV infection than the rest of the population and have therefore been designated a high risk group.

A common assumption in much of the AIDS literature is that prostitutes are always female. In some countries this is not the case and male prostitutes may be common. Yet women, particularly prostitutes, are frequently referred to as AIDS transmitters. While they may constitute a pool of infection, the role of their clients in transmission is rarely mentioned. Gabriella Leite, a prostitute in Brazil, put it bluntly:

> "As for AIDS, official bodies, society, attempt to define it in terms of people: prostitutes, homosexuals, the promiscuous, drug users. The political question is, what about the people who frequent prostitutes? They are not regarded as a high risk group . . . Sure AIDS kills, but so do many other things. Prostitutes have always been at risk of diseases and the government and health services have never lifted a finger before."[4]

The concern with prostitutes is as transmitters of AIDS, not as sufferers. This is not new or limited to AIDS. An article from Brazil draws a comparison with what happened previously with syphilis and gonorrhoea.[5] In the 1930s and 40s a poster aimed at soldiers in World War II portrayed a young woman and underneath the caption reads:

> "SHE MAY LOOK CLEAN—BUT . . . pick ups, 'good time' girls, prostitutes . . . Spread syphilis and gonorrhoea. You can't beat the Axis if you get VD."

This in spite of the fact that female to male transmission of gonorrohoea is documented to be around 20–25 per cent after a single exposure, and from male to female 50–80 per cent. The same article points out that although 95 per cent of the AIDS cases in Brazil are male, the official information on prevention portrays the face of a woman with the message, "You can't see AIDS when you see the face," i.e., she may look beautiful, but . . .

The possibility that a prostitute may catch HIV from an infected customer is rarely considered. For example, a study in *The Lancet* on the effectiveness of condom promotion and health education among prostitutes in Kenya concluded:[3]

> "We believe that this programme has prevented the transmission of a large number of HIV infections in men . . . In view of the sexual activity of these women and their high prevalence of HIV, every day approximately 3,750 men are sexually exposed to HIV through contact with them."

The phrasing makes one wonder whether the researchers were equally concerned about the health of the women. In the Philippines "hospitality girls" have identified this risk for themselves and together demanded testing for the men from the army who are frequent clients.

Men infecting women is never highlighted. However, in fact, the little information that is available on heterosexual transmission seems to suggest that male to female transmission is slightly higher than the other way around.[6] Also, in many African countries, men who have acquired the infection in the cities then return to their wives in rural areas and possibly start a new cycle of infection. There are anecdotal reports from some countries where HIV is prevalent in urban areas that some men are now looking for younger women in rural areas for the exchange of sexual favours, thinking that such women are less likely to be infected with HIV.

"Sex tours" for Western businessmen are well-known, particularly in some Asian countries, yet this group is not usually mentioned as a high risk group. A study of prostitutes in London showed that they were more likely to use condoms with their clients than with their own partners, even though these partners often engaged in high risk behaviour such as intravenous drug use.[7]

Harsh economic realities push women into prostitution, particularly in developing countries; for poor women on their own in urban areas there may be few choices other than becoming domestic servants or prostitutes. Often, they have been abandoned by a partner and have children to support. Women refugees also frequently end up resorting to prostitution, sometimes illegally, as their only survival strategy. With little education, or access to other resources, their opportunities are non-existent, and it is unrealistic to blame prostitutes and single them out for education and other programmes without offering them some kind of economic alternative. While education may help them to protect themselves (though even as prostitutes women are not always in a position to enforce the use of condoms by their clients), for many of these women abandoning prostitution would mean destitution.

Projects which aim to support women in prostitution or women sex workers should not limit themselves to giving health education; condoms need to be made available at an affordable price. General health services, including access to birth control, are also important. It is also essential to explore alternative income generating activities with these women and to provide the relevant assistance, as well as to explore other social and economic needs they may have.

Women and AIDS in Africa

The number of women infected with HIV in some African countries is high, particularly in certain urban areas. The female to male ratio is approximately one to one, i.e. at least 50 per cent, or sometimes slightly more, of those infected are women.[2] The peak incidence of infection for women in Africa is between 20 and 29 years while for men it is between 29 and 39, probably reflecting an earlier start of sexual activity for women. Yet few AIDS control programmes have considered women's particular needs; neither those of urban women nor of the wives of men returning to the rural areas bringing HIV with them.

AIDS cannot be separated from the extreme poverty, lack of resources and the heavy burden of work of women. For women the possibility of transmission to their babies is a cause for additional concern and when it occurs it adds to the guilt and worry.

Women traditionally have been the carers for children, the sick and the elderly and have already experienced the problem of caring for partners or others with AIDS. Who will take over this role for women when they themselves need to be cared for?

A research project in a capital city of an African country is following a sample of 1,500 women (selected from those attending antenatal care in the national hospital) for five years. The study, concerned with more than the research itself, has expanded to provide a valuable educational service, condoms, and spermicides, and counseling for the women as well as offering counselling and testing for their partners. Discussions with the women have helped to identify areas where they would like to receive some help. Testing was carried out, with informed consent and appropriate counselling. Approximately 25 per cent of the women were found to be seropositive. Marital conflict arising after disclosure of a positive result and the role of counselling in helping to overcome this have been particularly relevant.

This study exemplifies many of the problems faced by women in relation to HIV infection and AIDS. Many of these women were single and had little in the way of social or economic support. It is a generalised assumption that in Africa the extended family provides support and care for the sick. However, among the group of HIV seropositive women interviewed, 60 per cent of them said they would not be able to rely on husband or family for support.[8] Support from self-help groups, particularly with an income generation component, was very relevant to these women.

The same study identified the needs of women with AIDS. The provision of childcare, food and funeral services were major areas of concern to them. For women who were seropositive but asymptomatic, housing and employment assistance were a higher priority, although another important consideration was concern about preparing for the future in the event of illness or death. It is important to identify priorities and needs with the women themselves and to support projects which allow them to have more control over their situation and improve their economic status whenever possible.

Many of the women experience feelings of terrible isolation after being told they are seropositive; stigmatisation is real and many have been abandoned by friends, relatives or lovers; nurses and health workers have been known to refuse care. Hopefully, this rejection will decrease with appropriate information and education. Meanwhile, in the words of "Rosie" (a pseudonym), a sick woman in Zimbabwe:[9]

> "That's the worst part, the loneliness . . . I have it (AIDS). I can't change that, but if only I could talk about it openly, and stop hiding it. People think I've got cancer, because that's what I tell them, I can't admit I have AIDS, I would be stoned."

AIDS and children

The majority of women with HIV or AIDS are of childbearing age. HIV can be transmitted from an infected mother to her child, either during pregnancy or at birth.[10] There have been eight reported cases so far where transmission has been possibly related to breastmilk, all of them in special circumstances.[10] (Present evidence is that the benefits of breast-feeding far exceed the potential risks and breast-feeding should continue to be encouraged.)

The risk of a baby being infected is still not known with certainty. Results from different studies vary from less than 10 per cent to 30 per cent, and the risk of transmission appears to be associated with the stage of the disease.[10] The problem is bigger in those places in Africa and the Caribbean where a large number of women may be infected. In the West, women with HIV are advised to avoid pregnancy or to consider termination of pregnancy but for most women in developing countries these are not options. (And in some areas the risk of a baby dying of other diseases in the first year of life is probably higher than that of dying of AIDS.)

The debate on whether women should be offered testing for HIV as part of antenatal care is an ongoing one. In a survey in one African country about half the women said that knowing their HIV status would not affect their decision to become pregnant.[11]

In a clinic in London when women were offered a confidential test, 99 per cent of them declined.[11] In some developing countries women have been tested without their knowledge. In the USA some reports suggest that women, mainly from deprived or minority groups, accept testing because they fear they will be denied access to health care if they decline.[11] It is imperative that confidentiality be maintained if one is to encourage those women most in need of counselling and support to come forward. Even though it is now well recognised that pre- and post-test counselling is an essential part of testing for HIV, in many places it is often lacking. Doctors often have not informed patients of their diagnosis because they lack counselling skills and feel unable to provide the necessary support.

Policy implications

The above discussion has relevance to health and health education policies. Women's needs are different from men's and policy makers have to take this into consideration.

Women should be offered appropriate information and education so that they can make informed choices. This should take into account their particular social and economic circumstances, as information is not enough if women are not in a position to have control over their own lives and bodies. The messages will be different depending on which women are being addressed. Sex workers, women in stable relationships or adolescent girls about to start sexual activities need to be approached with messages that are relevant to their particular situation. In the case of prostitutes it is important not to make them scapegoats. Health education should be aimed at their clients as well.

Education on prevention of HIV infection/AIDS and other sexually transmitted diseases (STDs) should ideally be in the context of education and information on sexuality. There is a need for sex education which empowers women and encourages them to feel more confident to express their own needs and to negotiate over condom usage with a partner. Education with men on these aspects is necessary as well. Participation of the male sexual partner in an education and testing programme in Rwanda positively affected change to lower risk sexual behaviour. Access to family planning services offering appropriate choice and to early treatment of other STDs are also important.

The experiences of women who are beginning to organise themselves and to come up with their own solutions for support, sharing of childcare and income generating activities need to be taken into account. In relation to income generating activities, particularly for prostitutes, it is important to ensure that activities are genuinely productive. "Traditional" income generating projects like jam-making, knitting, weaving, etc., do not usually generate much money and large group activities are not profitable in most cases. It is difficult to find successful income generating projects but access to credit through revolving credit schemes could be explored. Access to childcare remains an important issue on which self-help groups could, with some external support, organise their own schemes.

Whatever the activity, it is essential to listen to what women and men identify as their needs and work out appropriate solutions in each particular situation.

Concluding comment

AIDS has been used to legitimise prejudices that already exist in societies. It is important therefore to consider carefully our attitudes and even the language that we use when dealing with the subject. The social, political and economic aspects of AIDS are as important as the medical and biological ones in improving the understanding of the disease and in decreasing transmission. Amongst these, gender is an important aspect and all of those involved in this field need to be aware of the existing biases.

Update on women and AIDS

This article was written in February 1989. Rather than update it, I have left it as it was (with only minor editorial changes) because it captures the issues as they were then. Also, because it exemplifies how in moments of crisis the specific problems of women are the last to be considered and taken into account.

Since it was written, much more attention has been paid to women in the AIDS literature. Women have been—and continue to be—the focus of various publications in the last year.[1,12,13] The fact that women are not just transmitters of AIDS or carers for people with AIDS, but also sufferers from HIV infection and AIDS has received attention. In fact, the theme for World AIDS Day in 1990 will be Women and AIDS. Dr Nakajima, the Director-General of the World Health Organisation, has said this "will reflect the increasing impact of AIDS on women, as well as the crucial role women play in preventing infection with the human immunodeficiency virus (HIV) and caring for HIV-infected people and people with AIDS."[14]

It is encouraging to note that the issue of AIDS and its impact on women is being recognised. However, the general situation of women still remains in most places that of second class citizens and many of the issues raised previously remain valid. Health policies in general and health education in particular still need to take gender issues more seriously.

Discrimination

Fear and stigma are still present, and people with AIDS continue to die in silence. "Rosie" the Zimbabwean woman who talked for the first time to a newspaper about her situation, and whom I quoted in the article, has since died at the age of 38. She was supported throughout her illness by Island Hospice who gave her loving care, but it was only in the last two weeks that she finally told a friend or two that she was not dying of cancer but of AIDS.[15]

Disturbing reports of discrimination in various forms (not just against women) continue.[16] An example which particularly affects women is the case of women prostitutes in India. They are detained under the Prevention of Immorality Act, and continue to be held past the expiry of their sentence if they are known to be HIV-positive. In March 1990, Shyamala Nataraj, an Indian journalist who had been researching the case, filed a writ in the Madras High Court seeking their release. The case is still pending.

In Thailand, although cheap sex and heroin are easily available, there had been very few reported cases of AIDS until 1988. Since then, the rates of seropositivity have increased at an alarming rate: from just over 100 in 1988 to 2,901 and then 13, 600 by the end of 1989. At the beginning of February 1990 the number of people with HIV reached 14,116.[17] Among prostitutes the rates of seropositivity varied depending on whether they were "low class" (72 per cent) or "higher class" (16–30 per cent). For a long time the government refused to do anything on AIDS education as they were worried about the adverse effects it would have on tourism. It is only now that the government is starting its AIDS education programmes. The blame continues to be laid on women, with little consideration of the economic and social realities faced by them. Health education continues to target the prostitutes rather than their clients, although presumably the latter are better educated, have more resources at their disposal and are more in control of the use of condoms.

Other disturbing occurrences have been reported. In Uganda "some Kampala men have begun to search out schoolgirl lovers in the belief that they will be free of HIV; the government has had to enact a law against sugar daddies."[18] In West Africa some men believe that sex with a virgin will cure AIDS.[19] In many countries women continue to be blamed for the transmission of AIDS even when it was their husband's behaviour that infected them in the first place. A married woman in Kenya wrote of her concern that in spite of being monogamous she could get AIDS through her husband's behaviour. In her words, married women remained "faithful but fearful."[20]

Women organising themselves

On the positive side, there are various groups which are attempting to deal with the problems of women in a different way. Some of these are particularly concerned with helping women sex workers. Empower is one such group in Thailand. It is an association of bar workers set up to help women working in Patpong (a sex centre in Thailand where about 4,000 women work). They have staged shows on safer sex aimed not just at sex workers but at their clients and bar and brothel owners. They also have a drop-in centre which gives information on AIDS and other STDs, nutrition, safe drug use and family planning, and they provide education for the women. The main problems they face are discriminatory attitudes towards sex workers who often get beaten up when they insist on the use of condoms. Yet women are still blamed for transmission (the local Thai expression for STDs is "woman's disease").[12,21]

Another example of positive activities are those undertaken by Gabriela, a national coalition of Filipino women's groups. This group has been involved in demanding the dismantling of US military bases in the Philippines and the compensation by the US government for "hospitality women" infected with HIV.[22] They have drop-in centres and provide information and education for sex workers. They also have formed a Task Force on AIDS to do advocacy work and attempt to educate people in the media and general public about the problems of AIDS in particular and the sexually prostituted in general.

In Zimbabwe a group of women have formed the Women's AIDS Support Network. The Network aims to make AIDS a concern for all organisations working with women in the country and to help women gain confidence to fight AIDS in a society where they have little control over the sexual behaviour of men.[12]

AIDS in children

As the number of women infected with HIV increases so will the number of children being born with HIV. While abortion may be an option for infected women in some developed countries, in many countries in the developing world having children is an important part of life for a woman. "The HIV positive woman must balance the chance she might infect her baby against the possibility that her husband might leave her if she refuses to give him children."[23]

Orphans

An added dimension to the problem is that of the social and economic consequences of AIDS which are now becoming evident in areas of high prevalence. One of them is the increase in the number of orphans. Precise figures are difficult to come by and there are problems of definition, but an increase in the number of orphaned children has been reported from parts of Uganda and Tanzania.[23]

Mission hospitals in the worst affected areas also report this and in some places the number of orphans is so large that it is difficult to envisage how to deal with the problem other than by creating welfare institutions.

One of the many issues related to orphans is that it usually falls on the extended family to care for these children. This burden of care has tended to fall on elderly grandmothers. It is difficult for elderly frail grandmothers to provide enough food and money for schooling. This is another issue in relation to women as carers and it is compounded by the loss of the main wage earners and its effects on family structures.

Conclusions

Some progress has been made on issues related to women and AIDS. Certainly, women's concerns have become an integral part of the "AIDS agenda." In practice though, gender biases still permeate health policies in general and AIDS "health messages" in particular. The links between AIDS and poverty are evident and poverty continues to affect women most severely. Prostitution continues to thrive, not usually from choice, but as a means of survival in an increasingly difficult economic situation.

At the same time women have organised themselves, and will continue to do so, in attempts to improve their (and their children's) situation. The solutions are not easy and daring thinking will be required of those involved in trying to find some. Let us hope we are up to the challenge.

References

1. Women and AIDS Resource Network (WARN) (June 1988), "Women *and AIDS: The Silent Epidemic,"* New York: WARN.
2. Mann J. (1988), "Global AIDS: Epidemiology, Impact, Projections and the Global Strategy," paper presented at the World Summit of Minis-

ters of Health on Programmes for AIDS Prevention, WHO, London, 26-28 January 1988.

3. Ngugi E.N., Plummer R.A. *et al.* (1988), "Prevention of Transmission of HIV in Africa: Effectiveness of Condom Promotion and Health Education Among Prostitutes," *The Lancet,* October, pp. 887-890.
4. McGrath J., "No Human Rights—Brazil," Interview with Gabriella, a prostitute, in Rio de Janiero, May 1988. Next article in this collection.
5. Ramos S., "Um Rostro de mulher," magazine article.
6. (Abstract) (1988/9), "Heterosexual Transmission of HIV," *The AIDS Letter* No. 10, Royal Society of Medicine, December/January, p. 4.
7. Day S., Ward H., Harris J.R. (1988), "Prostitute Women and Public Health," *British Medical Journal,* 297: p.1585 .
8. Keogh P., Allen S., Calle Almedal R.N., "Study of Needs of HIV seropositive women in Rwanda." Study completed in August 1988, report in progress.
9. Throncroft P.(1988), "Dying in Silence," *Parade,* Zimbabwe, December.
10. (Editorial), (1989) "Vertical Transmission of HIV," *The Lancet,* 2, pp. 1057-8.
11. Mariam J. and Radlett M. (1989), "Women face new dilemmas," *AIDS Watch 5,* IPPF.
12. Women and AIDS Action Issue 9, "Women, HIV and AIDS," AHRTAG, December 1989.
13. Campbell (1990), "Women and AIDS," *Social Scientist and Medicine* 30(4): pp 407-15.
14. Press Release WHO/5, 22 January 1990.
15. Thornycroft P. (1990), "AIDS Victim 'Rosie' is dead," *Parade,* Zimbabwe, January.
16. Panos Dossier (1990), "The Third Epidemic: Repercussions of the Fear of AIDS," Panos Institute in association with the Norwegian Red Cross, May.
17. Anderson J. (1990), "AIDS in Thailand," *BMJ, 17* February, pp. 415-6.
18. "The Terrible Trail of 'Slim'," *The Guardian,* April 12, 1990.
19. McFadden P. (1989), "AIDS—Who Is the Culprit?," SAPEM, April.
20. Anon, "AIDS and Married Women," *The Weekly Review,* Kenya, 12 September 1989.

21. (1989) "Empowering Bar Workers in Bangkok," *Community Development Journal* 24 (30): 202.

22. Tan M., de Leon A., Stoltzfus B. and O'Donnel C. (1989), "AIDS as a political issue: working with the Sexually Prostituted in the Philippines," *Community Development Journal* 24 (30): 202, pp. 186-193.

23. Panos Mini-Dossier No. 2, (1989), "AIDS and Children: a family disease," Panos Institute in association with Save the Children.

Claudia Garcia-Moreno is a Health Adviser for Oxfam, covering Latin America and Southern Africa. She has particular responsibility for AIDS work and policies and is interested in women's issues. She has experience of primary healthcare (PHC) in Mexico and Africa.

QUESTIONS

1. What damage is caused by the concentration on women as "carriers" rather than sufferers of HIV and AIDS? Why do prostitutes continue to be perceived as carriers, when their clients are not perceived that way?

2. If males "choose" to go to prostitutes just as some women may "choose" to be prostitutes, why are female prostitutes made scapegoats? Is this difference in attitude influenced by gender values? How much control do women have in ensuring that their male partners use condoms or viricides?

3. How do economic circumstances limit women's choices, forcing some into prostitution? How do issues raised for women with AIDS differ from those raised for men? What interventions and policies can improve conditions for women? What changes does Garcia-Moreno note from 1989-1990?

Asian Childhoods Sacrificed to Prosperity's Lust (1996)

Nicholas D. Kristof

This startling article, a 1996 special report for the New York Times, *describes child prostitution thriving in areas of Asia. Focusing primarily on Cambodian brothels, the author interviews a few of the 8 to 13-year-old girls that are regularly kidnapped or sold into the sex industry, and describes some of the factors that keep the business growing at such a steady pace. An issue complicated by the AIDS epidemic and a persistent demand for services, it also raises troubling questions about human rights.*

She giggled for a moment, a 13-year-old girl, all sparkling eyes and white teeth, her laughter washing over the grunts from a pornographic video playing a few feet away. Then the brothel owner strutted over.

The owner, a hearty, friendly woman in her late 20's, who paid good money to buy the girl, named Sriy, cheerfully and explicitly recommended her anatomical features and said the $10

---

fee was not so great because "she only just lost her virginity." In fact, that is a lie. Sriy was sold into prostitution two years ago.

As if to prove her point, the brothel owner reached out and, pushing Sriy's hand away, tugged down on the girl's dress to display her left breast, or rather the nipple of what will become a breast if Sriy survives to maturity. "You like?" the owner asked in broken English. "You take girl?"

Sriy endures these indignities, along with up to 10 customers a night, because she is considered the brothel owner's property. Sold by her step-father to another brothel, which then sold her to this one, the girl must work until the debt is deemed to be repaid. Or until she gets AIDS.

If she tries to escape, she will be caught, severely beaten, perhaps starved, and locked inside her room, while still being forced to have sex with many customers a night. A neighboring brothel burned down in mid-March, and the bodies of two girls were found in the wreckage. They had been locked up inside, forced to have sex with customers in their rooms, and never allowed out because they showed signs of wanting to escape.

Sriy is one of tens of thousands of children in Asia who are slaves working in the plantations of the 1990's: the brothels of Cambodia, India, China, Thailand, the Philippines, Taiwan and other countries.

Americans and other Westerners helped build the child prostitution trade in Asia, and many of the brothel districts date from R&R breaks from the Vietnam War, or surround former American military bases. Now they sustain it with an appetite for what at home would be child molestation and rape. A result is a partnership between local people, who run the brothels, and Westerners like the one who posted an item on the Internet informing sex tourists that in Cambodia "a six-year-old is available for US$3."

Family

Mother and Sister Pimp for the Kids

In the seedy Maleta district of Manila, near the waterfront and virtually under the shadow of a large church, lives a family with four daughters ranging from 8 to 18. Until a few months ago, the mother and oldest daughter procured for the 8-year-old and a 12-

year-old among foreigners, social workers say. When a customer was found, the oldest daughter would go to school to bring her sisters home early, telling the teachers that they had some family business.

The 8-year-old was raped by American, Australian and Japanese men. When the 12-year-old tried to resist, her sister held her arms and another pimp held her legs so the men could rape her more easily.

It was not supposed to be this way. Six decades ago, Asian cities like Shanghai, Hong Kong and Hanoi were notorious for their brothels, but it had seemed that economic development would allow countries to grow out of the worst of the squalor. Now Asia has enjoyed an historic economic boom, yet child prostitution is, by most accounts, increasing.

By estimates of social workers and Governments, more than a million girls and boys, aged 17 and younger, are engaged in prostitution in Asia, although all these figures are no more than wild guesses. The slaves, in the sense of those who are locked up or owned by a brothel, are a minority of the total. But even among those teen-agers who now offer themselves on street corners, many first entered the sex trade unwillingly, sold by parents or simply kidnapped off the street.

Three factors seem to be aggravating the problem of child prostitution in Asia: rising economic development, which initially seems to increase the appetite for children more quickly than it reduces the supply; the rise of capitalism in places like China and Indochina, so markets emerge not just for rice and pork but also for virgin girls; and, perhaps most important, the fear of AIDS, driving customers to younger girls and boys who are regarded as more likely to be disease-free.

All three factors merge into the person of a shy 14-year-old Vietnamese girl, Miss Nguyen, who one day recently was sitting in a brothel in the Cambodian town of Svay Pak, waiting to be sold for the very first time. Her brothel is one of dozens in Svay Pak, all nice two-story brick buildings that contrast with the rutted dirt streets and open sewers of the surrounding neighborhood.

Miss Nguyen was wearing a long purple dress, and the other girls in Svay Pak were also dressed lavishly and adorned with cosmetics and jewelry that looked out of place on their tiny figures. Miss Nguyen's story emerged slowly, because the brothel owners often beat girls for telling anyone about their backgrounds and because this brothel owner was paying particular attention to Miss Nguyen to make sure she does not escape.

The owner, a dour woman in her 30's, had bought Miss Nguyen three days earlier and was holding her off the market until she found a foreigner willing to pay $500 for her virginity. "It's not so expensive," the brothel owner said. "After all, she only loses her virginity once. This is a once-in-a-lifetime opportunity." Miss Nguyen was smuggled across the border from Vietnam, where, as in Cambodia, the collapse of strict Communist ideology has been accompanied by the rise of a huge flesh trade. The buyer of Miss Nguyen's virginity will probably be a foreigner, the owner said, most likely a newly prosperous ethnic Chinese from Taiwan, China or Singapore. A Chinese superstition holds that sex with a virgin helps make a man young again, or that it can cure venereal disease.

A 15-year-old Vietnamese girl who is also new to the brothel, having been sold by her mother, piped up to say that a Singaporean man paid $500 for her virginity a few days earlier. It is eerie to hear the girls speak of these topics because, to Western eyes, they look several years younger than their ages, not like sexual beings at all, more like American 10-year-olds than teenagers.

"It hurt a lot and I cried," the girl added. "It still hurts me, several days later. But it's not quite so bad now."

Miss Nguyen, whom the brothel owner was watching closely to insure that she does not escape, shuddered and leaned against the 15-year-old.

"I'm scared," she said softly. "I'm scared."

Fear

A Deadly Game of Sexual Roulette

In another Cambodian brothel, a 14-year-old girl also said she was scared—of AIDS. And with good reason. The girl said she was sold by her mother to the brothel a week earlier.

In this case, it was a Cambodian, not a foreigner, who purchased her virginity—a district police commander paid $500. The man, like many customers, did not use a condom.

Now the girl, as a fresh arrival, sells for $10, but in another week she will drop to $5 and then eventually to $2 or $3. She lay down on a bench, her long, pink dress flowing over her, full of anger and helplessness.

"My mother needed money, because she was sick," the girl said, staring at the ceiling. "How can I be angry with her? She's my Mom."

A decade ago, such a slight young girl would not have been in much demand. But now, men throughout Asia are turning toward younger and younger children, partly because they are deemed less likely to be infected with H.I.V., the virus that causes AIDS.

In fact, the children are greater risks because of their youth: their vaginas and anuses are easily torn, creating sores and bleeding that permit the AIDS virus to spread.

"Most men I know want younger girls, the younger the better, because then they can scare the hell out of us," said Tisay, a 14-year-old street-walker in Quezon City, the Philippines. "Older girls can set a price, can set conditions, but younger girls can't do that."

"I'd prefer safe sex," Tisay added. "But it's hard to insist that a man wear a condom. "I'm small and I'm alone and I can't do anything about it if he doesn't want to."

Tisay has contracted gonorrhea, which increases the risk of acquiring AIDS, but she refuses to be treated. Partly she is afraid that if the other girls find out that she is being treated, they will tell her customers and drive them away. And partly, her behavior is simply self-destructive.

"My life's worth nothing now," a social worker quoted Tisay as telling her. "It's better for me to die."

The AIDS virus is spreading extremely rapidly among prostitutes in Asia. India had its first AIDS case in 1986, yet already some 1.6 million Indians are infected with H.I.V. Thailand may have 800,000 people infected with the virus, and Myanmar—where condoms were banned until 1992 and are still rare—has some 400,000 infected people. In Cambodia, one study found that 39 percent of prostitutes are infected with H.I.V.

The virus spreads rapidly from country to country in part because of trafficking of prostitutes across borders, but also because customers tend to hop from place to place. Sex tours started in Japan, allowing groups of men to visit brothels in South Korea or Taiwan, and now other countries are doing the same. Indeed,

South Korean and Taiwanese men now are prosperous enough to travel on sex tours of their own to places like Bangkok or Manila.

Some Asian governments are beginning to prosecute foreigners caught having sex with minors, as Dr. Gavin A. M. Scott can attest. Dr. Scott, a tall, lean Briton who has lived in Cambodia practicing medicine since 1992, is still fuming over having to serve five months in a Phnom Penh prison last year on rape charges after paying five teen-age boys to have sex with him.

The police and court said that the boys were 14 to 16 years old, but Dr. Scott said that they were over 16 and that he simply engaged in sex with prostitutes.

"It was basically a case against homosexuality," said Dr. Scott, who is gay. "But it was misrepresented as a case about child sex, which it was not."

How do the customers regard their actions? From a conversation with Dr. Scott, who continues to practice medicine in Phnom Penh, and from materials published by pedophile organizations, it seems that customers sometimes offer two defenses.

First, they note that the age of consent in much of the world is 16—indeed, it is 14 in Pennsylvania and Hawaii—and suggest that there is nothing wrong with people of such an age engaging in sexual acts. Second, they sometimes suggest that young prostitutes are at least earning substantial sums to help their families, and that the alternative would be backbreaking jobs that would be even more demeaning and dangerous.

A growing number of Westerners are, like Dr. Scott, being arrested for sexual abuse of children in Asia, although usually they are simply fined and deported. Prison sentences are very rare.

Betrayal

Selling a Daughter For a Karaoke System

What kind of a mother would sell her daughters?

Leonilla Olayres is a 33-year-old mother in a slum near Manila's airport. She sat on a plastic chair in her hovel, nursing her youngest child as other children scampered around the tiny room and the dirt street outside. The stench of garbage and an open sewer wafted into the room. Although the family is poor, it is not starving. An expensive new karaoke music system, costing hundreds of dollars, sits in a place of honor in the middle of the wall.

Where did the family get the money for such a purchase? Apparently in part from Mrs. Olayres's oldest daughters, aged 10 and 12. On five occasions over the last year, by Mrs. Olayres's own count, she handed over the two girls to a Japanese man, Hisayoshi Maruyama, for cash.

The most recent time was Feb. 23 when, according to the police report, Mrs. Olayres delivered the 10-year-old to Mr. Maruyama's hotel room, accepted $60 and left.

The police say that they responded to a complaint from a relative and found Mr. Maruyama and the 10-year-old girl, both naked, in his hotel room. The police report says that Mr. Maruyama had kissed the girl, undressed her, sexually abused her, tied her up, photographed her and forced her to perform oral sex.

"I didn't know," Mrs. Olayres said matter-of-factly. She insisted that she had believed Mr. Maruyama's explanation that he wanted to take pictures for a Japanese foster-parent organization. Anyway, Mrs. Olayres added, many neighbors had also hired out their daughters to Mr. Maruyama.

The two girls were taken to a Government-run shelter, where, through a social worker, they declined to be interviewed about their mother. Mr. Maruyama, a 34-year-old with a mop of black hair and a modest paunch, who identifies himself as a medical doctor at a Tokyo institute that seems not to exist, insisted in an interview in the Manila city jail that he had been framed by the police.

Mr. Maruyama acknowledged that he had been arrested before in Manila, in 1991, in very similar circumstances. But he said he had been framed then, too.

Police reports from that time say that he forced a 10-year-old boy and his 11-year-old sister to engage in sexual acts together, and then further abused six young boys and a 7-year-old girl so he could take pornographic videos of them.

Mr. Maruyama argued that his main legal problem is that he did not have enough cash to pay a bribe. He said that when his hotel room was raided, he was not initially arrested, and police records confirm this. According to Mr. Maruyama's account, he was taken to a police office and asked for a $4,000 bribe. Only when he could not pay, he said, was he arrested.

Despair

Poisoned Cookies; Silent Fury

The way a child's fortunes can suddenly collapse was underscored by the case late last year of four Cambodian girls who tried to help a middle-aged woman who appeared to be ill on the road. According to a social worker who works with Cambodian prostitutes, the woman offered the girls a cookie each, in a show of gratitude, but the cookie was drugged and the girls passed out.

Then the woman hired a taxi to take them to a brothel, which she entered to negotiate a sale. The taxi driver realized what was happening and felt badly because he recognized one of the unconscious girls. So he drove off and took the girls home before the woman came out. Otherwise, they very likely would have finished their lives in the brothels.

The role of fate is fully evident in the Cambodian brothel that houses Sriy, the 13-year-old whose owner pushed down the neck of her dress to show off her chest. A moment later the owner did the same to Sriy's best friend, a 15-year-old Vietnamese girl who was sold to the brothel by a man who effectively kidnapped her.

That girl's mother finally tracked her daughter down in March, and found her working in the brothel. But since the brothel owner had paid for the girl—even if to a kidnapper—the mother could not take the girl home. Instead the mother had to settle for signing a contract with the brothel owner, stipulating that when the girl earns back enough money she will be returned to her family.

"If the mother tried to grab her daughter and take her out of the brothel, the owner would have them beaten up," said a Cambodian journalist who has written about the problems of child prostitution. "And if the mother takes on the brothel owner, she can't win. The brothel owner can just pay some money to the police, or give the girl to the police, and the parents will lose."

At least, Sriy seems to think, her friend eventually has a home to go back to. Sriy hates her stepfather, who used to beat her and who took the initiative in selling her to the brothel. All she has is the memory of her mother, who died recently.

What does she think of her mother, for allowing her to be sold into a brothel? Sriy's eyes grew distant as her 13-year-old mind sorted through memories of her mother.

"Mom was sick and needed money," Sriy finally said hesitantly. "She had a lung disease. I don't hate her."

Sriy's peaceful expression did not change, and she seemed lost in thought. But she began to play with a piece of brittle plastic on the table, breaking it with her slender fingers, violently crushing it into smaller and smaller pieces.

Questions

1. Although this article focuses on areas of Asia, how is this an "international" issue? How are other countries complicit in sustaining the sex industry? What other factors contribute to its growth? What role do women play? Should the industry be regulated?
2. What does the "age of consent" mean? How do the "age of consent" laws, varying by country, complicate the issue of what is "right" and "wrong"?
3. How does the AIDS epidemic complicate prostitution?